To Make Our World Anew

To live with and care for one's family without fear of separation—something that had been denied to slaves—was a goal for blacks after the Civil War. This family was photographed in 1886.

To Make Our World Anew

Volume One: A History of African Americans to 1880

edited by

Robin D. G. Kelley

and

Earl Lewis

OXFORD
UNIVERSITY PRESS

Oxford University Press, Inc., publishes works that further
Oxford University's objective of excellence
in research, scholarship, and education.

Oxford New York
Auckland Cape Town Dar es Salaam Hong Kong Karachi
Kuala Lumpur Madrid Melbourne Mexico City Nairobi
New Delhi Shanghai Taipei Toronto

With offices in
Argentina Austria Brazil Chile Czech Republic France Greece
Guatemala Hungary Italy Japan Poland Portugal Singapore
South Korea Switzerland Thailand Turkey Ukraine Vietnam

First published by Oxford University Press, Inc., 2000
198 Madison Avenue, New York, New York 10016
www.oup.com

First issued as a two-volume Oxford University Press paperback, 2005
Vol. 1 ISBN-13: 978-0-19-518134-0
Vol. 2 ISBN-13: 978-0-19-518135-7

The Library of Congress has cataloged the one-volume cloth edition as follows:
To make our world anew : a history of African Americans / edited by Robin
D. G. Kelley and Earl Lewis.
p. cm. Includes bibliographical references (p.) and index.
ISBN-13: 978-0-19-513945-7
1. Afro-Americans—History. I. Kelley, Robin D. G. II. Lewis, Earl.
E185 .T68 2000 973'.0496073—dc21 00-021131

5 7 9 10 8 6
Printed in the United States of America on acid-free paper

Contents

To You

To sit and dream, to sit and read,
To sit and learn about the world
Outside our world of here and now—
    Our problem world—
To dream of vast horizons of the soul
Through dreams made whole,
Unfettered free—help me!
All you who are dreamers, too,
Help me make our world anew
I reach out my hands to you.

—Langston Hughes

Preface to Volume One

Robin D. G. Kelley and *Earl Lewis*

The history of African Americans is nothing less than the dramatic saga of a people attempting to re-make the world. Brought to the Americas against their will as commodities to be bought and sold, Africans and their descendants struggled to change their conditions and thus turn the New World of their European masters upside down. Even when they did not succeed, the actions, thoughts, and dreams of Africans are responsible for some of the most profound economic, political, and cultural developments in the modern West. Black labor generated unprecedented wealth and helped give birth to capitalism; black resistance slowly destroyed the system of slavery and prompted new methods of coercion and punishment; black creativity influenced virtually all forms of Western art—from music and dance to theater and the plastic arts; black visions of freedom and efforts to realize them not only transformed American politics but inspired uprisings the world over—from South Africa to Tiananmen Square. Indeed, by invoking Langston Hughes's call to make "the world anew," we recognize that African Americans historically understood their plight and their possibilities in global terms. For if this book demonstrates anything, it is that African Americans saw themselves as both Americans and part of a larger, international black diaspora. *To Make Our World Anew* tells the story of the nation but places the struggles and achievements of black people in a larger international framework.

The history of African Americans begins on the African continent, a huge and varied land bounded by the Atlantic and Indian Oceans. It was home to people with different languages, traditions, histories, and religions. They called themselves Twi, Yoruba, Ethiopian, Zulu, Ashanti, and Kumba among other names. Some lived in ancient kingdoms as old as the annals of recorded history, and others lived in small family groupings. Some worshipped one god, and others many gods. Some lived in societies headed by powerful men, and others by powerful women. Whether in cities or rural areas, whether Muslim, Christian, or other, the peoples of this amazing continent had long played a central role in world affairs. Egyptian advances in medicine, language, and architecture greatly influenced the Greek and Roman worlds. Gold from the Bure and Bambuk goldfields of West Africa made its way into the Mediterranean world, where the accumulation of significant quantities enabled the merchants of Genoa (Italy) to underwrite European exploration and expansion. Likewise, notable learning centers like Timbuktu attracted visitors from Europe and the Orient, and greatly enriched the Islamic world.

The roles of Africans in world affairs changed significantly with the rise of the South Atlantic System. As European explorers made their way to the Americas, they expected to find streets paved with gold. The Americas were indeed rich in natural resources, but the bounty had to be excavated, cultivated, and processed. Labor was needed. The Europeans had already begun exploiting African labor on plantations in the Mediterranean and off the coast of West Africa, so the modern world's turn to Africa as a reservoir of slaves was not surprising. What followed was the forced migration and enslavement of several million Africans of varied ethnic backgrounds. Although scholars debate the exact numbers, it is understood that somewhere between ten and twenty million people became part of the system of enslavement that ultimately led to the making of an African diaspora and African Americans. Many died in the trek from the interior to the coast, others during the wait for a slave ship, and scores of others during the harsh Middle Passage. Out of the crucible of their suffering was forged a new people—no longer simply Twi, Yoruba, Ashanti, or Kumba. In the Americas, they first became Africans and then African Americans. This process of people making is central to a complete understanding of African-American history.

To the countless numbers of Africans who survived the trans-Atlantic journey and were forced to disembark at one of the many ports along the coast of Britain's North American colonies, what lay before them was indeed a "strange new land." The seemingly infinite landscape, the cooler climate, the European settlers whose station in society ranged from vagabond to plantation owner, and their new neighbors—the Native peoples who had occupied the land for centuries—were all unfamiliar to these new arrivals. More than the land itself, the relationships they entered into must have seemed especially peculiar. Although forms of bondage had existed in West and Central Africa long before the trans-Atlantic slave trade, human beings were rarely the main commodity at the marketplace. Here in the modern world, the enslaved African was inspected, assessed, auctioned, bought, sold, bartered, and treated in any manner her or his auctioneer or owner saw fit.

By the end of the eighteenth century, African slaves came to be property, pure and simple, and the color of their skin had everything to do with their unique status. This had not always been the case, however. During the first half of the seventeenth century, the planters and colonial administrators had few hard and fast rules about what it meant to be a slave. Some Africans were treated like European indentured servants and emancipated after a designated period of time. Others were slaves for life, but their children were born free. Over time, however, owners realized how valuable their investments were and proceeded to support laws that tightened the bonds of racial slavery—most notably laws that made African slavery an inherited condition and denied black people the most rudimentary human rights.

The slaves did not always cooperate, however. They fought the masters and overseers, ran away, and made the business of commercial farming more difficult by not working efficiently. Some white indentured servants supported their fellow laborers, especially at the beginning of the seventeenth century, but as the laws changed and blackness became the primary mark of slavery, most poor white servants learned that the consequences of interracial solidarity had become much more severe. Being white, even a poor white, meant immunity from absolute slavery.

Yet, in spite of their condition, enslaved Africans were still thinking and feeling human beings endowed with intellect, creativity, and vision. They came to these shores from various ethnic groups and speaking many languages, but through it all they forged a strong sense of community. Here in this strange new land the Africans learned the English language and made it their own. They learned Christianity, if they had not before arrival, and transformed it. Others held fast to Islam or combined their own spiritual beliefs with the faith of the master. Sometimes the masters words served as their sharpest weapons, for all around them, especially into the late eighteenth century, they heard talk of liberty and freedom, of the rights of man. Not surprisingly, many enslaved Africans embraced the idea of liberty as a fundamental right, and some even presented petitions to colonial administrators insisting on their right to be free. But nobody had to read a declaration or a treatise to have a yearning for freedom. Indeed, the slaves themselves authored the earliest declarations of freedom, and they were written in blood in the form of slave insurrections. The majority simply stole themselves to freedom.

In the 150 years since their forced arrival in the seventeenth century, little exposed the contradiction between slavery and freedom for Africans as much as this nation's fight for independence from Great Britain. It was a contradiction many resolved to settle. Some, such as Crispus Attucks, joined with others colonists in striking direct blows for liberty. Others, meanwhile, heard the pleas for loyalty to the British crown, and with the promise of emancipation as their reward, remained faithful to the old order only to see it vanish before them. But whether in the poems of Phillis Wheatley, the legal action of Qouk Walker, or the efforts of Paul Cuffee, Americans of African descent helped define what it meant to be revolutionary citizens.

In fact, as the clamor for independence from Great Britain intensified, so too did the debate over slavery. Many who participated recognized that slavery remained a central form of labor in both the North and the South. Although a minority view, some American colonists favored emancipation. They ably pointed to the few blacks who purchased their freedom and gained an economic foothold before the 1760s. But in a land where dark skin signaled a subordinate social position, the few who lived as other than slaves represented the exception. For the enslaved, independence was not a philosophical debate; it stood as an alternative to permanent bondage.

As a result African Americans took a keen interest in public affairs. A small group of Africans in Massachusetts, for example, vigorously asserted their right to freedom, telling the provisional House of Representative so as early as 1773. Such petitions increased in frequency and cogency after the Declaration of Independence. Others acted individually, suing their masters for manumission and thereby insisting that they were citizens with the right to seek redress. And after five generations on North American soil, the promise of freedom seemed tantalizingly close so a few clung to the potential for British citizenship, trading loyalty to the crown for freedom. Irrespective of which side they supported, African people saw in the war an opportunity to escape slavery, pursuing different routes to possible full citizenship.

The Revolutionary era, however, did more than accelerate the push for freedom. It also midwifed the birth of a people called African Americans. In the crucible of the United States's birth, Africans claimed they too were Americans. They emphasized the role they played in building the infant nation and in securing its freedom. From their embrace of the religious awakening to the formation of independent institutions, they inserted themselves into the social and cultural life of the country. Ever aware of the implication of freedom, they spread word of their own efforts throughout the Americas, and took pleasure as other members of the African diaspora liberated themselves in Haiti.

The age of Revolution ended with a tightening of the Southern slave regime along with an intensification of resistance to slavery. As the industrial revolution got underway in the Northeastern states and England, the market for cotton was more profitable than ever. And after inventor Eli Whitney created a machine that could easily remove the seeds from cotton bolls—a slow and tedious chore slaves had to do by hand—plantation owners were able to grow even more cotton with fewer hands. However, they were not about to give up the slave system so easily. Even after the United States abolished the slave trade in 1808, plantation owners in the less fertile "upper South" added a new twist to the business of human bondage by breeding their slaves like cattle and selling them to the growing cotton plantations of the South and Southwest.

In the in-between zones of a harsh existence many African Americans struggled to build lives of value and dignity. Men and women renamed themselves, expressed love for their children, engaged in local economy when and where possible, and generally refused to follow all of the directives handed down by masters. Some earned funds to purchase their own freedom and that of loved ones. They built churches and other institutions, and not only in the North after the gradual abolition of slavery between the 1780s and the 1810s, but also in the South. And to the degree possible, they built the framework, if not the complete workings of a community. This enabled men and women to live on rather than die off, to leave progeny determined to end the abominable condition called slavery.

Not surprisingly, the African-American struggle to be free—and remain free—in the United States clashed with the slaveholders's efforts to keep the system alive and profitable. Indeed, the central goal of free blacks in antebellum America, beyond their very survival as a people, was to fight for the complete abolition of slavery. And fight they did, often in concert with fellow slaves, sometimes in alliance with progressive white abolitionists, sometimes all alone. Free and enslaved African Americans, including notable figures like Gabriel Prosser, Denmark Vesey, and Nat Turner, attempted to launch slave rebellions. David Walker, Frederick Douglass, Maria Stewart, Henry Highland Garnet, and a host of others, wrote militant books, pamphlets, and speeches calling for the abolition of slavery and condemning the United States for its hypocritical claim to being a "land of the free."

The clash between slaveholders and their opponents (most notably, the slaves themselves) ultimately escalated into a full-scale war. The years of Civil War and Reconstruction challenged the very foundations of American democracy and established the place of African Americans in that democracy. The war raised the intriguing question of whether a state or collection of states had the right to leave the union when residents felt their way of life was under attack. It eventually raised the question of whether a nation, founded on the deep belief in freedom, could deny those same rights and privileges to others because of a difference in color and status. Fundamentally, the years bound by the Civil War and Reconstruction raised extremely important questions about the place of African Americans in a newly reconstructed nation.

When Southern forces fired on Fort Sumter, South Carolina in 1861, sparking a confrontation between the federal government and Southerners, the end of a way of life was at hand. The country had grown increasingly polarized over the issue of slavery. Some favored total abolition; others simply wished to contain slavery, halting its further spread. Yet, after the war's start and over the pleas of prominent African Americans such as Frederick Douglass, President Lincoln and members of Congress hesitated to make the struggle a referendum on slavery. Initially, Lincoln sought to reunite the country. But with growing pressures from some whites, after several important defeats, and in light of African-American agitation, the freedom of African Americans became a paramount concern.

The emancipation of slaves and the abolition of slavery were neither immediate nor universally applied. As important, a shift from slavery to freedom introduced a number of searching questions for Southern blacks. While the majority favored freedom over enslavement, a few feared such a dramatic change in status. Many, for example, ran away to join army units, where they encountered Northern blacks heading South to aid in their liberation. Others filled the contraband camps—so called because fleeing slaves had no legal status and were considered contraband—that flanked Northern encampments. Even after Lincoln signed the Emancipation

Proclamation in 1863, blacks living in border states such as West Virginia were not freed until passage of the 13th Amendment to the Constitution in 1865. Still, a few served in the Confederate Army, which is not surprising since a few blacks had been slave owners.

When the war ended in 1865 many African Americans anticipated their inclusion into the nation's civic culture. With ratification of the 14th Amendment in 1868, which granted blacks citizenship, and the 15th (1870), which extended the franchise, they were free and optimistic. Scores anxiously searched for family members sold during slavery; others exercised their right to form labor associations, and to build schools, churches, and other institutions. Families withdrew women and children from the labor force, thereby asserting a right to be treated as paid, free labor. Although continued racial violence tempered some of this optimism, blacks voted and played an active role in the affairs of the nation. African Americans were free at last! They were finally full-fledged members of the republic.

So they thought. "The slave went free; stood a brief moment in the sun; then moved back again toward slavery." This is how W. E. B. DuBois, the great black scholar and activist described the plight of black people in 1877—the year Reconstruction officially came to a close. Federal troops were withdrawn from the South, freed slaves were not given the land promised them, white terrorist groups ran rampant, and the same defenders of slavery who led the Civil War against the North returned to positions of power. It was a sad moment, for it marked the end of a decade and a half of effort to create a true democracy in the South.

To Make Our World Anew, volumes one and two, are the product of a truly collective endeavor. We have combined the efforts of eleven leading historians who authored the original *Young Oxford History of African Americans* to produce the two-volume paperback edition. In this volume, Colin A. Palmer authored the first chapter, "The First Passage: 1502–1619;" Peter H. Wood wrote "Strange New Land: 1619–1776;" Daniel C. Littlefield, "Revolutionary Citizens: 1776–1804;" Deborah Gray White, "Let My People Go: 1804–1860;" and Noralee Frankel, "Breaking the Chains: 1860–1880." Each of these authors deserves full credit as a co-author of *To Make Our World Anew.*

To Make Our World Anew

CHAPTER 1

The First Passage

1502–1619

Colin A. Palmer

Without exception, the contemporary societies of North and South America and the Caribbean include peoples of African descent. They form the numerical majority in the Caribbean, are about one half of Brazil's population, and make up a significant minority in the United States. In other countries, such as Canada, Mexico, Venezuela, and Colombia, blacks are present in smaller numbers. Regardless of the societies in which they live, these peoples share a common historical origin and ancestral homeland. Their experiences in the Americas have also been remarkably similar since the sixteenth century, when they began to arrive from Africa in ever-increasing numbers.

Black Africans were brought as slaves into the Caribbean islands and the mainland colonies of Central and South America, first by the Spaniards and later by the Portuguese. Beginning in 1502, the slave trade gathered momentum as white colonists came to rely on this forced black labor. During the early years of the trade, Africans passed through Spain (where many remained) to the Americas. By 1518, however, a direct trade route from Africa to the Americas was introduced.

Not all Africans in the Americas, even in the sixteenth century, served as slaves for the duration of their lives. Some managed to achieve their freedom; others were born free. In 1617 the first town or settlement controlled by free blacks in the Americas was established in Mexico. This was a major development in black life in the Western Hemisphere; it was the first time that a group of Africans gained the right to live as free people. These pioneers had successfully thrown off the yoke of slavery through their own efforts, setting the stage for the eventual liberation of other enslaved Africans. But almost three centuries passed before this goal would be accomplished everywhere in the Americas.

Two years after this free Mexican town—San Lorenzo de los Negros—received its charter, about twenty Africans disembarked from a Dutch ship at Jamestown, Virginia. These people were the first Africans shipped to the new and permanent settlement that the English colonists had established in North America. They came 117 years after Africans were first enslaved in the Americas, in Hispaniola.

From Africa to the Americas

Modern archaeological research has established that Africa was the birthplace of human life. No precise date can be given for the emergence of early humans, or the hominid species, but it may have taken place about two million years ago. The earliest of these hominid fossils were discovered at Lake Turkana in Kenya, at Olduvai Gorge in Tanzania, and at the river Omo in Ethiopia. Consequently, it is possible to claim that east and northeast Africa formed the cradle of human society. In time, over hundreds of thousands of years, early humans moved to other parts of Africa and to other continents.

The first Africans were nomadic peoples who made simple stone tools to aid them in their struggles for survival. With the passage of time, these tools became more sophisticated. The hand ax, for example, appeared around a million years ago. Its sharp cutting edges were more effective in the killing of prey than the earlier tools. Probably about sixty thousand years ago, Africans started using fire. This development meant that meat could be cooked, and fire may even have been used to clear land for settlement or other purposes.

Human life in Africa, or elsewhere for that matter, was always changing. The people developed new tools, moved around, and organized their lives and societies in a variety of ways. There was much diversity among the African peoples in terms of their culture and skin color. In northeastern Africa, for example, the people tended to be lighter in complexion than those who lived in the tropical areas. Much of this difference in skin color was a result of living in different climates. Individuals who lived in areas of intense heat and sunlight developed the kind of dark skin pigmentation that provided more effective protection against the ravages of heat and allowed them to survive.

The black peoples of Africa, however, should not be characterized as belonging to a single race. In fact, many scholars have abandoned the use of the concept of "race" as a way of categorizing peoples. Skin color and other physical features do not reveal much about the genetic makeup of an individual or group. Two individuals with the same skin color and hair texture may be more genetically different from one another than they are from two persons with another pigmentation. For this reason, scholars have concluded that Africans, and other peoples as well, are so internally different that the old way of classifying people according to physical appearance or "race" is no longer useful.

It is more useful to look at the African peoples according to language groupings. Different languages make up a family if their structures are basically similar. In most cases, the similarities in these languages result from the interaction among the speakers and the mutual borrowing of words. Using this method of studying languages, scholars have fitted the African peoples into five language families: the Afro-Asiatic family in North Africa; the Nilo-Saharan languages spoken in areas south and east of the Sahara and around the Nile River valley; the Congo-Kordofanian family spoken in West and West Central Africa; and the Khoisan group of languages spoken in southern Africa and parts of East Africa. A sixth family, the Austronesian, is found in Madagascar but is not native of Africa (having originated in Southeast Asia).

African societies varied in the pace of their development and the nature of the changes that they experienced over time. Egypt, for example, was the first society to begin cultivating food crops, probably about 5500 B.C. Other societies followed. By 3000 B.C., the people living in the savanna were producing a variety of grains and yams. The development of agriculture made it possible to support larger populations and contributed to the rise of settlements.

Throughout the continent, the people organized themselves in political units of various sizes and degrees of complexity. Egypt was the first great African civilization. Located in an area fertilized by the Nile River, Egypt made rapid strides in agriculture and commerce by 3000 B.C. Before 3100 B.C., however, several small states existed in the area. These political divisions came to an end when the states formed one kingdom ruled by the pharaohs. This national unity paved the way for an impressive civilization that would last for several centuries.

Egyptian civilization was characterized by a hieroglyphic writing system, complex religious ideas, and monumental stone pyramids. Although historians disagree on this matter, it appears that the Egyptian peoples consisted of black Africans as well as lighter-skinned peoples from the Mediterranean area. Their civilization had a major impact on Greek culture and ultimately on Western civilization.

Ancient Egypt is the best known of the early African societies, but it did not stand alone. Elsewhere, Africans developed a variety of states ranging from a few hundred people to large kingdoms and empires. These states were not all alike; there were variations in their political and social structures, the nature of the power exercised by the rulers, their religions, and so on. Many Africans believed that the authority and power of their ruler derived from the gods. Most of these societies had their own bureaucracies, taxation systems, and armed forces.

Some of the best-known states and empires were located in the western and central Sudan. Ghana, located in West Africa north of the Niger and Senegal valleys, was probably the earliest of them all. Noted for its great wealth and the power of its ruler, Ghana was said to have had an army of more than two hundred thousand soldiers around A.D. 1068. Later, the empire of Mali rose to prominence in the fourteenth century, occupying areas that are now part of Nigeria and the Guinea forests.

Mali's most famous ruler was Mansa Kankan Musa, who came to the throne in 1312. Bold and aggressive, he extended the frontiers of the Mali Empire to the Atlantic Ocean, incorporating several smaller states along the way. A Muslim, Mansa Musa undertook a pilgrimage to Mecca, which was then a part of Egypt, in 1324. On this journey, Mansa Musa made a lavish display of his wealth. He was

ANCIENT KINGDOMS OF THE WESTERN SUDAN

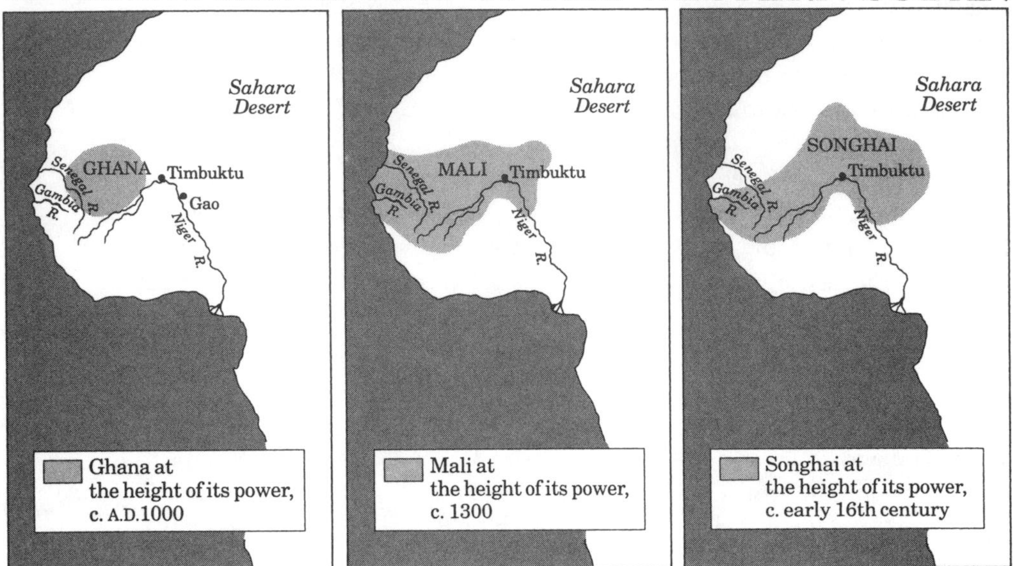

In the western Sudan, the kingdom of Ghana was the first important African empire to emerge. The Mali empire came to power in the fourteenth century and later, in the early sixteenth century, the Songhai kingdom dominated the region.

accompanied by five hundred slaves, each one bearing a staff of gold that weighed six pounds. In addition, one hundred camels carried thirty thousand pounds of gold. Mansa Musa's extravagance in Egypt created an accurate perception that his empire was one of the wealthiest then in existence.

The African peoples also developed cultural traditions that met their needs. The family was the basis of their social organization. Kinship ties, which united members of an ethnic group, were particularly strong. African societies were also deeply religious; most had a supreme god and other lesser deities. There was hardly any distinction between the religious and the secular, or civil, aspects of life. Religious beliefs determined when almost all activities, such as the planting seasons, harvest time, or the naming of children, would take place. Not surprisingly, the African peoples who came to the Americas brought very strong family and religious traditions with them.

African societies were never free from influences that originated outside of the continent. The Egyptian civilization enjoyed much interaction with the societies of the Mediterranean. There was a great deal of contact between the East African societies and those of Asia. Ethiopians had lived in Greece from about the fifth century B.C. Other Africans, usually traders, had visited various European countries for centuries.

In the eighth century, the new and aggressive Islamic religion began to gain converts in North and sub-Saharan Africa. With the embrace of Islam came important changes in the beliefs of the Africans and the nature of their legal systems. The Islamization of West Africa was aided by traders who converted to Islam in the north and brought their new religious ideas across the Sahara to the south. The pace of religious conversion and the number of converts varied, but few states remained untouched by Islam at the start of the Atlantic slave trade in the early sixteenth century. This did not mean, however, that most West Africans became Muslims and abandoned their traditional religious ideas. For many of the converts to Islam, ancient beliefs existed alongside the new ones, although these beliefs were undoubtedly modified in some way over time. Some of the Africans who were enslaved in the Americas were Muslims, but most were not.

Some scholars think that some West African peoples had established trading relationships with the native peoples of the Americas before the arrival of Columbus in 1492. Such contacts may have begun as early as the seventh century B.C. This conclusion is based on skeletal remains found in Central America that appear to be African, representations of African features in the art of some of the first Americans, as well as similarities in some African languages and those spoken in the Americas before Columbus. Because these kinds of evidence are subject to different interpretations, it cannot yet be established conclusively that Africans arrived in the Americas before the Europeans did.

Historians can never be certain of the number of Africans who were brought to the Americas as slaves. Reliable records were often not kept, some have disappeared, and there is no firm data on those persons who were imported illegally. Those Europeans and Americans who engaged in illegal slave trading did so in order to avoid paying taxes on the slaves that they carried. Others traded without receiving permission to do so from the authorities or began smuggling slaves after laws were passed abolishing the human traffic. In spite of these difficulties, most historians now estimate that the number of Africans who arrived as slaves from 1502 to the mid-nineteenth century amounted to between ten and twelve million. Most of these people were shipped to Latin America and the Caribbean.

The foundations of the Atlantic slave trade were established in the sixteenth century by Spanish colonists, who were no strangers to the institution of slavery. Prior to Columbus's voyages to the Americas, the Spaniards held Muslims, black Africans, Slavs, and even other Spaniards as slaves. In fact, the number of African slaves in Spain and Portugal was increasing during the years preceding Columbus's voyages, reflecting a decline in the use of other groups as slaves.

Under the circumstances, it is not surprising that the Spaniards in Hispaniola, the first colony in the Caribbean, asked the Crown to send them African slaves once the need for labor arose. This request was made in 1501, a mere seven years after the island had been colonized. Unwilling to perform menial and backbreaking tasks, the Spaniards had expected to depend on the forced labor of the native peoples. The Indians, at least those who fell under the control of the colonists, were enslaved and required to work in the fields, households, and mines. But many Indians soon died from mistreatment and disease, which created a shortage of labor.

Faced with a declining supply of Indian laborers, the Spanish colonists pondered their options and decided to introduce African slavery. Not only were Africans performing unpaid labor in Spain and elsewhere in Europe at the time, but as a group they were placed at the bottom of the social order as well. The terms *black* and *slave* had become increasingly interchangeable in Spain in the fifteenth century. The country's moral climate justified African slavery. In other words, black Africans had occupied a decidedly inferior place in Spanish society prior to Columbus's expeditions. In addition, the notion that Africans could be enslaved and were suited for that condition had become widely accepted and deeply rooted in Spanish society.

It is not entirely clear why this was the case. Spaniards, and by extension the Portuguese and other Europeans, may have attributed negative qualities to the Africans because they were different culturally, had black skin, and were not Christians. Africans were people set apart as the "other," persons whose differences the Europeans neither appreciated, respected, nor understood. Not until the nineteenth century, however, did a full-blown racist ideology develop to promote the biological claims to superiority by whites and to defend the treatment of blacks by alleging that they were inferior members of the human species. No such "scientific" claims were made at the time of Columbus. Perhaps none was needed. By purchasing Africans and using them as slaves, the Europeans were already asserting power over them. In time, the Africans' inferior place in society came to be seen as normal, and few voices were raised to challenge their treatment and condition.

In response to the request from the governor of Hispaniola for African slave labor in 1501, the Spanish Crown authorized the shipment of slaves in 1502. The slaves in this first cargo had lived in Spain for some time before they were shipped to the Caribbean. Not until 1518 would slaves be transported to the Americas directly from Africa.

The Portuguese were the pioneering European slave traders. Portugal was the first country in Europe that had developed the technology to conduct a seafaring trade. Unlike some of the other European countries, Portugal was politically united by the fifteenth century and free from the sorts of serious internal conflicts that weakened its neighbors. As a result, its leaders could focus their energies on overseas expansion and trade. Situated on the Atlantic Ocean, the Portuguese had also made significant advances in shipbuilding, thereby giving them the ability to participate actively in overseas trading ventures. Portugal had also developed a class of merchants and entrepreneurs with the wealth, skill, and experience to conduct a slave trade.

Prince Henry, who would later be called "the Navigator," was one of the earliest of the Portuguese explorers. His explorations along the African coast in the 1420s opened the way for the development of a European-African trade in black slaves. The first organized Portuguese expedition to capture black Africans and enslave them appears to have occurred in 1441. Led by Antão Gonçalves and Nuno Tristão, the members of the expedition captured twelve Africans off the coast of northern Mauritania and presented them at the Portuguese court.

This initial Portuguese success at people-stealing encouraged additional attempts. A few kidnapped Africans were brought to Portugal in succeeding months, but the single largest group was unloaded in Lisbon on August 8, 1444. There were between 235 and 240 captives in this party. In time, Genoese, Florentine, and Castilian traders joined the Portuguese kidnappers on the West African coast. But the Portuguese remained the principal carriers of Africans to Europe for the next century and more. The process by which these Africans were acquired in the early years cannot be characterized as a trade. The evidence does not show that the Europeans bargained with anyone; the Africans were simply abducted. Portuguese authorities, however, imposed a tax on all Africans sold in their country.

Not surprisingly, the Europeans could not continue to kidnap Africans indefinitely, and a trade with its own rules would have to be developed. To this end, the Portuguese built a fort on the island of Arguin to serve as a base for trade with the Africans. This did not mean that raids for African slaves ceased; it indicated that the contact with Africa was being placed on a more formal footing and that the abductions decreased even if they did not disappear. By 1450 the Portuguese had begun to transport an average of one thousand to two thousand African slaves to Europe each year. Most of these people came from the Senegambia, but a few were from other nearby areas.

Portugal's domination of the Euro-African trade deepened as the fifteenth century wore on. In 1452, Pope Nicholas V granted the Portuguese king the authority to attack and enslave "the Moors, heathens and other enemies of Christ" who lived south of Cape Bojador. Although this and other papal grants did not necessarily lead to an increase in the number of slaves, they gave the approval of the church to the institution of slavery and paved the way for Portuguese conquest and occupation of societies that were not Christian. In 1479, Spain recognized Portugal's supremacy in the slave trade by signing the Treaty of Aláçovas. The treaty granted Portugal the right to supply Spain with African slaves and accepted its monopoly of the African trade. Three years later, in 1482, the Portuguese built a fort on the Gold Coast (modern Ghana) to encourage, assist, and protect the expanding African commerce. Known as Elmina Castle, the fort could hold hundreds of slaves.

Clearly, when the Spanish Crown agreed to send African slaves to Hispaniola in 1502, the bureaucratic machinery of treaties and established practices was already in place to acquire them. Under the terms of the 1479 treaty, the Portuguese had already agreed to supply African slaves to the Spaniards. So the decline of the

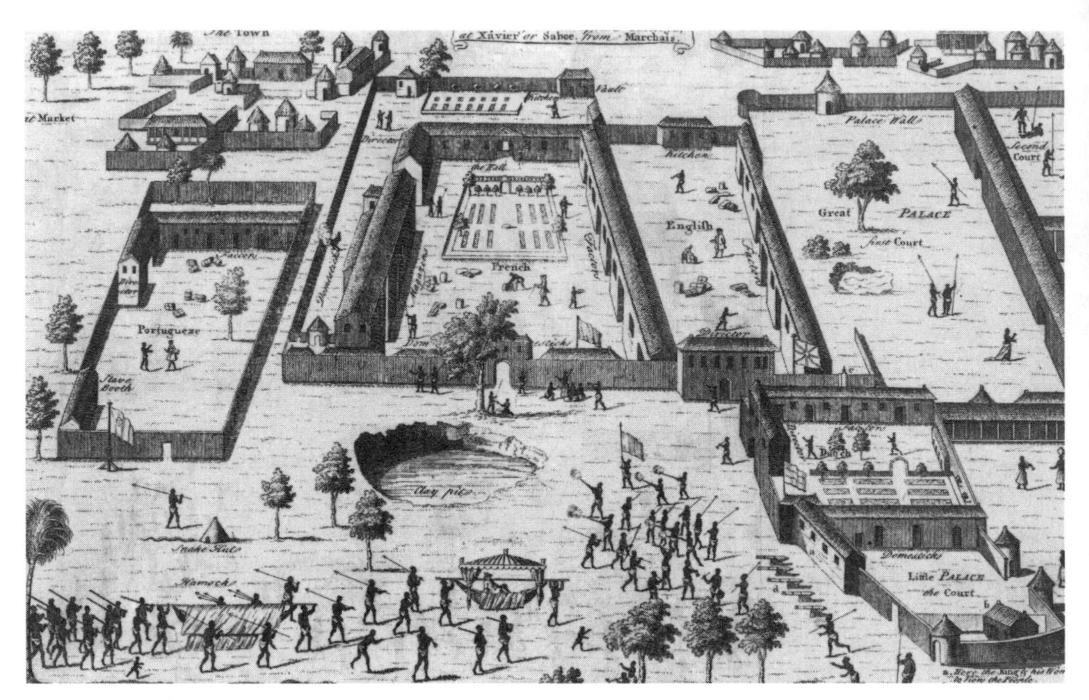

This drawing shows the layout of a European slave-trading center in West Africa. By the mid-seventeenth century, Portugal, England, France, Holland, and other European countries were involved in the trade of African slaves.

Indian population of the Americas and the Spanish colonists' insistence on a new labor force did not create the African slave trade and slavery. Both were already in existence. The demand for slaves in the Americas did, however, lead to an expansion of the trade and a change in its direction. Instead of going up to Europe, the majority of the Africans would soon be sent across the Atlantic to the Americas.

The increase in the demand for slaves, coupled with the expectation that huge profits could be made, led several other European nations to participate in the slave trade. By 1650, the Dutch, the English, and the French, among others, had joined the Portuguese in this human commerce. Spain, whose colonies consumed most of the African slaves during the first century and a half of the slave trade, did no trading on the African coast until the late eighteenth century. This was not by design. It was a consequence of another treaty signed by Spain and Portugal in 1494. Known as the Treaty of Tordesillas, the agreement permitted the Portuguese to trade on the African coast and in Asia and Brazil. The Spaniards were confined to the rest of what became known as the Americas. The other European nations, however, were not parties to this division of the known world. They did not feel themselves bound by the treaty, and they ignored it.

Once the Spanish Crown authorized the introduction of African slaves in the Americas, it issued licenses, for a fee, to individual traders to supply the slaves. These traders were likely to be either Portuguese, Genoese, or Spaniards. The license specified the number of slaves that would be delivered and the destination. A new license was required for each slave-trading journey because the Crown wanted to exercise control over the supply of slaves and to receive the tax revenue that the trade generated. Most traders received permission to deliver fewer than twenty or thirty slaves. There were exceptions, of course, and some traders were allowed to ship hundreds of slaves at one time. Spaniards who intended to settle in the colonies were also allowed to take with them any slaves that they already owned.

The system of awarding licenses did not satisfy the growing demand for unfree African labor. Some traders did not fulfill their contractual obligations for one reason or another. Slave deliveries were often delayed, and Africans never arrived in adequate numbers to meet the demand.

In spite of the bureaucratic and other problems that the licensing system produced, it was not replaced until 1595. In that year, the Spanish Crown introduced a monopoly system known as the *Asiento,* or "contract." Under this system, a trader or a trading company was granted the sole right to supply a given number of slaves, usually several thousand each year, to the colonies for a specified number of years. These contracts were awarded only after the Crown received bids from prospective traders. The traders who were chosen had to pay a sizeable fee when they received the contract.

Most, if not all, of these traders failed to meet the terms of their agreements. Some ran into financial difficulties, and others were more interested in engaging in other forms of commerce, such as trading in silver and other precious metals or in textiles. The failure of the *Asentistas* to meet their contractual obligations paved the way for other traders to smuggle slaves into the colonies. The smugglers were likely to be Portuguese, Spanish, Dutch, or English traders.

The business of the Atlantic slave trade was helped by the existence of slavery and a slave trade inside Africa. As was the case with various societies in Asia, Europe, and the Americas, forms of servitude existed among African ethnic groups. Captives taken in war, debtors, and persons convicted of certain crimes, such as homicides, could lose their liberty. These people still had some rights, however. They could marry, inherit property, and participate extensively in the life of the host society. Over time, most slaves could expect to receive their freedom. The pace at which this occurred must have varied, but the expectation that freedom was within reach probably made their condition more endurable.

Still, the Atlantic slave trade did not develop *because* slavery already existed in Africa. Such a claim would place the primary responsibility for the human traffic on the shoulders of the African peoples. The European and American traders joined hands with their African counterparts to conduct a mutually beneficial

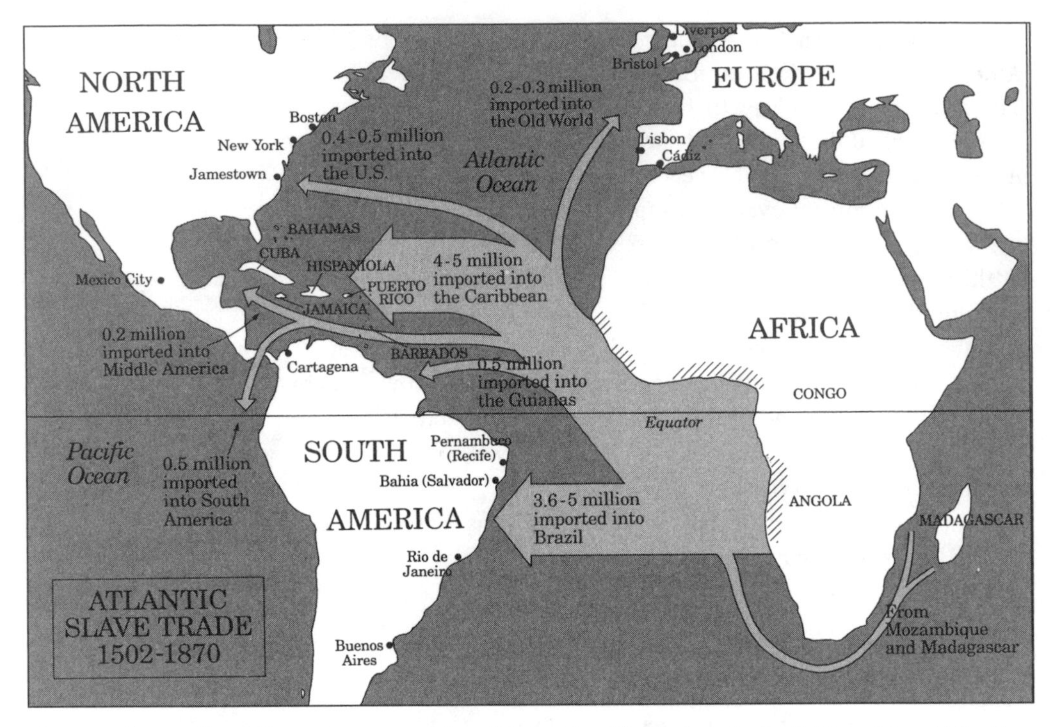

This map shows where African slaves were shipped during the Atlantic slave trade. Between 10 and 12 million African slaves were imported into the Americas.

commerce. It was a trade like any other, bound by the rules of supply and demand, profit and loss. But the slave trade differed from other forms of business in one important respect: The trading goods were other human beings. It is this crucial difference that explains the horror of the slave trade and the moral revulsion that it would later produce.

The rules governing the slave trade took their distinctive shape during the second half of the fifteenth century. Once the external demand for African workers began to increase, the process by which they were acquired fell under the control of the local traders. Although European traders continued to abduct unsuspecting Africans, the number of such raids diminished. The African leaders and their peoples had to assert control over what was taking place in their territory and could not allow foreigners to kidnap their citizens at will. Such atrocities undermined the stability of the society and constituted an assault on the people. The African rulers also realized that if the developing trade were organized and regulated, they could make money from it. Among other things, a tax was imposed on the sale of each slave.

Portuguese traders obtained their slave cargoes for the Americas from West Africa as well as from the Congo and Angola, which are located in West Central Africa. Until about 1600, the majority of the slaves came from West Africa, from a vast area north of the equator. This region includes modern Senegal, Gambia, Guinea-Bissau, and Sierra Leone. The ethnic groups that made up these slave cargoes included the Wolof and the Serer from Senegal; the Mandinka from the Gambia; the Bram, Banyun, and Biafada from Guinea-Bissau; the Baga, Temne, and Landuma peoples from Sierra Leone; and the Congo-Angola region provided the Bakongo, Teke, and Ambundu peoples. Probably about one-third of the slaves originated in the Congo-Angola region, and about twenty-five percent each came from both the Senegambia and Guinea-Bissau.

The sources for the supply of slaves kept shifting throughout the entire history of the African slave trade. Much depended on political developments in the various societies. Whenever states were at war, and if these wars continued for long periods of time, the captives would be made available for sale to European traders. Such was the case of the states in the Senegambia in the sixteenth century and of the kingdom of Kongo during the same period. Angola increasingly became the chief source of slaves as the sixteenth century progressed. This was the result of the political disorder that wracked the various states in the area. By 1600, slave cargoes also included the Akan from the Gold Coast (modern Ghana), the Fon from coastal Dahomey, and the Ibo from eastern Nigeria. A few persons also came from southeastern Africa, principally from Mozambique. Overall, West Central Africa supplied about forty percent of the slaves between the sixteenth and nineteenth centuries.

The political divisions among the African peoples largely accounted for the availability of slaves for the Atlantic market. Africa has never been a politically united continent whose peoples had a common identity and consciousness—either during the sixteenth century, or at any time during the course of the slave trade, or later. Hardly anyone would have described himself or herself as an "African." Residents of the continent were more likely to think of themselves as belonging to specific ethnic groups, such as the Ibo, Biafada, Bram, or Mandinka. The concept of an African identity above and beyond ethnic and geographic boundaries is a relatively recent development.

West and West Central Africa, from which most of the captives were taken, consisted of a large number of states. Some of these were relatively small, while others, such as the kingdom of Kongo and the Jolof Empire in the Senegambia, were very large and included various mini-states that they had absorbed. These states frequently had disputes that led to warfare. In some cases, larger and more powerful states attempted to overrun their smaller neighbors. These instances of territorial expansion often led to prolonged conflicts and the taking of prisoners. Other conflicts between states arose from commercial rivalries, struggles to control trade routes, and even efforts to determine who would succeed to the leadership of bordering states. The political fragmentation of the different regions, coupled with the varieties of conflicts that led to war, created a constant flow of human victims for the trade.

The vast majority of the slaves were prisoners of war. The seller and the victim usually belonged to different states and were enemies. Accordingly, Africans did not "sell their own people," as some historians have maintained. Such a claim ignores the culturally and politically diverse nature of the regions from which the slaves came as well as the diversity of the African continent as a whole. The overwhelming majority—perhaps eighty percent—of the victims of the human traffic were likely to be persons who had no ties to the state of their sellers, had no rights, and were vulnerable to the traditional fate of wartime prisoners—imprisonment, enslavement, or death.

Little is known about the process by which the slaves were traded during the early years. (Information is much more readily available for the years after 1650.) Still, it is known that the European traders exchanged textile products, guns, gunpowder, alcohol, pots and pans, and a range of other consumer goods for the slaves. The value of each slave was arrived at after much bargaining between the black and the white traders. The process evidently became more complicated in the seventeenth century, when more Europeans entered the trade, bringing a wider variety of products with values expressed in their own currency. Thus, in addition to the Portuguese escudo, the Africans had to get accustomed to the English pound sterling, the Dutch guilder, and the French franc. The Africans, too, had different monetary systems. There was the iron bar in Sierra Leone, gold in Ghana, cowrie shells in Dahomey, and Loango cloth in Angola.

Once the African was sold, he or she was usually branded with the identification mark of the purchaser. Whether this was a regular practice in the early years is uncertain, but it would become so in the seventeenth century and later. A slave who was branded could be identified in the event of escape or if the individual were stolen by a European competitor. There was, understandably, not much honor in the slave-trading business.

The slaves' journey to the coast and to the waiting ships could be quite hazardous. Prodded by their captors, some perished along the way as a consequence of disease and wounds infected by branding. Death was an ever-present feature of the trade. Many more would die as they awaited departure on the coast for the Americas, and others would succumb during the Atlantic crossing.

The length of time that the human cargoes waited in the forts on the coast prior to their departure for the Americas varied. Much depended on the supply of slaves to be purchased. This, in turn, was related to whether the states were at war, which would generate captives who could be sold. Once the traders had acquired their full cargo, the long and terrible journey to the Americas began.

The journey from Africa to the Americas was known as the Middle Passage. It derived its name from the second, or middle, segment of a European-based slave ship's triangular route. The first leg was the trip from Europe to Africa, and the third was the ship's return journey from the Americas to Europe. The Middle

Passage, however, remains the most horrible symbol of the traffic in human beings. Chained together and confined to the cramped, hot, and humid holds of the ships, these Africans were lucky if they survived the ordeal. The sanitary conditions aboard these slave ships were appalling, producing the perfect environment for the spread of disease. Some slaves were already ill before they embarked, and others were tormented by disease on board the ship. Dysentery, measles, smallpox, yellow fever, dehydration, and a variety of "fevers" proved to be the scourge of every journey.

It was, of course, impossible to predict how many slaves would die during the crossing. The *Asiento* contracts that the Spaniards awarded usually made allowances for a death rate of between ten percent and forty percent on each cargo. But it is not entirely clear whether this was an accurate estimate for the sixteenth century.

The death rate not only reflected the sanitary conditions aboard the ships, but it was also related to the general health of the slaves before the journey began. Chance, or luck, played a part as well. If there was no one on board who carried an infectious disease, such as smallpox, the cargo would most likely experience a lower than average death rate.

There was also a relationship between the time the ship took to cross the Atlantic and the death toll. The faster the sailing time, the lower the death rate. During the sixteenth century it took anywhere from twelve to twenty weeks to reach the American ports. Such a long confinement at sea in close quarters aided the spread of disease. With the construction of faster ships in the eighteenth and nineteenth centuries, the sailing time ranged between five and eight weeks. The average death rate in the eighteenth century was between ten percent and fifteen percent; by the nineteenth century it had fallen to somewhere between five percent and ten percent. Sanitary conditions had improved aboard the ships, and better medical care was provided.

Thoughtful captains took care to provide their human cargoes with a diet consisting of the foods to which they were accustomed. The composition of these foods varied, depending on the part of Africa from which the slaves came. In general, however, such foods included corn, yams, palm oil, rice, and potatoes. Slave ships also stocked foodstuffs that they brought from Europe, such as bread, cheese, beef, beans, and flour. However, these supplies sometimes proved inadequate to feed a cargo of slaves, particularly if the journey to the Americas lasted longer than had been expected. Reports from the eighteenth century and later described voyages that ran out of food and slaves who arrived thin and hungry.

The slaves must have engaged in forms of resistance on board ships during this early period, but the surviving records shed no light on this issue. Ships did, however, carry a variety of gadgets—such as mouth openers, thumb screws, chains, and whips—to punish those who resisted their condition. During the eighteenth and nineteenth centuries slaves participated in rebellions and hunger strikes, jumped overboard, and verbally abused the crew. Such physical challenges to slavery on the high seas were seldom successful, but they often resulted in considerable loss of life.

The arrival of the slaves in such places as Hispaniola, Lima, and Vera Cruz signaled the end of one awful experience and the beginning of another. The Africans were purchased yet again and became the property of strange people in a strange land. Their prospects of returning to their homeland were virtually nonexistent. Their ties with their kith and kin were severed forever, and their sense of alienation in their new lands must have been paralyzing.

Where did the slaves who arrived in the Americas go? The vast majority, approximately ninety-five percent, were distributed to the societies of Latin America and the Caribbean. Only about five percent ended up in the British colonies of North America, or what is now the United States. The following figures are a reasonably accurate accounting of the distribution patterns of the trade based upon present knowledge:

British North America	550,000
Spanish America	2,000,000
British Caribbean	2,500,000 to 3,000,000
French Caribbean	1,600,000
Dutch Caribbean	50,000
Brazil	4,000,000 to 5,000,000
Danish Caribbean	50,000

Almost all of the slaveholding societies of the Americas experienced an annual decrease in population as the Africans fell victim to hard work and disease. As a result, they had to depend on the slave trade to replenish their labor supply. The only exception to this pattern was English North America. By the first decades of the eighteenth century, the North American slave population began to reproduce itself, and it sustained this growth until emancipation came in the 1860s. For this reason, North America was much less dependent on the slave trade than the other slave societies of the Americas, which had a profound influence on the culture of the black population in this region. The North American slave population by the nineteenth century was essentially a creole, or locally born, population. Although only about five hundred thousand Africans had been imported into that society, the slave population numbered almost four million in 1860, just before the outbreak of the Civil War.

The Worlds of Slavery and Work

African slaves were first brought to the Americas in the sixteenth century to meet the economic needs of Spanish and Portuguese colonists. The first slaves arrived in Hispaniola in 1502; thousands more would experience a similar fate as the century progressed. From Hispaniola the institution of slavery spread to the other islands in the Caribbean that were colonized by the Spaniards—Puerto Rico, Cuba, and Jamaica. Eventually, such mainland colonies as Mexico, Peru, Venezuela, Bolivia, and those in Central America became the new homes of thousands of unfree African workers. Brazil, a Portuguese colony, was no exception; by 1600 it joined Mexico and Peru as one of the three largest slaveholding societies.

The Spaniards and the Portuguese were not the only slaveholders in the Americas. In time, African slaves were used in all of the European colonies. By 1650, for example, the English had begun to use enslaved Africans in their Caribbean and North American colonies. The Dutch, the French, and the Danes would soon do likewise. So great was the demand for African labor that an average of 60,000 slaves were imported annually during the eighteenth century.

Of the 300,000 Africans who arrived before 1620, the greatest number, probably around 80,000, went to Mexico. This colony received most of its slaves after 1570, when the Indian population began a rapid decline. Once the local population began to recover in the mid-seventeenth century and a racially mixed group emerged (mestizos, the children of Spaniards and Indians), fewer Africans were imported. The other mainland colonies and the Caribbean islands received another eighty thousand to ninety thousand slaves before 1620. Portuguese Brazil did not begin to import Africans until the mid-sixteenth century, but it received an ever-increasing number throughout the rest of that century and in succeeding years. By 1620 that colony had imported an estimated 130,000 slaves.

Regardless of where the slaves went, the colonial authorities introduced laws that defined their status and regulated their behavior. Because the Spaniards and the Portuguese owned slaves before they came to the Americas, they had already developed rules governing their behavior, rights, and treatment. The Spanish slave laws were a part of a larger body of laws and moral principles that formed the basis of the Spanish legal system. Known as *Las Siete Partidas* (the Seven Parts), these laws granted slaves the right to marry, inherit property, and to be freed under certain conditions. The *Partidas* imposed limits on the masters' ability to mistreat their slaves, and slaves could appeal to the local authorities if their rights were violated. It is not known whether the law was always enforced.

The situation in Portugal, at least in theory, was somewhat different. At the time when Brazil was colonized in the sixteenth century, the mother country did not have a body of laws similar to the *Siete Partidas.* Rather, each town had its own rules, and there does not appear to have been much uniformity in content or enforcement. Accordingly, the Crown filled the breach by issuing appropriate laws when the need arose. The English, French, and Dutch had no preexisting law of slavery. As a result, these nations developed their colonial slave laws in a piecemeal fashion.

The slave laws that the Spanish colonists introduced in the sixteenth century in Hispaniola, Mexico, Peru, and elsewhere shared many features. In general, these laws were much harsher than those existing in Spain. Outnumbered by a servile population of Indians and Africans in the sixteenth century, the colonists tried to impose rigid controls over those whom they exploited and enslaved. Essentially, the laws were designed to protect the slaveholding class from the angry reprisals of their human property.

The earliest legislation concerning black slaves that the colonial governments introduced prohibited them from owning or carrying weapons. In Mexico, for example, such laws were placed on the books at various times beginning in 1537. Peru issued its first series of restrictive measures in 1545 and repeated the measures in succeeding years to ensure enforcement. Such restrictive legislation also established the punishment for assaulting whites. According to a 1552 law, slaves who took up arms against a Spaniard in Mexico were liable to receive one hundred lashes in addition to having a nail driven through their hands. Slaves would have their hands cut off if they repeated the offense.

As the slave populations increased, colonial authorities imposed a series of controls on almost every aspect of the Africans' public lives. Although the details varied, slaves were forbidden to be out of doors after dark, and could not travel freely or gather in large groups except for religious purposes. Insecure masters wanted to take no chances; they had to ensure that their human property lacked the opportunity or the means to launch movements to claim their freedom. But such restrictions did not always have the desired results.

Although the slave owners and other whites feared black slaves, colonial society increasingly became dependent on them for a variety of services. As soon as blacks began to arrive in the colonies, the Spaniards used them to help subjugate the native peoples and to explore for new territories to seize. Hernan Cortés, who defeated the Aztecs, is said to have had three hundred African slaves with him in Mexico in 1522. African slaves accompanied the Spaniards on their various military invasions of Peru beginning in 1524. A number of them participated in explorations into Chile and other areas on the coast and in the interior. A black man was among the four Spanish soldiers chosen by the Spanish conquistador Francisco Pizarro to be in the advance party to survey the Inca capital at Cuzco, Peru. Slaves also participated in the Spanish military expeditions against the Indians in Honduras in the 1550s.

The role of blacks in such military expeditions, however, paled in comparison to their sustained importance as workers. As soon as they began to arrive in Hispaniola in 1502, slaves assumed the most strenuous tasks, setting a precedent for other slaveholding societies. The colonists in these early years were particularly interested in mining for precious metals and constantly appealed for black slaves. The Crown was willing to agree because it received a one-fifth share of the proceeds of the mines. In 1505, for example, King Ferdinand informed the governor of Hispaniola that "I will send more Negro slaves as you request. I think there may be a hundred. At each time a trustworthy person will go with them who may share in the gold they may collect."

Without a doubt, black slaves played the most important roles in the mining industry during the sixteenth century. Mining was a particularly hazardous activity, and the death rate of those involved in it tended to be quite high. The Indian workers died quickly, and the Spaniards as a group did not find the occupation attractive. African slaves were imported as substitutes, and they, too, suffered a high death rate.

The Africans were used first in the copper and gold mines of Hispaniola, but these metals were not abundant there. The industry soon collapsed. On the other hand, the mainland colonies of Mexico and Peru were extremely rich in silver deposits. By 1550 the colonists had found silver in northern Mexico at Zacatecas, Guanajuato, and Pachuca. Deposits of silver were also uncovered at Michoacan, Tasco, Temascaltepec, and other places. In Peru, silver veins were struck in the highland areas of Potosí and Porco, and rich gold deposits were discovered at Chachapoyas and Carabaya.

Shortly after the discovery of the first silver veins in Mexico, Viceroy Antonio de Mendoza requested that the authorities in Spain send Africans because "the silver mines are increasing, as each day more and more are discovered while the [Indian] slaves continue to decrease." A sympathetic Crown responded favorably to these pleas, but the supply of Africans could not keep abreast of the demand for them in the mines and other economic enterprises. The high death rate of the Africans and Indians employed in the mining industry from accidents (such as collapsing underground roofs) and lung diseases also made the labor problem more severe.

Some of those who advocated the importation of Africans wanted to relieve the Indians of the burdensome labor of the mines. Another Mexican viceroy, the Marques de Villamanrique, was one such person. In 1586, for example, he noted the "dangerous" and "excessive" nature of the work in which the Indians were engaged in the mines. In order to protect them from such exploitation he asked that three thousand or four thousand Africans be sent. Four years later, in an attempt to increase the servile labor force, the viceroy recommended that all free blacks and mulattoes (children of Spaniards and blacks) in the colony be forced to labor in the mines. Not only would they serve as a substitute for Indian workers, the viceroy reasoned, but they would also earn wages and "their children growing up in that life would become fond of it."

Black slaves also played critically important roles in the textile factories of Mexico and, to a lesser extent, Peru. These workshops, known as *obrajes*, manufactured cloth for the residents of the colonies. The workers in these factories were often physically abused and forced to labor for long hours in cramped, hot, and humid quarters. The Crown was concerned about the poor working conditions in these hell houses and wanted to protect the Indians in Mexico from being employed in them. In 1601, the Crown prohibited Indian workers from laboring in the Mexican *obrajes* and repeated the ban in 1609, probably because it was not being enforced. In both instances, the Crown decreed that black slaves should replace the Indians. Clearly, the Crown saw black workers as suited for the most difficult tasks in society and seemed unconcerned about the inhumane conditions under which they worked. There was nothing particularly new about this attitude; black workers in Spain had experienced a similar fate.

As soon as it became clear that the early mining economy in the islands would collapse because of the depletion of the mineral resources, the Spanish colonists embraced other pursuits. The climate and soil of the Caribbean proved ideal for sugarcane cultivation, and in 1506 the colonists in Hispaniola began to experiment with growing that crop. The Spaniards and the Portuguese had been familiar with sugarcane cultivation for centuries before the Columbus voyages. By the mid-fifteenth century, the Portuguese had begun to use African slaves on their sugarcane plantations in the Atlantic islands of Madeira, São Tomé, the Azores, the Canaries, and Cape Verde. Africans who were experienced in the techniques of sugarcane cultivation and the sugar industry must have comprised some of the slave cargoes to the Americas.

The first sugar mill (*ingenio*) in the Caribbean was constructed in Hispaniola in 1516, and by 1548 the island had thirty-five of them, the most that would exist there at any one time in the sixteenth century. Sugarcane cultivation also spread to the other islands of Puerto Rico, Jamaica, and Cuba. Although Hispaniola began to export sugar in 1521, the sugar industry did not flourish anywhere in the Caribbean in the sixteenth century. Not until after 1650 did sugar become "king" in the islands, particularly in the English, Dutch, and French colonies.

Sugarcane cultivation, aided by the extensive use of African slave labor, underwent its greatest expansion on the mainland during the sixteenth century. Mexico and Brazil became particularly important as sugar-producing colonies, but cane was also cultivated in Peru, Venezuela, and elsewhere. Because the Portuguese dominated the slave trade, Brazil received an ever-expanding supply of African labor. By 1580, this colony not only boasted a large black population but was the principal supplier of sugar to European markets.

Mexico was the earliest of the mainland colonies to grow sugarcane. Because of their agreeable climates, the tropical areas surrounding Vera Cruz and the warm valleys of Michoacan, Huatusco, Córdoba, and Oaxaca quickly became major centers of sugarcane cultivation. Historians are not certain when the colonists first started to grow the cane; contemporary sources indicate that it began between 1524 and 1530. African slaves seemed to have been used in the industry from the outset.

Sugarcane plantations in sixteenth-century Mexico were of various sizes, depending on the availability of capital, land, and labor. There were some extremely large ones by the last decades of the sixteenth century, employing scores of African

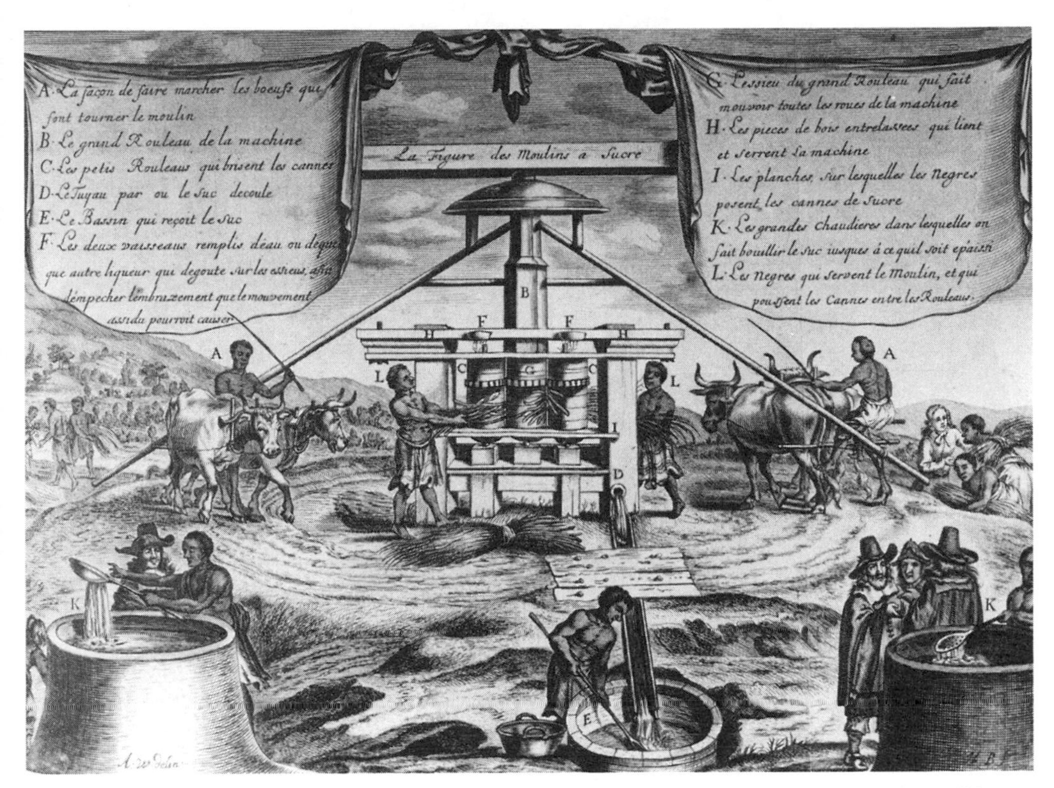

This seventeenth-century French engraving shows slaves laboring at an outdoor sugar mill in the Caribbean. Most sugar mills were actually inside buildings.

workers. In 1580, a plantation at Orizaba reported the presence of 123 African slaves, and in 1606 the Santísima Trinidad plantation in Jalapa had two hundred. Most plantations probably employed fewer Africans, and almost all appear to have had Indian workers as well.

The Crown did not take kindly to the use of Indians on the sugar plantations. The work was demanding, and it was believed that the native peoples lacked the physical strength to do the work. In fact, Spanish colonists on the mainland and in the Caribbean islands believed that one African could do the work of four Indians. This kind of mythology ensured that blacks would not only be in great demand but would be assigned the most strenuous tasks.

Work on the sugar plantations in Mexico and elsewhere extracted a heavy toll from the Africans. At the Xochimaneas hacienda in southern Mexico, owned by the Society of Jesus,

> slaves were generally awakened at four in the morning and worked until ten or eleven o'clock at night. Upon arising, the slaves went to the sugar mill where they ground eight, nine, or ten caldrons of sugar "depending on the

> cane and the season." At daybreak the sound of a bell summoned the slaves to take the sugar from the boiling house (casa de calderas) to the refinery (casa de purgar) and to put the "white sugar" in the sun to be dried. When there was no sugar to be sunned, the slaves occupied themselves with other tasks. When this work was completed, they returned to their homes for breakfast and to ready themselves for the fields.

Accidents occurred in the *ingenios* and the overall death rate in the sugar plantations seemed to have been as high as that in the mines, if not higher. The Mexican viceroy confessed in 1599 that African slaves who worked in the sugar industry had a death rate in excess of "that in any other kind of work."

As in Mexico, the cultivation of sugarcane began in Brazil shortly after the Europeans settled there. The exact date is uncertain, but it may have started as early as 1516. There is some evidence that Brazilian sugar was being exported to Europe in 1519. By the 1540s sugar plantations existed all along the coastal area extending from Pernambuco in the north to São Vicente in the south. Pernambuco would become the most important sugar-producing area in the colony by the 1580s, and by 1600 it had two hundred sugar mills. In fact, by the beginning of the seventeenth century, Pernambuco produced more sugar than any other place in the world.

African slaves played an important role in the latter part of the sixteenth century in Pernambuco's (and Brazil's) rise to prominence in the sugar industry. It is believed that Africans first came to Brazil with the Portuguese explorer Pedro Álvares Cabral in 1500. Brazil was sparsely populated by the native peoples, and it did not, at first, appear very attractive to the Portuguese as a place to settle and accumulate wealth. A few colonists trickled in after 1500, some bringing one or two African slaves, mostly domestic servants and artisans. Not until 1539 did the Crown receive a request from a colonist for permission to import Africans to work on his sugar plantation.

The Crown did not approve Duarte Coelhós's request, and he repeated it in 1542. This time, the colonist emphasized that the success of the sugar industry depended upon black labor. Up until that point, and for the next four or five decades, Indians provided most of the labor services on the sugar plantations. But the colonists would, at various times, press their argument that Africans were superior and hardier workers.

The first groups of slaves to arrive in Brazil directly from Africa, as opposed to being sent from Portugal, arrived at the city of Salvador in 1550. This was a momentous development, because it was the start of a formal slave trade between Brazil and Africa that would last for the next three hundred years. In response to the increasing demand for African workers as a result of the expansion of the sugar industry, the Crown issued a decree in 1559 allowing the owners of sugar plantations to import a maximum of 120 slaves for each sugar mill that they owned.

This *Alvará*, or decree, gave a tremendous boost to the slave trade. Accurate records are lacking, but it is clear that Portuguese traders responded to this demand for Africans with considerable vigor. In time, African workers would replace the Indians on the plantations, and Brazil's human and cultural landscape would be irreversibly transformed. It has been estimated that after about 1580 between 10,000 and 15,000 slaves landed in Brazil annually. Most were destined to serve on the sugar plantations, and most would come from Angola. The lot of the African on a Brazilian sugar plantation in the sixteenth century and later was a difficult one. With extremely hard work, long working hours, inadequate diet, and exposure to debilitating diseases, slaves faced an early death.

The work in the mines, *obrajes*, and sugar plantations must rank as the most demanding of the tasks that slaves had to perform in the sixteenth century and later. Their death rates were higher than those of slaves engaged in other tasks. This was a consequence of the terrible working conditions that prevailed in them. The sugar, mining, and textile industries were capitalist enterprises that were driven by the profit motive. Each used a combination of free and slave labor, and each depended on a great deal of labor and capital for its survival. Each was a form of industrial slavery. These enterprises, because of the need for profits, drove the slaves to their maximum, extracting as much labor from them as possible. Poorly fed and overworked, these human machines were wracked by ill health and suffered an early death.

Slaves who were used in the pearl-fishing business also faced an early death as a result of the hazardous nature of their work. They seemed to have been assigned this task in all of the coastal areas where the waters were considered particularly rich in pearls. But the divers frequently ran the risk of drowning or colliding with underwater objects. An order issued by the authorities in Vera Cruz, Mexico, in the 1550s unwittingly shows the relationship between pearl fishing and the incidence of death by drowning. The order was designed to clear the waters of sharks, not to protect the slaves. It noted that "because the bodies of drowned Negroes have not been removed from [the waters of] oyster fisheries, many sharks are present and haunt the places with grave danger to life." Given the risks involved, the colonial authorities sought to prevent Indians from pearl fishing for the colonists. In 1572, for example, Indians were forbidden to dive for pearls off the Venezuelan coast. Statistics are not available for the sixteenth century on the number of Africans who died while engaged in pearl fishing, but its dangerous nature was widely recognized.

African slaves were also used extensively as artisans. Many were already skilled in metalworking, cloth making, leatherwork, arts and crafts, and carpentry, to name a few skills, before they were brought to the Americas. Some acquired specialized skills in the Americas by virtue of the tasks that they were assigned. The *maestro de azucar* (sugar master) was one of the most highly respected slaves because he was in charge of processing the cane in the *ingenios*. Such skilled workers determined the success or failure of the sugar-making industry.

Not all colonists, whether in Brazil or Spanish America, welcomed the participation of African slaves—or even free persons—in the skilled trades. They feared that the competition from slave labor would lower the wages that they received. In addition, skilled whites wanted to confine blacks to manual labor, believing that the prestige of their trades would be lessened if they were open to slaves. As a result, several guilds that licensed tradesmen or provided specialized training excluded blacks from membership. Those that admitted blacks frequently confined them to the rank of journeyman, denying them the privilege of becoming masters.

Still, colonists who were hard-pressed for skilled labor used their slaves in a variety of capacities. Black carpenters, for example, were used extensively in the construction industry. They helped build houses, churches, monasteries, hospitals, bridges, shops, and public buildings. Others served as bricklayers, plasterers, and blacksmiths. African slaves engaged in ironworking, made hats, baked bread, and sewed clothes, in addition to other skilled tasks. The image of Africans confined exclusively to field work, mining, or household chores is not accurate for the sixteenth or for any other century. During the sixteenth century most skilled slaves appear to have been located primarily in urban areas, such as Santo Domingo, Mexico City, Lima, and Salvador. Most of the European colonists were also urban residents, and they were the ones who depended on the specialized skills of the free and unfree African labor force. Black slaves and free persons were also used significantly in their households. Domestic workers, who were chiefly women, cooked, washed, cleaned, and cared for the children. Some scholars maintain that slaves in the urban areas had an easier life than those in the rural areas, particularly in the case of those who were engaged in sugar cultivation or mining.

Not all slaves in the rural areas were agricultural workers, although most of them were during the sixteenth century and later. In Hispaniola, Cuba, and Jamaica, blacks helped to grow the foods, such as maize and plantains, that sustained the islands' populations. They were also engaged in cultivating ginger on the three islands, but chiefly in Hispaniola.

There was also much diversity in the agricultural activities of the slaves on the mainland. In Mexico, for example, slaves were engaged in the cultivation of the cocoa bean in Colima, Oaxaca, and Huatulco. In Peru, slaves worked in the vineyards in the south; others grew wheat, olives, and other foodstuffs. The colonists in Venezuela used their African labor to produce cacao, cotton, vegetables, and other provisions. Most Brazilian slaves were involved in the sugar industry during the period, but some must have cultivated the crops that would feed them.

Rural slaves everywhere had to engage in pastoral activities, usually tending sheep and cattle. By 1550, the colonists in the Caribbean islands had developed a vibrant grazing economy. In Hispaniola, some families owned as many as thirty thousand head of cattle by the 1540s. Slaves also worked on Mexican ranches during the sixteenth century, although they were not as numerous as the free laborers. Slaves seem to have been more important in Peru and may even have constituted the majority of the herdsmen on some of the larger ranches. Ranching may have afforded the slaves a greater degree of control over their lives than some of the other occupations. Charged with tending livestock over huge areas of land, the slaves were quite likely free from the constant supervision of their owners.

Because slaves were expensive property, most colonists lacked the resources to purchase them. But they still needed the services of additional hands from time to time. In order to supply such colonists with the labor that they wanted, the practice of hiring out slaves developed in the sixteenth century. Those who needed slave labor contracted with the owners to use their human property for a fixed period of time and for a determined rental fee. As property, slaves probably had no choice in the matter; they had to go where they were sent and to work for whoever hired them. Some people bought Africans for the sole purpose of renting them to others.

It appears that the slave owners in Spanish and Portuguese America assigned tasks in accordance with the gender of the workers. Males were more likely to be employed in the mining industry, in the *ingenios,* and as artisans and pearl fishers. Women were used primarily as domestics and performed the same duties as the men on the plantations. There is also some suspicion that women formed the majority of the labor force in the textile factories. Because the majority of the slaves in the early period were males, women appear less frequently in the records.

Africans, both men and women, played a crucial role in building the economies of the Americas in the sixteenth century. They endured the terrible conditions of the *obrajes,* the heat of the *ingenios,* and the physical hazards of the mines. Many engaged in the skilled trades and planted the food that would help feed the society as a whole. The sugar that they manufactured and the silver and other metals that they mined would cross the ocean to Europe with profound consequences for the diets and economies of the importing countries. The African presence would continue to grow in these societies in succeeding centuries. But the sixteenth-century pioneers laid the foundations of the new societies then in formation. Africans were present at the birth of the Americas as we know them today, not as colonizers but as the coerced hewers of wood and drawers of water.

Slave Society and Culture

European colonists in every part of the Americas came to depend on the labor of Indians and Africans in the sixteenth century. The Indians were enslaved as soon as the Spaniards established effective control of the Caribbean islands. When Mexico, Peru, and other areas fell under Spanish control, the colonists converted the Indians on the mainland into a servile labor force. The Portuguese would do the same once they settled Brazil. In effect, the European outsiders became the ruling elite in these societies, imposing their will on the original residents and taking their land in the process. Not all of the Indians were enslaved, however. Some simply lived beyond the reach of the colonists and refused to submit to them, and in Mexico and Peru, at least in the immediate aftermath of the colonial occupation, the sheer size of the Indian population made complete control by the European conquerors impossible.

Slavery was only one of the labor systems that the Europeans employed. The Spaniards also introduced the *encomienda.* Under this system, a number of Indians were assigned by colonial authorities to work for the Spaniards without receiving wages. In return, the colonists were expected to teach the workers Spanish customs, language, and religion. These Indians were not slaves because they were not owned; the Spaniards had access only to their labor, and the condition was not hereditary. But in time, the colonists began to treat these Indians as if they were slaves, abusing them and denying them basic rights.

Faced with mounting criticism of Indian slavery and the *encomienda* system from humanitarians, the Spanish Crown abolished both in 1542. They were replaced with a system that rotated Indian workers among the Spanish colonists who needed their labor. Workers would be assigned to employers for a specified period of time, for designated tasks, and for a wage. Once the time had expired and the duties had been completed, the Indians could be allocated to other colonists. This system was called the *repartimiento* (or *mita* in Peru). It, too, proved to be an unsatisfactory response to the labor problem. Workers were often not paid, and some were held by the colonists longer than they were supposed to work.

The *repartimiento* system all but disappeared by the seventeenth century. In some societies, a system of debt passage emerged. Under this system, Indian workers borrowed money from their employers to purchase necessities but could not leave their job until the debt was repaid. Many people fell further and further behind because their wages were so low. Because these debts were considered hereditary, generations of Indian workers were tied to the colonists and had no option but to work for them. Not all labor services in the Spanish empire were coerced, however. Wage labor existed alongside the various unfree systems.

Like the Spanish, the Portuguese in Brazil also enslaved the Indian peoples who fell under their control. Portuguese colonists received grants of land from the Crown, under which they could enslave the Indians who resided on them. Other Indians were simply pursued, captured, and enslaved. Before 1600 almost no one doubted the right of the Portuguese colonists to treat the native peoples in this fashion. With the Indian population diminishing and the sugar industry expanding in the second half of the sixteenth century, Africans would come to form the dominant group of exploited workers by 1600.

Thus, Africans were not the only peoples whom the Europeans would enslave or exploit in one fashion or another. But they were the only peoples imported as permanent, unfree laborers. The sixteenth century was a particularly ugly one in the Americas. It saw the military defeat of the Indian peoples, their colonization, the astounding decline in their number, the introduction of oppressive labor systems, and the start of African slavery. It was a century of chaos, disaster, and crises for the native peoples. For the Africans, it was the beginning of an awful odyssey in these societies. Arriving as involuntary workers, African slaves confronted the challenge of helping to build societies in which they were, and would continue to be, persons with few if any rights. They also had to struggle to maintain, as best they could, a measure of human dignity, and to develop the social institutions that would sustain them.

African slaves occupied the lowest rank in the social order of the colonial societies. Imported as human property, their sole function was to work for those who had purchased them. Though the colonists valued Africans for the agricultural and craft skills that they possessed, they were nevertheless considered of "bad race" and "bad caste" by those who had come to depend on their labor. Such unflattering descriptions originated in Europe, but they assumed an added intensity and strength in the Americas as slavery expanded.

The European colonists also embraced negative images of the Indians whom they encountered. There was no inclination to see them as equals and to treat them accordingly. In fact, there was some doubt among the Spanish colonists whether the Indians were rational beings. But the pope resolved these doubts in 1537 by declaring that "the Indians are truly men."

The papal pronouncement did not lead to an end to the mistreatment of the Indians, nor did it mean that the colonists embraced them as equals. Driven by the desire to acquire wealth, the colonists wanted only to be left alone to exploit the native peoples. Still, there were some voices raised to denounce the colonists for their behavior. Chief among them was Bishop Bartolomé de las Casas, a member of the Dominican religious order who became enraged at Spanish cruelty toward the Indians. He was not the first, however, to publicly chastise his fellow Spaniards. That honor fell to Friar Antonio de Montesinos. In 1511, he denounced the mistreatment of the Indians in Hispaniola and questioned the moral basis for their inhumane treatment.

Although the Crown introduced measures to protect the Indians, or at least reduce the level of their mistreatment, these laws were never adequately enforced. Las Casas never lost his concern for the plight of the Indian peoples and kept up an active campaign to promote their rights and reduce the degree of their exploitation. He debated one of the foremost proponents of the view that the Spaniards were superior to the Indians and were entitled to exercise control over them. This important debate was held in Valladolid, Spain, beginning in late 1550. Juan Ginés de Sepúlveda, a noted scholar, was Las Casas's opponent. The two men debated

Bartolomé de las Casas, who appears as the savior of the Indians in this heroic depiction, argued that Indians were not inferior to Spaniards.

before a panel of judges and addressed the question, "What rights do the Indians have and what are the obligations of the Spaniards to them?"

A fervent admirer of the Indians, Las Casas argued that the Indians were not inferior to the Spaniards in any way. He maintained that they were "prudent and rational beings, of as good ability and judgment as other men and more able, discreet, and of better understanding than the peoples of many other nations." He believed that the Spaniards should do their own work and cease their exploitation of the Indians. Sepúlveda, on the other hand, was certain that the Spaniards were superior to the Indian peoples. The Indians lacked the capacity, he argued, to attain the level of development that the Spaniards had reached. They should be forced to work for the Spaniards and, in time, they would acquire some of the customs and habits of their superiors.

We do not know who won the debate, but the Spanish Crown seemed to have been more influenced by Las Casas's arguments. Subsequent laws were more respectful of the rights of the Indians and often limited the power of the colonists over them. Yet such laws were often not enforced, and the colonists still abused the Indians. There was a considerable difference between what the law said and how it was applied.

The debate at Valladolid and the spirit of the Spanish legislation concerning Indians underscores the fact that there was no similar concern shown by Spanish officials toward the fate of the Africans. The Indians were new peoples to the Spaniards. Africans, by contrast, had long been familiar to the Spaniards, and their image of Africans had already been framed. Even Las Casas recommended in 1517 that black slaves should be imported to replace Indian workers. He would later renounce this position.

The society that the Spaniards and the Portuguese created in the sixteenth century recognized racial and class distinctions. Everyone knew his or her place in the social order. Whites as a group formed the elite, followed by the mixed peoples—mestizos and mulattoes. Then came the Indians and the Africans. Africans may have been set apart from the other groups because of their status as property and their racial heritage. Colonial society reserved the most difficult and hazardous jobs for Africans, sanctioned the most horrendous forms of punishment for them, and for three hundred years held generations of them as property.

Black slaves consisted of three principal groups, the distinctions based primarily on the place of their birth. First, there were people who were born in Africa but spent time in Europe before they were transported to the Americas. The Spaniards called them *ladinos.* They knew some Spanish and, in varying degrees, were familiar with Spanish culture. The second category consisted of people who were born in Africa and came directly to the Americas. Known as *bozales,* these individuals had little or no familiarity with the ways of the Europeans. As soon as they began to speak the languages of the Europeans and accepted Christianity, they could be called *ladinos.* The third major group of slaves comprised those who were born in the Americas. They were called *criollos* (creoles). Unlike the *bozales,* they were exposed to the cultural influences of the Europeans and other groups, such as Indians and mestizos, from birth. The *bozales* formed the majority of the slave populations once a direct slave trade with Africa was instituted in 1518. Although the *bozales* were called *ladinos* once they became accustomed to the ways of their owners, no one can say how long this process lasted. Some *bozales* probably never became *ladinos.* In any event, *ladinos* probably never lost all of their African heritage, even though they embraced aspects of the way of life in the Americas.

Early records show that the African-born slaves were renamed in the Spanish colonies and elsewhere in the Americas. These persons had no say in the selection of a new name because it was forced upon them by the person who purchased them. In some cases, they may have been renamed by the priest who baptized them. The Africans who were renamed had to begin the difficult process of adjusting to a new identity. Their previous names had deep emotional, cultural, and ceremonial meanings, so the loss of their names must have resulted in much anguish. These Africans probably never abandoned their former names and used them among their friends and peers.

In renaming the Africans, the colonists seemed to have confined their choices to the most popular first names in usage. Thus, males were named Fernando, Juan, Jaime, Ricardo, José, Cristobal, and so on. Women were frequently called Mariá, Catarina, Luisa, Margarita, and Ana, to name just a few. Most slaves were given only one name; only a small minority had a last name, usually that of the person who owned them. In order to make their identification easier, the designation *"criollo," "ladino,"* or *"bozal"* would be listed after the slaves' names on official documents. In other cases, their ethnic or national origin would be added. Thus, official documents would list a slave as María Biafada, Ricardo Congo, or Juan Angola.

The imposition of a new name was just one of the many changes that the Africans had to endure. In order to communicate with their owners, they had to learn Spanish or Portuguese, depending on the colony. Africans spoke many different languages, but some of these languages were similar enough that the speakers could usually understand one another. In the Americas, however, the Africans had to learn the languages of the Europeans, which was the primary means of communication. Some slaves became reasonably fluent in these languages, although they probably spoke their own languages whenever possible. The African languages spoken by the slaves must also have had an impact on Spanish and Portuguese—on the vocabulary, the meanings of words, and the intonation. The slaves must have Africanized these languages, particularly in those colonies, such as Brazil, where they formed a large share of the population.

Torn from their homeland, ethnic group, family, and kin, the Africans experienced a sense of profound shock, loss, and alienation in the Americas. Kinship ties were the core of the societies from which the slaves came. Marriages united not only the husband and the wife but also the lineages to which they belonged. In most instances, the bond between the two lineages was more important than that which existed between the couple. To be without ties of kinship was to be socially dead; an individual could exist meaningfully only as part of a network of blood relationships. The slave trade and slavery destroyed these bonds, and the individual faced the enormous challenge of re-creating them in the Americas.

The task of developing new relationships in the Americas was made more difficult by the very wide geographic distribution of the slaves in the sixteenth century. Few slave owners owned more than two or three Africans, although there would be very large concentrations of them in the mines, *obrajes,* and on the sugar plantations as the century wore on. There were, however, enough Africans living in easy reach of one another in some places so that extensive family relationships were reconstructed by 1580. In addition, strong emotional bonds united the Africans who crossed the Atlantic in the same ship. They had endured terrible times together, and those experiences fostered strong ties among the survivors. These shipboard bonds formed the beginnings of the struggle by the Africans to create relationships among themselves and to replace those that had been severed.

As a rule, the colonial authorities did not oppose formal marriages of their slaves. In fact, the church and the state in Spain's colonies encouraged unions among the population at large, including slaves. The family was seen as the foundation stone of society. In theory, at least, once slaves were married they could not be separated through sale. Slaves whose marriages were broken up by their masters could appeal to the civil or religious authorities for redress.

This did not mean that African slaves waited for the state or the Catholic church to sanction their intimate relationships. Most slaves probably chose their partners whenever and wherever they could and had their own marriage ceremonies in accordance with their own customs and practices. Africans came from societies with complex traditions and rules that governed all aspects of human relationships, including family life, and there is no reason to believe that these were abandoned quickly, if at all, in the Americas. In their choices of marriage partners and in other ways, they responded to universal human tugs and emotions.

Beginning in the sixteenth century there are numerous examples of Africans getting married in Catholic ceremonies. But such marriages probably represented a minority of the unions that the slaves made. Most of them, it can be guessed, did not accept the authority of the church in this matter, because they still maintained their own traditions. Marriages that did not receive the approval of the church were, of course, considered illegal—and therefore nonexistent—by the colonial authorities.

In order to have a marriage sanctioned according to colonial rules, the Africans had to apply for a license. The prospective bride and groom had to appear with two

This document contains an application for marriage by two slaves, whose names are at the top, and a grant of permission by an official (bottom). African slaves had to make such applications to have their marriage recognized by colonial authorities.

witnesses before an official to make the request. They had to declare their ethnic backgrounds, stating whether they were Mandinka, Bram, Biafada, and so on. Creole slaves also had to indicate where they were born. The witnesses had to verify the accuracy of the statements made by the couple, and they also had to state how long and under what circumstances they had known the man and woman. The authorities were not interested in whether the bride and the groom had ever been married in Africa. Such prior unions were never recognized by the church as valid because they had not occurred under Christian authority. The bride and groom had only to establish that they had never been married in the Americas or that they had been widowed.

An analysis of the surviving marriage licenses from Mexico and Peru suggests that Africans tended to marry individuals from the same ethnic group or from the same geographic area. Such a pattern of ethnically based choices should not be particularly surprising. As foreigners in strange lands, these Africans sought to reconstruct and nurture their ethnic ties and heritage. They chose partners with whom they shared a cultural heritage and who had similar life experiences. For the same reasons, creole slaves were also more likely to marry other creoles. Ethnicity, as reflected through marriage choices, remained an important part of the lives of African slaves.

Slave owners were not always respectful of the marriages of the Africans. The unions were sometimes broken up and families separated through sale. The church opposed such atrocities, railing against these practices from time to time but with little effect.

Africans who avoided the Catholic marriage ceremonies simply lived together as man and wife, if the circumstances allowed. The Spanish colonial and religious authorities frowned on this practice, declaring it worthy of punishment. The Holy Office of the Inquisition, an institution created to pursue religious offenders of all sorts, was established in Mexico in 1570. It had been in existence in Spain for a century, and its principal targets included Jews, Muslims, and others accused of a variety of religious crimes. In Mexico, in addition to its customary victims, the Holy Office pursued blacks accused of concubinage (unmarried couples living together), bigamy, witchcraft, sorcery, and other offenses. Individuals convicted of *amancebado* relationships (concubinage) could be flogged, imprisoned, or humiliated in various ways. Bigamists received similar punishments.

By punishing those accused of bigamy and *amancebado* relationships, the Holy Office and other colonial authorities failed to understand the meanings of such behavior for the Africans. The Catholic authorities viewed church-approved marriages as the norm and refused to recognize any other form of marital arrangement as legitimate. Thus Africans who may have had private marriage ceremonies according to their own rules ran the risk of being accused of *amancebado* and punished.

Similarly, the frequency of what the Spaniards called bigamy shows how African cultural traditions endured in the New World. It was the norm in many African societies for one man to have several wives. In others, it was acceptable if the number of women of marriageable age exceeded the number of men. Because having children was the highest service one could render in many African societies, men and women faced enormous pressure to marry and start families. If there were not enough men to go around, polygyny (having more than one wife) was a culturally proper way of solving the problem. These cultural obligations did not die in the Americas of the sixteenth century. African men continued to take several wives whenever that was possible. Failing to understand the larger meaning of such a practice, the colonial authorities responded in horror, broke up the unions, and punished the individuals involved. In this way they applied Western and Catholic norms to a people whose traditions and values were fundamentally different. Creoles who were accused of bigamy, particularly in the seventeenth century, may not have been immune to the continuing influences of their African ancestry. Judging from the testimony offered at their trials, however, some of them understood the Christian precepts against two spouses but chose to engage in that practice anyway.

Like their family arrangements, the traditional religious ideas and beliefs of the Africans were very much alive in sixteenth-century America. Regardless of their ethnic origins, African peoples came from societies where religious beliefs influenced all aspects of the life of individuals and the community. Unlike Western societies, there was no distinction between secular and religious spheres. Religious ideas determined the timing of important occasions, naming ceremonies, planting seasons, harvesting practices, the nature of art and dance, and a thousand other aspects of life. The African who converted to Christianity would have to undergo a profound internal rebirth as well as changes in his everyday life. In other words, the religious ideas of Africans were deeply imbedded in their human fabric, forming an central part of their being and profoundly influencing and shaping their behavior. To embrace Christianity meant, in effect, the acceptance of a new identity.

The Catholic church, with the support of the Crown and other state officials, believed that its duty was to Christianize the Africans. They had no respect for the Africans' religious ideas and practices. Muslim slaves were particularly feared, and their importation into the Americas was discouraged. The Spaniards and other Catholics had been the foes of the Muslims for centuries, and they did not want religious competition and conflicts to arise in the Americas. In addition, the Spaniards believed that Muslim slaves would indoctrinate the Indians with their religious ideas.

Both the Spanish Crown and the religious authorities required that Africans be baptized prior to their departure for the Americas. It is doubtful whether this had anything more than a symbolic value because the Africans would not have received much, if any, instruction in the Catholic faith. A few slaves who came from the

Two Catholics of African descent worship in Peru. Many Africans became formal members of the Catholic church in Latin America.

Congo-Angola region may have already been exposed to Christianity, because Portuguese missionaries and citizens had arrived there in the fifteenth century. From the complaints that the priests in the Americas made throughout the sixteenth century, it is clear that many slaves, contrary to what the Crown wanted, left the African coast without being baptized. The situation was not much better in the Americas. There were frequent reports that some Africans had not been baptized even after they had been in residence for several years.

This was probably a welcome development for the Africans. Undoubtedly, most of them would have preferred to continue to practice their religious beliefs without the interference of the Christians. Conscientious priests and friars, however, wanted to do their duty as Christians to instruct the Africans about their faith and to baptize them. With the permission of the owners, they conducted classes for the slaves on Sundays or at other mutually convenient times. Not all slaveholders cooperated, some believing that the time that their human property spent receiving religious instructions should be devoted to working at their various tasks.

Still, many Africans were baptized and became formal members of the church. They participated in the various festivals and had marriages and funerals performed by a priest. Some Africans became active members of the religious brotherhoods known as the *cofradía.* In essence, these were mutual aid organizations that were devoted to the memory of a particular saint. The members paid dues and received financial help in times of difficulty. *Cofradías* took part in the various religious processions that occurred from time to time.

The authorities in the colonies kept a careful watch on the activities of black *cofradías.* The spectacle of hundreds of blacks congregating to hold meetings or to participate in processions raised white fears of conspiracy and insurrection. In 1572, for example, the Mexican viceroy was concerned that "recently the negroes have had a *cofradía* and have assembled and held processions with their members as the others do, and these are always increasing . . . and it seems that they may create problems." On occasion, intoxicated members did create problems in Mexico and Peru and probably elsewhere. In 1612, members of a black *cofradía* in Mexico City played a leading role in a rebellion that slaves and free persons had planned. Such rebellious activity led to the temporary suspension of the organization by the authorities. The potential of the *cofradías* to lead violent assaults on slavery must have led to an increase in their surveillance. In general, however, *cofradías* were more likely to meet the needs of the slaves for social interaction and communal activities.

The first black *cofradías* may have been established as soon as enough Africans were baptized in a particular colony and lived close to one another. The church encouraged the formation of separate *cofradías* for Africans, probably for racial reasons. The Africans may also have wanted their own organizations, free from the direct control of whites, reflecting their own needs and bearing their cultural stamp. In fact, the *cofradías* in Peru, and perhaps in other colonies as well, were organized along African ethnic lines in the sixteenth century. This could only have occurred in those places where individuals from particular ethnic groups existed in significant numbers. The existence of ethnic-based *cofradías* clearly suggests the continuing strength of an African heritage in the Americas.

Although the Catholic church succeeded in making converts among the slaves, Christianity did not replace African religious beliefs in the sixteenth century or at later times. Christianized Africans did not abandon their core religious beliefs. In other words, their African religious ideas existed alongside the dogma of the Christianity that they embraced. African slaves could draw upon their Christian beliefs when it suited their purposes. On other occasions, they drew upon their African beliefs.

Practitioners of African religions used a variety of charms and amulets in their rituals. These could be herbs, sticks, bags, cloth, or bones. Africans believed that these objects carried certain mystical powers or were the objects through which the supernatural operated. Dirt from cemeteries, perhaps because of its association with the ancestors, also possessed revered qualities. When used in the appropriate fashion and accompanied by the relevant ceremonies, the charms, objects, and dirt could be used to avenge a wrong, win the affections of a man or woman, solve a crime, get a slave owner to treat his slaves well, and accomplish a variety of other objectives.

The use of these objects and charms was based on the belief that certain forces or events could be manipulated and controlled by resorting to the appropriate ritual acts. This is similar in some respects to the Christian belief that prayer can be used effectively to achieve a desired end. What is important, however, is not any perceived similarity to Christianity, but the persistence of African beliefs and ways of influencing the supernatural in the Americas. Over time, of course, some of these ideas and practices would be modified or altered in some fashion.

In addition to their kinship systems and religious ideas, Africans brought their music, songs, dances, art forms, and cooking methods with them. The colonists viewed many of these cultural practices negatively, and tried to suppress them. Slaves danced in the streets on festive occasions, drawing upon their African styles of movement. Others were skilled at drumbeating and played such stringed musical instruments as the banjo and marimba.

We possess little information on the diet of the slaves during their early years in the Americas. The principal ingredients appear to be corn, sweet potatoes, plantains, beef, and a variety of legumes. The nutritional adequacy of the diet is also unknown because of the absence of information about the quantity of the foods provided to each slave. Similarly, we can make no definite comment on the relationship between diet, disease, and the death rates of the slaves. Slaves, like other members of society, fell victim to the frequent epidemics of measles and smallpox. Workers in the mines and the *ingenios* had a higher death rate than other blacks, a result of the physical hazards of such employment and perhaps of overwork and a poor diet. The unhealthy climate of such places as Vera Cruz may also have taken its toll on the health of the slaves.

Medical care, such as it was, was available for sick slaves, particularly those who lived in urban areas. In Lima, for example, a hospital run by the Jesuits welcomed slaves and gave them the same care that they provided to whites. Hospitals run by municipalities also accepted slaves in Mexico City and Lima. Some large plantations in the rural areas had infirmaries attached to them. Given the state of medical knowledge during the sixteenth century, it is doubtful whether these hospital stays did any good if serious illnesses were involved. African slaves had their own traditional remedies, and many of them may not have availed themselves of the services that the hospitals offered. They also seemed to have borrowed freely from the medical lore of the Indians. This is hardly surprising, given their often close interaction with one another.

Indians and Africans also fell in love with each other, got married, or lived together without the approval of the church or the state. The Spanish Crown, in particular, opposed such unions, preferring that individuals choose partners from among their own "races" or groups. But such a restriction was impossible to enforce. Male Africans greatly outnumbered the females, so Indian women often became the sexual partners of black men. Because the Indian women were likely to be free, the children of such unions, known as *zambos,* took the mother's legal status and were born free. This was probably an added incentive for male slaves to choose Indian women as partners.

The early colonial records indicate, however, that there was some tension in the relationship between the Africans and the native peoples of the Americas. It may very well be that colonial officials focused much more on the difficulties between them, ignoring the many areas and instances of cooperation. In particular, the Peruvian and Mexican authorities accused blacks of physically assaulting Indians, taking their possessions, and generally mistreating them.

In order to correct this problem, the Crown and the local authorities attempted to prevent the two peoples from living in the same communities. Although these restrictions were sometimes not enforced, they were repeated with regularity throughout the sixteenth century. The Crown also forbade blacks from trading with Indians on the grounds that they took advantage of them. It is doubtful, however, that the commercial activity between the two groups ceased.

Regardless of the colony in which they lived, Africans were placed at the bottom of the social order. Forced to work for others, they nevertheless tried to maintain their humanity, doing the things that gave meaning to their lives. They toiled, married, reproduced, worshiped their gods, and made the best of their situation. Their burdens were never easy, and the forced separation from their homeland created much physical suffering and emotional anguish. Plus those Africans who arrived in the sixteenth century faced, in retrospect, an additional challenge. It was they who had to lay the cultural and institutional foundations of the modern black societies of the Americas.

The Struggle for Freedom

Perhaps the Africans could have eased their emotional pain in that terrible first century of their enslavement in the Americas if they had been present in larger numbers in the various colonies. This would have provided them with the opportunity to associate more intimately with one another and establish meaningful support systems. But even when relatively large numbers of slaves arrived in such colonies as Mexico, Peru, and Hispaniola, they were widely scattered. Most lived in small groups of their peers. Not until the mid-seventeenth century did the large sugar plantations, with their huge concentrations of slaves, become increasingly regular features of the Caribbean islands. The silver mines of Mexico and Peru and a few sugar plantations had employed high numbers of slaves before 1600, but most blacks still lived in smaller communities.

An African population living in larger groups would not have automatically ended the alienation that its members felt or have fostered a sense of community among them. The African-born slaves were divided along ethnic lines, which was an obstacle to cooperative relationships between them and the development of a sense of oneness. In addition, there were cultural differences between those people who had become familiar with the ways of Europeans and those who were newly arrived from Africa bearing their traditional culture.

Thus, the slave population had to overcome many obstacles before it could pose an organized challenge to the institution under whose control it lived. Such challenges took different forms, depending on the local circumstances, the size of the slave population, the degree of interaction among its members, and their level of political consciousness. Slaves who lived within easy reach of wooded, mountainous, or other inaccessible areas often chose flight as their principal means of resistance. Where their numbers permitted, others conspired and participated in revolts. Still others engaged in day-to-day acts of sabotage, such as working slowly, that punctured the efficiency of the institution of slavery.

Slaves were inclined to resist their condition when they came to the recognition that a profound wrong had been committed against them. Resistance occurred when the individual had decided to reclaim control over his or her life. Such a decision could come after much careful thought, or it could occur in a moment of passion, such as when the person was being mistreated. Once a decision to resist had been made, whether individually or collectively, the slave reached an important turning point, and his or her life would not be the same again.

During the seventeenth century, when black cultures in the Americas were taking firm shape, slaves engaged in flight more frequently than any other form of physical resistance. This was the case in all of the colonies, and there were several reasons for its appeal. Regardless of whether the slaves were shipped from Spain or came directly from Africa, the overwhelming majority were African-born. They were, therefore, unaccustomed to the demands and rigors of plantation, mining, and other forms of labor that they were required to perform. Not surprisingly, they sought to escape from the sources of their oppression as soon as the opportunity presented itself. Often few in numbers and separated from their peers by long distances, flight also had a certain practicality. It did not depend significantly on the cooperation of others for its success. Slaves could escape alone or in a group. Small groups were best because slaves ran the risk of detection and capture if the number in the escape party was too large.

The physical environment of the colonies also aided escape. Hispaniola, Jamaica, Cuba, Mexico, and Brazil, to name just a few places, all had mountainous, inaccessible, and wooded areas—the ideal terrain for those who wanted to create sanctuaries away from their pursuers. The Sierra Maestra mountain range in eastern Cuba, the densely wooded Cockpit Country in central Jamaica, the hilly Orizaba zone adjacent to Vera Cruz in Mexico, and the densely forested regions of northeastern Brazil beckoned and protected the escapees.

Adult males were the most likely to escape. Women constituted a minority of the slave population, so it is not surprising that they remained a small proportion of those who fled. Perhaps women were less inclined to risk the hazards of the escape than the men. They may also have chosen to remain behind with their children. Because infants and older children slowed the pace of escape and increased the risk of capture, parents had to face difficult choices in this regard.

The incidence of escape began as soon as the first slaves arrived in Hispaniola in 1502. In 1503, the governor of the colony, Nicolás de Ovando, reported to the Crown that a number of slaves had fled. There is no additional information on this first group of runaways, but they probably fled to a remote area of the colony. Whatever their fate, these people established a pattern that would be followed by other slaves everywhere in the Americas.

These escaped slaves were called *cimarrones* by the Spaniards. The origin of this term is not entirely clear, but some scholars believe that the word *cimarrón* originally referred to cattle that roamed in the hills of Hispaniola. Eventually, it was applied to Indians who had fled from slavery. As Indian slavery declined and blacks arrived in increasing numbers, the word came to be associated with those who escaped. It is not certain, however, when *cimarrón* began to be applied exclusively to black runaways, but it appears that was the case by the 1530s. In time, the English equivalent became *maroon,* and the French used the word *marron.* The word *cimarrón,* at least in the eyes of the Spaniards, had negative connotations. It was generally a synonym for "wild," "fierce," or "untamed." On the other hand, the escapees may have worn it as a badge of honor, in the same way that the descendants of the maroons in the English-speaking Caribbean do today.

There was a close relationship between the number of escapes and the size of the black population. As more and more Africans arrived, the flight to an uncertain freedom in the mountains and other remote areas accelerated. Slaves who were inclined to escape probably ran off quietly, perhaps not even telling friends of their plans for fear of betrayal. The colonists may even have come to expect that some of their slaves would flee. The surviving documents from these early years often mention *cimarrones* in an offhand manner. It is only when the escaped slaves began to attack their former masters or entice other slaves to escape that their existence became a matter of grave public concern.

It was not until the 1520s that the references to *cimarrones* in the letters of the colonists and in official reports became more frequent and urgent. There were reports of *cimarrones* not only in Hispaniola, but also in Mexico in 1523, in Puerto Rico in 1529, and in Cuba in 1534. By the 1550s, additional reports of the presence of *cimarrones* had come from Panama, Venezuela, Peru, and Honduras. In general, the *cimarrones* were accused of murdering Spaniards, participating in rebellions, and theft. In 1546, a Spanish official in Hispaniola, for example, noted that the *cimarrones* in one part of the island were so dangerous that "no one dared to venture out unless he was in a group of fifteen to twenty people."

Colonial authorities everywhere saw the *cimarrones* as a threat to public order. As a result, the descriptions of them in the records are overwhelmingly negative. Given the fact that the *cimarrones* in all of the colonies were depicted as assaulting the colonists and, in some cases, the Indians, such charges must have had some merit. Because such accusations were often followed by requests for resources to strengthen the law-enforcement agencies, it is also conceivable that the reports gave exaggerated accounts of the behavior of the escapees.

Some historians have attempted to make distinctions between the motivations of the *cimarrones* and those who remained in slavery but participated in revolts. They suggest that the *cimarrones* did not pose much of a threat to slavery because they escaped from the institution and returned only now and then to carry out hit-and-run attacks on it. On the other hand, slave revolts threatened slavery from within and were designed to destroy it. This distinction does not hold for the early years, when *cimarrones* played the most significant roles in a large number of the early challenges to slavery.

With the possible exception of a few urban areas such as Mexico City and Lima, slaves were so sparsely distributed in the sixteenth century that they lacked the numbers necessary to organize and launch rebellions. Slaves apparently escaped individually or in small groups and eventually formed maroon communities of varying sizes. In 1542, one estimate in Hispaniola placed the number of *cimarrones* at "about two thousand or three thousand." Several hundred were reported to be in Puerto Rico at various times in the sixteenth century. The same could be said of Mexico, particularly in the mountainous area between Mount Orizaba and Vera Cruz. Accounts from Peru, Cuba, and Venezuela also suggest significant runaway populations in those early years.

The existence of these communities gave the *cimarrones* the confidence to challenge the slave owners and their colonial society. The *cimarrones* were, for the most part, interested not only in preserving their own freedom, but in destroying slavery as well. The first slave rebellion in the Americas occurred in Hispaniola in 1522. Three years earlier, in 1519, Indians were reported to have been joined by escaped slaves in an attack on the Spaniards. But when the first all-black revolt occurred in 1522, it included *cimarrones* and slaves who had never fled. The forty slaves and *cimarrones* who participated were, however, defeated by the Spaniards. Several lost their lives in the fighting, and the Spaniards hanged those who were captured.

This early assault on the Spaniards was followed by others. It is doubtful, however, that the runaways always united with the slaves. Nor is it entirely clear if all of the disturbances were designed to destroy slavery or whether they were a consequence of the *cimarrones* defending their communities from invasions by the Spanish authorities. It is certain, nonetheless, that there were serious confrontations between the Spaniards and the *cimarrones* in Puerto Rico in 1529; Cuba in 1534; Mexico, Columbia, Hispaniola in the 1540s; and Panama in the 1550s.

The Mexican *cimarrones* were probably the most active during the sixteenth and early seventeenth centuries. Mexico's slave population steadily increased after the Spanish occupation, and the native peoples declined in number. There were about twenty thousand African slaves in Mexico by 1570 and perhaps as many as fifty thousand by 1600. The Mexican terrain, with its numerous mountain slopes, provided ideal sanctuaries for escaped slaves. The number of escapes increased after the 1550s, and there were frequent reports from the silver mines in the north and the east that *cimarrones* were engaged in attacks on the colonists. In some cases, Indians joined the *cimarrones* in acts of arson and theft. By 1580, *cimarrones* could be found almost everywhere in rural Mexico.

Relatively speaking, a great deal is known about a community of *cimarrones* that lived in the area of Mount Orizaba adjacent to Vera Cruz during the late sixteenth and early seventeenth centuries. The community had developed a reputation for attacking the Spaniards, taking their possessions, and enticing other slaves to flee. Their leader was Yanga, an African-born man who had escaped shortly after arriving in Mexico. Evidently a skilled military tactician, he had successfully repulsed several attempts by the Spaniards to destroy his settlement and return the residents to slavery. By 1608 there were about five hundred *cimarrones* in the community. They supported themselves by planting such crops as corn and potatoes and by rearing animals.

Despite their best efforts, the *cimarrones* were unable to withstand an aggressive assault on their camp in 1609. An invading army of 450 men forced Yanga and his people to accept a truce. Under the terms of the agreement, the Spanish authorities recognized the freedom of the *cimarrones* and allowed them to establish and govern their own town. Yanga would become governor of the town, and the position could only be held by those descended from him. The *cimarrones* promised to defend the colony if it were ever attacked by Spain's enemies and agreed to return all future runaways to their owners. It is not clear whether this part of the agreement was kept. In accordance with the terms of the agreement, the town of San Lorenzo de los Negros received its charter in 1617.

SOULEVEMENT DES NEGRES
à la Jamaïque.

Cimarrones kill colonists in a revolt against the English in 1758. Starting in the early seventeenth century, large communities of escaped slaves were powerful enough to sign peace treaties with colonial authorities in Mexico, Jamaica, and other colonies.

The treaty that these *cimarrones* signed with the Spanish set a model for other societies. In later years, maroons signed peace treaties with the authorities in Jamaica, Cuba, Suriname, Venezuela, and other places. Many of these large maroon communities came into existence after 1600. In Jamaica, for example, one group of maroons signed a peace treaty with the English in 1739 that affirmed their freedom. Similar treaties would be signed with other maroon groups in succeeding years.

The slaves in Brazil also embraced escape as an effective form of resistance. Portuguese assaults on some of their settlements killed many of the residents but failed to destroy them. The most resilient of these early maroons were those who established a settlement known as Palmares in Pernambuco. In 1612 a Portuguese official noted that "some thirty leagues inland, there is a site between mountains called Palmares which harbors runaway slaves . . . whose attack and raids force the whites into armed pursuits which amount to little for they return to raid again."

Palmares had between eleven thousand and twenty thousand residents at its peak in the seventeenth century. After maintaining their freedom for almost a century, however, the residents of the settlement were finally defeated by the Portuguese in 1694. The disappearance of Palmares as an organized community of maroons did not end this form of resistance in Brazil. Known as *quilombos,* such settlements became more numerous as the slave population increased. Some of these communities still survive in contemporary Brazil.

Slave owners and the colonial authorities attempted to curb the incidence of runaways. Several colonies, such as Mexico and Peru, established civil militias primarily to catch runaways and prevent their attacks on Spanish life and property. In addition, the authorities introduced a series of measures for the punishment of those who escaped and were recaptured. Some of these laws permitted the castration of the *cimarrones* and even authorized their deaths if they had escaped for long periods of time. According to a 1535 law passed in Lima, an absence of more than six days carried the death penalty. Runaways could also be whipped, chained, imprisoned, tortured, or have a foot or hand cut off. Such horrible punishments reflected the seriousness with which the authorities viewed the slaves' efforts to claim their freedom. On the other hand, by escaping in the face of such reprisals, the slaves demonstrated the powerful nature of their desire to live as free people.

Although the *cimarrones* and the slaves who did not flee joined together sometimes to challenge slavery, there were occasions on which this was evidently not the case. In fact, several slave revolts during this early period and later do not appear to have involved the participation of *cimarrones.* There were organizational difficulties that stood in the way of such collaboration. Maroons lived in remote areas, and communication between them and the slaves was usually not easy. Nor should it be assumed that the *cimarrones* always wanted to involve themselves in such conflicts. They had fled from slavery; the struggle to destroy it remained the primary responsibility of those who were left behind.

The first major conspiracy involving slaves acting alone occurred in Mexico City in 1537. The conspirators elected a king and planned to kill the Spaniards, liberate themselves, and seize control of the colony. The plot, however, was discovered by the authorities, and those involved were arrested. A frightened government extracted confessions from the accused and hanged them. The threat of rebellion never declined in Mexico, and the Spaniards always feared that the Indians would join the black slaves in any confrontation.

Spanish fears were fulfilled in 1608 when thirty-one free blacks and slaves gathered in Mexico City to elect a king and queen and to plot a revolt. One of the conspirators reported the details to the authorities. Predictably, the participants were arrested, although it is not clear what punishment they received. Four years later, in 1612, blacks in Mexico City once again planned a revolt. When the authorities heard of the plans they arrested a large number of people and tortured them to obtain more information on the conspiracy. In the end, thirty-five blacks were hanged and others were sent out of the colony.

Slaves continued to escape in all societies of the Americas, and many were successful in building their own communities and maintaining their freedom. Maroon communities united slaves from different African ethnic groups as well as the creoles. The first settlements, however, consisted almost exclusively of African-born persons. These communities probably understood that the ethnic divisions such as the Ibos, the Coromantee, the Mandinka, and others had to cooperate with one another in order to survive. These communities of runaway slaves represented the first truly black societies in the Americas. Free from white control and responsible for their own decisions, these societies were the first attempts by African peoples in this hemisphere to order their lives in their own way. Their societies were always insecure, however, because they faced the constant threat of invasions from the outside. Yet many of them survived for long periods of time because the desire for freedom gave them the necessary resolve to confront, and in many cases overcome, the obstacles that stood in their path.

The communities that these maroons established appear to have been patterned along the lines of African societies. Although information on this subject is still rather sketchy, such communities could be characterized as centralized kingdoms with a ruler, such as Yanga, wielding absolute or near-absolute power. These communities, of course, were also influenced by the conditions the escapees encountered in the Americas. Consequently, they were never exact copies of the Africa that they remembered. In any event, the maroons created communities that met their needs and bore their own cultural and political stamp.

No slave revolt, however, achieved any success during this first century. The slaves could not successfully contest the armed might of the colonial states. Not

Wearing Spanish clothes and native jewelry, *zambos* from Esmeraldas (in present-day Ecuador) visit Quito in 1599. Some *zambos,* children of blacks and Indians, were among the many free Africans in the Americas.

until two centuries later were slaves in Haiti able to claim their freedom through their own efforts. Still, the incidence of revolts and conspiracies shows that the enslaved never resigned themselves to their condition and never saw it as just. Although relatively few in number, these individuals gave slave owners everywhere notice that they could never be taken for granted.

The enslavement of the African peoples in the Americas finally ended in 1888. In that year, Brazil became the last society to emancipate its slaves, bringing to an end a process that had begun in the first decades of the nineteenth century. The Haitian slaves began a successful revolution in 1791 and finally defeated the French slave-owning colonists in 1803. When they achieved their independence from Spain in the early 19th century, the former Spanish colonies began a slow process of liberating their slaves. The British passed an Emancipation Act in 1833, and the French followed suit in 1848. In North America, all of the slaves were freed in 1865 as a result of a bloody civil war. Puerto Rico ended the institution in 1873, and Cuba acted similarly in 1886.

There were, of course, a number of slaves who managed to become legally free before slavery formally ended in the various societies. This process began in the sixteenth century, but its extent varied, depending on the society and the forces that encouraged freedom for some slaves. In all of the slaveholding societies of the Americas, a child born to a free woman but fathered by a male slave was legally free. Some slave owners freed their own children born of slave women and sometimes those women as well. Others liberated slaves who had grown too old to work or who had served faithfully for a period of time. Some slaves purchased their freedom; others had it done on their behalf by a sympathetic citizen or humanitarian. Children born to parents who were already free also added to the size of the free black population.

The Spanish legal code, the *Siete Partidas,* encouraged liberty for slaves. It stated that slavery was "the most evil and the most despicable thing that can be found among men." As a result, according to the *Siete Partidas,* "all of the laws of the world should lead toward freedom." Owners who freed their slaves, the document maintained, rendered a service to God. In 1540, the Crown echoed these sentiments and advised its officials in the Americas that if slaves "should publicly demand their liberty, they should be heard and justice done to them, and care be taken that they should not on that account ... be maltreated by their Masters." There was, of course, a tremendous gulf between these ideals and actual practice both in Spain and in the colonies. The Portuguese never produced a document similar to the *Siete Partidas* and did not embrace, at least in legal theory, the notion that property in persons was not to be encouraged.

In general, the enslavement of the Africans in the Americas was not an issue about which sixteenth-century Spaniards and Portuguese worried. Only a few enlightened voices raised questions about the morality of African slavery, but their objections had no effect. One of the first people to do so was Alonso de Montufár, the archbishop of Mexico. In 1560 he wrote to the king of Spain complaining that "we do not know what reason exists that the Negroes should be enslaved more than the Indians ... because they receive the holy faith and do not make war against the Christians." Nine years later, Friar Tomás de Mercado denounced the abuses of the slave trade and urged his fellow Spaniards not to participate in it. In 1573, Bartolomé de Albornoz, a professor who lived in Mexico, wrote a well-known treatise condemning slavery. He pointed out that the institution violated natural law, or the basic "natural" rights of all human beings. These were lonely voices; it was not until the second half of the eighteenth century that a movement to abolish the slave trade—and eventually slavery—gathered momentum, particularly in England and France.

The slaves who gained their freedom in the sixteenth century, therefore, benefited from individual arrangements and not from any formal end of slavery. While some slaves were freed by their owners, others worked hard, saved whatever money came their way and, if the master were agreeable, bought their freedom. On occasion, slaves could not readily meet the price the master asked, so they purchased their freedom over a period of years.

Young men between the ages of fourteen and twenty-five were the group least likely to be freed. They were in the most productive years of their lives physically, and slave owners were not particularly eager to part with their strongest and healthiest workers. At the other extreme, the mulatto children of the slave masters and the mistresses of these men stood the best chance of acquiring their freedom. Liberty was clearly not within the reach of everyone in quite the same way. Most African-born slaves and their children could expect to spend their entire lives in bondage.

It is impossible to say how many persons received their freedom in the Spanish empire and in Portuguese Brazil in the sixteenth century. The proportions probably never exceeded five percent to ten percent of the black population at any time. It may be guessed, however, that the number of freed persons in the Spanish colonies increased steadily after 1550 simply because of the continuing growth of the black population, the incidence of owners freeing their children and mistresses, and the fact that some slaves by that time had been in the colonies long enough and received their freedom because of advancing age.

There were no laws in the colonies that prevented slaves from being freed. This did not mean, however, that free blacks were accorded equal rights with whites. The white colonists dominated the colonies, and blacks and Indians, regardless of their legal status, occupied subordinate places. The free peoples of African descent were expected to pay taxes, serve in the armed forces, and generally assume the responsibilities of full citizenship, but they were the victims of discriminatory legislation because of their racial heritage.

As soon as the numbers of free blacks began to increase, the Spanish crown and the colonial authorities sought to control their lives and limit their opportunities. Such actions were based on the racist notion that blacks needed white supervision. Unlike the slaves, free blacks could, at least in theory, choose their employers and move from place to place. The colonists feared the loss of control over them, as well as loss of access to their labor. Beginning in the 1570s free blacks were ordered to live with Spaniards and work for them for a wage. This was a serious curtailment of their liberty and made them little better than slaves. Other measures required that all freed persons be registered with the local authorities in order to make it easier to collect taxes from them. Failure to be registered brought severe physical punishments. The order was repeated from time to time, an indication that some free persons successfully evaded it.

Most free blacks performed menial and unskilled tasks during the period, but some were artisans much in demand. The various guilds—associations of craftsmen, such as carpenters—either refused membership to free blacks or allowed them to become only apprentices. They were also excluded from high schools and universities, a fact that also limited their economic and social opportunities.

The Spanish-American societies went to extraordinary lengths throughout the period to emphasize the inferior status of the free persons of African descent. In 1614, for example, the authorities in Lima ruled that free blacks should be buried without coffins. Evidently, burial in a coffin blurred the social distinctions between whites and blacks. The authorities in Mexico and Peru also prevented free black women from adorning themselves with gold and other jewelry and wearing silk. Such finery was the preserve of white women, as a mark of their social superiority.

Very little is known about the texture of the lives of the free peoples of African descent in this early period or about the social institutions that they created. Scattered evidence suggests that as a group they were likely to choose their marriage partners from among their peers. Few males married slave women, probably because their children would take the mother's status. There was considerable interaction at other levels, however. Free blacks and slaves often belonged to the same *cofradías,* or mutual aid organizations, participated in conspiracies, established friendships, and worked together in *obrajes,* households, on sugar plantations, and so on.

The relationships of the free peoples with one another, however, was not always harmonious. There is evidence that some of them adopted the racist views of Spanish society and gave a higher value to those who had a lighter skin color by virtue of a mixed ancestry. Some *cofradías* that free persons established in Lima, for example, admitted only mulattoes. Yet, in spite of such divisions, a similar heritage bound the free and the slave—a fact that none could forget. Slavery and discriminatory treatment in the Americas produced enormous stresses and strains in the lives of the freed people, but their common identity was never destroyed.

Shaping America

For the black populations in the Americas, the sixteenth century represented the start of their unique historical odyssey. The estimated 300,000 Africans who arrived during that first century made crucial contributions to the shaping of the colonial societies. They also laid the foundations of the present-day black societies of the Americas. Whether they came in groups large or small, Africans brought their languages, religious beliefs, musical styles, cooking practices, and a thousand other aspects of their societies with them. Because Africans came from many different ethnic groups, they did not all share the same culture or ways of doing things. As a result, a variety of African beliefs and cultural forms went into the making and shaping of the societies of the Americas.

Although their number was small at first, the labor of the Africans was indispensable in the mining industries, textile factories, and in sugar cultivation and other agricultural enterprises. By the second half of the eighteenth century, African workers had helped make sugarcane "king" in the Caribbean and Brazil. Vast numbers of slaves would by that time, or shortly thereafter, be used on the coffee plantations in Haiti and Brazil and in the cotton industry in the southern United States.

In terms of labor, African slaves made the principal contribution to the construction of the plantation economies of the Americas. But they were not the beneficiaries of their efforts. They formed an exploited labor force, and their energies went into the creation of wealth for those who owned them. Because they did not benefit materially from what they produced, the slaves really had no stake in the economic systems. Their labor was both forced and unpaid. Still, the roles that they played as workers in the building of the American societies must be recognized, even as the slave systems that defined Africans and their children as property and tried to debase them at every turn should be condemned.

The economic benefits of slavery and the slave trade, even in the sixteenth century, went beyond the Americas. The European slave traders, slave owners, and their societies reaped economic rewards as well. These rewards increased as the slave trade and slavery expanded in the seventeenth and eighteenth centuries.

Starting in the sixteenth century, a number of European-produced goods—such as guns, textiles, woolen products, and pots and pans—were used in the African trade. The increased demand for these products benefited the economies of the areas that manufactured them. The construction of slave ships created jobs for carpenters, sail makers, painters, and other artisans. Slave traders brought African gold, ivory, and redwood back to Europe, imports that were in great demand. Then, too, the profits from the slave trade were frequently invested in other areas of the European economies.

Historians are not in agreement on the degree to which the slave trade was profitable. Several joint stock companies went bankrupt in the first two hundred years. But the independent traders who dominated the human traffic after about 1700 seemed to have done much better. The rate of profit or loss varied from trader to trader or from voyage to voyage. A great deal depended on the business sense and skills of the trader, the price of slaves on the African coast, their selling price in the Americas, the number who perished during the Atlantic crossing, and the state of their health upon arrival. With these qualifications in mind, most of the existing studies show a return of somewhere between five percent and twenty percent on the investment made by the traders.

In the end, it may not be possible to separate the profitability of the slave trade from that of slavery. The two business practices were intricately interrelated. The funds that the slave trade generated were used to purchase the products that were produced with slave labor. Thus, a slave trader would sell his slaves in the Caribbean and use the funds to buy sugar, which he would then sell in Europe.

There are no reliable estimates of the returns that slave owners made on their investments in slaves in Latin America and the Caribbean. Investments in slaves in the United States in the nineteenth century yielded an average rate of profitability of ten percent, making for a very healthy business. Some Caribbean slave owners were heavily in debt by the beginning of the nineteenth century, but others must have continued to turn a profit. In fact, some scholars have argued that the economies of European countries owed their expansion to the slave trade and the financial benefits of slave labor.

The impact of the slave trade on the African societies is also a highly controversial issue. Some scholars maintain that the removal of millions of people from West and West Central Africa led to the depopulation of certain societies. Others conclude that the African populations did not decline during the almost four centuries that the slave trade existed. They suggest that new food crops introduced during the period led to improved diets and helped to account for a steady increase in the population, even though millions were being drained away by the trade. These two points of view do not necessarily rule each other out.

The slave trade did not affect all African societies in the same way, and its impact varied over time. Some weaker societies disappeared, while the stronger ones with access to guns and gunpowder increased their power and size. They were able to incorporate other societies into their own, often selling the captives whom they took in the process. The fact that most of the slaves who were sold were young males must have had severe negative consequences in some societies. There were probably imbalances in the number of men to women in some societies and a shortage of persons available for such male-assigned duties as defense.

The slave trade may also have increased the incidence of wars in the African societies. African societies in the sixteenth century and later went to war for their own local reasons. The popular view that the Europeans created wars between the Africans for the purpose of acquiring slaves is highly exaggerated. Nor is it generally true that the Africans fought primarily for the purpose of obtaining captives to be sold as slaves. It is very likely, however, that the availability of European-supplied weapons led to an increase in the frequency of wars.

The slave trade, according to most scholars, had a negative economic effect on the African societies that were involved in it. This was because the Africans developed a taste for the consumer goods provided by the Europeans in exchange for the slaves. Because these goods could be obtained without undue difficulty and the prices were not excessive, some Africans developed a dependence on them and neglected their own local industries. In the long run, the Africans' failure to develop their own industries helps to account for their falling behind the Europeans in manufacturing.

The Atlantic slave trade left a lasting and bitter legacy for all groups involved in it. It has remained a source of embarrassment and guilt for them. Some have sought to establish blame and responsibility for its origins and continuation. The unpleasant fact is that there were African sellers and European and American buyers. The African sellers came from many different societies and so did the purchasers. The contemporary reader looks back in horror at human beings buying and selling other members of the human family. But most people at the time did not see anything wrong with the slave trade. Still, there were others, undoubtedly a small minority, who denounced the human traffic and reacted to it with disgust.

Blame and accusation aside, the extraordinary burdens that the enslaved endured must be recognized. They were human property, subjected to the whims of their owners, humiliated, and abused. As unfree workers, they labored long hours, often at dangerous tasks. Overworked and underfed, many died prematurely. Their life chances were limited, and few could expect to acquire their freedom. Yet, there is ample evidence that the enslaved called upon their inner strength to survive their ordeal. Beginning in the sixteenth century, they escaped and rebelled, challenging the power of those who denied them freedom. The enslaved everywhere established the cultural institutions that became the core of black life in the Americas. Theirs is a tale of extraordinary suffering; but it is also a timeless lesson in endurance and survival.

CHAPTER 2

Strange New Land

1619–1776

Peter H. Wood

In the summer of 1619, a 160-ton ship from the port of Flushing in Holland sailed into Chesapeake Bay. This Dutch vessel was under the command of Captain Jope and piloted by an Englishman named Marmaduke Raynor. They were seeking to obtain provisions after a season of raiding in the West Indies. In exchange for supplies, Jope and his crew sold more than twenty Negroes to the local authorities in the struggling English colony of Virginia. These black newcomers came ashore twelve years after the founding of Jamestown and one year before the *Mayflower* arrived at Plymouth in New England. The people brought to Virginia by the Dutch man-of-war are often cited as the first persons of African ancestry to set foot on North America. But, in fact, others had come before them and had traveled widely through the southern part of the continent.

Africans were present in the early Spanish forays onto the continent of North America, as Juan Ponce de León and his successors probed Florida and the Gulf Coast in search of slaves, wealth, and a passage to the Pacific. In August 1526, for example, six Spanish ships landed on the coast of what is now South Carolina. Their commander, Lucas Vásquez de Ayllón, brought at least five hundred people—men, women, and children—along with one hundred horses and enough cattle, sheep, and pigs to start a settlement. They pushed south along the coast to find a suitable location, and they constructed a small village of thatched-roof huts. But within months Ayllón died, and bitter tensions arose over who should succeed him. In the midst of this struggle for control, African slaves set fire to some of the houses at night. Divided and embittered, 150 survivors straggled back to the Caribbean as winter set in. Almost all the rest—more than 350 people—died because of sickness, violence, hunger, or cold. But it was rumored that some of the Africans had escaped their bondage and remained to live among the coastal Indians.

That same winter the Spanish king approved another expedition to the Florida region, and five ships, commanded by Pánfilo de Narváez, set sail from Spain in June 1527. The following spring more than four hundred soldiers and servants, including some men of African descent, landed near Tampa Bay and marched northwest. They hoped to make great conquests, but they were poorly prepared and badly led. The Indians fought fiercely to defend their own lands, and soon the invaders were separated from their supply boats and from each other. Most died in the Gulf Coast wilderness, but a few survived long enough to be taken in by local tribes. Miraculously, four such men encountered one another on the Texas coast in 1534. They evaded the tribes with whom they were living and set off across the Southwest in hopes of reaching Mexico City, the capital of the Spanish colony of New Spain.

One of these four survivors was a Spanish-speaking African named Esteban—the first African to emerge clearly in the pages of North American history. Another survivor was a Spanish officer named Álvar Núñez Cabeza de Vaca who wrote down their incredible story. He told how they had been enslaved by Indians and forced to haul wood and water, living on nuts, rabbits, spiders, and the juice of prickly pears. Heading west, they viewed the rolling Texas prairie with its herds of buffalo. "Over all the region," they reported, "we saw vast and beautiful plains that would make good pasture." They also marveled at the variety of languages they encountered among Southwestern Indians. Cabeza de Vaca noted that "there are a thousand dialectical differences," adding that Esteban served as their primary go-between. "He was constantly in conversation, finding out about routes, towns, and other matters we wished to know."

After eight years in America, including two years traveling together through the Southwest, the four men finally reached Mexico City in 1536—the first newcomers from Europe and Africa to cross the huge expanse of North America. When they described the massive Indian apartment dwellings they had seen (known as *pueblos*), gold-hungry listeners assumed they had glimpsed the legendary and wealthy Seven Cities of Cíbola. Soon the Spanish viceroy, Governor Antonio de Mendoza, organized a new exploration to seek out these seven mythical towns, which were supposedly surrounded by turquoise-studded walls of gold. Since the black man was a skilled translator and a seasoned guide who remained enslaved, Mendoza purchased Esteban and presented him to a Spanish friar named Marcos de Niza, who had been selected to lead the expedition. In March 1539, the friar's party, "with the Negro and other slaves, and Indians," headed northward toward what is now Arizona in search of Cíbola. According to an official report:

> The Lord Viceroy having . . . news and notice of such land sent a friar and a negro, the latter having come from Florida with the others . . . as survivors of the party taken there by Pánfilo Narváez. These set out with the knowledge the negro had in order to go to a very rich country, as the latter declared, and told the friar . . . that there are seven very populous cities with great buildings. . . . They have houses built of stone and lime, being of three stories, and with great quantities of turquoises set in doors and windows.

Esteban, familiar with the region, proceeded ahead with his two dogs and a number of Indians. As the summer heat increased, he sent wooden crosses back to the Christian friar to assure him of their progress. Finally he approached a large community—probably the pueblo of Zuni in western New Mexico. Hoping to have reached "Cíbola" at last, Esteban sent messengers ahead as usual, carrying "his great Mace made of a gourd," which "had a string of belles upon it, and two feathers one white and another red, in token that he demanded safe conduct, and that he came peaceably." But the Zunis quickly recognized the bells as Spanish. They linked this party advancing from the south with rumors of Spanish slave raiding and violence that were already circulating in the Indian markets of the region. Zuni leaders blamed the appearance of foreigners for deaths that had already occurred, and they feared a plot by which "neither man nor woman of them shall remaine unslaine."

When Esteban's messengers returned, they reported handing over the "great gourd" to the Indian magistrate. He "tooke the same in his hands, and after he had spyed the belles, in a great rage and fury hee cast it to the ground, and willed the messengers to get them packing with speed, for he knew well ynough what people they were, and that they should . . . in no case enter the citie, for if they did hee would put them all to death." Determined in his course and confident that diplomacy could prevail, Esteban dismissed this initial rejection as "no great matter" and proceeded to approach the town. But armed men blocked his entrance to the city and confined him to an outlying building. They denied him food and water overnight, and they confiscated his trade goods. Negotiations proved unsuccessful, and when Esteban emerged the next morning, he and most of his company were attacked and killed by an angry crowd. Though "bloody and wounded in many places," several of his Indian companions managed to survive. They returned southward to inform Fray Marcos of the death of his experienced black guide.

The failure of the expeditions of Ayllón, Narváez, and Fray Marcos only increased the ambitions of other explorers. Their ventures into the American interior would also include the presence of Africans at every stage. Even before the death of Esteban at the Zuni pueblo, other black Hispanic soldiers and slaves were among those preparing to accompany Francisco Vázquez de Coronado into the Southwest and Hernando de Soto into the Southeast, and a few remain visible in the surviving accounts. Among those marching with de Soto, for example, was a man named "Gomez, a negro belonging to Vasco Gonçalez who spoke good Spanish." In 1537, de Soto had received permission to invade Florida and carve out a province for himself and his followers in the southern interior. The Spanish crown had authorized him to raise an army, to establish three fortified towns, and to include as many as fifty enslaved Negroes in his plans. Gomez was among the black men forced to take part in this ambitious design.

When the expedition landed in Florida in May 1539, it contained 330 foot soldiers and almost as many others—artisans, carpenters, cooks, servants, and priests. They also brought herds of hogs and other livestock that would accompany their army to provide fresh meat. De Soto had taken part in Pizarro's successful campaign against the golden cities of the Incas in Peru. Now he was anxious to discover an equally wealthy kingdom of his own. But long marches through the swamps and forests of the Deep South revealed no such prize, even when he tortured local leaders for information and pushed his own company to extremes. The more de Soto's ambition was frustrated, the more ruthless his invasion became. At the Indian town of Cofitachequi near the Savannah River, he finally received gifts of pearls in the spring of 1540. But he thanked the young woman leader (or *cacica*) who had presented the pearls by making her a captive in her own region and obliging her to march with his soldiers to assure their safe passage in her domain.

De Soto's repeated cruelty toward the Native Americans ensured that few would give him a kindly reception. His ruthlessness with his own army meant that many were willing to risk desertion in a strange land, especially slaves who stood to gain nothing from the entire enterprise. Several weeks after de Soto's departure from Cofitachequi, his royal Indian prisoner stepped off the path with several servants and made good her escape. Several members of de Soto's company also disappeared, including three Spanish-speaking slaves: an Indian boy from Cuba, a Berber from North Africa, and a West African—Gomez. The first two slaves eventually returned to camp and begged forgiveness, reporting that Gomez had elected to remain behind with the young Indian.

Regarding the black man and the Native American woman, these informants said, "it was very certain that they held communication as husband and wife, and that both had made up their minds" to go to Cofitachequi.

So by 1540, less than fifty years after the arrival of Columbus in the Caribbean, an African ex-slave and an Indian *cacica* were living together in the southern forest. By now other European countries, jealous of Spanish wealth in the New World, were beginning to show an interest in the coast of North America. Several explorers sailing for the French king envisioned the possibility of discovering a short "Northwest Passage" from the Atlantic to the Pacific. Giovanni da Verrazzano hoped to find a route to the Orient when he examined the Outer Banks of Carolina and the mouth of New York harbor in 1524. Jacques Cartier had similar ambitions when he sailed up the broad St. Lawrence River in 1535. Even if they could not discover access to the Pacific, Spain's rivals could take advantage of the excellent fishing grounds in the North Atlantic. Or, if they dared, they could go after grander targets, attacking the Spanish galleons that sailed homeward regularly from Mexico.

The annual Spanish fleet, carrying gold and silver from the New World to Seville, followed the currents of the Gulf Stream northward along the Florida Peninsula. Foreign ships, lying in wait along that coastline, could easily attack and capture stray vessels before they headed across the Atlantic. In 1565, therefore, the Spanish established a garrison at St. Augustine on the east coast of Florida. The purpose of this small port town was to help protect the passing gold fleet from marauders and to secure Spain's claim to the Florida region against European rivals. It became the first permanent non-Indian settlement in North America, and Africans were present there from the beginning.

By 1600, roughly forty Africans had been transported to the small outpost of St. Augustine as property of the royal garrison; another sixty had arrived in the households of private individuals. These early African Americans—mostly men and mostly Spanish-speaking—were involved in erecting more than one hundred Spanish-owned shops and houses and in building Fort San Marcos on the northern edge of town. They planted gardens and fished in the Matanzas River, selling their catch in the local fish market. Those who had accepted Christianity worshipped at the local Catholic church, and some drew token pay for themselves and their owners as drummers, fifers, and flag bearers in the local militia.

But living conditions were harsh, and controls at the remote outpost were limited. So some Africans escaped to live among the Indians, as Gomez and others had done several generations earlier. A Spanish document from 1605 complained that slaves had slipped away toward the south and intermarried with the Ais tribe living along the Florida coast. Those who remained in town had little reason for allegiance to their owners. The authorities feared that they would support any invader who offered them their freedom, and one official, writing in 1606, warned others to be wary of "persons of their kind, who are the worst enemies we can have." More than a century later St. Augustine would be viewed as a potential haven by a later generation of black Southerners, but that day was still far in the future.

Just as blacks, both enslaved and free, took part in the exploration and colonization of Spanish Florida, they also participated in the creation of a new colony in the Southwest. There, from the time of Esteban, Spanish raiding parties had carried Indian captives back to Mexico to work in the silver mines alongside enslaved Africans. Before the end of the sixteenth century, Mexican adventurers pushed to gain control of the populated region along the upper Rio Grande. Their reasons for immigrating to this region were many and varied: Some hoped to limit the exploitation of local Indians; some hoped to convert the Indians to Christianity; some hoped to control them and extract a profit. Government officials hoped to prevent European rivals from discovering wealth that had so far eluded the Spanish. But most of the settlers simply hoped to escape harsh conditions in *old* Mexico and take their chances on the rough frontier in a colony to be called *New* Mexico.

In 1595, a contract for this northern venture was awarded to Don Juan de Oñate, one of the last in a long line of ambitious and violent conquistadors stretching back to Cortés and Pizarro, de Soto and Coronado. Oñate put up the enormous wealth his father had gained from silver mining (largely with Indian and African labor) in exchange for the right to conquer, control, and exploit a vast region. His tactics proved strikingly ruthless, even in an era known for its brutality, and his grandest ambitions were never realized. In 1599 he crushed a desperate Indian revolt at the pueblo of Acoma so ferociously that he was reprimanded for his acts, and eventually he was forced to withdraw from his newly founded colony. By 1608 there was serious talk of abandoning the settlement of New Mexico altogether.

Nevertheless, by 1610 a permanent mission had been established at Santa Fe, and many of those who had accompanied Oñate had demonstrated their determination to remain in New Mexico.

In 1598, the first contingent of five hundred colonists heading north included persons of varied racial backgrounds and social ranks. These newcomers to the Southwest included black and mulatto men and women, both enslaved and free. Authorities in Mexico, anxious to prevent runaways from escaping to another province, ordered the death penalty for any Indian or mulatto attempting to migrate without presenting clear identification. So when several hundred reinforcements headed north in 1600, nonwhites had to obtain clearance to depart.

In the century before the first Dutch slave-trading ship arrived in Virginia, Africans in North America had experienced all of the hardships and some of the opportunities associated with transatlantic colonization.

The Uncertain Century

During the first half of the sixteenth century, while Gomez and Esteban encountered the wilderness of America, Europe was shaken by a religious upheaval. The disruption was so large that its shock waves had a lasting influence on all parts of the Atlantic world, including Africa and North America. Members of Europe's Catholic church, led by German minister Martin Luther, "protested" against practices of the established priesthood and challenged the authority of the Pope. These dissenters, called Protestants, broke away from the Catholic church in Rome and organized their own Christian churches. Their mass movement, aiming to "reform" Christianity to a purer and simpler pattern of earlier times, became known as the Reformation. Encouraged by the theologian John Calvin in Geneva, this rebellion against papal authority soon gained its strongest support in northern Europe.

There were more than religious motivations for defying papal power in Rome. The Catholic church was also a major economic and political force across Europe. Its large cathedrals and numerous monasteries made it a dominant landholder throughout the continent, and the Pope supported, and benefited from, the enormous spoils that flowed to Europe as a result of Spanish conquest in the New World. Both England and the Netherlands, two lands caught up in the Reformation, were small countries with excellent ports and long seagoing traditions. By the second half of the sixteenth century they each had enough ships and sailors, backed by private capital and encouraged by government leaders, to dare to challenge the awesome sea power of Catholic Spain. The Protestant Reformation's ideas about humanity's relationship to God and about papal authority added a religious and political dimension to this challenge.

Defending its economic power and its religious ties, Spain emerged as the leader of an extended "Counter-Reformation," and by the 1580s this struggle had erupted into international warfare in Europe. Among the Dutch, the northern provinces rebelled successfully against Spanish control (becoming the country we know as Holland or the Netherlands). Among the English, Queen Elizabeth's seamen, led by Sir Francis Drake, repelled a huge invasion by an armada of Spanish ships in 1588. Emboldened by such triumphs and jealous of Spanish and Portuguese success overseas, Dutch and English sea captains became increasingly active in Atlantic waters and beyond.

As a result, these religious and political rivalries in Europe took on a much wider and more lasting significance, reaching out to touch and shape the lives of many distant peoples, including early African Americans. Reformation rivalries helped determine where Africans would be transported in the New World and by whom, as well as which new languages they would hear and what forms of Christianity they would encounter. Most importantly, these struggles meant that for an entire uncertain century, from the 1560s to the 1660s and beyond, it was by no means clear how many Africans would reach North America or what their exact status would be when they arrived.

One way for Englishmen to gain access to Spain's closely guarded dominions and profits in the New World was to seek a role in shipping non-Christians between Africa and Latin America. Englishmen first tried transporting Africans across the Atlantic for gain in the 1560s, when an Elizabethan "sea dog" named John Hawkins made several slaving voyages from Africa to the Caribbean. Spanish reluctance, not English scruples, cut short this approach. Alternative ways for England to undermine the powerful Spaniards involved plundering their gold fleet in the waters of the Gulf Stream, or—even more dangerously—attacking their Central American ports and inciting discontented Indians and enslaved Africans to revolt against their Spanish overlords. Raiding Panama for treasure in 1572, Francis Drake received valuable aid from the *cimarrones,* several thousand "valiant" Negroes living in the mountains who had, according to one English account, "fled from their cruel masters the Spaniards."

When Drake returned to the Spanish Caribbean on a similar mission in 1585, his countryman Sir Walter Raleigh sent a related expedition to the Atlantic Coast. Raleigh's men established an outpost at Roanoke Island. The spot (in modern-day North Carolina) was not far from Florida and was protected by the Outer Banks. From there, the colonists hoped to support raids against the Spaniards. In addition, the Protestant Englishmen intended to treat neighboring Indians and imported Africans with greater respect and humanity than their Catholic rivals had shown. The opportunity came sooner than they expected. Drake, having narrowly missed the Spanish treasure fleet, attacked several major Spanish ports, siding openly with local *cimarrones* and embittered slaves. In Santo Domingo and Cartagena he extracted huge ransoms, captured valuable ships, and liberated hundreds of enslaved men and women—Indians, Africans, Turks, and Moors. Frightened Spanish officials reported "the pains he took to carry off launches and frigates, implements, locks and all sorts of hardware and negro labourours who in his country are free."

Drake's next stop was at St. Augustine, where his men attacked the fort and encouraged local Indians to burn the town. The victorious little fleet, carrying people from three different continents, then headed north up the coast to Roanoke. Three black men who remained behind at St. Augustine confirmed to authorities that their liberator "meant to leave all the negroes he had in a fort and settlement established . . . by the English who went there a year ago." But when Drake reached Roanoke in June 1586, he found the officers and men ready to give up their enterprise as a failure. Before he could unload his newly freed reinforcements and captured hardware, a summer storm scattered his fleet from its unprotected anchorage. Within days Drake sailed for England in his remaining ships, taking most of the garrison with him. A further settlement effort on the same spot the following year with more than one hundred new colonists had disappeared by 1590, largely because boats carrying much-needed supplies were held in England to help resist the Spanish Armada.

The real mystery of this so-called "Lost Colony" is not what became of the English settlers; evidence suggests that most were absorbed peacefully into neighboring tribes. Instead, the most fascinating, and unanswerable, question concerns several hundred ex-slaves from the Caribbean. These people, mostly Africans, apparently vanished in the sudden storm, and records give no indication of their fate. But one wonders: What might have become of these "lost colonists" if they had managed to go ashore before the tempest struck? They would certainly have been put to work along with everyone else, for the outpost was short on supplies and needed additional hands. But the English, to score a propaganda victory, might have gone out of their way to convert these men and women to the Protestant religion and to make sure they lived more freely than under Spanish rule. Grateful for liberation and relative independence, these newcomers might have served in future Caribbean ventures, eager to gain revenge upon the Spanish, liberate fellow Africans, and share in possible spoils.

The transition to rigid and unwavering racial enslavement in North America still lay in the future. Black arrivals before 1680, several thousand in number, came from varied backgrounds and often had extensive Caribbean experience. Most had been denied their freedom in the West Indies and had been forced to work as slaves, but this did not mean that their status was fixed for life in the fledgling colonies of the mainland. Frequently they spoke one or more European languages; often they were of mixed European and African ancestry. They entered a world where religious identity and the practical demands of daily survival still counted for far more than one's physical appearance or ethnic background. Between 1600 and the 1670s, the status of Africans in North America remained varied and uncertain, as the Protestant English and Dutch pushed to establish new settlements along a coastline that the Spanish had once claimed as their own.

In 1609, the Dutch laid claim to the area now known as New York when Henry Hudson sailed up the river that now bears his name. Their colony, called New

During the seventeenth century, Dutch ships transported several thousand Africans to the New World each year. Most were enslaved on Brazilian and Caribbean sugar plantations, but a few hundred labored in New Amsterdam.

Netherland, began as a fur trading outpost, and African Americans appeared there aboard the earliest ships.

By 1628, the Dutch had constructed a crude fort at the tip of Manhattan Island. They planned to import enslaved Africans to augment the supply of farm laborers in the little village of New Amsterdam, which had a population of fewer than three hundred people. Several years later the Dutch West India Company imported additional slaves from the Caribbean to rebuild the fort, and by 1639, a company map showed a slave camp five miles north of the town housing newcomers from the West Indies. Though most black settlers were legally enslaved and some apparently lived in a separate settlement, these few initial Afro-Dutch residents did not lead a life totally apart from other colonists in New Amsterdam. Some were granted "half-freedom" (they lived independently but continued to pay an annual tax); others were manumitted, or freed, by their owners and possessed their own land and labor. Indeed, it was possible for a European woman to work for an African freeman as an indentured servant.

Early Dutch records make clear that blacks were active in the courts. In June 1639, for example, a freeman named Pedro Negretto, who worked as a day laborer alongside Dutch farmhands, sued Jan Celes for failing to pay him for taking care of his hogs. Similarly, religious documents show that the few Africans who professed Christianity were permitted to marry within the Dutch Reformed church. Among fifty marriages recorded by the New Amsterdam church from 1639 to 1652, thirteen involved unions between black men and black women. When Indian wars threatened, as in 1641, Africans found themselves recruited by the governor and council to venture out in teams against Indian hunting parties.

Though Holland steadily expanded its role in transporting Africans to the Americas, the population of New Netherland grew slowly at first. For the most part, the powerful Dutch confined their major traffic to the burgeoning plantation economies of the South Atlantic. They focused particularly on Portuguese Brazil, seizing temporary control there in 1637. They also took from the Portuguese several ports in Africa (Elmina on the Gold Coast and Luanda in Angola), and soon they were transporting twenty-five hundred Africans per year west across the South Atlantic. A few of these people eventually ended up in New Amsterdam, as suggested by the presence in the records of such names as Paulo d'Angola, Simon Congo, and Anthony Portuguese.

In 1654, the Dutch lost control of Brazil, where they had been shipping thousands of Africans, so distant New Netherland suddenly became a more attractive destination for Dutch slavers from the South Atlantic. The first shipload of several hundred people brought directly from Africa arrived at the mouth of the Hudson in 1655. More shipments followed, and many of the enslaved passengers were promptly resold to English planters in the Chesapeake colonies seeking additional workers. By this time the Dutch had made peace with the Spanish and found themselves at war with their former ally, England. In 1664, when the English seized New Netherland and renamed it New York, there may have been as many as seven hundred Dutch-speaking black residents in a population of nine thousand. The Dutch soon turned their colonizing attention to other places—such as South Africa, where they had established a colony at the Cape of Good Hope in 1652.

It would be the English who expanded their hold on the Atlantic Coast of North America and steadily increased the number of blacks living there. As more black newcomers appeared in the English mainland colonies, racial designations gradually took on new significance. Eventually, legal codes would impose hereditary enslavement, and profit-conscious traders would undertake the importation of slaves directly from Africa.

An early muster roll from the Plymouth Colony in New England, founded by the Pilgrims in 1620, shows that at least one African—or "blackamoor," the old English term for a dark-skinned African—was present in the community by the early 1630s and was serving in the militia. The journal of John Winthrop, governor of the larger Massachusetts Bay Colony (founded in 1630), makes clear that in 1638, not long after the English defeat of the neighboring Pequot Indians, a Boston sea captain carried Native American captives to the West Indies and brought back "salt, cotton, tobacco, and Negroes." Six years later, in 1644, Boston merchants sent several ships directly to the West African coast, a small beginning to a pattern of New England slave trading that would continue for a century and a half.

At the start of the seventeenth century, Christian Europeans still tended to see political and religious, not physical, differences as the key divisions among mankind. Enemies in foreign wars and adherents to different faiths could be captured and enslaved. For this reason, John Smith, a leader of the English colony at Jamestown, had been forced briefly into slavery by the Muslims when fighting in Eastern Europe as a young man; "infidel" Pequots who opposed Winthrop's men in New England were sold into bondage in the Caribbean. Such enslavement was not always for life; conversion to the religion of the captor and other forms of good behavior could result in freedom. A law passed in the colony of Rhode Island in 1652 even attempted to limit the term of involuntary servitude to ten years.

By mid-century, however, the condition of unfree colonists in North America had started to change. In the older colonies of the Spanish New World to the south, a pattern of hereditary servitude based upon race had long ago evolved into a powerful and irresistible system of exploitation. Now, slowly, this destructive institution began to gain a substantial foothold in the small colonies of the North American mainland as well. Its emergence would have a devastating effect on the next generation of Africans to cross the Atlantic, and upon all of their descendants for several long centuries to come.

The Terrible Transformation

During the second half of the seventeenth century, a terrible transformation, the enslavement of people solely on the basis of race, occurred in the lives of African Americans living in North America. These newcomers still numbered only a few thousand, but the bitter reversals they experienced—first subtle, then drastic—would shape the lives of all those who followed them, generation after generation.

The timing and nature of the change varied considerably from colony to colony, and even from family to family. Gradually, the terrible transformation took on a momentum of its own, numbing and burdening everything in its path, like a disastrous winter storm. Unlike the changing seasons, however, the encroachment of racial slavery in the colonies of North America was certainly not a natural process. It was highly unnatural—the work of powerful competitive governments and many thousands of human beings spread out across the Atlantic world. Nor was it inevitable that people's legal status would come to depend upon their racial background and that the condition of slavery would be passed down from parent to child. Numerous factors combined to bring about this disastrous shift. It is worth exploring how all these human forces swirled together during the decades after 1650, to create an enormously destructive storm.

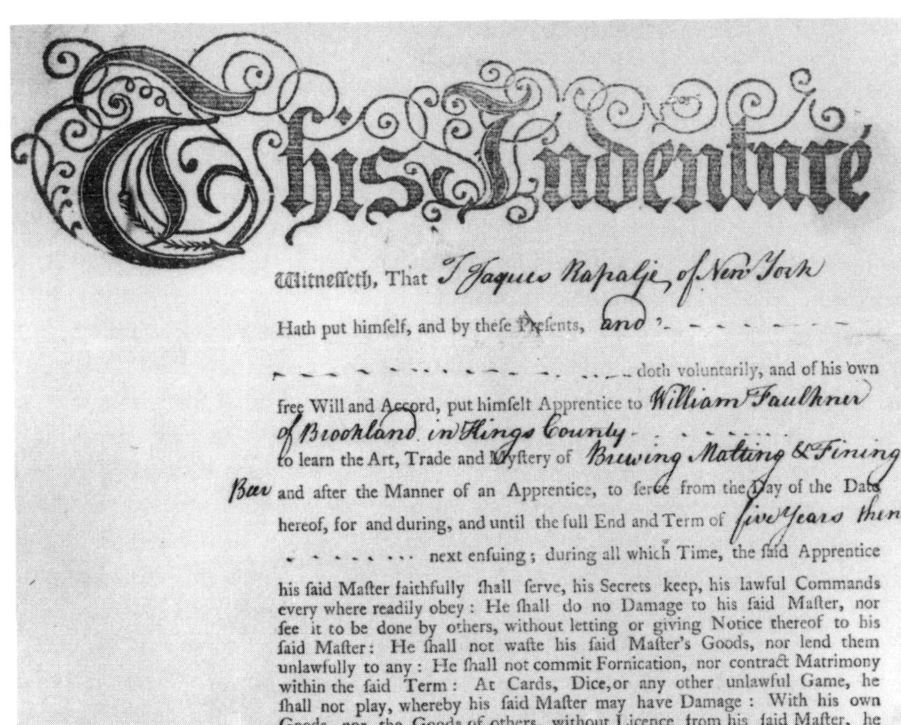

This Indenture

Witneſſeth, That *I Jaques Rapalje of New York*

Hath put himſelf, and by theſe Preſents, *and* - - - - - - - -

- - - - - - - - - - - - - - doth voluntarily, and of his own free Will and Accord, put himſelf Apprentice to *William Faulkner of Brookland in Kings County* - - - - - - to learn the Art, Trade and Myſtery of *Brewing Malting & Fining Beer* and after the Manner of an Apprentice, to ſerve from the Day of the Date hereof, for and during, and until the full End and Term of *five Years then* - - - - - - - - next enſuing; during all which Time, the ſaid Apprentice his ſaid Maſter faithfully ſhall ſerve, his Secrets keep, his lawful Commands every where readily obey: He ſhall do no Damage to his ſaid Maſter, nor ſee it to be done by others, without letting or giving Notice thereof to his ſaid Maſter: He ſhall not waſte his ſaid Maſter's Goods, nor lend them unlawfully to any: He ſhall not commit Fornication, nor contract Matrimony within the ſaid Term: At Cards, Dice, or any other unlawful Game, he ſhall not play, whereby his ſaid Maſter may have Damage: With his own Goods, nor the Goods of others, without Licence from his ſaid Maſter, he ſhall neither buy nor ſell: He ſhall not abſent himſelf Day nor Night from his ſaid Maſter's Service, without his Leave; nor haunt Ale-houſes, Taverns, or Play-houſes; but in all Things behave himſelf as a faithful Apprentice ought to do, during the ſaid Term. And the ſaid Maſter ſhall uſe the utmoſt of his Endeavour to teach, or cauſe to be taught, or inſtructed, the ſaid Apprentice in the Trade or Myſtery of *Brewing Malting & Fining Beer* and procure and provide for him ſufficient Meat, Drink, Lodging and Waſhing, fitting for an Apprentice, during the ſaid Term of *five Years To be found by Garret Rapalje,*

AND for the true Performance of all and ſingular the Covenants and Agreements aforeſaid, the ſaid Parties bind themſelves each unto the other firmly by theſe Preſents. IN WITNESS whereof the ſaid Parties have interchangeably ſet their Hands and Seals hereunto. Dated the *First* - - - Day of *August* - - - in the *Eight* Year of the Reign of our Sovereign Lord GEORGE the Third, King of *Great-Britain*, &c. *Annoq; Domini*, One Thousand Seven Hundred and *60*

Sealed and delivered in the Preſence of

Robt Wilson

Andrew Van Tuyl

Jaques Rapalje

The indenture papers of Jacques Rapalje, a white immigrant who agreed to work for a New York brewer for five years. Many Europeans arrived in America as indentured servants. Their labor belonged to their master for a set number of years, after which they were free.

Consider the situation at mid-century along the Atlantic Coast. Except for St. Augustine in Florida, there were no colonial settlements south of Chesapeake Bay. The English and Dutch colonies remained extremely small. As growing communities, they felt a steady need for additional hands, but their first priority was to add persons of their own religion and nationality. Many newcomers labored for others, but most of them were "indentured"—they had signed contracts to work under fixed conditions for a limited number of years. Their term could be shortened for good service or lengthened for disobeying the laws, but when their indenture expired they looked forward to having land of their own. Ships sailing back to England and Holland regularly carried letters describing the pluses and minuses of each colony. As a result of this continuous feedback, European migrants learned to avoid the settlements that had the longest indentures, the poorest working conditions, and the least amount of available land.

Conditions in the Caribbean and Latin America were strikingly different. There, for well over a century, Spanish and Portuguese colonizers had enslaved "infidels": first Indians and then Africans. At first, they relied for justification upon the Mediterranean tradition that persons of a different religion, or persons captured in war, could be enslaved for life. But hidden in this idea of slavery was the notion that persons who converted to Christianity should receive their freedom. Wealthy planters in the tropics, afraid that their cheap labor would be taken away from them because of this loophole, changed the reasoning behind their exploitation. Even persons who could prove that they were not captured in war and that they accepted the Catholic faith still could not change their appearance. So by making color the key factor behind enslavement, dark-skinned people brought from Africa to work in silver mines and on sugar plantations could be exploited for life. Indeed, the servitude could be made hereditary, so enslaved people's children automatically inherited the same unfree status.

By 1650, hereditary enslavement based upon color, not upon religion, was a bitter reality in the older Catholic colonies of the New World. But this cruel and self-perpetuating system had not yet taken firm hold in North America for a variety of reasons. The same anti-Catholic propaganda that had led Sir Francis Drake to liberate Negro slaves in Central America in the 1580s still prompted many colonists to believe that it was the Protestant mission to convert non-Europeans rather than enslave them. Apart from such moral concerns, there were simple matters of cost and practicality. Workers subject to longer terms and coming from further away would require a larger initial investment.

By 1650, however, conditions were already beginning to change. For one thing, both the Dutch and the English had started using enslaved Africans to produce sugar in the Caribbean and the tropics. English experiments at Barbados and Providence Island showed that Protestant investors could easily overcome their moral scruples. Large profits could be made if foreign rivals could be held in check. After agreeing to peace with Spain and giving up control of Northeast Brazil at mid-century, Dutch slave traders were actively looking for new markets. In England, after Charles II was restored to the throne in 1660 he rewarded supporters by creating the Royal African Company to enter aggressively into the slave trade. The English king also chartered a new colony in Carolina. He hoped it would be close enough to the Spanish in Florida and the Caribbean to challenge them in economic and military terms. Many of the first English settlers in Carolina after 1670 came from Barbados. They brought enslaved Africans with them. They also brought the beginnings of a legal code and a social system that accepted race slavery.

While new colonies with a greater acceptance of race slavery were being founded, the older colonies continued to grow. Early in the seventeenth century no tiny North American port could absorb several hundred workers arriving at one time on a large ship. Most Africans—such as those reaching Jamestown in 1619—arrived several dozen at a time aboard small boats and privateers from the Caribbean. Like Mingo, who was working among white indentured servants on a Virginia farm in 1648, they tended to mix with other unfree workers on small plantations. All of these servants, no matter what their origin, could hope to obtain their own land and the personal independence that goes with private property. In 1645, in Northampton County on Virginia's Eastern Shore, Captain Philip Taylor, after complaining that "Anthony the negro" did not work hard enough for him, agreed to set aside part of the corn field where they worked as Anthony's plot. "I am very glad of it," the black man told a local clerk, "now I know myne owne ground and I will worke when I please and play when I please."

Gradually, it was becoming harder to obtain English labor in the mainland colonies. Civil War and a great plague reduced England's population, and the Great Fire of London created fresh demands for workers at home. Stiff penalties were imposed on sea captains who grabbed young people in England and sold them in the colonies as indentured servants. (This common practice was given a new name: "kidnapping.") English servants already at work in the colonies demanded shorter indentures, better working conditions, and suitable farmland when their contracts expired. Officials feared they would lose future English recruits to rival colonies if bad publicity filtered back to Europe, so they could not ignore this pressure, even when it undermined colonial profits.

Nor could colonial planters turn instead to Indian labor. Native Americans captured in frontier wars continued to be enslaved, but each act of aggression by European colonists made future diplomacy with neighboring Indians more difficult. Native American captives could easily escape into the familiar wilderness and return to their original tribe. Besides, their numbers were limited. African Americans, in contrast, were thousands of miles from their homeland, and their availability increased as the scope of the Atlantic slave trade expanded. More European countries competed to transport and exploit African labor; more West African leaders proved willing to engage in profitable trade with them; more New World planters had the money to purchase new workers from across the ocean. It seemed as though every decade the ships became larger, the contacts more regular, the departures more frequent, the routes more familiar, the sales more efficient.

As the size and efficiency of this brutal traffic increased, so did its rewards for European investors. Their ruthless competition pushed up the volume of transatlantic trade from Africa and drove down the relative cost of individual Africans in the New World at a time when the price of labor from Europe was rising. As their profits increased, slave merchants and their captains continued to look for fresh markets. North America, on the fringe of this expanding and infamous Atlantic system, represented a likely target. As the small mainland colonies grew and their trade with one another and with England increased, their capacity to purchase large numbers of new laborers from overseas expanded. By the end of the century, Africans were arriving aboard large ships directly from Africa as well as on smaller boats from the West Indies. In 1698, the monopoly held by England's Royal African Company on this transatlantic business came to an end, and independent traders from England and the colonies stepped up their voyages, intending to capture a share of the profits.

All these large and gradual changes would still not have brought about the terrible transformation to race slavery, had it not been for several other crucial factors. One ingredient was the mounting fear among colonial leaders regarding signs of discontent and cooperation among poor and unfree colonists of all sorts. Europeans and Africans worked together, intermarried, ran away together, and shared common resentments toward the well-to-do. Both groups were involved in a series of bitter strikes and servant uprisings among tobacco pickers in Virginia, culminating in an open rebellion in 1676. Greatly outnumbered by these armed workers, authorities were quick to sense the need to divide their labor force in order to control it. Stressing cultural and ethnic divisions would be one way to do that.

A second crucial ingredient contributing to worsening conditions was the total lack of feedback within the stream of African arrivals. If masters mistreated their English servants, word of such abuses could reach England and influence future migration. Whether this information traveled by letter or by word of mouth, it provided an incentive for fair treatment that did not exist for migrants brought from Africa. Once deported across the Atlantic, Africans had no prospect of returning to their homeland, and few European sailors possessed the will, or the language skill, to carry the full story of New World enslavement back to the seaports of West Africa. Therefore, when an English master misused his African workers, it had no influence upon the future supply of labor from that continent. He was therefore tempted to hold them for life, reasoning that they had been enslaved for life long before he ever saw them. Once they were held for life, he could not extend their term of service for bad behavior (the usual punishment for indentured servants), so he resorted increasingly to harsh physical punishments, knowing that this year's brutality would not effect next year's supply of African labor.

Lifetime servitude could be enforced only by removing the prospect that a person might gain freedom through Christian conversion. One approach was to outlaw this traditional route to freedom. As early as 1664, a Maryland statute specified that Christian baptism could have no effect upon the legal status of a slave. A more sweeping solution, however, involved removing religion altogether as a factor in determining servitude. Therefore, a third and fundamental key to the terrible transformation was the shift from changeable spiritual faith to unchangeable physical appearance as a measure of status. Increasingly, the dominant English came to view Africans not as "heathen people" but as "black people." They began, for the first time, to describe themselves not as Christians but as whites. And they gradually wrote this shift into their colonial laws. Within a generation, the English definition of who could be made a slave had shifted from someone who was not a Christian to someone who was not European in appearance. Indeed, the transition for self-interested Englishmen went further. It was a small but momentous step from saying that black persons *could* be enslaved to saying that Negroes *should* be enslaved. One Christian minister was dismayed by this rapid change to slavery based on race: "these two words, *Negro* and *Slave*," wrote the Reverend Morgan Godwyn in 1680, are "by custom grown Homogeneous and Convertible"—that is, interchangeable.

As if this momentous shift were not enough, it was accompanied by another. Those who wrote the colonial laws not only moved to make slavery *racial;* they also made it *hereditary.* Under English common law, a child inherited the legal status of the father. As Virginia officials put it when looking into the case of Elizabeth Key in 1655: "by the Comon Law the Child of a Woman slave begott by a freeman ought to bee free." Elizabeth, called Black Bess by her neighbors, was the mulatto daughter of Thomas Key and his Negro servant. As a child, she had been indentured by her father for nine years to Colonel Humphrey Higginson, but after Thomas Key died others had attempted to extend her term of service indefinitely.

Bess was in her mid-twenties and anxious to prove her free status in court before marrying William Greensted. After hearing sworn testimony, the authorities ruled that "the said Elizabeth ought to bee free and that her last Master should give her Corne and Cloathes and give her satisfaction for the time shee hath served longer than Shee ought to have done." Bess did indeed have the same status as her father and was free to marry William. But within seven years that option had been removed. Faced with similar cases of "whether children got by any Englishman upon a negro woman should be slave or Free," the Virginia Assembly in 1662 decided in favor of the master demanding service rather than the child claiming freedom. In this special circumstance, the Assembly ignored all English precedents that children inherited the name and status of their father. Instead, the men in the colonial legislature declared that all such children "borne in this country shal be held bond or free only according to the condition of the mother." In Virginia, and soon elsewhere, the children of slave mothers would be slaves forever.

(121)

Ent: this 21th Feb: Ano Dni: 1680/81 per me Jos: Oldys Dep: Regist.

John Lord Berkley Pallatine and the rest of the Lords and absolute Proprietors of the Province of Carolina doe hereby grant unto Edward Evance a plantacon conteyning seaventie acres of land English measure now in the possession of the said Edward Evance scituate lying and being upon that tract of land called the Oyster point and butting and bounding as appeares by a plott thereof hereunto annexed, to have and to hold the said plantacon to the said Edward Evance his heires and Assignes for ever Yeilding and paying yearly to the sd Pallatine and the rest of the Lords Proprietors aforesd their Heires and Assignes every nine and twentieth day of September wch shall be after the nine and twentieth day of September in the yeare of our Lord One thousand six hundred eightie and nine one penny of lawfull money of England or the value thereof for every of the said acres to be holden in free and comon soccage Given under the great Seale appoynted for that purpose at Charles Towne in the Province of Carolina aforesaid this fourteenth day of July in the yeare of our Lord one thousand six hundred seaventie and seaven

Joseph West Governor

Mau: Mathews
Richard Conant
And: Percivall
John Godfrey } Depties

(Endorst)

To all people to whome these presents shall come I Edward Evins Ordnayner of the Province of Carolina doe assigne and sett over the within mentioned seaventy acres of land unto Thomas Hart of the Province aforesd his Heires and Assignes for ever as Witness my hand the nine and twentieth day of October 1677

Edward Evans

Testis John Hopkins
John Bodycott

Carolina

Ent: 4th Feb 1681 per me Jos: Oldys Depty Registr

To all Xtian people to whome these presents shall come Know ye that I James Moore of the above Province doe hereby Manumiss, make free and for ever release and discharge from all services whatsoever for me my Heires, Executors Administrators & Assignes Negro Harry, In Wittness hereof I hereunto putt my hand this 21st day of February 1680

Ja Moore

This 1680 document contains a land grant at the top, and at the bottom a manumission document for "Negro Harry" from South Carolina. As the nature of slavery in the colonies changed, such routes to freedom became less available.

To satisfy their huge demand for labor in America, colonial empires developed the vicious circle depicted here. Europeans offered guns, rum, and trade goods to Africans for enemies captured in local wars. With profits from reselling these enslaved workers in the New World, they imported more guns and rum to encourage further conflict, which in turn provided additional African captives.

Now the terrible transformation was almost complete, with the colony of Virginia leading the way. An additional legal sleight of hand by the land-hungry Virginia gentry helped speed the process. For several generations, as an incentive toward immigration, newcomers had received title to a parcel of land, called a "headright," for every family member or European servant they brought to the struggling colony. By expanding this system to include Africans, self-interested planter-magistrates, who were rich enough to make the initial investment in enslaved workers, managed to obtain free land, as well as valuable labor, every time they purchased an African worker.

A Nation of Newcomers

In 1976, the African-American writer Alex Haley traced the story of his black family in the popular book *Roots.* He discovered that his "furthest-back-person" in America was Kunte Kinte, a Gambian who had been brought in chains from West Africa to Annapolis, Maryland, in the 1760s aboard the English slave ship *Lord Ligonier.* Haley was fortunate in knowing the name of his first American forebear and in being able to locate the exact ship on which he arrived. But the facts themselves are remarkably typical. On average, the furthest-back New World ancestor for any African American today would have reached these shores shortly before the American Revolution, just as Kunte Kinte did. (By comparison, the largest migrations of Europeans and Asians to the United States began in the late nineteenth century and grew larger in the twentieth century.)

Newcomers like Kunte Kinte were part of a large forced migration that started in earnest shortly before 1700 and ended, for the most part, shortly after 1800. By the time the government of the young United States prohibited further importation of enslaved Africans in 1807, well over six hundred thousand people had been brought to North America directly from Africa or indirectly via the Caribbean. (Most of these people were transported to English-speaking settlements on the East Coast, although some entered Florida and Louisiana; many fewer entered Canada and the Spanish Southwest.) Roughly two hundred thousand of these enslaved people arrived during the final generation of the slave trade, between 1776 and 1807. This means that more than four hundred thousand Africans reached North America during the century stretching between 1675 and 1775. They were described at the time as "Saltwater Negroes," Africans who had endured the Atlantic crossing. This diverse group of men and women occupies an important place in American history.

Even though these black ancestors arrived in North America *early* compared to most white ancestors, they arrived *late* in comparison with Africans elsewhere in the New World. In addition, these ancestors represent a surprisingly small part—less than seven percent of the entire transatlantic movement from Africa.

Moreover, even within the British portion of the vast African trade, Africans sent to North American ports represented only a small portion of the total exodus. Between 1690 and 1807, English captains deported nearly 2.75 million slaves from Africa. Most were sold in foreign ports, but English planters on the tiny island of Barbados purchased more African slaves than all the mainland British colonies combined, and English-controlled Jamaica absorbed fully twice as many workers. Finally, unlike their countrymen dispersed through the sugar cultures of the tropics, the Africans transported to North America managed to live longer on average and bear more children. Almost from the start, the number of births regularly exceeded the number of deaths in most places over the course of each year, meaning that the black population grew steadily, regardless of new importations from Africa.

The conditions faced by these saltwater slaves were less horrendous than those encountered by their black contemporaries entering the sugar colonies of Latin America. But they were decidedly worse than those faced by the few thousand Africans reaching North America before 1675 (or by the numerous Europeans who arrived in increasing numbers throughout the eighteenth century). Diverse forces combined in the late seventeenth century to slowly and terribly transform the status of African arrivals from bad to worse.

Two further adjustments assured that this system of race-based exploitation would endure across North America for generations—and in some regions for more than 150 years. The first shift involved the creation of strict legal codes in one colony after another, spelling out the organized practice of discrimination and giving it the full force of the law. Wealthy white assemblymen, representing the landowning gentry who would benefit the most financially from these changes, enacted statutes that destroyed the legal standing of African Americans. The laws of the land they had entered viewed them not as humans with rights but as property to be controlled by others. Specific statutes prohibited enslaved blacks from earning wages, moving about freely, congregating in groups, seeking education, marrying whites, carrying firearms, resisting punishment, or testifying in court. In 1705, Virginia legislators gathered diverse laws aimed against blacks into a single comprehensive "slave code," and other colonies followed this example.

English colonists took another step as well—less formal but equally destructive. Brutal and dehumanizing treatment of African newcomers was approved not only in the colonial courts of law, but also in the broad court of white public opinion. The phenomenon all Americans know as "racism"—which peaked in the nineteenth century and lingers even at the start of the twenty-first century—first emerged as a solid feature of North American society in the early eighteenth century. In Boston, the prominent Puritan minister Cotton Mather (himself a slaveholder) generalized about what he viewed as the "stupidity" of Negroes. In 1701, another Bostonian refused to free his African slave on the grounds that the "character" of every black person was innately deficient.

Unquestionably, signs of European prejudice and discrimination toward Indians and Africans had been present in the English colonies from the start. But this poisonous pattern of mistrust and abuse became widespread and central within the culture only after 1700, as race slavery rapidly expanded. One indication of this racism was the increased hostility toward marriages between Africans and Europeans. Such interracial unions became illegal in Virginia in 1691, in Massachusetts in 1705, in Maryland in 1715, and soon after in most other colonies.

Another indication was the sharp prejudice exhibited toward free blacks. A law passed in Virginia in 1699 required black persons receiving their freedom to leave the colony within six months. The assembly argued that additional free blacks would represent "great inconveniences . . . by their either entertaining negro slaves . . . , or receiving stolen goods, or being grown old bringing a charge upon the country."

City of New-York, *ſs.*

A LAW

For Regulating Negroes and Slaves in the Night Time.

B*E It Ordained by the Mayor, Recorder, Aldermen and Aſſiſtants of the City of* New-York, *convened in Common-Council, and it is hereby Ordained by the Authority of the ſame,* That from hence-forth no Negro, Mulatto or Indian Slave, above the Age of Fourteen Years, do preſume to be or appear in any of the Streets of this City, on the South-ſide of the Freſh-Water, in the Night time, above an hour after Sun-ſet; And that if any ſuch Negro, Mulatto or Indian Slave or Slaves, as aforeſaid, ſhall be found in any of the Streets of this City, or in any other Place, on the South ſide of the Freſh-Water, in the Night-time, above one hour after Sun-ſet, without a Lanthorn and lighted Candle in it, ſo as the light thereof may be plainly ſeen (and not in company with his, her or their Maſter or Miſtreſs, or ſome White Perſon or White Servant belonging to the Family whoſe Slave he or ſhe is, or in whoſe Service he or ſhe then are) That then and in ſuch caſe it ſhall and may be lawful for any of his Majeſty's Subjects within the ſaid City to apprehend ſuch Slave or Slaves, not having ſuch Lanthorn and Candle, and forth-with carry him, her or them before the Mayor or Recorder, or any one of the Aldermen of the ſaid City (if at a ſeaſonable hour) and if at an unſeaſonable hour, to the Watch-houſe, there to be confined until the next Morning) who are hereby authorized, upon Proof of the Offence, to commit ſuch Slave or Slaves to the common Goal, for ſuch his, her or their Contempt, and there to remain until the Maſter, Miſtreſs or Owner of every ſuch Slave or Slaves, ſhall pay to the Perſon or Perſons who apprehended and committed every ſuch Slave or Slaves, the Sum of *Four Shillings* current Money of *New-York*, for his, her or their pains and Trouble therein, with Reaſonable Charges of Proſecution.

And be it further Ordained by the Authority aforeſaid, That every Slave or Slaves that ſhall be convicted of the Offence aforeſaid, before he, ſhe or they be diſcharged out of Cuſtody, ſhall be Whipped at the Publick Whipping-Poſt (not exceeding *Forty Lashes*) if deſired by the Maſter or Owner of ſuch Slave or Slaves.

Provided always, and it is the intent hereof, That if two or more Slaves (Not exceeding the Number of Three) be together in any lawful Employ or Labour for the Service of their *Ma*ſter or Miſtreſs (and not otherwiſe) and only one of them have and carry ſuch Lanthorn with a lighted Candle therein, the other Slaves in ſuch Company not carrying a Lanthorn and lighted Candle, ſhall not be conſtrued and intended to be within the meaning and Penalty of this Law, any thing in this Law contained to the contrary hereof in any wiſe notwithſtanding. *Dated at the City-Hall this Two and Twentieth Day of* April, *in the fourth year of His Majeſty's Reign,* Annoq; Domini 1731.

By Order of Common Council,

Will. Sharpas, *Cl.*

Towns and colonies drafted elaborate legislation controlling the activities and limiting the mobility of enslaved workers. This law, passed by the Common Council of New York City in 1731, prohibited any "Negro, Mulatto or Indian slave" above the age of fourteen from appearing on the streets of the city at night alone without a lantern. Those caught breaking this law could receive as many a forty lashes at the public whipping post.

Ironically, as the situation worsened and the options diminished for African Americans, their population in certain English mainland colonies rose dramatically. In the forty years between 1680 and 1720, the proportion of blacks in Virginia's population jumped from seven percent to thirty percent, as white landowners shifted from a labor system of indentured servitude to one of chattel slavery. "They import so many Negros hither," observed planter William Byrd II, "that I fear this Colony will some time or other be confirmed by the Name of New Guinea." In South Carolina during the same four decades the African increase was even more pronounced: from seventeen percent to seventy percent. During the 1740s and 1750s, an average of five thousand Africans per year were being sold into bondage on American docks. In 1760, Virginia had more than 130,000 black residents, and fifteen years later the number had jumped beyond 185,000. By the eve of the American Revolution, the proportion of African Americans in the population of North America was higher than it would ever be in any subsequent generation.

Several hundred thousand Africans appear as nameless statistics in ship logs and port records from eighteenth-century North America. Only in exceptional cases can we reconstruct the life of an individual saltwater slave with much certainty. Ayuba Suleiman Diallo, best known as Job ben Solomon, is one such exception. He was born around 1702 to Tanomata, the wife of a Fula high priest named Solomon Diallo, in the region of Bondou between the Senegal and Gambia Rivers of West Africa, more than two hundred miles inland from the Atlantic Ocean.

Raised as a Muslim, Job could read and write Arabic easily; by the time he was fifteen this exceptional student had committed the Koran to memory and could copy it by heart. His education proved his salvation after March 1, 1731, when he suddenly found himself in chains aboard an English slave ship. He was no stranger to the slave trade, for French captains on the Senegal and English captains on the Gambia further south bartered regularly for captives, and merchant families like the Diallos often took advantage of this stiff competition to drive profitable bargains. Indeed, by his own later account, Job had just sold two persons into slavery in exchange for twenty-eight cattle. He was beginning the long trek home with his new herd when he was suddenly kidnapped by a group of Mandingo men and sold to an Englishman on the Gambia, Captain Pyke of the *Arabella*. Job sent a message to his wealthy father asking for help, but before the distant priest could ransom his son (by providing two replacement slaves), the *Arabella* had set sail across the Atlantic.

For Captain Pyke, the transit from Africa to America was the middle leg of a three-part voyage that began and ended in England and was designed to bring profit to investors Henry and William Hunt. But for the Africans crammed below decks, this middle passage was a terrifying one-way journey from which no one could expect to return. The voyage from James Fort on the Gambia River to Annapolis, Maryland, on Chesapeake Bay was long and hard, as Kunte Kinte would discover three decades later. The men and women were kept in separate, foul-smelling holds. They were given terrible food and almost no chance to move about. For some, the endless motion of the ship brought seasickness; for others, the constant chafing against hard boards created open sores that could not heal. The threat of infection and epidemic disease hung over the captives constantly, made worse by their crowded conditions and the daily changes in temperature below decks, from scorching heat to damp chill.

When the crew, in its daily inspections, found that some had died, their bodies were literally "thrown to the sharks." This prompted further despair, and some, if they shared a common language, spoke of violent revolt. They were physically weakened, narrowly confined, and closely watched. Moreover, they were totally unarmed, uncertain of their whereabouts, and innocent of the workings of the large ship, so an uprising seemed nearly suicidal. Despite these odds, a shipload of passengers occasionally attempted to rebel. But most, however desperate, struggled simply to endure, praying to be saved from this nightmare into the unknown.

For Job ben Solomon, almost alone among more than one hundred thousand prisoners transported from the Senegambia region to the New World aboard British ships, this prayer would eventually be answered. When Pyke reached Annapolis, he turned over saltwater slaves to Vachell Denton, a local "factor," or agent, who was paid by merchant William Hunt of London to sell the *Arabella*'s human cargo at a profit. When Denton put Job on the auction block, he was purchased for forty-five pounds by Alexander Tolsey, a planter from Queen Anne's County. Job's new master attempted to change his name to Simon and put him to work picking tobacco and herding cattle. This latter task was a thoroughly familiar one, and it gave him time to pray regularly in the woods and also to plan an escape. But when he ran away in desperation, he was captured easily and confined to jail in the back of a local tavern. While there he was visited by an elderly saltwater slave who could still speak Wolof, Job's native language, and the old man explained to Job the full outlines of his predicament.

The ingenious young Fula now wrote a note in Arabic to his important father, explaining his dilemma and requesting Captain Pyke to deliver the letter on his next voyage to the Gambia River. Against all odds, Job sent it to Mr. Denton in Annapolis, who forwarded the curiosity to Mr. Hunt in London, who in turn showed a copy to friends until a translation was obtained from a professor of Arabic at Oxford University. Officials of the Royal African Company, including James Oglethorpe, the idealistic founder of the Georgia colony, took an immediate interest in the note. The author clearly had powerful relatives in Africa who might be of use in future trading ventures, if only the captive could be bought in Maryland and returned safely to Gambia. Tediously, the sum of forty-five pounds passed from Oglethorpe to Hunt to Denton to Tolsey, and by the spring of 1733 Job was aboard a ship sailing from Annapolis to London. During the eight-week voyage, between bouts of seasickness, he practiced his English and mastered the European alphabet.

In London, officials of the Royal African Company prepared a certificate "setting forth that Simon otherwise called Job the Gambia black lately brought from Maryland, is . . . to be a free man; and that he is at liberty to take his passage to Africa in any of the Company's ships." They assured Job they would avoid taking Muslim slaves in the future. In return, he agreed to assist them in their competition with the French to gain access to his homeland and its traffic in gold, gum, and non-Muslim slaves. He reached the Gambia River in August 1734, after four years away from Africa, and was met by Francis Moore, the Royal African Company's agent at James Fort.

Moore was eager to benefit from Job's return, so he sent a messenger to Bondou. The man returned in several weeks with disheartening news. According to Moore, he reported that Job's father had recently died and his prosperous country, once noted for its "numerous herds of large cattle," had been ravaged by such a terrible war "that there is not so much as one cow left in it." On top of all that, one of Job's wives had given him up for lost and had married another man. As Moore recorded in his journal, Job "wept grievously for his father's death, and the misfortunes of his country. He forgave his wife, and the man that had taken her; for, says he, Mr. Moore, she could not help thinking I was dead, for I was gone to a land from whence no Pholey [Fula] ever yet returned; therefore she is not to be blamed, nor the man neither."

Though Job ben Solomon's personal sorrows seemed heavy, his biographer rightly calls him "the fortunate slave." Thousands upon thousands were less fortunate, torn away from Africa unwillingly and sold into bondage overseas, with no hope of return. Some of these men and women had already been slaves in their own lands—captured in war, condemned for a crime, or purchased for a price. But they had been treated as people, not as property. They had been allowed to marry and raise families, and their children did not face continuous servitude. Captives deported across the ocean faced a new kind of slavery. They entered a system driven by enormous profits, tolerated by the Christian churches, bolstered by increasing racism, and backed by the full sanction of the law. Very few found ways to tell their story, but one who did was named Olaudah Equiano, who was seized with his sister at age eleven and shipped to Virginia via Barbados.

Equiano claimed to be born in 1745 among the Ibo people living near the lower Niger River, an area under the loose control of the king of Benin. Like Job ben Solomon, Equiano grew up in a slave-owning family. Like Job, he was captured in his native land and shipped to Chesapeake Bay, eventually gaining his freedom and making his way to England. Unlike Job, he did not return to Africa and become a participant in the slave trade from which he had escaped. Instead, he sailed extensively during the era of the American Revolution—to Jamaica, Portugal, Turkey, Greenland. He spoke frequently in Britain about the evils of slavery, and in 1789 he published a vivid autobiography, in which he described the circumstances of his arrival in the New World.

> At last we came in sight of the island of Barbadoes, at which the whites on board gave a great shout, and made many signs of joy to us. We did not know what to think of this; but as the vessel drew nearer, we plainly saw the harbor, and other ships of different kinds and sizes, and we anchored amongst them, off Bridgetown. Many merchants and planters now came on board, though it was in the evening. They put us in separate parcels, and examined us attentively. They also made us jump, and pointed to the land, signifying we were to go there. We thought by this, we should be eaten by these ugly men, as they appeared to us; and, when soon after we were all put down under the deck again, there was much dread and trembling among us, and nothing but bitter cries to be heard all the night from these apprehensions, insomuch, that at last the white people got some old slaves from the land to pacify us. They told us we were not to be eaten, but to work, and were soon to go on land, where we should see many of our country people. This report eased us much. And sure enough, soon after we were landed, there came to us Africans of all languages.
>
> We were conducted immediately to the merchant's yard, where we were all pent up together, like so many sheep in a fold, without regard to sex or age. As every object was new to me, everything I saw filled me with surprise. What struck me first, was, that the houses were built with bricks and stories, and in every other respect different from those I had seen in Africa.
>
> We were not many days in the merchant's custody, before we were sold after their usual manner.... I now totally lost the small remains of comfort I had enjoyed in conversing with my countrymen; the women too, who used to wash and take care of me were all gone different ways, and I never saw one of them afterwards.
>
> I stayed in this island for a few days, I believe it could not be above a fortnight, when I, and some few more slaves, that were not saleable amongst the rest, from very much fretting, were shipped off in a sloop for North America. On the passage we were better treated than when we were coming from Africa, and we had plenty of rice and fat pork. We were landed up a river a good way from the sea, about Virginia county, where we saw few or none of our native Africans, and not one soul who could talk to me. I was a few weeks weeding grass and gathering stones in a plantation; and at last my companions were distributed different ways, and only myself was left. I was now exceedingly miserable.

Those Africans like Equiano who were shipped to North America made up only one small portion of an enormous stream. But their numbers grew rapidly, particularly in the Southern colonies. Between 1770 and 1775, Charleston, South Carolina, was receiving four thousand Africans per year. All of them were held for several weeks at the so-called pest house on Sullivan's Island, a quarantine station designed to prevent the arrival of epidemics from overseas. So many people arrived there that it has been called "the Ellis Island of black America." Yet unlike the Europeans who poured into New York City through Ellis Island in the late nineteenth and early twentieth centuries, the saltwater slaves of the eighteenth century could have little hope for a life that was more self-sufficient or humane than the one they left behind.

A World of Work

Most immigrants coming to North America arrive with high hopes. They expect to work hard, and they assume their efforts will somehow yield tangible rewards for themselves or their children. Over the centuries the dream has not always been fulfilled, but the dream exists. It did not exist, however, for Africans arriving in colonial North America after the terrible transformation. They had no choice in their deportation and no knowledge of their destination. From the hold of a slave ship, they could only speculate about the reason for their abduction and the nature of their impending fate.

What awaited them was a world of work—lifetimes of unending labor, rigidly controlled. Equiano and thousands of other people like him soon came to the realization that they were to be kept alive, but only in order to work. Their labor would benefit others, rather than themselves. They would be granted minimal food and clothing and shelter in exchange for their toil; there would be no wages and no possibility to save for a better future. Indeed, it seemed clear there would be no better future. The incentive for parents to work hard so that their children could enjoy a better life had been removed for almost all Africans by the terrible transformation to race slavery, which obliged each generation to inherit the same unfree status as the last.

The servitude facing African newcomers was the horrible outgrowth of unprecedented economic warfare on an international scale. With the rise of European exploration overseas, the battles for supremacy among a few rival monarchies had spread far beyond Europe. Their struggles to establish profitable colonies abroad took on new intensity after the religious Reformation divided Europe into competing Protestant and Catholic powers. By creating diverse colonial settlements, each country hoped to provide itself with a steady flow of resources—gold and silver, furs and fish, timber and tobacco, sugar and rice. At the same time, they would prevent rivals from obtaining access to the same goods, unless they were willing to pay a high price.

By 1700, mounting competition had led to the creation of numerous New World colonies, and during the eighteenth century rival European powers would establish additional outposts in all corners of North America. In successive generations the French colonized Louisiana, the English settled Georgia, the Spanish entered California, and the Russians laid claim to Alaska. Though very different in location and purpose, each new European settlement demanded a steady supply of labor in order to survive and grow as a profitable colony. In many places accessible to the transatlantic slave trade, it was Africans who filled that growing demand for labor during the century before the American Revolution.

Work, therefore, dominated the lives of all enslaved African Americans—men and women, young and old. But the nature of that work varied significantly from one place to the next, from one season to the next, and from one generation to the next. Cotton agriculture, though present in Africa, did not yet exist in North America. Later generations of African Americans would be obliged to pick cotton all across the Deep South after 1800, but their ancestors in colonial times faced a very different array of tasks. Most lived in the Chesapeake region and the coastal southeast, where the lengthy growing season promised enormous profits to aggressive white investors once the land had been cleared for plantation agriculture. African newcomers—women as well as men—soon found themselves cutting and burning trees, splitting rails and building fences. Using an axe and a hatchet, each individual was expected to clear several acres of southern wilderness in a single season.

For some, the work with wood never ended. Buildings were needed, and workers spent long hours felling trees and then squaring the logs with an adze. Guided by an African parent or a white overseer, a skilled black youth might learn to be a wheelwright, a house carpenter, a shingle cutter, a boat builder, or a cabinetmaker. But he was most likely to make barrels, for these huge containers were crucial to the safe shipment of valuable products over long distances. Barrels pieced together from separate staves of wood were needed for fish and rum in New England, for grain and tobacco in the Chesapeake, for rice and indigo in South Carolina. By the eighteenth century, timber, which had been cleared to make room for plantations, was scarce on Caribbean islands, so staves shaped from American trees were sold to the West Indies, where they were assembled into barrels for shipping Caribbean sugar and molasses.

The transportation needs of the expanding colonies demanded various sorts of labor. Africans found themselves pressed into service building wagons, hammering horseshoes, stitching saddles, and mending harnesses. Amos Fortune, an African who ended his days as a free leatherworker in Jaffrey, New Hampshire, worked for a tanner in Woburn, Massachusetts, for two decades before gaining his freedom. Black South Carolinians built dugout canoes from cypress logs and fashioned larger boats to float the rice crop to Charleston via the winding rivers. After crops were harvested every fall, planters in South Carolina's coastal low country were required to send enslaved workers to dig ditches. Over several generations they created an amazing network of canals—a web of waterways linking local rivers for travel and irrigation. Near Chesapeake Bay, slaves constructed roads along which huge round wooden "hogsheads" of tobacco could be rolled to ships waiting at harbor docks and riverside piers. In Maryland one of these thoroughfares is still known as "Rolling Road" after more than two hundred years.

Sooner or later, all colonial roads led down to the sea and ships. England's North American colonists clustered around rivers and ports. They sold their surplus produce to Europe and received a steady supply of manufactured goods in return—everything from hats and hatchets to china and window glass. They also sent to the West Indies quantities of salt fish, to be used as food for enslaved workers, and supplies of firewood, to be used in boiling sugarcane into molasses. In return, they brought back slaves who had not yet been sold in Caribbean markets, along with barrels of molasses to be made into rum and shipped to Africa as a commodity in the slave trade. In North Carolina, slaves cut pine trees filled with resin and then burned the wood in closed ovens to produce tar and pitch for use by English sailors. French seamen needed similar materials for protecting the hulls and rigging of their ships. In 1724, an English report suggested that rival French colonists in Louisiana were producing pitch and tar and had "already settled four Plantations with fifty Negroes on each to carry on that Work."

Besides working in the dangerous production of tar and pitch, African-American artisans were involved in all aspects of the colonial boat-building trade. It was one thing to build ships, but quite another to sail on them. Numerous ingenious colonial slaves found ways to leave shore and become harbor pilots and deep-sea sailors. Equiano, for example, was purchased by the captain of a British merchant ship shortly after his arrival in Virginia, and he spent decades sailing the Atlantic, working for different owners on various ships, before finally securing his freedom.

Equiano had never seen the ocean, or even a large river, before being taken from his small village as a boy, but many Africans arrived in America with a knowledge of the sea. Those from coastal regions were experienced swimmers, not as afraid of bathing and diving as most eighteenth-century Europeans. Others were expert fishermen, and they put their skills to good use in the fish-filled bays and rivers of the American coast. Black newcomers in South Carolina and Georgia found an abundance of shrimp (a delicacy well-known to many Africans but foreign to Europeans) in the waters surrounding the coastal Sea Islands. They wove casting nets and hauled in schools of tasty shrimp just as they had done in West Africa. In Southern swamps and rivers, the Europeans proved frightened by the strange alligators. Africans, on the other hand, were familiar with killing and eating crocodiles, so many of them knew how to confront such dangerous reptiles without fear.

Black women often worked in the fields, as many of them had done in Africa, but they also assumed primary responsibility for a great deal of domestic labor. House servants were forced to cook and clean, wash and press, sew and mend, to suit the demands of their colonial mistress. With varying degrees of oversight, a plantation cook handled all aspects of food preparation, from tending the garden or visiting the town market to washing the dishes and throwing leftovers to the pigs. Indeed, when it came time to slaughter the hogs and cure their meat, she supervised that complex process as well. Day after day, year after year, she was obliged to balance the endless demands of the white household and the ongoing needs of her own family. Nothing illustrates this conflict more dramatically than the fact that the mother of a black infant was sometimes required to stop suckling her own baby and to serve instead as the wet nurse to a newborn child in the family of her master.

Southern planters noted approvingly that African women were generally experienced agriculturalists, while women coming from Europe usually were not. They also realized that Africans were less troubled by the seasonal bouts of malaria that often sickened European workers (though no one yet understood that a distinctive blood trait now known as sickle cell contributed to this difference). In addition, they observed an obvious benefit in the fact that West Africans were generally familiar with survival in a warm and humid climate. They knew how to take advantage of shade trees and summer breezes in locating their dwellings, and they were familiar with many of the plants and animals that existed in the subtropics.

Where the flora and fauna differed from the Old World, enslaved Africans could turn to local Indians for knowledge. Indian slaves still made up a portion of the colonial work force in the early eighteenth century. Moreover, Africans were involved in the early Indian wars on the frontier and participated in the extensive fur trade.

These frontier activities brought black men into frequent contact with Native Americans, and eventually this aroused the fears of white authorities. They worried about any black person who was carrying a gun, exploring the countryside, and gaining the acquaintance of Indians willing to harbor runaways. Therefore, they passed laws limiting the participation of enslaved Africans in frontier warfare and the Indian trade. They even went so far as to offer handsome rewards to Indians who brought back runaway slaves, dead or alive. By the 1720s, of course, African Americans had already been in contact with Indians for more than two hundred years, and this complex and important relationship would continue throughout North America regardless of such laws.

The extent of Indian-African contact in the eighteenth century is evident in the way the Southern diet evolved in colonial times. Such African foods as okra, yams, peanuts, and sesame seeds made their way into Southern cooking. Often they were combined with traditional Indian delicacies, as in gumbo, the famous specialty of Louisiana cuisine. The thick base is made by cooking sliced okra (an African dish) or powdered sassafras (a Choctaw Indian staple) in slowly heated oil. Even the word *gumbo* may come from the Angolan *guingombo* for okra or the Choctaw *kombo ashish* for sassafras powder.

Food containers and utensils also revealed traditions from Africa, reinforced by New World Indian practices. The palmetto tree of coastal Carolina, which appeared strange and exotic to Europeans, was familiar to African newcomers as well as Indian residents. Soon black Carolinians were using strips from the long palmetto leaves to bind together circular baskets of all shapes and sizes, much as they had in Africa. Gourds, like palmetto trees, were familiar to Africans and Indians, as the experience of Esteban in an earlier century made clear. Southern Indians had long used light, durable gourds for bowls, dippers, and storage containers, as had arriving Africans. In contrast, English colonists, coming from a cool climate, had little familiarity with gourds and their practical possibilities. In addition, we now know that African-American artisans were fashioning their own clay pots and bowls, which were different from European earthenware but similar to much Native American pottery. These simple vessels, now known as "colonoware," have been correctly identified only in recent years.

In short, the Africans who survived the middle passage brought numerous skills with them and acquired others from Indian neighbors, who already knew which local plants were edible and which had special medicinal value. Ironically, the slaves' ability to persevere and subsist under harsh conditions often benefited their self-styled "owners." Obviously, workers who raised their own food in small garden plots and caught fish in the local stream saved a planter the expense of supplying provisions. A strong man who had hammered iron in Africa needed little instruction in metalworking at a colonial forge. Occasionally Europeans seized and exploited much more than African labor; they took advantage of superior African knowledge as well. The story of profitable rice cultivation in colonial South Carolina is a good example.

After the founding of Carolina in 1670, English colonists spent a full generation seeking a suitable staple crop. In order to have enough food, a few of the earliest enslaved Africans in the settlement began growing rice in the wet swampland, as they had done in their homeland. English planters, who were largely unfamiliar with rice, realized that conditions were excellent for this crop and began to learn more. Production grew rapidly as Africans showed them how to irrigate the plants in the field, pound the rice kernels with a wooden mortar and pestle, and winnow the chaff with a "fanner" basket. Soon slave merchants were advertising workers from the so-called Rice Coast of West Africa, and profits from the sale of Carolina rice were making local plantation owners the richest gentry in North America. French Louisiana began importing Africans aggressively around 1718—the year New Orleans was founded. French officials promptly urged captains to import several Africans "who know how to cultivate rice," along with "hogsheads of rice suitable for planting."

By 1775, roughly half a million African Americans were living and laboring in North America. Throughout the colonies a small proportion were free blacks, but most were legally enslaved, and most lived in the South. As their numbers increased, so did the profits from their work. Wealthy planters acquired more land and bought additional slaves, so an increasing number of enslaved black colonists found themselves working on large plantations. This was especially true in the Chesapeake region, where nearly half of the entire African-American population labored in the tobacco fields of Virginia and Maryland. Thomas Jefferson, still in his early thirties, owned nearly four hundred black Virginians on the eve of the Revolution, and George Washington's enslaved labor force was even larger.

A Division of the Negros made, and agreed to by between Col.o George Lee, and the Brothers of the deceased Maj.r Lawrence Washington the 10th day of Decem.br Anno Domini 1754—

Col.o Lee's part		The Estates Part	
Old Moll	£25	Phebe	£25
Lawrence	60	Peter	60
Ben	40	Pharo	40
Will	40	Abram	40
Frank	40	Couta	40
Barbara	40	Nell	40
Moll	25	Sall	25
Milly	20	Bella	20
Hannah	15	Barbara	15
Penny	10	Anteno	10
Will	10	Dicer	10
Nan	15	Aaron	15
Nan	31	Judah	35
James	40	Ned	40
Dula	40	Camero	40
Dublin	40	Sambo	40
Acco	40	Sando	40
Harry	35	[illegible]	[illegible]
Roger	40	Tomboy	40
Grace	40	Lett	40
Phillis	40	Jenny	40
Kate	40	Judah	40
Cesar	25	Tom	15
Jarra 1 mth old	F S	Phill	F S
Charles	4.7½	Tom	4-1
Doll	3-4	Prince	3-7½
Sue	2-11½	Betty	3-1
George	3-7½	Lucy	4-1
[illegible]	[illegible]	[illegible]	[illegible]

When Lawrence Washington died in 1754, his African slaves, including infants, were divided "evenly"—with regard to market value rather than family or kinship. Half went to Colonel George Lee and the other half ("the estate's part," right column) went to his brothers, including twenty-two-year-old George Washington.

Washington, Jefferson, and other members of the Virginia gentry were dismayed to see so much of the wealth generated by their African workers passing into the hands of London merchants instead of into their own pockets. The grievances of white colonists would eventually prompt their demands for freedom from English rule. But eighteenth-century African Americans gained few rewards from the revolutionary struggle. Nevertheless, black Americans had been engaged in a successful revolutionary battle of their own over several generations. Throughout the eighteenth century they had been struggling, against tremendous odds, to build the cultural framework that would allow their survival in a harsh and alien land.

Building a Culture

The growing number of black colonists in America varied dramatically in their backgrounds and experiences. Gambians differed from Angolans, and "saltwater" slaves differed from "country-born." Obvious and important contrasts emerged between field hands and house servants, Northerners and Southerners, town dwellers and rural residents—not to mention the gulf often separating the many who were enslaved from the few who were legally free. Among most of these very different people, however, there began to appear during the eighteenth century one identifiable African-American culture.

In certain ways, the emergence of African-American culture can be compared with the later appearance of other ethnic cultures in pluralistic America. All newcomers—from the earliest African Americans down to the most recent immigrants from Asia, Latin America, the Caribbean, or the Middle East—try to hold on to certain elements of life from their "old country." In addition, all newcomers confront the hard questions posed by American geography. Is the land hotter or colder, wetter or drier, than the home they left behind? How different are the foods and smells, the hills and rivers, the cities and towns? Each group, in short, must adapt to the possibilities and limits of the varied American landscape and climate. Moreover, all new arrivals must confront the world of white, English-speaking Protestants. This portion of the diverse American population gained the upper hand during the colonial era, grew with the country in the nineteenth century, and has dominated the nation's mainstream culture from its beginning.

In other ways, however, the emergence of black culture is unique in American history, for the influx of Africans was *early, large,* and *involuntary.* The fact that most Africans, in contrast to other distinctive racial, ethnic, or religious groups, arrived during the eighteenth century means that their roots in America are older and deeper. Black culture has had more than two centuries to influence other parts of the society. Though later migrations to North America have been bigger, none has been so large in comparison to the total American population of the time. Most important of all, no other migration to America was involuntary and based entirely upon exploitation. Black immigrants to the strange new land of North America faced lives of physical hardship and constant psychological hurt from one generation to the next. In order to endure in this isolated and confining world of work, it was necessary to forge links that would allow families to form and communities to develop.

Racial slavery as practiced in colonial North America made the creation of stable families extremely hard. Slave captains usually purchased their captives one by one from several African ports. If a husband and wife or mother and daughter somehow managed to stay together and survive until they reached America, they were likely to be separated at the auction block. Creating new families proved almost as difficult as preserving old ones. Newcomers who overcame the deep sense of grief and loss created by the middle passage had to weigh the risk of fresh relationships in the New World. Intimacy was difficult in a realm where neither husbands nor wives controlled their own lives.

Nevertheless, durable families and extensive networks of kinfolk gradually came into being. Masters realized that people with vulnerable and needy loved ones depending on them often proved more obedient and hardworking than single people who lacked local ties. Because it would have limited their power, masters did not recognize legal marriage among slaves, but they encouraged long-term relationships from which they expected to benefit, both through the work of the couple and the labor of their eventual children.

More important than the pressures of the masters were the desires of the people themselves. The harshness and insecurity of their situation increased the need to share the numerous sufferings and rare pleasures with another person. Raising one's own children, even under trying circumstances, could be a greater affirmation than living without children at all. If family members could suddenly be killed or disappear, there was all the more reason to honor each new union, delight in every healthy birth, and extend the network of relations as widely as possible.

Extended slave families reached across generations and linked separate plantations. They were constantly being broken apart and reformed in new ways, adapting to meet the changing and unkind circumstances of plantation life. These emerging family networks played an important role in transmitting cultural patterns and conserving African values. Many slaveowners welcomed these ties as a way to limit black independence, but family bonds were not always such a conservative force for preserving the slavery system as most masters thought. After all, families fostered loyalty and trust; they conveyed information and belief; they provided a strong shelter within which to hide and a reliable launching pad from which to venture forth.

By providing much-needed solace and support, the positive ties of family gave encouragement to individuals and groups who were coming together, against formidable odds, to forge the beginnings of a common culture. Over time, they built a unique and varied way of life of their own that gave them the faith to carry on.

Music undoubtedly provided one crucial starting point for this complex process of cultural building. Certainly no element was more central, or illustrates the process more clearly. Recognizable African harmonies, intonations, and rhythms sounded familiar to strangers from different regions who could not converse with one another. This shared musical background drew together people who still spoke different languages. Songs of grief, worship, love, and work could reassure listeners even before they discovered other common ground. A musical tradition that stressed improvisation provided a welcome hearth where the sharing process could begin. Eventually, a similar sharing process would touch almost every aspect of cultural life, but for many the earliest common links were through music.

Drums, universal among African societies, served as one common denominator, and different styles of drumming and diverse ways of making drums were soon shared. Moreover, this kind of exchange through an emphasis on percussion instruments reached beyond diverse Africans. Native Americans found that the use of drums and rattles represented one of many cultural elements they shared with people from sub-Saharan Africa. Europeans, startled by the extent of African drumming and fearful that this skill sometimes provided a secret means of communication, outlawed the use of drums by slaves in various colonies. South Carolina's strict Negro Code of 1740 prohibited slaves from "using or keeping drums, horns, or other loud instruments, which may call together, or give sign or notice to one another of their wicked designs and purposes."

Such fears did not prevent white colonists from recruiting free blacks to serve as military musicians (as they were already doing in England). Virginia's Militia Act of 1723 allowed that "Such free Negroes, Mulattos or Indians, as are capable, may be listed and emploied as Drummers or Trumpeters." Learning to play European instruments allowed a black person to gain status in the community, avoid harsh tasks, and travel widely. Notices in colonial newspapers suggest such slave musicians were in constant demand.

For each person who learned to make and play European instruments, there were many others who recalled how to make and play African instruments. Besides manufacturing a variety of drums, African Americans also re-created various string and percussion instruments used on the other side of the Atlantic. The most popular import was the banjo (often called a bandore, banjer, or banjar). "The instrument proper to them is the Banjar," wrote Thomas Jefferson, "which they brought hither from Africa."

When William Smith visited West Africa as a surveyor for Britain's Royal African Company in the 1720s, he described the xylophone known as a balafo (also ballafoe, barrafou, or barrafoo) and later published a picture of it. The instrument consisted of eleven thin planks of differing lengths, supported over large gourd resonators of various sizes. The music of this unusual instrument was well known locally, as suggested by a sarcastic comment in the *Virginia Gazette* the following year, when many blacks were joining the British rather than supporting their masters' push for independence. With obvious irritation, the editor observed that these people expected to "be gratified with the use of the sprightly and enlivening *bar-*

rafoo" behind British lines, rather than being stirred by "the drowsy fife and drum" of the patriot cause.

The pattern is clear. Black colonists learned from one another and from non-Africans as well. They recalled old songs and sounds and instruments, and they borrowed new ones. Over several generations, they gave birth to a fresh and changing musical tradition. They drew heavily upon their varied Old World heritage, but they also built, necessarily, on the novel influences and sorrowful circumstances of their strange new land. The result was a range of musical expression that was both African and American. It varied widely in its forms from New Orleans to Philadelphia, or from a Georgia slave cabin to a Boston kitchen. But it contained unifying threads that became stronger over time. After 1800 this consolidation would become clearer still, as access to African roots diminished, communication among black Americans increased, and full entry into the dominant culture remained off limits.

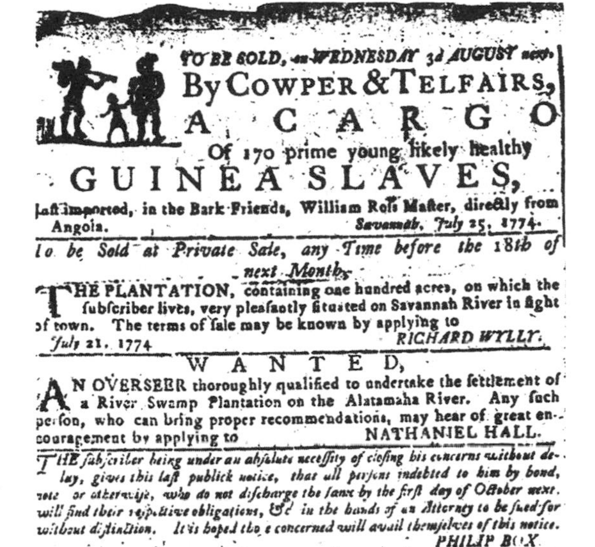

TO BE SOLD, on WEDNESDAY 3d AUGUST next,

By COWPER & TELFAIRS,

A CARGO

Of 170 prime young likely healthy

GUINEA SLAVES,

Last imported, in the Bark Friends, William Ross Master, directly from Angola. *Savannah, July 25, 1774.*

To be Sold at Private Sale, any Time before the 18th of next Month,

THE PLANTATION, containing one hundred acres, on which the subscriber lives, very pleasantly situated on Savannah River in sight of town. The terms of sale may be known by applying to

July 21, 1774 *RICHARD WYLLY.*

WANTED,

AN OVERSEER thoroughly qualified to undertake the settlement of a River Swamp Plantation on the Alatamaha River. Any such person, who can bring proper recommendations, may hear of great encouragement by applying to NATHANIEL HALL.

THE subscriber being under an absolute necessity of closing his concerns without delay, gives this last publick notice, that all persons indebted to him by bond, note or otherwise, who do not discharge the same by the first day of October next, will find their respective obligations, &c in the hands of an Attorney to be sued for without distinction. It is hoped those concerned will avail themselves of this notice.

PHILIP BOX.

RUN AWAY the 20th of May last from John Forbes, Esq.'s plantation in St. John's parish, TWO NEGROES, named BILLY and QUAMINA, of the Guinea Country, and speak good English. Billy is lusty and well made, about 5 feet 10 or 11 inches high, of a black complection, has lost some of his upper teeth, and had on when he went away a white negroe cloth jacket and trowsers of the same. Quamina is stout and well made, about 5 feet 10 or 11 inches high, very black, has his country marks on his face, had on when he went away a jacket, trowsers and robbin, of white negroe cloth. Whoever takes up said Negroes, and deliver them to me at the above plantation, or to the Warden of the Work-House in Savannah, shall receive a reward of 20s. besides what the law allows.

DAVIS AUSTIN.

African newcomers to America, such as those reaching Savannah from Angola in July 1774, would learn the strange language of their oppressors from earlier arrivals such as Billy and Quamina, who were said to "speak good English."

The same conditions applied to much more than music. All elements of life in the strange new land seemed to depend upon involvement with other Africans and with non-Africans as well. Language provides a dramatic case in point. Even before they reached America, enslaved Africans began to learn words and phrases from one another. Shipmates from the same area often found they could comprehend portions of their neighbors' languages. In the New World, black newcomers were soon forced to assimilate at least one European language—whether English, French, German, Dutch, Spanish, or Portuguese—and often learned more than one. If an African girl lived on a large plantation in South Carolina, where blacks were in a majority and contact with whites was limited, she might speak Gullah, a complex blend of African languages and English. But if she lived in a white household in New England, she would learn the English of that region.

Certain African words were especially likely to survive. Some, for example, were common to numerous African tongues, such as *Cudjo,* the day name for a boy born on Monday. Others happened to coincide closely in sound with an English word.

An African girl born on Thursday and given the traditional day name *Abba* became known in America as *Abby*. A few terms overlapped in both sound and meaning and therefore had a strong chance of survival. In the Mende language of West Africa, *sasi* could mean "a prideful boaster," or "to ridicule contemptuously." In the Gullah speech of the South Carolina low country, therefore, *sasi* continued to mean "proud one" or "to ridicule," but this matched so closely the common English term "saucy" that it probably reinforced the use of "sassy" and "to sass" in American English. Other words endured simply because they were used so often. In the Congo region, *tota* means "to pick up," and enslavement involved so much lifting and carrying that "to tote" became a universal Southern term.

The same factors that shaped how newcomers might speak also determined other aspects of life. The clothes they wore and the homes they built, how they styled their hair and cooked their food—all these things were influenced by many forces, even in the confining world of enslavement. Obviously one powerful force—though not always the most important one—was the rule of the masters. Colonial assemblies passed laws defining the cheap fabrics suitable for slave clothing and forbidding fancier apparel. But appearance was difficult to legislate. When Peter Deadfoot ran away in Virginia in 1768, his master advertised that this versatile man (a shoemaker, butcher, plowman, sawyer, boatman, and "one of the best scythemen . . . in America") was also "extremely fond of dress."

On certain holidays, colonial blacks were allowed to dress in extravagant English finery. By the 1770s, for instance, a tradition of black celebrations had grown up around the annual white election day in such New England towns as Newport, Rhode Island; Hartford, Connecticut; and Salem, Massachusetts. Once a year, during these sanctioned "Negro Election Days," elegantly dressed black "kings" and "governors" borrowed fine horses, large hats, or dress swords from the whites who endorsed the entertainment. On other special occasions, particularly in the South, blacks often chose to dress in styles and colors and materials that invoked their free African past. By the nineteenth century, and perhaps even earlier on some plantations, slaves in certain localities were dressing in African costumes and dancing to African rhythms during the event that would become known as Jonkonnu. These festivities usually occurred during the Christmas season, and the lead dancer often wore an elaborate mask or headdress and had colorful rags and ribbons swirling from his costume.

Like clothing, hairstyles also represented a complex area for cultural negotiation. Some black men became barbers for whites, learning to cut the hair and powder the wigs of their master; some black women attended to the hair of their mistress and her children, according to the latest European fashions. But how African Americans wore their own hair depended upon the individual's preference, an owner's rules, and the limits of time. For girls to braid their hair in elaborate cornrows—then as now—was satisfying and attractive, but also very time-consuming. For men to tease their hair into swelling "Afros" drew comments—and even punishments—from white masters who were often offended by such "foreign" styles. Hats and bonnets, bandannas and braids often provided varied and colorful compromises in the realm of hairdressing.

In some areas, necessity may have agreed with preference. Many early slave cabins, for example, had dirt floors and yards without grass. Did this represent simply an unwillingness of the planter to provide boards for floors and seeds for grass? Probably not, for many blacks preferred the African tradition of a clay floor, pounded hard and kept clean, just as they valued a carefully swept yard, even though these practices demanded considerable work. Similarly, the thatching of houses with palmetto leaves and the weaving of baskets with coils of sweet grass represent cherished traditions remembered from Africa and practiced in America. What are we to make of the presence of simple handmade pottery at eighteenth-century slave sites across the South? Though iron cooking pots and cracked dishes and pitchers from the big house are also evident, archaeologists now believe many African Americans may have preferred to fashion their own bowls for cooking in a more traditional way.

Finally, consider how these early African Americans fashioned the mental and moral aspects of their emerging culture. In short, what did they think and believe? The question is challenging, and the full answer remains to be found. But in the realm of ideas, as in the material domain, their lives seem to have been varied and creative, despite overwhelming constraints. At the center of black thought throughout the eighteenth century, a crucial debate was occurring over the acceptance of European Christianity. Many "saltwater slaves"—including some, like Job ben Solomon, who had been raised in the Muslim faith—held firmly to their African religious beliefs. A white missionary in South Carolina recalled the answer of one elderly African when asked why he refused to take part in the rituals of the Church of England. The old man replied simply, "I prefer to live by that which I remember."

On the other hand, certain slaves who had left Africa at an early age or had been born in the New World, accepted the Protestant Christian faith of the whites around them. But most African Americans fell somewhere in the middle. Torn between the remembered belief systems of their ancestors and the dominant religion of their masters, they combined these two worlds in a process of evolution that took many generations.

Over time, white masters increasingly demanded, and even rewarded, an outward profession of Christianity among many second- and third-generation African Americans. But they had little control over the forms that religion might take, and black colonists, slave and free, gradually began to shape a faith that gave special meaning to traditional Protestant beliefs. Black Christians favored music and song; they emphasized baptism and down-to-earth preaching. Denied the right to read, they stressed Old Testament stories that suited their situation, such as the Hebrew captivity in Egypt. Most of all, they considered carefully the New Testament portrait of Jesus Christ as a friend of the afflicted and a redeemer of the weak. We know that George Liele, the slave of a Baptist deacon in Burke County, Georgia, used to preach to fellow slaves on the text: "Come unto me all ye that labour, and are heavy laden, and I will give you rest."

By the mid-eighteenth century—during a period of revitalized Protestant zeal among whites known as the Great Awakening—a minority of black Americans were beginning to embrace Christianity. Black preachers appeared as early as 1743, and by the mid-1770s, George Liele and a small group of converted slaves along the Savannah River established the Silver Bluff Baptist Church, the first black Protestant church in America. Under the influence of both white and black itinerant Methodist and Baptist ministers, the number of African-American converts would grow during the next generation. But even those who accepted Christianity retained certain African spirit beliefs and burial customs that would become vital aspects of the emerging African-American culture.

Breaking the Bonds

Challenging arbitrary rule is the world's most difficult task, especially when undemocratic control has become firmly established. Faced with overwhelming odds, many in bondage elect survival over open resistance, and their choice is as logical and understandable as it is painful. For those who choose to defy the odds and test the boundaries of their confinement, no one effective model exists. Therefore, they try all imaginable modes of resistance: calculated and spontaneous, covert and direct, psychological and physical, individual and collective. Despite the monotony of enslavement, no two circumstances are ever exactly alike, so the best tactic yesterday may be the most costly or foolhardy today. Adaptability is crucial, and bravery is a constant ingredient, for even the smallest gesture of defiance can result in cruel punishment and lasting consequences.

Small acts of resistance, though dangerous, were regular events in the house of bondage. The slightest command could be wrongly interpreted or carelessly carried out. The easiest task could be purposely bungled or endlessly extended. By breaking a tool or pretending to be sick, slaves could avoid a whole day's work, gaining needed rest for themselves and undercutting steady profits for their owner. Workers forced to labor to support the life of a master often felt justified in appropriating some of the food they had grown and prepared, even if the planter viewed this activity as stealing. Elaborate trading and marketing networks grew up to exchange such goods. Though the owner might encourage slave gardens to reduce his own expense in feeding his work force, he objected when these gardens received more attention than his fields or when the slaves sold their own produce and defiantly pocketed the profits.

No act of defiance was more commonplace than running away. Even brief departures could provide relief from an oppressive overseer. But such disappearances also

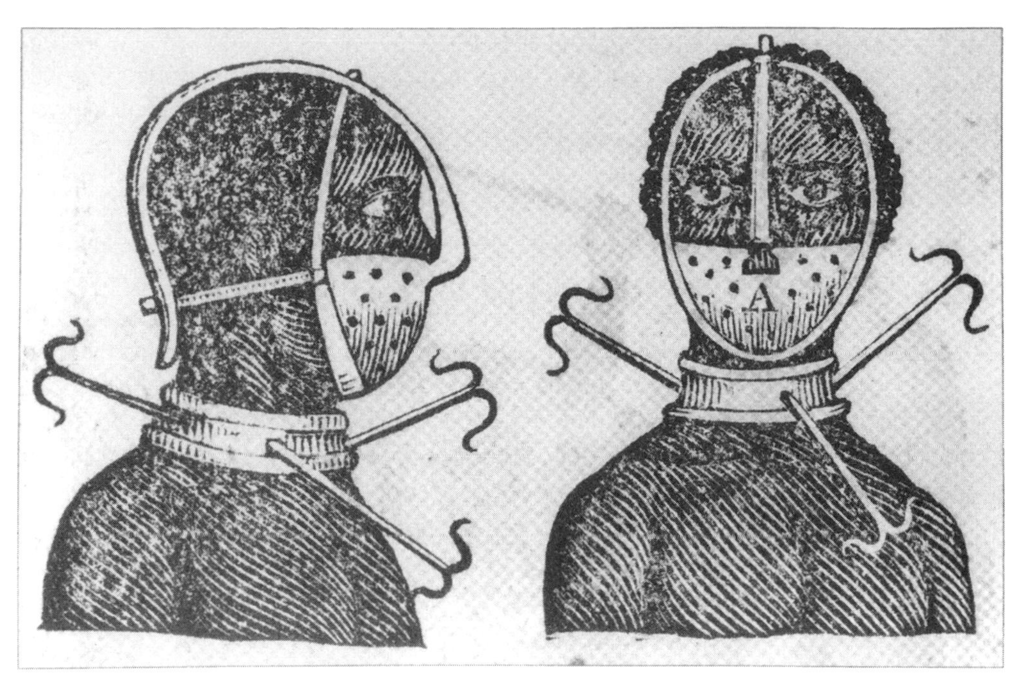

When he arrived in Virginia from Africa, Equiano was shocked to see a black woman forced to wear an iron muzzle "which locked her mouth so fast that she could scarcely speak; and could not eat nor drink."

deprived the owners of their daily profits, so penalties were often harsh, especially for repeat offenders. Magistrates could not assess fines against persons who were forbidden to own property. Therefore, minor acts of defiance prompted harsh physical punishment, such as whipping, branding, or the wearing of shackles. Moreover, masters were free to inflict their own forms of retribution. Equiano never forgot the horrible sight that confronted him the first time he entered a white dwelling, just days after he had arrived in Virginia:

> I had seen a black woman slave as I came through the house, who was cooking the dinner, and the poor creature was cruelly loaded with various kinds of iron machines; she had one particularly on her head, which locked her mouth so fast that she could scarcely speak; and could not eat nor drink. I was much astonished and shocked at this contrivance, which I afterwards learned was called the iron muzzle.

Seeing or experiencing such inhuman treatment could only sharpen the resentments and deepen the bitterness of a worker in bondage. The resulting rage often found expression in acts of extreme violence. Overseers were beaten to death by angry workhands in the fields; masters and their families were poisoned by desperate servants in the kitchen. Setting fires also became a favored act of defiance, since arson, like poisoning food, was difficult to prove and easy to deny.

Burning a loaded barn at harvest time was a way to avoid unwelcome work and deprive the owner of a year's profits. Even the desperate act of suicide took on a double meaning, for it freed the black worker from bondage and deprived the white owner of a valuable investment.

Black violence against the system of slavery ranged from spontaneous individual acts to elaborate conspiracies involving numerous people. Among enslaved African Americans, as among any people living under totalitarian control, thought of rebellion was universal; open talk of such matters was far more guarded; and the undertaking itself was the bold and rare exception, for a variety of reasons. Urban slaves were closely watched, and rural slaves were widely dispersed; organized patrols were commonplace, and informants were everywhere. Long working hours and wide distances made communication difficult, as did forced illiteracy and diverse ethnic backgrounds. Despite such huge obstacles, brave individuals joined in risky coalitions to attempt mass escape or armed insurrection.

Occasionally, an event took on a life of its own, as rumors of revolt fueled fears among whites and raised hopes among African Americans. Word of a foreign war, a heavenly sign, or a slave rebellion in some other colony could quickly bring matters to a head, increasing the sense of urgency among enslaved blacks and the feelings of paranoia among those who exploited them. In New York City, in 1712, workers desiring their freedom set fire to a building and attacked those summoned to put out the blaze. They managed to kill nine persons and wound seven others, but they failed to spark a larger revolt. Half a dozen accused conspirators committed suicide after their capture, and more than twenty were put to death, some by being burned alive.

Capital punishment was also used in the small French colony of Louisiana, when several hundred Bambara people, who had recently been brought from Africa, planned a revolt that was to begin in late June 1731. The rebellion might have succeeded, but a remark by a defiant African woman tipped off authorities. They were surprised to learn that the leader was a man known as Samba Bambara, who had worked as an interpreter for the slave traders at Galam on the Senegal River in West Africa. After falling out of favor with French authorities there, he had been thrown aboard the slave ship *Annibal* in 1726 and shipped to Louisiana, where he was soon put to work as a trusted overseer. According to Le Page du Pratz, who investigated the case, eight suspected leaders, including Samba, were "clapt in irons" by authorities and then "were put to the torture of burning matches; which, though several times repeated, could not bring them to make any confession." When further evidence prompted an admission of guilt, du Pratz reported that "the eight Negroes were condemned to be broken alive on the wheel"—tied to a wagon wheel and battered severely until they gradually died of shock. Meanwhile, the woman who had revealed the plot was sentenced "to be hanged before their eyes; which was accordingly done." Even then, rumors of revolt continued, but an uprising predicted to begin during midnight mass on Christmas 1731 never materialized.

Meanwhile, slaves had been escaping occasionally from South Carolina and making their way to St. Augustine in northeast Florida. Spanish officials had bestowed freedom on some of the refugees, in hopes of disrupting the neighboring English colony, while others, such as a Mandingo man named Francisco Menendez, were resold into servitude. In 1728, Menendez was made captain of the slave militia, a unit organized to help protect St. Augustine from English attack. In 1733, the Spanish king issued an edict granting freedom to runaway slaves reaching St. Augustine, and in 1738, the local governor granted these newcomers a townsite several miles north of the port city. In return, dozens of converted freedmen pledged to shed their "last drop of blood in defense of the Great Crown of Spain and the Holy Faith, and to be the most cruel enemies of the English." With Menendez as their leader, they constructed a fortification known as Mose (or Moosa or Mosa). Two decades later this small fort (which has recently been located and excavated) still sheltered a community of sixty-seven men, women, and children.

By 1739, a great many of the forty thousand African Americans in bondage in South Carolina were aware that the Spaniards in Florida had offered freedom to slaves from English colonies. In September, when word reached Charleston of the outbreak of open war between England and Spain, the news helped trigger an uprising at Stono Landing south of the city. During the brief and bloody Stono Rebellion, scores of slaves killed their English masters and began marching toward Fort Mose and Spanish St. Augustine, only to be intercepted before their numbers could swell. Fearful of the colony's expanding black majority, officials displayed the heads of executed rebels on poles to discourage future revolts. In addition, they placed a prohibitive duty, or tax, on slaves imported from abroad for several years, and they passed a new Negro Act further restricting the movement and assembly of black South Carolinians. A suspected slave plot in New York in 1741 led to even more fearsome reprisals, fueled by suggestions of underground support and encouragement from Spanish Jesuits and local poor whites.

British conflict with Spain had given hope to slaves in England's North American colonies. Similarly, when England and France became locked in an all-out imperial war in the 1750s, white colonists again became anxious. They feared that enslaved African Americans would take advantage of warfare on the frontiers and seek to challenge their miserable condition. In 1755, British troops under General Edward Braddock suffered a shocking defeat in the backcountry at the hands of the French and their Indian allies. When word of the setback at Fort Duquesne reached the governor of Maryland, he immediately circulated a notice that slaves should be "well observed & watched," and he ordered the colony's militia units "to be prepared to quell it in case any Insurrection should be occasioned by this Stroke."

Officials in Virginia also worried about the potential for rebellion. More than one hundred thousand blacks now made up well over a third of the total population in that province, and many of the white militiamen were absent in the war. The lieutenant governor reported that local slaves had become "very audacious" in the wake of Braddock's defeat in the Ohio Valley. In South Carolina, where blacks outnumbered whites by roughly three to two, authorities made plans to separate Charleston from the mainland with a canal (to be dug by slaves), so the city might be somewhat "protected against an Insurrection of the Negroes" in the surrounding countryside or an attack by Indians from the frontier.

The end of the great war of empire brought dramatic changes to the colonies. In Paris in 1762, British representatives sat down with envoys from France and Spain to negotiate a final peace. Their treaty, completed the following year, gave decisive advantages to the victorious British under their young monarch, George III. From the king of France, they received control over Canada. From Spain, the Catholic ally of France, they gained hold of what had for two hundred years been Spanish Florida. These sweeping shifts in the colonial landscape had an immediate impact on all the peoples of eastern North America. Among Indians, for example, it is no coincidence that a major uprising known as Pontiac's Rebellion began in 1763, as Native Americans in the Great Lakes region lost their strategic bargaining position between French and English colonizers.

Many African Americans also felt an immediate impact from the peace settlement. In Florida, hundreds of blacks had been imported as laborers from the West Indies or had escaped from slavery in the neighboring English colonies. Most of them departed with the Spanish as they evacuated St. Augustine in 1763. At the same time, thousands of African Americans enslaved in nearby Georgia and South Carolina saw a sudden end to their dream of escaping to Fort Mose. Florida quickly changed from an outpost of possible black liberty to a new frontier for English plantations. Rich investors in Charleston and Savannah transported several thousand workers to British Florida in hopes of earning quick profits from slave labor. A few of these African Americans managed to escape and join bands of Creek Indians in what would soon be known as the Seminole Nation. The rest died in bondage.

Elsewhere on the British colonial frontier, the end of the so-called French and Indian War also brought immediate change for African Americans. In the North, numerous servants and free blacks had taken advantage of the turmoil of war to travel more freely. Some served white officers, while others cut roads, built fortifications, and transported supplies. Still others enlisted as soldiers. Garshom Prince, for example, had been born in New England in 1733 and apparently went to war with Captain Robert Durkee. He must have been issued a musket to fight, for he inscribed a traditional powder container made from a cow's horn, when the soldiers paused at Crown Point in 1761 following their victory over the French. Seventeen years later, at age forty-five, Prince was back in service in the American Revolution, fighting for the patriot side. When he was killed in the Battle of Wyoming, Pennsylvania, in 1778, he was once again carrying his carved powder horn. The years between the end of one great war and the beginning of another would be eventful ones for African Americans in their strange new land.

To the west of the English colonies, the end of the war with France also brought change for African Americans. George III and his government ministers were fearful that expanding settlement would encroach on Native American lands and provoke an expensive Indian war. Britain, deeply in debt after the struggle with France, wanted to avoid such a costly undertaking. So the king proclaimed a boundary line running along the top of the Appalachian mountains to divide the Atlantic colonies from Indian nations living in the Ohio and Mississippi river valleys. This so-called Proclamation Line, plus the willingness of colonial officials to pay bounties to Native Americans for capturing runaways, held down the number of enslaved blacks who risked seeking freedom in Indian country. An act by the Virginia Assembly "thought it good Policy . . . to keep up and increase that natural aversion which happily subsists between Negroes and Indians."

Efforts to prohibit interracial mixing on the frontier were not new. When a German named Christian Priber had gone to live among the Cherokees in the 1730s, announcing his plans for an interracial utopia without private property where all races would be welcome, he was hunted down by authorities and imprisoned in Georgia until he died in 1744. Nevertheless, the backcountry was so large and so thinly populated that it was impossible for white authorities to prevent nonwhites from settling together along the frontier. In 1740, Molly Barber, daughter of a wealthy white New England family, eloped with James Chaugham, a Narragansett Indian. The couple established the small community of Barkhamsted in northwest Connecticut, which soon drew a number of Indians, poor whites, and free blacks. In 1758, Mary Jamison, a Scots-Irish immigrant girl, was captured by Indians and lived most of her life among the Senecas in what is now upstate New York. She later told of staying briefly with two African-American runaways at their remote cabin near the Genesee River. She and her children helped harvest their corn crop and passed the winter in their frontier homestead.

Besides affecting African Americans on the borders of the empire, Britain's dramatic triumph over France also had a swift impact upon blacks living in the heart of the mainland colonies. Soon after 1763, the political climate began to change dramatically.

"Liberty! Liberty!"

England's war with France had been a long and expensive struggle; it had taken place on land and sea, and it had extended to several continents. As a result, the British crown had built up an enormous public debt. Therefore, no sooner had victory celebrations ended than the government in London began pressing for new taxes to replenish empty coffers. With residents of England already heavily taxed, Parliament turned its attention to the colonies. Their economies had grown and prospered under the protection of the British crown and had benefited directly from the recent war. In the past, England had asked its colonists to pay only duties designed to regulate trade. Now, however, officials suggested that perhaps it was

THE

Massachusetts Spy

Or, AMERICAN ORACLE of LIBERTY.

"Undaunted by TYRANTS we'll DIE or be FREE."

WHEREAS the NEGROES in the counties of Briſtol and Worceſter, the 24th of March laſt, petitioned the Committees of Correſpondence for the county of Worceſter (then convened in Worceſter) to aſſiſt them in obtaining their freedom. THEREFORE,

In County Convention, June 14th, 1775.

RESOLVED, That we abhor the enſlaving of any of the human race, and particularly of the NEGROES in this country. And that whenever there ſhall be a door opened, or opportunity preſent, for any thing to be done toward the emancipating the NEGROES; we will uſe our influence and endeavour that ſuch a thing may be effected,

Atteſt. WILLIAM HENSHAW, Clerk.

Although African Americans had dreamed of liberty for generations, it took the idealism of the revolutionary era to prompt some white Americans to accept the political goal of black emancipation. In the June 21, 1775, issue of the *Massachusetts Spy,* the Committee of Correspondence for Worcester County published this notice stating its desire to see an end to slavery.

time to levy taxes to raise revenues, even if the colonists were not directly represented in the English Parliament.

In 1765, Parliament approved the controversial Stamp Act, taxing the colonists by obliging them to purchase a government stamp for such simple transactions as buying a newspaper, filing a will, or selling a piece of property. Extensive protests forced the law to be repealed, but it was followed by other revenue measures that intensified debate. British soldiers and sailors paid to maintain order became objects of scorn, and the king's troops were frequently attacked. When Parliament passed the Tea Act in 1773, suspicious local leaders saw the offer of cheap tea as a device to trick the colonies into accepting the principle of taxation by Parliament. Colonists vowed not to purchase English tea and even threw boxes of tea into Boston harbor. In 1774, an irate Parliament responded with a series of "Coercive

Acts," prompting colonial leaders to organize a Continental Congress that would work out the American response to the intrusive British legislation. British troops met armed resistance when they attempted to secure government powder supplies in Lexington, Massachusetts, in April 1775, and in July 1776 the Continental Congress voted to declare independence from Great Britain.

As participants or observers, African Americans were close to all these important events leading up to the American Revolution. They witnessed firsthand the mounting pressures for an armed revolt against the strongest empire on earth. During a Stamp Act protest in Wilmington, North Carolina, for example, the royal governor sent food and drink in an effort to placate white demonstrators. Not willing to be bought off, the crowd "immediately broke in the heads of the Barrels of Punch and let it run into the street." According to a firsthand account, they refused to roast the ox offered to them by the governor. Instead, they put its head on display "in the Pillory and gave the Carcass to the Negroes" who were looking on. Equiano was working as a slave on a small vessel in the Caribbean when word reached America that such protests had brought an end to the Stamp Act. He recalled sailing into Charleston harbor at night and seeing "the town illuminated; the guns were fired, and bonfires and other demonstrations of joy shown, on account of repeal of the stamp act."

Crispus Attucks, son of a black man and an Indian woman, played a central role in the Boston Massacre of 1770, in which British redcoats killed five colonists. Described as "Six Feet two Inches high" with "short curl'd hair," Attucks had run away from his master in Framingham, Massachusetts, in 1750. Twenty years later, at age forty-seven, he was working as a sailor out of the Bahamas, aboard a boat bound from Boston to North Carolina. On the evening of March 5, 1770, Attucks played a leading part in the bloody skirmish on King Street. When attorney John Adams (later the second President of the United States) defended the British soldiers at their trial, he argued they had been provoked by a "mob" made up of "a motley rabble of saucy boys, negroes and mulattoes, Irish teagues [slang for Irishmen] and outlandish jack tarrs [sailors from foreign ports]." "Attucks," he told the court, "appears to have undertaken to be the hero of the night, and to lead this army with banners, to form them in the first place in Dock square, and march them up to King street with their clubs."

Andrew, a slave witness who testified at the same trial, recalled seeing Attucks and his band arrive on the scene, where a bitter scuffle was already in progress. The new contingent was shouting loudly and crying, "Damn them, they dare not fire, we are not afraid of them." According to Andrew, "one of these people, a stout man with a long cordwood stick," whom he later identified as Attucks, "threw himself in, and made a blow at the officer," crying out, "kill the dogs, knock them over." Similarly, John Adams argued that the "stout Molatto fellow" waded into the fray "and with one hand took hold of a bayonet, and with the other knocked the man down." Attucks's actions cost him his life. According to published accounts, he was the first to fall—"killed on the Spot, two Balls entering his Breast." When Boston staged an elaborate public funeral for the martyrs killed in this clash, "all the Bells tolled in solemn Peal" throughout the town. In subsequent years colonial radicals invoked the name of Crispus Attucks as the first person who had given his life for the patriot cause.

Other African Americans would risk their lives, even before the Declaration of Independence. When Paul Revere summoned the Minutemen to oppose British troops at Concord and Lexington in April 1775, a number of black men living in Massachusetts responded to the call. They included Cato Stedman, Cuff Whitemore, and Cato Boardman from Cambridge, Job Potama and Isaiah Bayoman from Stoneham, Peter Salem from Braintree, Prince Easterbrooks from Lexington, Pompy from Brookline, and David Lamson, an elderly mulatto who had fought in the French and Indian War. Later that same year, at the Battle of Bunker Hill, Cuff Whitemore and Peter Salem again saw action, along with nearly twenty other African Americans. Salem Poor, a black freeman from Andover, fought so bravely that some of his white colleagues later petitioned that this "Brave & gallent Soldier" deserved a reward, since he had "behaved like an Experienced officer" throughout the conflict.

Crispus Attucks has become a remembered figure in American history, and a picture of Peter Salem at Bunker Hill has appeared on a U.S. postage stamp. But there are other black men and women from the decade before the revolution who are less well known and who deserve greater recognition. Individually and collectively, they were involved in their own struggle for liberty. They faced tremendous odds and they took enormous risks. Loyal to the principle of freedom, they listened to the competing rhetoric of white patriots and the British crown. Would either side in the mounting debate include African Americans as free and equal members of society? Unfortunately, the response turned out to be "no." But during the decade before 1776 (and the decade after as well) this fateful answer remained uncertain.

After all, there were moral and logical arguments why Englishmen on one or both sides of the Atlantic might finally decide to renounce race slavery. For one thing, a few whites, led by pioneering Quakers such as John Woolman and Anthony Benezet, were showing an interest in abolishing the institution of slavery—an idea that enslaved African Americans had supported unanimously for more than a century. Not only were notions of human equality beginning to gain favor, but politicians and strategists on both sides of the Atlantic were anxious to appear consistent in arguing over "British liberties." White colonists who claimed they were being "enslaved" by British tyranny were frequently reminded of their hypocrisy. How could they pretend to be "advocates for the liberties of mankind," one critic asked, when they were "trampling on the sacred natural rights and privileges of Africans" at the same moment? How indeed, wondered Abigail Adams in

Boston. She reminded her husband, John Adams, that white colonists were preparing to fight for the same liberty that "we are daily robbing and plundering from those who have as good a right to freedom as we have."

Black colonists were ready to fight for their own freedom. They knew they might gain from any dissent that divided the whites who dominated their lives. Even distant events could provide rays of hope. In 1772, a judge in London ruled, in the well-publicized case of a slave named Somerset, that it was illegal to hold anyone in bondage in England, regardless of race. While this case did not actually end slavery in England, word of this stunning decision reached the southern colonies, and created a predictable stir among enslaved workers. Virginia newspapers soon carried ads for black runaways who had disappeared in hopes of securing passage to England.

A year later, four slaves in Boston seeking independence for blacks in Massachusetts had petitioned the colonial legislature. Whether out of irony or flattery, they began by stating: "We expect great things from men who have made such a noble stand against the designs of their *fellow-men* to enslave them." They asked for the right to "leave the province" as soon as they could earn enough money to buy passage "to some part of the coast of *Africa*, where we propose a settlement." At the same time other black New Englanders, both slave and free, were petitioning successive governors, hoping to induce the British crown to show sympathy to their cause. In 1774, African Americans in Massachusetts reminded Governor Thomas Gage, "we have in common with all other men a naturel right to our freedoms." They asked him to abolish slavery and to provide them with "some part of the unimproved land, belonging to the province, for a settlement."

In the Southern colonies, with enslavement more widespread and black literacy generally forbidden, the chances for a petition or public appeal remained slim—unless it came from an outspoken visitor. In the tumultuous spring of 1775, an African-born preacher named David visited Charleston. The young evangelist spoke to a private gathering of black and white Christians, and he refused to utter gentle pieties. Instead, David assured his audience that "God would send Deliverance to the Negroes, from the power of their Masters, as He freed the Children of Israel from Egyptian Bondage." White listeners suspected that "he meant to raise rebellion amongst the negroes," and David had to flee the town rapidly to avoid being hanged.

If enslaved Africans were finally to win deliverance in 1775, perhaps it would be with the aid of British forces. When shots were fired at Lexington in April, and later at Bunker Hill, blacks like Peter Salem joined the patriot forces, and eventually thousands more would follow during the course of the Revolutionary War. But many more, particularly in the South, saw the British as their likely ally, as court testimony reveals. In April, Thomas Jeremiah, a free black who worked as a pilot in Charleston harbor, took aside an enslaved dockworker named Sambo and told him

BOSTON, APRIL 20th, 1773.

SIR,

THE efforts made by the legiſlative of this province in their laſt ſeſſions to free themſelves from ſlavery, gave us, who are in that deplorable ſtate, a high degree of ſatisfaction. We expect great things from men who have made ſuch a noble ſtand againſt the deſigns of their *fellow-men* to enſlave them. We cannot but wiſh and hope Sir, that you will have the ſame grand object, we mean civil and religious liberty, in view in your next ſeſſion. The divine ſpirit of *freedom*, ſeems to fire every humane breaſt on this continent, except ſuch as are bribed to aſſiſt in executing the execrable plan.

WE are very ſenſible that it would be highly detrimental to our preſent maſters, if we were allowed to demand all that of *right* belongs to us for paſt ſervices ; this we diſclaim. Even the *Spaniards*, who have not thoſe ſublime ideas of freedom that Engliſh men have, are conſcious that they have no right to all the ſervices of their fellow-men, we mean the *Africans*, whom they have purchaſed with their money ; therefore they allow them one day in a week to work for themſelve, to enable them to earn money to purchaſe the reſidue of their time, which they have a right to demand in ſuch portions as they are able to pay for (a due appraizment of their ſervices being firſt made, which always ſtands at the purchaſe money.) We do not pretend to dictate to you Sir, or to the honorable Aſſembly, of which you are a member : We acknowledge our obligations to you for what you have already done, but as the people of this province ſeem to be actuated by the principles of equity and juſtice, we cannot but expect your houſe will again take our deplorable caſe into ſerious conſideration, and give us that ample relief which, *as men*, we have a natural right to.

BUT ſince the wiſe and righteous governor of the univerſe, has permitted our fellow men to make us ſlaves, we bow in ſubmiſſion to him, and determine to behave in ſuch a manner, as that we may have reaſon to expect the divine approbation of, and aſſiſtance in, our peaceable and lawful attempts to gain our freedom.

WE are willing to ſubmit to ſuch regulations and laws, as may be made relative to us, until we leave the province, which we determine to do as ſoon as we can from our joynt labours procure money to tranſport ourſelves to ſome part of the coaſt of *Africa*, where we propoſe a ſettlement. We are very deſirous that you ſhould have inſtructions relative to us, from your town, therefore we pray you to communicate this letter to them, and aſk this favor for us.

In behalf of our fellow ſlaves in this province,
And by order of their Committee.

PETER BESTES,
SAMBO FREEMAN,
FELIX HOLBROOK,
CHESTER JOIE.

For the REPRESENTATIVE of the town of *Thompson*

A committee of slaves circulated this carefully worded request to the Colonial Assembly of Massachusetts in 1773. They applauded the anti-British legislature's "noble stand against the designs of their fellow-men to enslave them" and went on to request their own release from bondage and the chance to return to Africa.

"there is a great war coming soon." He urged Sambo to "join the soldiers," because the impending war "was come to help the poor Negroes." Several months later Jeremiah was accused of smuggling guns from a British warship to slaves in the Charleston vicinity. Fearful of black rebellion, patriot leaders in control of the town had Jeremiah publicly hanged and then burned as a brutal example to other African American freedom fighters.

In other Southern colonies black hopes for successful armed rebellion also ran high during 1775, and white fears of a slave uprising proved equally strong. In eastern North Carolina, rumors of revolt were widespread. When a plot was discovered in early July, the patriot Committees of Safety rounded up scores of African Americans, many of them armed. Suspected slaves were severely whipped in public, and some had their ears cut off. All those who spoke to their captors told a similar story. According to Colonel John Simpson, they said they were to rise up on the night of July 8, destroy the local community, and march toward the backcountry, where they expected to be met by armed British officials and "settled in a free government of their own." Blacks in Maryland had similar hopes of overthrowing their bondage. Their bold talk and actions infuriated the patriot leaders in Dorchester County, who finally moved to confiscate their weapons. In one day, they claimed to have taken up "about eighty guns, some bayonets, swords, etc."

As 1775 unfolded, black aspirations for freedom and English desires to frighten white radicals in America seemed to coincide. "Things are coming to that crisis," wrote British commander Thomas Gage in June, "that we must avail ourselves of every resource, even to raise the Negros, in our cause." This practical alliance emerged most dramatically in Virginia. The royal governor in Williamsburg, Lord Dunmore, had hinted in May his intention of "proclaiming all the Negroes free, who should join him." By autumn, the patriots had forced him to take refuge on a vessel from His Majesty's Navy, and Dunmore was sailing the coastline, encouraging black Virginians to escape to British ships. In November he issued a proclamation emancipating any slaves who would join his forces, and black Virginians flocked to his banner. Within a month he had more than three hundred persons enrolled in his "Ethiopian Regiment," with the words "Liberty to Slaves" emblazoned across their uniforms.

Patriot leaders and Virginia planters expressed deep concern over the success of Dunmore's proclamation. Up and down the Chesapeake, and as far away as Georgia, enslaved blacks were making desperate efforts to elude their owners and come under the protective wing of the Royal Navy. On November 30, the *Virginia Gazette* spoke of "boatloads of slaves" struggling to reach British ships. When a contingent of blacks in Georgia gathered on Tybee Island near the mouth of the Savannah River, the local Committee of Safety secretly paid a band of Creek Indians to destroy them before they could reach British protection. Likewise, some of the South Carolina runaways who set up camp on Sullivan's Island near Charleston harbor were hunted down before they could board British ships.

Despite the high risk, hundreds of African Americans clamored safely aboard English vessels in the months after Lord Dunmore's proclamation. In late December 1775, George Washington expressed his fear of Dunmore's plan. The patriot commander wrote that if "that man is not crushed by spring, he will become the most formidable enemy America has; his strength will increase as a snow ball by rolling; and faster, if some expedient cannot be hit upon to convince the slaves and servants of the impotency of his designs." But during the spring of 1776, it was not General Washington who stopped the dramatic flow of black Virginians to join Lord Dunmore. Instead, an outbreak of smallpox in the crowded camps finally reduced the tide of hopeful refugees.

During the Revolutionary War that followed, numerous slaves took advantage of the continuing turmoil to seek their freedom, but most were disappointed. The new nation that was born out of the struggle over independence would fail to honor, in its Constitution, the stirring words of Thomas Jefferson's declaration that "all men are created equal." The vast majority of the country's half million African Americans were still living in the South and still bearing the yoke of slavery in 1776. It would take more than three long generations before the expectations for freedom raised by the American Revolution could be met through the bloodshed of the Civil War.

CHAPTER 3

Revolutionary Citizens

1776–1804

Daniel C. Littlefield

In October 1772 a young Boston woman wrote a poem dedicated to William Legge, earl of Dartmouth, who lived in London. A man reputedly of humane character, the earl had recently been appointed by the British king as secretary of state for the colonies. He took charge during this troubled period in relations between Britain and its North American possessions. The young Boston woman hoped that the earl would respond favorably to the difficult issues that prevented harmony between the king and his colonial subjects. She flattered him as a friend of "Fair *Freedom*" who would end the "hated *faction*," or dissension, that the crisis created.

Ironically, the young woman who wrote so knowledgeably about the colonial struggle for liberty and who was so aware of the political affairs and personalities of the day was not free herself. Her bondage gave her an acute sensitivity to issues of slavery and freedom. As she wrote the earl:

> Should you, my lord, while you peruse my song,
> Wonder from whence *my love of Freedom sprung,*
> I, young in life, by *seeming cruel fate*
> Was snatched from Afric's fancy'd happy seat;
> Such, such my case. And can I then but pray
> Others may never feel *tyrannic sway*?

The poet's name was Phillis Wheatley, and she was brought from the West Coast of Africa, probably from the Senegambia region, to Boston, Massachusetts, in 1761. Her life spanned the era of America's revolutionary struggle with Great Britain, and her death in 1784 followed by one year Britain's recognition of America's independence. She wrote a poem lauding George Washington as well as one praising King George III, and she attracted the attention of revolutionary patriots such as Benjamin Franklin, Thomas Jefferson, Thomas Paine, John Hancock, and the American naval hero John Paul Jones. She was the first African American to publish a book of poetry and she gained international notice. Yet she was also a slave and composed most of her poetry while in that condition. Her color, enslavement, keen intelligence, and, quite likely, her gender all contributed to her fame. She was seen as unique because many people at that time did not think that Africans had intelligence or capability equal to that of Europeans. Many believed that Africans could not be educated, that they had no capacity for original or creative thought, and that they were best suited to servitude.

Phillis Wheatley began early on to disprove these notions. She was only seven or eight years old when she landed in Boston, but as John Wheatley, her purchaser, related, "Without any Assistance from School Education, and by only what she was taught in the Family, she, in sixteen Months Time from her Arrival, attained the English Language, to which she was an utter Stranger before, to such a Degree, as to read any, the most difficult Parts of the Sacred Writings, to the great Astonishment of all who heard her." Doubtless her owners quickly saw a chance to test the proposition that Africans were unable to learn and encouraged her to persist in educating herself. John Wheatley bought Phillis to aid his wife, Susannah, whom friends described as a woman of unusual refinement, sensitivity, and religiosity. She also had an interest in missionary activity, particularly among Africans and Native Americans. These characteristics help explain why Susannah encouraged Phillis to get an education. Besides studying Latin and English classics, she was tutored in astronomy, ancient and modern geography, and history. When one considers that she was a slave and also a woman in a period when most women and even more slaves received no such attention, her situation and accomplishments are remarkable. She was almost certainly one of the most highly educated young women in Boston at the time.

She was also well connected, for her mistress encouraged her religious interests and introduced her to leading advocates of the eighteenth-century evangelical Christian movement in America and Britain. Evangelical religion has been described as more a feeling and an attitude about religion than a strict religious system. Evangelicals refused to be bound by the rules of formal church organizations. They placed great emphasis on a personal knowledge of the Bible, a direct and emotional experience of God's grace, and the unity and equality of those saved by faith in the Holy Spirit. Consequently, they weakened existing distinctions between masters and slaves and undercut the traditional Christian toleration of slavery. Though not all evangelicals opposed slavery, the most radical among them did, particularly those of the Baptist and Methodist denominations that began a rapid expansion in England and America during Phillis's lifetime. They directed a particular appeal to the slaves.

The English noblewoman Salina Hastings, countess of Huntingdon, friend of Susannah Wheatley, and patron of Phillis, was a supporter of evangelical Methodism. Her personal chaplain, George Whitefield (whom Phillis celebrated in an elegy), was the leading figure in the Great Awakening religious revival movement (1739–45). It was characterized by highly emotional preaching, often delivered by itinerant ministers who sometimes preached in fields or tents as well as in churches. It united black and white people in religious community and inspired some to reflect upon the blacks' secular condition, including speculations concerning their mental capabilities.

Phillis's achievements, therefore, had more than personal significance. She was embraced by abolitionists, many of whom were evangelicals, and offered as evidence that black people had the same possibilities as white people and deserved the same opportunities. After her *Poems on Various Subjects, Religious and Moral* was published in London in 1773, the Philadelphia physician and abolitionist Benjamin Rush extravagantly praised her "singular genius and accomplishments."

Her book, dedicated to the countess of Huntingdon, was printed a year after the famous Somerset decision of 1772, a court case that placed severe limits on slavery in England and caused considerable unease for her young master, Mrs. Wheatley's son Nathaniel, when they traveled there together in the summer of 1773. At the center of the case was James Somerset, an American slave taken to London by his Boston master in 1769. In England, Somerset escaped, only to be recaptured and as punishment threatened with relocation to the more rigorous slave environment of Jamaica. His plight came to the attention of Granville Sharp, an abolitionist committed to ending slavery in Britain. Chief Justice Lord Mansfield, who heard the case, was reluctant to make the decision for liberty toward which he felt the law leaned, because he feared the reactions of colonial planters if all the servants they had brought to England were suddenly declared free. He also feared the social and economic consequences of freeing all the slaves. He therefore delayed and attempted to get the case dismissed. When this tactic failed, he ordered Somerset's master to release him from service and established the precedent that in Britain slaves could not be compelled to serve. Although this case did not actually end slavery in Great Britain, as historians so often maintain, it did make the atmosphere uncongenial for slaveholders. Moreover, it brought the issue of slavery before the public and excited much sympathy for the slaves. Phillis Wheatley, however, did not take advantage of the situation. Instead, she cut short her stay and returned to Boston when her mistress, then ailing, requested her presence.

Her popular success in Britain notwithstanding, not everyone was impressed by Phillis's accomplishments. Despite his stirring affirmation in the Declaration of Independence that all men were created equal, Thomas Jefferson had severe reservations about blacks' abilities. Moreover, he readily discounted whatever evidence he found that discredited his opinion. Consequently, he dismissed Phillis Wheatley as being incompetent as a poet. "The compositions published under her name," he said, "are below the dignity of criticism."

A Jamaica planter, Edward Long, was even more harsh. He intended to parody Wheatley's verse and the uses to which she had been put by abolitionists when he wrote:

> What woeful stuff this madrigal would be
> In some starv'd, hackney sonneteer, or me!
> But let a *Negroe* own the happy lines,
> How the wit brightens! How the Style refines!
> Before his sacred name flies ev'ry fault,
> And each exalted stanza teems with thought!

Long clearly intended to suggest that the merits of Wheatley's poetry derived solely from the fact that she was black. Yet he exhibited a certain illogic because, while she may not have been, in his estimation, a genius, the common assertion was that blacks had not even a minimal competence.

The New World in which these commentators lived seemed to support such doubts, because by the middle of the eighteenth century, Africans were enslaved throughout the Americas. Abolitionist sentiment began to develop and have its first effects in Britain's American colonies. There were several reasons for this: First, British victories against France in the Seven Years' War (1756–63) extended Britain's possessions in the Caribbean and allowed for an increase in the supply of sugar reaching the mother country, temporarily forcing down its price. But the decline was not permanent because the British returned captured French sugar islands after the war, and the commodity's price in the British market, protected by restrictive regulations, recovered. However, increasing absentee ownership, rising slave prices, soil exhaustion in older islands, natural disasters, and slave unrest caused a rise in production costs. The outbreak of the American Revolution in the 1770s, which cut off the major source of island supplies, aggravated the situation. Planters, however, did not curb but rather expanded production, spurred by an economic boom in the 1790s. Jamaican planters, particularly, extended cultivation. Nevertheless, the French island of Saint Domingue produced more sugar, more cheaply, and undercut the British sugar price in Europe. The British simply could not compete because of the high production costs associated with their sugar industry. Some people began to question the whole process of British sugar production, and the most glaringly expensive factor in this production was slavery.

But economic stress does not adequately explain the British anti-slavery movement. Indeed, the movement achieved its first successes during a period when the sugar industry had, however briefly, regained its profitability. Moreover, similar crises among the Spanish or Portuguese had not led to the same questioning of human bondage. One historian explains the distinctive British reaction as being the result of a different historical background than that of the Iberian nations. Spain and Portugal had experienced slavery continuously from the time of the Roman Empire, and Iberians transported the institution to their colonies overseas as an ancient practice.

But slavery had died or was dying in northwestern Europe, and Englishmen readopted it in the sixteenth century mainly as a way to secure profits in tropical climes. They did not, however, approve of it at home. Where Iberians saw a familiar pattern of relationships because of their long slave tradition, Britons saw something new and relatively strange. Slavery was an institution for the colonies but not for Britain or the British. This does not mean that there were no slaves in Britain, for an estimated fourteen thousand resided there in the eighteenth century. But slaveholding was increasingly seen as an immoral choice, not part of British tradition.

One of the social, intellectual, and religious currents that forced people within the British Empire to look more closely at bonded labor was evangelical Protestantism. Millennialism (taken from the biblical prophecy in Revelations of Christ's one-thousand-year reign on earth), which suggested the idea that man's sinful nature can be changed and that the world can be transformed into a heaven on earth, was an important feature of this outlook. It prompted much self-reflection. Millennialists equated slavery with sin and reform with virtue, and thus many of them became abolitionists. The ideas of the equality of all men before God and the necessity of free will for salvation were also sources of anti-slavery beliefs. Many Protestants considered free will to be essential to a conversion experience that emphasized personal commitment, and slavery permitted no free exercise of will.

Another intellectual concept that forced a reconsideration of slavery was the Enlightenment. Beginning in the late seventeenth century, this European philosophical movement developed around a number of concepts. The most important of these were a confidence in human reason as a guide to wisdom, a rejection of ignorance and superstition, a firm belief in the basic goodness of humankind, and a certainty that society, through reason, could be perfected. Eighteenth-century Enlightenment thought, particularly the idea of natural equality and the notion that society departed from that principle when it instituted slavery, supported abolition. These philosophical ideas intersected with religious ones: From both perspectives, slavery was seen as wrong and society could and ought to be reformed.

But it took economic change, which placed increasing emphasis on free labor and free trade, and a move away from the restrictive trading system derived from mercantilism, to make the arguments of abolitionists most effective. Mercantilism was an economic philosophy based on the concept that a nation's wealth depended on its supply of precious metals or other commodities, such as gold and silver (bullion) or jewels. These could be obtained through trade or conquest. A nation's colonies existed to aid the mother country in achieving wealth by supplying these commodities directly or by producing items that could be traded for them. Ideally, a colony that did not yield bullion directly produced raw materials that could be rendered into products that would bring in bullion. Slavery was not a necessary component of mercantilism except that it came to be considered the most effective and efficient means of raising the tropical products that created the wealth of eighteenth-century European empires.

The Scottish philosopher Adam Smith cast doubt on this relationship. In his *Theory of Moral Sentiments* (1759) and *The Wealth of Nations* (1775), he argued that slavery was inefficient as well as brutal and, in fact, not the most profitable system. "The experience of all ages and nations," Smith claimed, "demonstrates that the work done by slaves, though it appears to cost only their maintenance, is in the end the dearest of all." It encouraged idleness, Smith argued, and retarded progress. Neither enforced labor nor restricted trade brought the greatest material or social reward.

In North America, even before the revolutionary era, the beliefs of some Protestant sects led them to consider the injustice of slavery. As early as 1688 a Quaker group in Germantown, Pennsylvania, spoke out against the institution, and in 1693 Quakers published the first anti-slavery tract in America. Quakers were not only concerned about their personal salvation but had a commitment to social reform as well. Their anti-slavery sentiments increased in the eighteenth century as individual meetings, or congregations, took a stand against holding slaves. They were joined in their stance by members of other sects as a result of the Great Awakening.

Having ousted the French from the continent, the British government developed reorganization schemes designed to govern the empire more effectively and economically. These efforts ended a practice that had left colonials largely to their own affairs. In practical terms, the new policies brought much greater interference by the British Parliament in the colonists' daily lives—an intrusion the colonists resented. Most disturbing was Parliament's claim of the power to tax, formerly assumed by provincial legislatures. Americans viewed these innovations as disruptive of harmony, running counter to an ancient and valuable relationship, and corrosive of traditional liberties. What began as a struggle for traditional English rights (such as the principle that they could not be taxed without their consent), however, was extended under the influence of Enlightenment philosophy into a struggle for liberty as a natural (rather than an English) right. This struggle forced white Americans to consider the plight of blacks.

The Massachusetts patriot James Otis made this connection most clearly in 1764 when, in response to the Sugar Act, he declared that "the Colonists are by the law of nature free born, as indeed all men are, white or black." Skin color, hair texture, or other physical characteristics were not a logical basis on which to base enslavement. Or, as another revolutionary put it, "That all black persons should be slaves is as ridiculous as that law of a certain country that all red-haired persons should be hanged." He referred to *The Spirit of Laws* (1748), a book by the French Enlightenment philosopher Baron de Montesquieu that made fun of prejudice by describing a country where that was the custom.

But blacks were not satisfied to let others make their case for them. They, too, were affected by revolutionary ideology and were quite prepared to use it to argue for their own freedom. This was particularly the case for New England blacks, who, of all slaves, had the greatest opportunity to attain literacy. Thus in April 1773 four Massachusetts slaves addressed a letter to the Colonial House of Representatives stating that "the efforts made by the legislature of the province in their last sessions to free themselves from slavery, gave us, who are in that deplorable state, a high degree of satisfaction." They went on to suggest that they, too, desired freedom.

They adopted a peculiar strategy in pressing their case: "We are very sensible that it would be highly detrimental to our present masters, if we were allowed to demand all that of *right* belongs to us." But, they continued, "Even the *Spaniards*, who have not those sublime ideas of freedom that Englishmen have, are conscious that they have no right to all the services of . . . the *Africans*, who they have purchased." So they simply asked to be allowed one day a week to work for themselves to accumulate the money to buy their freedom. The House tabled the petition. When the blacks appealed to Governor Thomas Hutchinson, he said that he could do nothing for them.

After the Declaration of Independence was signed, petitions to the Massachusetts legislature from blacks became a little more aggressive. In New Hampshire blacks argued that "the God of nature gave them life and freedom, upon the terms of the most perfect equality with other men" and that "private and public tyranny and slavery are alike detestable to minds conscious of the equal dignity of human nature."

At the same time, free blacks moved against other aspects of discrimination. Although they were subject to taxation, free blacks in Massachusetts and elsewhere could not vote or hold office. Consequently, in February 1780 a group of blacks, under the leadership of a prominent local businessman, Paul Cuffe, and his brother John, took further advantage of revolutionary philosophy. They suggested to the legislature that "while we are not allowed the privilege of freemen of the state, having no vote or influence in the election with those that tax us, yet many of our own color, as is well known, have cheerfully entered the field of battle in defence of the common cause, and that as we conceive against a similar exertion of power in regard to taxation." In other words, they desired to extend to themselves the principle of no taxation without representation. Indeed, as part of the struggle, the Cuffes refused to pay taxes in 1778, 1779, and 1780. As a result, in December 1780 they were jailed. Three months later they admitted defeat and paid their back taxes, but they renewed their complaint.

Because blacks refused to let the argument die, it was difficult for New Englanders and other colonials to escape the logic of the revolution. Moreover, as the Cuffes noted, blacks were among the first to shed their blood in the common cause. Phillis Wheatley had a good chance to view the Boston Massacre on March 5, 1770—in which Crispus Attucks became celebrated as the first to die for colonial liberty—for it took place just down the street from the Wheatley mansion at King Street and Mackerel Lane, where she still lived.

Other blacks fought more personal battles. In April 1781, twenty-eight-year-old

The 29th Regiment have already left us, and the 14th Regiment are following them, ſo that we expect the Town will ſoon be clear of all the Troops. The Wiſdom and true Policy of his Majeſty's Council and Col. Dalrymple theCommander appear in this Meaſure. Two Regiments in the midſt of this populous City; and the Inhabitants juſtly incenſed: Thoſe of the neighbouring Towns actually under Arms upon the firſtReport of the Maſſacre, and the Signal only wanting to bring in a few Hours to the Gates of this City manyThouſands of our brave Brethren in the Country, deeply affected with our Diſtreſſes, and to whom we are greatly obliged on this Occaſion—No one knows where this would have ended, and what important Conſequences even to the whole Britiſh Empire might have followed, which our Moderation & Loyalty upon ſo trying anOccaſion, and ourFaith in the Commander'sAſſurances have happily prevented.

Laſt Thurſday, agreeable to a general Requeſt of the Inhabitants, and by the Conſent of Parents and Friends, were carried to their *Grave* in Succeſſion, the Bodies of *Samuel Gray*, *Samuel Maverick*, *James Caldwell*, and *Criſpus Attucks*, the unhappy Victims who fell in the bloody Maſſacre of theMonday Evening preceeding!

On this Occaſion moſt of the Shops in Town were ſhut, all the Bells were ordered to toll a ſolemn Peal, as were alſo thoſe in the neighboring Towns of Charleſtown Roxbury, &c. The Proceſſion began to move between the Hours of 4 and 5 in the Afternoon; two of the unfortunate Sufferers, viz. Meſſ. *JamesCaldwell* and *Criſpus Attucks*, who were Strangers, borne from Faneuil-Hall, attended by a numerous Train of Perſons of all Ranks; and the other two, viz. Mr. *Samuel Gray*, from the Houſe of Mr. Benjamin Gray, (his Brother) on the North-ſide the Exchange, and Mr. *Maverick*, from the Houſe of his diſtreſſed Mother Mrs. *Mary Maverick*, in Union-Street, each followed by their reſpective Relations and Friends: The ſeveral Hearſes forming a Junction in King-Street, the Theatre of that inhuman Tragedy! proceeded from thence thro' the Main-Street, lengthened by an immenſe Concourſe of People, ſo numerous as to be obliged to follow in Ranks of ſix, and brought up by a long Train of Carriages belonging to the principal Gentry of theTown. The Bodies were depoſited in one Vault in the middle Burying-ground: The aggravated Circumſtances of their Death, the Diſtreſs and Sorrow viſible in every Countenance, together with the peculiar Solemnity with which the whole Funeral was conducted.

This account of the burial of the victims of the Boston Massacre appeared in the *Boston Gazette and Country Journal.* The coffin on the far right bears the initials of Crispus Attucks, the former slave who became a hero of the revolutionary era for his role in the incident.

Quok Walker left his master's service. He did so without permission and was sheltered by a neighbor, who employed him. His master discovered Walker, assaulted him with a whip handle, and charged the neighbor with enticing away his property. For his part, Walker brought suit against his master for assault and battery. The case came down to the issue of whether slavery was legally defensible, justifying the use of force. The master's lawyer argued that custom and usage of the country made slavery legal. Walker's lawyer argued, however, that custom and usage were unsustainable when they went against reason. The case eventually went to the Massachusetts Supreme Court. In coming to its decision in 1783, the court declared that since the state constitution of 1780 declared in its preamble that all men were born free and equal, slavery in the state was illegal. At the same time, it gave blacks who were taxed the right to vote. New Hampshire followed Massachusetts's lead when it decided that its Bill of Rights of 1783 forbade slavery, at least for those born after its adoption. Vermont was more forthright and prohibited slavery in its constitution of 1777.

While the judicial process worked its way in Massachusetts, Pennsylvania faced the problem head-on and became the first state to adopt a manumission, or freedom, law. As the home of Quakers, anti-slavery sentiment there was strong; many German immigrants, such as the Amish and Mennonites, also opposed the institution.

Perhaps no single person was more important in this process than Anthony Benezet. Born in France but forced to

Quaker leader Anthony Benezet actively supported the anti-slavery cause and sought to educate blacks in Philadelphia. He established integrated schools and published pamphlets attacking slavery and the slave trade.

flee because of religious persecution, he and his family eventually settled in Pennsylvania. Converting to the Quaker faith, he early became active in the anti-slavery cause. He published a number of pamphlets attacking slavery and the slave trade, dramatizing the evils of the trade and removing all doubts that it had any humanitarian features. Moreover, he studied the history of Africa to prove that Africans had cultures and civilizations comparable to those of other people in the world, and he argued that the chains of bondage alone were responsible for any failings they showed in America. He undertook to educate Philadelphia blacks, establishing integrated schools for that purpose. His writings had influence far beyond his locality. Thomas Clarkson, a leader in the British anti-slavery campaign, took his stance after reading Benezet's *A Short Account of that Part of Africa, Inhabited by the Negroes* (1762). John Wesley, founder of the Methodists, used Benezet's *Some Historical Account of Guinea* (1771) as the basis of sermons he preached in Britain against the slave trade. When Pennsylvania's manumission bill reached the Assembly, Benezet worked with the legislators to ensure passage.

As the first abolition law passed in America, Pennsylvania's 1780 statute was viewed as the perfect expression of American revolutionary philosophy. It provided for a gradual freeing of slaves over a period of years, yet it was not the most liberal such law to be passed. It merely came in advance of the rest, and along with Massachusetts and Vermont, Pennsylvania was one of the few states to end slavery before Britain's formal recognition of American independence.

But while blacks made use of revolutionary rhetoric to advance their freedom, and gave their blood in the colonial cause, they could not help but be reminded, even as they fought, that they were different. Thus, when blacks joined a crowd of Boston whites in an attack upon British soldiers in 1769, a Boston newspaper commented, "To behold Britons scourged by Negro drummers was a new and very disagreeable spectacle."

This consciousness of difference caused a group of slaves in the town of Thompson, Massachusetts, to end their request for freedom in 1773 with the statement: "We are willing to submit to such regulations and laws, as may be made relative to us, until we leave the province, which we determine to do as soon as we can, from our joynt labours procure money to transport ourselves to some part of the Coast of *Africa,* where we propose a settlement." Even before the end of the eighteenth century, then, there was the feeling among some blacks that a return to Africa was desirable. These emigrationists felt that because racial oppression in America was so great, black people could develop only if they returned to the land of their forefathers. They also thought that a return to Africa would help them to free their enslaved brethren in the New World by illustrating the competitiveness of tropical products grown with free labor. Finally, they believed that they could take with them to Africa the gifts of Christianity and civilization and serve as the means to uplift what common prejudice held to be a backward continent.

These ideas found resonance among the Christian evangelists of Phillis Wheatley's acquaintance. In 1773, one conceived a plan for educating two New England blacks, a free man named John Quamino and a slave, Bristol Yamma, and sending them to Africa as missionaries. The outbreak of the Revolutionary War doomed the project, yet not before Wheatley was asked to join the venture. She responded to the request with a statement that expressed the opinion of most American blacks, who, born and bred in the country, felt they had a right to consider it their own:

> Why do you hon'd Sir, wish those poor men so much trouble as to carry me [on] so long a voyage? Upon my arrival, how like a Barbarian shou'd I look to the Natives; I can promise that my tongue shall be quiet for a strong reason indeed, being an utter stranger to the Language.... Now to be Serious, This undertaking appears too hazardous and [I am] not sufficiently Eligible to go—And leave my British & American friends.

Wheatley's British and American friends would soon be at war, but the warfare provided other opportunities for blacks to achieve their freedom.

Battle Cry of Freedom

Eight months before the American Declaration of Independence was proclaimed in Philadelphia on July 4, 1776, a man named Lymus declared his own independence. He told his master in Charleston, South Carolina, as his master reported in the *South Carolina Gazette,* that he would "be free, that he w[ould] serve no Man, and that he w[ould] be conquered or governed by no Man."

In the year following the Declaration, two black men in Massachusetts advanced a different claim to liberty. They "ship'd on board the Armed Brigantine *Freedom,*" as their friends related the story, "to fight ag[ains]t the Enemies of America." They thereby justified a claim to *personal* freedom. As their white compatriots announced, they "were volentieers [*sic*] in the business & ought to be considered in the same light as any other Sailors & by no means liable to be sold meerly because they are black." Somewhat earlier, a group of slaves in Boston devised still a different course. They petitioned the governor to propose, so Abigail Adams informed her husband John, that "they would fight for him provided he would arm them, and engage to liberate them if he conquered." The governor was General Thomas Gage, British commander in chief in America, and these slaves were clearly willing to fight on the British side if that would guarantee their emancipation. These people exemplify the claim of one noted African-American historian that black people in the revolution were more concerned about a principle than any one place or people—that principle being the natural right of human beings to their own person.

African Americans were motivated by the same desire for "life, liberty, and the pursuit of happiness" that animated other Americans. They were equally conscious of the natural rights philosophy of the Enlightenment and of the meaning of the phrases that Thomas Jefferson addressed to King George III. Thus black New Hampshire petitioners proclaimed: "Freedom is an inherent right of the human Species, not to be surrendered, but by Consent, for the sake of social Life." Abigail Adams expressed the same sentiments somewhat differently to her husband, John. "I wish most sincerely," she wrote, "there was not a slave in the province; it always appeared a most iniquitous scheme to me to fight ourselves for what we are daily robbing and plundering from those who have as good a right to freedom as we have."

When the fighting broke out, therefore, African Americans were among the first to rally to patriot banners. As they fought to free their country, they also fought to free themselves. Thus the slave of New Hampshire General John Sullivan, told by his master that they were going to join the patriot army to fight for liberty, responded "that it would be a great satisfaction to know that he was indeed going to fight for *his* liberty." Sullivan, impressed by the justice of his cause, freed him on the spot. Peter Salem, of Framingham, Massachusetts, was freed by his owners so that he could enlist. He fought in the battles of Lexington and Concord in April 1775 and helped to fire the "shot heard round the world" that heralded the beginning of America's military struggle. In June he fought at the Battle of Bunker Hill, where the colonials were forced to retreat after inflicting heavy losses on the British. Salem is credited with killing a British officer who led the final assault, and his musket is preserved at the Bunker Hill Monument.

Salem Poor, a free black, also fought at Bunker Hill. He came to the attention of fourteen officers who petitioned Congress to reward him for his bravery: "We declare that A Negro Man Called Salem Poor . . . behaved like an Experienced officer, as well as an Excellent Soldier." Although there is no record that Congress ever acknowledged him, he remained with the Continental army.

New England blacks were well situated to offer their services, for, despite laws prohibiting the practice, they had a history of duty in local militias. There simply were not enough white men willing or able to fill the ranks. African Americans served in twenty-five percent of Connecticut's militia companies and in noticeable numbers in other New England colonies. In spite of its relatively small black population, therefore, New England contributed more blacks to the Continental army than any other region. Rhode Island offered an all-black regiment, reported to be one of the few American regiments that enlisted for the entire war. Patriot General Philip Schuyler, on a military campaign in upstate New York, however, expressed a general objection to the presence of blacks. "Is it consistent with the Sons of Liberty," he asked, "to trust their all to be defended by slaves?"

Indeed, that was a question the colonials had to face as soon as the contending parties came to blows. In a country where slavery remained an important economic and social institution, few whites wanted the army to become a haven for runaway slaves. After the Continental army was formed in June 1775, commanding general Horatio Gates ordered that recruiters should not enlist "any stroller, negro, or vagabond," nor any deserter from the British army. He did not distinguish between slaves and free blacks. In September, the Continental Congress rejected a proposal of Edward Rutledge of South Carolina that blacks be totally excluded, but a council of generals in Cambridge, Massachusetts, adopted just such a policy the following month.

They took this position apparently in deference to George Washington, newly arrived commander in chief of the Continental army. Having scarcely ever been outside the confines of slaveholding Virginia and Maryland, he was appalled to find large numbers of blacks among the troops besieging the British in Boston in 1775. New England generals insisted that they made good soldiers, but Washington persuaded them that the use of African-American troops would hinder cooperation with southern colonies. Washington, however, did not have the same emotional dislike of blacks that affected Thomas Jefferson. Both from inclination and

VIRGINIA, *Dec.* 14, 1775.

By the **REPRESENTATIVES** *of the* **PEOPLE** *of the Colony and Dominion of* **VIRGINIA,** *aſſembled in* **GENERAL CONVENTION.**

A DECLARATION.

WHEREAS lord Dunmore, by his proclamation, dated on board the ſhip William, off Norfolk, the 7th day of November 1775, hath offered freedom to ſuch able-bodied ſlaves as are willing to join him, and take up arms, againſt the good people of this colony, giving thereby encouragement to a general inſurrection, which may induce a neceſſity of inflicting the ſevereſt puniſhments upon thoſe unhappy people, already deluded by his baſe and inſidious arts; and whereas, by an act of the General Aſſembly now in force in this colony, it is enacted, that all negro or other ſlaves, conſpiring to rebel or make inſurrection, ſhall ſuffer death, and be excluded all benefit of clergy: We think it proper to declare, that all ſlaves who have been, or ſhall be ſeduced, by his lordſhip's proclamation, or other arts, to deſert their maſters' ſervice, and take up arms againſt the inhabitants of this colony, ſhall be liable to ſuch puniſhment as ſhall hereafter be directed by the General Convention. And to the end that all ſuch, who have taken this unlawful and wicked ſtep, may return in ſafety to their duty, and eſcape the puniſhment due to their crimes, we hereby promiſe pardon to them, they ſurrendering themſelves to col. William Woodford, or any other commander of our troops, and not appearing in arms after the publication hereof. And we do farther earneſtly recommend it to all humane and benevolent perſons in this colony to explain and make known this our offer of mercy to thoſe unfortunate people.

EDMUND PENDLETON, preſident.

In response to Lord Dunmore's proclamation, Virginia's General Convention issued this statement threatening death to any slave caught trying to join the British side, while offering pardons to any slave who surrendered to the Continental army.

considerations of policy, Washington was convinced to listen when free blacks expressed their dissatisfaction at exclusion. He authorized their reenlistment and put the matter before Congress. Congress backed the decision but forbade any new black enlistments. That policy, however, was to change.

Among the considerations influencing Washington was the proclamation of the royal governor of Virginia, Lord Dunmore, offering freedom to slaves and indentured servants who joined the British troops. Although it applied only to the slaves of rebellious subjects and only to those able to join and fight, it nevertheless offered a clear choice that many accepted.

But neither Lord Dunmore's proclamation nor the Declaration of Independence caused any immediate change in the colonials' determination to keep slaves out of the war. States from New England to Georgia forbade blacks to enlist. Manpower shortages alone caused these prohibitions to be overlooked. Free blacks often took the place of whites when states drafted soldiers, and recruiting officers, sometimes paid by the head, were not particular about the inductees' color. When, beginning in 1777, Congress ordered the states to meet quotas to fill patriot ranks, the process of black recruitment picked up speed. African Americans were commonly enlisted in New England after 1777, and Rhode Island became the first state to authorize slave enlistment in 1778. Maryland took the same step in 1780, and New York in 1781. Virginia refused to follow Maryland's lead in enlisting slaves but did permit the service of free blacks. Nevertheless, some Virginia masters sent slaves to serve in their stead, promising freedom but frequently not making good on those promises after the war. In 1783, when it became aware of the situation, the state government freed those people.

Only the Lower South resisted the trend to enlist black soldiers. Greatly outnumbered by their slaves, planters who inhabited the coastal lowland regions of South Carolina and Georgia (often simply referred to as the low country) feared the consequences of permitting slaves to bear arms. They were more dependent than their neighbors on black labor and proved correspondingly less receptive to the logic of revolutionary reasoning. Yet even there it had effects.

No one better exemplified this fact than John Laurens, an aide to George Washington and son of South Carolina planter Henry Laurens, a former slave trader and president of the Continental Congress. Educated in Geneva, Switzerland, John had become influenced by anti-slavery sentiments. Early in the revolution he proposed recruiting slave soldiers in exchange for their freedom. He wrote his father in January 1778 asking that he be given his inheritance in able-bodied slaves, whom he would form into a battalion to be freed at the war's close. Henry asked Washington's opinion. John replied: "He is convinced that the numerous tribes of blacks in the southern part of the continent offer a resource to us which should not be neglected." The following year the Continental Congress gave its assent to the project and recommended the course to South Carolina and Georgia. But the Lower South would not be moved.

The issue of slave soldiers was controversial because it offered a threat to slavery itself. And the threat to slavery was important because it involved rights of property. The right to be secure in possession of their property was one of the things the colonists accused the British king of taking away from them when he taxed them without their consent. Thus when the Virginia legislature formally rejected the use of slaves as soldiers it was because, as one man reported, it was "considered unjust, sacrificing the property of a part of the community to the exoneration of the rest." Or, to put it another way, it was not fair to ask some people to give up their property in order to save the property of others.

The outbreak of fighting provided blacks some say in the matter. They had a choice of sides, and an estimated five thousand ultimately stood in Continental ranks. But the conflicted nature of their response was illustrated at the Battle of Great Bridge, fought on December 9, 1775, and described as the "Lexington of the South." This battle compelled Lord Dunmore to leave the soil of Virginia and operate thereafter offshore from naval vessels. Almost half of the British force of six hundred consisted of African Americans of Dunmore's "Ethiopian Regiment," who went into battle wearing sashes emblazoned with the words "Liberty to Slaves."

On the other side, a black spy for the Virginians tricked Dunmore into attack, and a free black from Portsmouth, William Flora, distinguished himself in the engagement against the British. Flora was "the last sentinel that came into the breast work," an officer remembered, and "he did not leave his post until he had fired several times. Billy had to cross a plank to get to the breast work, and had fairly passed over it when he was seen to turn back, and deliberately take up the plank after him, amidst a shower of musket balls." At least thirty of the blacks on the British side were captured.

Although Dunmore was forced away, the specter of his proclamation hung over the region, and periodic raids conducted by the British produced numerous slave defections. Thomas Jefferson had a reputation as a kind master, but when redcoats visited his estate in 1781, thirty of his slaves left with them. Robert "Councillor" Carter (so called because of his position on the governor's council from 1758 to 1772, where he had advisory and legislative functions), another kindly patriarch, was unusual in that he had accepted the Baptist faith and was united with his servants in a religious community. He made a special plea to his slaves to stay. But when royal troops arrived at one of his outlying farms, the lure of personal freedom proved too great. Jefferson estimated that about twenty-five thousand Virginia slaves left their owners during the war, and many had to endure considerable danger and hardship to do so. Yet they were willing to pay the cost. As a correspondent to a Pennsylvania newspaper suggested, "the defection of the Negroes, [even] of the most indulgent masters . . . shewed what little dependence ought to be placed on persons deprived of their natural liberty."

Conflict between families and neighbors was more frequent in the Lower South than in the Chesapeake, and it created a violent atmosphere in which slaves had to tread lightly. British invasion provoked a bitter struggle between supporters and opponents of the crown. Indeed, several Georgia and South Carolina planters moved their families and slaves to more peaceful Virginia after the redcoats came at the end of the 1770s. As in Virginia, blacks were cautiously welcoming. A slave guide helped British forces in Georgia to outflank and defeat patriot forces in 1779, and when royal troops landed along the Carolina coast in 1780 they likewise had to depend on slave knowledge of the terrain. Many landowners abandoned their farms and plantations, leaving servants and white women and children to fend for themselves.

The British recruited blacks as guides or spies, as laborers to perform the heavy and exhausting work of building roads and fortifications, and some to serve as soldiers. Perhaps as many as twenty thousand African Americans served with the British in one capacity or another, and five thousand to six thousand left with them when they evacuated Charleston in 1782. A large number of slaves—maybe most (like many whites)—took no side but pursued their well-being as best they could in a situation of military uncertainty and social upheaval. Some fled to Charleston or Savannah and tried to pass as free people. Some continued to run plantations, with or without a white man's presence, assuming greater independence in the process. These were, after all, their homes, and the only places—outside of one of the contending armies—where they had any chance to secure a livelihood. In a period of chronic shortages of food, clothing, and other supplies, their old homesteads were sometimes the safest place to be. Of course, no guarantee existed even there, for marauding forces of one side or the other regularly confiscated whatever they needed and frequently destroyed the rest.

The remaining alternative for blacks (as for whites) was to migrate to some region away from the fighting. Some did so, retreating into the wilderness to form independent communities of their own. Some formed or became members of roving bands, occasionally interracial, that added to the disorder. They roamed the countryside, taking what they could for their own benefit. Some joined patriot fighting units such as that of South Carolina's "Swamp Fox" Francis Marion, who bedeviled the British with lightning raids and then melted away into Carolina's forests, marshes, or swamps. No slave was safe roaming about, however; capture could mean being sold, punished, or executed. It took considerable courage, therefore, even to run to the invader. In view of all the upheaval, some blacks welcomed the return of landowners and peace.

But warfare weakened slavery and provided bondsmen with at least a few options. They were limited because neither Britons nor white Americans were prepared to allow open black rebellion. Neither Britons nor white Americans could envision or accept a black republic. The only practical choices were to seek as much freedom as possible within the framework of revolutionary ideology in America or to trust the word of the British when they promised an eventual emancipation, there or elsewhere. Those who stayed on plantations accepted the realities of their condition but extended the boundaries of their servitude considerably, often acting virtually as free men.

Despite the planters' nightmares, war and revolution provoked no formal slave insurrection. About one-quarter of South Carolina slaves fled, however, and there was even more movement in Georgia. There, in response to British invasion, more than a third of the slave population walked away. No previous event in North American slavery equaled the slave exodus from Georgia, either in its size or consequences for undermining the institution. In the South as a whole, slave flight during the Revolution was of such an extent and character that it can almost be viewed as a kind of slave revolt.

While slaveholding colonials were zealous about guarding their claims to bondsmen they already possessed, they were less secure about arguing for the right to buy and sell them. They were particularly squeamish about the purchase of those newly brought from Africa. If the works of Anthony Benezet did anything, they dramatized the horrifying conditions under which the overseas slave trade was conducted. In those circumstances, the human rights of the captive were magnified and the property rights of the slave catcher or of the prospective buyer were greatly diminished.

Virginians had no difficulty, therefore, in attacking the slave trade. The Virginia constitution of 1776 accused the British king of an "inhuman use of his negative" in preventing the colony from excluding slaves, and Thomas Jefferson made the same charge in the Declaration of Independence. King George, Jefferson wrote, had "waged cruel war against human nature itself, violating its most sacred rights of life and liberty in the person of a distant people who never offended him, captivating and carrying them into slavery in another hemisphere, or to incur miserable death in their transportation thither." Never mind that the king had never forced any Virginian to buy slaves, nor that the prohibitive duties or taxes that Virginians and other colonists had placed on slaves before the Revolution (which is what Jefferson referred to) had been assessed for economic and social rather than humanitarian reasons. The fact is that the Atlantic slave trade was a horror difficult to ignore in a period of heightened humanitarian sensitivity.

For a combination of reasons, then, Americans moved against the slave trade. In New England, where slavery was relatively less important, legislatures began to terminate the trade with the first stirrings of revolutionary ardor. Rhode Island made the connection plain with a comment in its abolition law that "those who are desirous of enjoying all the advantages of liberty themselves, should be willing to extend personal liberty to others." When the Continental Congress decided in October 1774 to prohibit the import of slaves, however, it did so as part of a nonimportation agreement designed to bring economic pressure against British merchants rather than because the trade was morally objectionable. Colonials intended these merchants to put pressure on Parliament to change its policies. When Virginia, North Carolina, and Georgia prohibited the trade, it had more to do with economic considerations and political pressure against the British government than with humanity. Nevertheless, the Congress reaffirmed its prohibition in 1776 and no state reopened the trade thereafter, except those in the Lower South. By their activities, therefore, blacks forced their masters to see some of the contradictions in their fight against England and laid the groundwork for a new birth of freedom.

Blacks and the British

As Americans wrestled with the question of what to do about the slaves, the British, unhampered by any inconvenient declaration of human equality, did likewise. Their West Indian empire as well as the southern portion of the North American colonies, which they still claimed, were based on slave labor. They had little interest in encouraging a social revolution that, if successful on the continent, might affect their holdings in the Caribbean. Moreover, they shrank from the prospect of being part of a bloody slave insurrection. Finally, they, too, generally accepted principles of white superiority that prevented them from considering a workable alliance with African Americans on terms approaching equality. It was clear, however, that blacks would have to be taken into account in a conflict in which they were an inevitable part.

An initial strategy was to use the black presence as a threat against the colonials. Thus General Gage warned South Carolinians that if they continued their opposition to Great Britain "it may happen that your Rice and Indigo will be brought to market by negroes instead of white people." This was not a pleasing prospect for either Britons or Americans, and proposals for emancipating southern slaves were not favorably received in Parliament. Lord Dunmore's proclamation and various other proposals to arm and free slaves caused public debate in England, for they were viewed as a shameful departure from a tradition opposed to using slaves against free people. Edmund Burke, a member of Parliament who supported the Americans, even considered such a policy hypocritical. Why, he wondered, should blacks accept "an offer of freedom from that very nation which has sold them to their present masters?" Doubts about the slaves' level of "civilization," an unwillingness to take the slaves of loyalists, and a fear of driving Americans to extremes beyond hope of reconciliation, all argued against a slave alliance. In both Virginia and North Carolina, royal governors who sought to use slaves spurred colonials to rage and brought royal forces to defeat.

Unfortunately for the British and their American opponents, African Americans were not prepared to stand idly by while others decided their fate. If they were to be pawns in a game of chicken or chess, they would not be passive ones. They forced the hands of both Lord Dunmore and George Washington, and the use of blacks by one side reinforced the use of blacks by the other. But it was the shift of warfare to the South, particularly the Lower South, where blacks frequently outnumbered whites in the general population, that sealed the British decision to utilize blacks, and changed their outlook toward the employment of black troops in other regions.

When Sir Henry Clinton, who replaced Gage as commander in chief of British forces in America, prepared to invade South Carolina in 1779, he began with the Philipsburg Proclamation. It was issued from his headquarters, Philipsburg Manor on the Hudson River in New York, on June 30. He declared that blacks taken in service with the patriots would be sold for the benefit of the crown, but that those who ran away to the British would be protected.

A policy provoked by military considerations rather than by humanitarian motives, it nevertheless chipped away at the foundations of slavery. It challenged blacks to take the British side. It did not formally offer them freedom but promised self-determination that was little short of it. Moreover, those who signed on as "pioneers," or laborers, to perform the drudgery of cleaning camp, building or repairing roads or bridges, constructing fortifications, or simply being on hand to take care of whatever undesirable tasks came up, were promised manumission in return for their devotion to duty. The same gift was held out to those who worked under British direction on agricultural estates or public works, or to the few enrolled as soldiers. African Americans took the bait in significant numbers.

Service with the British was not always to their liking, however. A policy prompted by military necessity was guided by military reasoning, and neither humanity nor fair play stood in the way of decisions that treated blacks harshly. They received fewer and inferior rations than white soldiers. They were not as well clothed. Their housing was inadequate and overcrowded. They were often overworked. They were consequently highly susceptible to disease, particularly various smallpox epidemics that afflicted the low country. Large numbers of them died. Nor were they exempt from sale for the use of the army when circumstances suggested that course.

Since the British army sought to maintain social order in regions it conquered, it had no philosophical objection to suppressing slave rebellions, particularly those directed against loyal subjects. It pledged to return the slaves of those whites who had remained loyal to the crown or to replace them with those of patriots. The degree to which slaves could view the British army as an army of liberation, therefore, was very limited indeed. No wonder it did not evoke wholesale desertions from the colonials.

Nonetheless the pull of freedom was great and the chance of leaving bondage improved as the British moved toward defeat. Manpower shortages and a demonstrated black resistance to tropical diseases prompted General Alexander Leslie to recruit black troops seriously beginning in 1779. The successful use of blacks in South Carolina caught the attention of other British officers and served as the precedent for the use of black soldiers in the West Indies. Shortly before the British left the Carolina coast, Jamaica's governor enrolled a battalion of troops from among the free black and colored, or mixed race, people of Charleston. They formed the Black Carolina Corps, which served in Jamaica and elsewhere, and they took with them American ideas about the rights of man. By the 1790s, Britain utilized black troops extensively to support its Caribbean empire.

When the British left the United States at the end of the war, the question of what to do about blacks who had sought their protection proved a source of controversy. Planters wanted their human property returned, but the new British commander in chief, Sir Guy Carleton, felt that the commitments made in previous proclamations of freedom to slaves who joined them ought to be honored.

The old slave dealer Henry Laurens, despite periodic expressions of sympathy for the Africans—and notwithstanding his son's championship of slave battalions—remained keenly aware of the property interests involved. He inserted a provision in the treaty ending the war, the Treaty of Paris of 1783, that obliged the British to return fugitive slaves. Sir Guy thought that would be dishonorable. He interpreted the clause to mean that he should shelter no more fugitives and gave orders to turn back any who had newly come in. Only those who had been with the army for a year or more would receive his protection. But those already with the army were, in his opinion, already free and no longer to be considered property. Or if they were, that issue would have to be solved by some kind of money transaction, for he was not prepared to violate the word of British officers by returning them. Nor could he believe that had been the intention of the government. British ministers, he said, could not possibly have agreed to such a "notorious breach of the public faith towards people of any complection." If the royal army's relationship with blacks had not always been the most admirable, at least at the end one general took the high ground and saved many blacks from a return to servitude.

George Washington stuck with the American position that the British ought to return fugitive slaves to their former owners. Yet compared to others who insisted firmly on the return of all slaves, Washington was unusually sensitive in this regard. He seemed resigned to the inevitable. "[S]everal of my own are with the Enemy," he reflected, "but I scarce ever bestowed a thought on them; they have so many doors through which they can escape from New York, that scarce any thing but an inclination to return . . . will restore many." He thereby indicated a property awareness strongly modified by a revolutionary spirit that was rapidly diminishing in the wake of American victory. If Thomas Jefferson most clearly expressed the ideals of the revolution, Washington, of all the slaveholding leaders of the revolution, came closest to practicing these ideals insofar as blacks are concerned. He certainly desired the return of property, but he was prepared to accept a black man's rejection of that status. In contrast to Jefferson, he provided in his will for the freeing of many of his slaves.

Boston King exemplifies the reasons many slaves left for the British side and also why many others did not. He was born in South Carolina, and as a child he performed many of the ordinary tasks common to plantation life, such as running errands and minding cattle. After an apprenticeship to a carpenter, he became a skilled laborer. He also had an uncommon experience. At one point he worked around racehorses, which permitted him a degree of travel. The job occasioned some hardship because the head groom was unkind and once made him go without shoes through the winter because he happened to lose a boot. His mentor in carpentry was also mean and mistreated him until his owner, Richard Waring, threatened to withdraw him from service.

Although King had an easygoing master, his experiences with other white folk made him wary of slaveholders' kindness and conditioned him to be receptive to British offers of freedom. He accompanied his master outside of Charleston—or Charles Town as it was then known—during the redcoats' occupation. But, he wrote in his memoirs, "having obtained leave one day to see my parents, who lived about twelve miles off, and it being late before I could go, I was obliged to borrow [a horse]; but a servant of my master's took the horse to go a little journey, and stayed two or three days longer than he ought. This involved me in the greatest perplexity, and I expected the severest punishment, because the gentleman to whom the horse belonged was a very bad man, and knew not how to show mercy. To escape his cruelty I determined to go to Charles-Town, and throw myself into the hand of the English . . . altho' I was most grieved at first, to be obliged to leave my friends, and remain among strangers."

Boston King eventually followed the British to New York City and there married Violet, a fugitive from North Carolina. Recaptured by the Americans, he was treated well but "sorely distressed at the thought of being again reduced to slavery, and separated from my wife and family." He managed to escape and return to his English protectors. Unlike white Americans, Boston King was not filled with joy at the end of the war, "for a report prevailed at New-York that all the slaves, in number two thousand, were to be delivered up to their masters, altho some of them had been three or four years among the English. This dreadful rumour filled us with inexpressible anguish and terror, especially when we saw our old masters coming from Virginia, North-Carolina, and other parts, and seizing upon their slaves in the streets of New-York, or even dragging them out of their beds. Many of the slaves had very cruel masters, so that the thoughts of returning home with them embittered life to us." King and other slaves were therefore highly appreciative of the position taken by British General Sir Guy Carleton. King and his wife received certificates of freedom and left with other loyalists for Nova Scotia.

Large numbers of blacks accompanied British forces when they departed the coastal cities of Savannah, Charleston, Philadelphia, Boston, and New York at various times during the war and especially during the final evacuations. Besides Nova Scotia and the West Indies, London was also a destination for several hundred North American blacks. In London, which had a significant black population in the eighteenth century, these new arrivals attracted the attention of anti-slavery activists and fueled a concern about the treatment of blacks in England and the British Empire. The Somerset case of 1772 had established that English law did not recognize slavery in the kingdom itself, but it had not applied to the colonies.

Blacks on the streets of London, however, could not be ignored, particularly since so many were destitute and reduced to begging. For unlike white loyalists, who were frequently compensated for their losses and supported until they were reestablished in Britain and elsewhere, African Americans were given little assistance. The British government assumed that since they had nothing to begin with, former slaves should be thankful merely for their freedom.

In the absence of governmental concern, a group of humanitarian businessmen formed the Black Poor Committee in 1786 to provide temporary relief. They also persuaded the Lords of the Treasury to grant aid to the most needy, although, as it turned out, this was not enough for bare subsistence. At this point Henry Smeathman, an amateur botanist who had spent some time on the coast of Africa, offered to rid the committee and the government of their unwanted charges by settling them in Sierra Leone, on the West Coast of Africa. Abolitionist Granville Sharp became involved with the scheme and even drew up a plan of government.

In spite of Sharp's involvement, the initial idea seems to have been to get blacks out of England over all other considerations. The humanitarian and religious reasons usually associated with the settlement of Sierra Leone were not much in evidence when the colony was first proposed.

Nevertheless, once the scheme was advanced, it became the focus of antislavery groups as a possible means of attacking the slave system by introducing free labor into Africa. Quakers had begun petitioning Parliament against the slave trade and formed the majority of the Society for Abolition of the Slave Trade, founded in 1787, in which they were allied with other evangelicals. Their activities made the slave trade a public issue by 1787, at the time the Sierra Leone expedition was getting under way.

Despite Sharp's continued activity, the men around whom the movement focused were Thomas Clarkson and William Wilberforce. Clarkson's interest resulted from his decision in 1785 to enter a contest sponsored by Cambridge University. It offered a prize for the best essay on the question, "Is it lawful to make slaves of others against their will?" As he knew nothing about slavery or the slave trade, he read, among other things, Anthony Benezet's *Short Account of Africa* and set to work. He won the prize and a short time later received what he considered to be a divine mission to devote his life to abolition. He joined with Granville Sharp and others in the Society for the Abolition of the Slave Trade.

The role of Clarkson was primarily as researcher and writer. He was not a very good speaker, had little sense of humor, was somewhat petulant, and showed little inclination to compromise. Still, he had an immense capacity for work. He visited Liverpool, Bristol, and other slaving ports to gather data for use against the trade. He began a collection of horror instruments, such as thumbscrews, handcuffs, leg shackles, and mouth openers (which were used to force-feed slaves who sought to starve themselves to death) to illustrate the cruelty of the trade. He realized his limitations, though, and knew that, lacking oratorical skills, he was unlikely to become a captivating national leader. Someone would have to be found who had a gift for public speaking, preferably someone wealthy and well connected whom the slaving interests could not buy or intimidate. Such a man was William Wilberforce.

Born in Hull, England, Wilberforce was the son of a wealthy merchant. He was physically frail but brilliant and charming. His grandfather bequeathed him a fortune and he grew up addicted to the good life. He frequented the best clubs, kept company with prominent people, and took to gambling and heavy drinking. However, he was also an eloquent speaker as well as an amiable companion, and when he tired of dissipation he decided to enter Parliament. But Parliament bored him, too. He took a tour of Europe with a religious friend who converted him to evangelical Christianity and gave his life more meaning. He intended to resign from Parliament and find more useful employment until his friend Prime Minister William Pitt suggested that he involve himself in the abolitionist cause. A few parliamentary speeches brought him to the attention of the Society for the Abolition of the Slave Trade and he agreed to become its spokesman. He and Clarkson became close friends.

The two were dedicated to a common goal and complemented each other because each had qualities the other lacked. Together they mapped out a strategy. They decided to concentrate on the misfortunes suffered by English sailors engaged in the trade rather than on the Africans they enslaved, because they felt the English public would more likely be moved by the former. They also agreed to limit their attack to the trade and not malign slavery itself so as to avoid alarming West Indian planters. They assured planters that their slave property would be more valuable and insurrections less likely if the trade were abolished.

The first of these conclusions they derived from the fairly obvious relationship between supply and demand: If the supply ceased and the demand remained constant, the value of bondsmen already on, or capable to be put on, the market would rise. The second conclusion was put forward because newly imported Africans were frequently thought to be responsible for slave rebellions. But Wilberforce and Clarkson also felt that they could undermine the argument for slavery if a free labor colony in Africa, raising competing tropical products, proved successful. Such a colony would benefit English industrialists by furnishing raw materials for English manufacturers and providing a market for English goods. Moreover, such a colony would be only the starting point for opening a much larger African market, one that would absorb much more of Britain's production than its West Indian colonies. An African market would provide more work for English workingmen and more wealth for the wealthy. In other words, the abolitionists hoped to convince the English public and English business interests that they had more to gain than to lose by ending the slave trade and, ultimately, slavery.

A total of 459 people left Portsmouth, England, for the African coast on February 23, 1787, to found the colony of Sierra Leone. Most were black, but almost a quarter were white, most of them white women married to black men. At least half of the emigrants were former slaves from North America. Olaudah Equiano had been appointed by the navy commissioners as commissary for the voyage. He was responsible for the settlers' supplies. He complained, however, that preparations were inadequate. Moreover, he charged the white man who supervised the venture with incompetence, dishonesty, and racism. The supervisor misappropriated funds for his own use, Equiano said, and treated blacks "the same as they do in the West Indies." Although Equiano's charges had merit, he was recalled, and white men were left in control.

The voyage, therefore, did not have an auspicious beginning and the settlement came close to failure. The settlers came at the wrong time of year for building and brought the wrong kind of seeds for planting. They quickly succumbed to disease. By September almost half the original colonists were dead and only a supply ship sent by Granville Sharp the following year saved the remainder.

Abolitionists now began to take a serious interest in the African enterprise, for

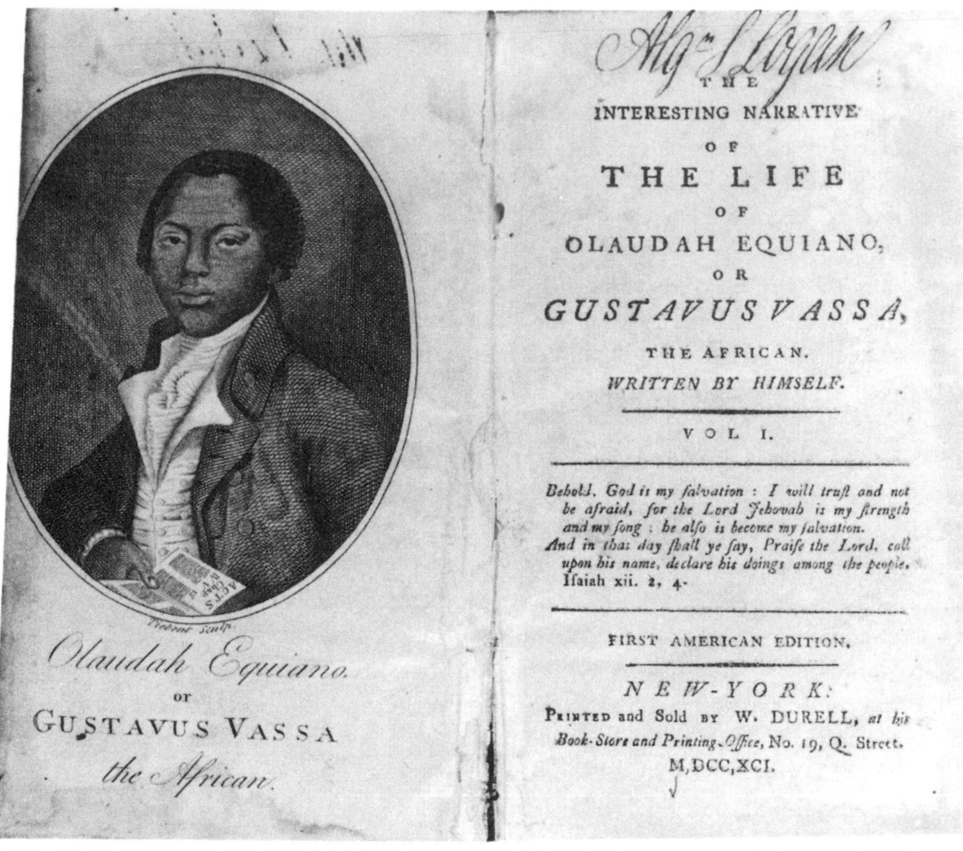

Olaudah Equiano.
OR
GUSTAVUS VASSA
the African.

THE
INTERESTING NARRATIVE
OF
THE LIFE
OF
OLAUDAH EQUIANO,
OR
GUSTAVUS VASSA,
THE AFRICAN.
WRITTEN BY HIMSELF.

VOL. I.

Behold, God is my salvation: I will trust and not be afraid, for the Lord Jehovah is my strength and my song; he also is become my salvation.
And in that day shall ye say, Praise the Lord, call upon his name, declare his doings among the people.
Isaiah xii. 2, 4.

FIRST AMERICAN EDITION.

NEW-YORK:
PRINTED and Sold BY W. DURELL, *at his Book-Store and Printing-Office,* No. 19, Q. Street.
M,DCC,XCI.

Olaudah Equiano was taken from his African home as a child and sold into slavery in the Americas. The extraordinary details of his life, described in his autobiography, captivated readers in England and in America.

it was clear that its failure would harm their cause. Among other things, it would support the pro-slavery argument that blacks could not rule themselves and would work only under the threat of force; it would also ruin the vision of a free-labor society in Africa as a market for British manufactured goods. Thomas Clarkson, Granville Sharp, and William Wilberforce, therefore, were appointed as three of the directors of a new enterprise, the Sierra Leone Company.

What gave the colony a new lease on life was the arrival of immigrants from Nova Scotia, Canada. African-American migrants to that region had found harsh winters, rocky and infertile land, starvation, discrimination, and political limitations. Hardship faced both white and black refugees, but the blacks came with less of everything needed for their survival and were given less upon their arrival. In the meantime, Boston King recalled: "Many of the poor people were compelled to sell their best gowns for five pounds of flour, in order to support life. When they had parted with all their clothes, even to their blankets, several of them fell down dead in the streets through hunger. Some killed and eat [*sic*] their dogs and cats; and poverty and distress prevailed on every side."

John Clarkson, brother of Thomas, accompanied Thomas Peters, who had been a leader of the Black Pioneers, a British military unit formed in 1776, back to Canada, and in January 1792 they left Nova Scotia with almost 1,200 passengers for the Province of Freedom, as Sierra Leone was called. One of these was Henry Washington, who had run away from the American commander-in-chief in 1776. He proved to be a successful farmer in Sierra Leone until he was banished for involvement in a dispute over issues of taxation and representation in the African colony. His quarrel offers clear evidence that the settlers had not forgotten their American revolutionary experience.

Already the fight against slavery and the slave trade was beginning to have some impact. Britain was now the leading slave-trading nation, with the French not far behind. Prime Minister William Pitt attempted to negotiate an agreement with the French in 1787 for mutual abolition of the slave trade, but that attempt failed. Among other reasons, the French were not anxious to hamper the prosperity of their thriving sugar colony in Saint Domingue, in the Caribbean, which was heavily dependent on slaves.

The British Parliament nevertheless passed a law in 1788 to limit the number of slaves its own vessels could carry relative to their size. This law was designed to make the slave trade somewhat more humane by providing the captives more room and comfort. In 1789 Wilberforce introduced a motion in Parliament to abolish the British trade and began a series of hearings into the issue. Meanwhile, Clarkson set off for the continent to make contact with the Society of the Friends of the Blacks in France, formed in 1788 for the same purpose. He, like Pitt, hoped to coordinate the abolitionist activities of the two nations so that their opponents could not use a failure in one nation as an excuse for failure in the other. The outbreak of the French Revolution in 1789 and the subsequent slave rebellion in Saint Domingue made the slave trade's abolition impossible in the 1790s. Nevertheless a start had been made and African Americans had had something to do with it.

The influence of African Americans on this worldwide movement to end slavery operated at various levels. The American Revolutionary War provided African Americans a chance to fight for their freedom by playing one force against another. No other group more clearly saw the contradiction between revolutionary ideals and American practice. Occasionally, they succeeded in convincing their white compatriots to live up to their stated ideals of the natural equality of all people, or at least to recognize their inconsistency when they did not. Of course, the war also provided blacks an alternative course to liberty. Those who left the country took revolutionary notions with them—to Africa, to the West Indies, and elsewhere.

The war also cut off West Indian planters from supporters in North America and left them to fight the rising tide of abolitionism within the British Empire unaided. This was true not solely in political terms but in economic and social terms as well. They lost easy access to American supplies and to the American market for their molasses. They therefore became more dependent on the mother country and more vulnerable to imperial pressure. African-American immigrants in Britain forced the issue of slavery and caused people there to take a stand. They therefore helped to breathe new life into British abolitionism, contributing to the British attack on the slave trade and eventually on slavery itself. In their American homeland, however, the revolution had only limited success.

Slavery and Freedom in the New Nation

Revolution and war in America, based on principles of natural rights and human equality, created an environment destructive to slavery. Yet there were definite limits to the effectiveness of these forces. Among the revolutionary generation there was no clear line drawn between human rights and property rights; no feeling that the one ought to come before the other.

Thus Pennsylvania's chief justice, denying a slave woman's claim to emancipation in 1815, wrote, "I know that freedom is to be favoured, but we have no right to favour it at the expense of property." Significantly, this case came from one of the nation's most liberal states. The judge's statement accurately captures the spirit of the earlier age. Rather than being banned by the state on the grounds of immorality, slavery was seen as something that had to be abolished voluntarily, usually with some form of compensation to the former slaveowners. This was not a direct compensation from the government. Most people thought that would be too great a public expense. Indeed, some radicals felt that, in a moral sense, if such a payment were to be made it ought to go to the bondsman in return for his unrequited toil rather than to his master.

Instead, the gradual emancipation laws enacted in most northern states provided for freedom for children of existing adult slaves born after a certain date, but not to those slaves themselves. In addition, the children were bound to serve their parents' master until sometime in their twenties, depending on the state. Slave owners thus continued to benefit from slave labor for some years after these acts were passed. Nevertheless, in the northern states, where the institution was not economically crucial nor its abolition regarded as too socially disruptive, slavery gradually ended.

By 1784 the new nation was already well along the way toward a division between a northern region of free states and a southern one of slave states. Yet that vision is most clear in hindsight. A person who lived at the time may not have considered that result a foregone conclusion. For one thing, slavery was still fairly strongly entrenched in New York and New Jersey. Proposals to end the institution there in 1785 and 1786, respectively, failed. Indeed, slavery expanded rapidly in New York during the 1790s, particularly in New York City. The surrounding rural population, which was largely Dutch, remained strongly wedded to bound labor.

In Virginia, by contrast, there was widespread anti-slavery sentiment and the legislature passed a law in 1782 making it easy for individuals to follow their conscience and free their slaves. Moreover, Delaware and Maryland, like New York and New Jersey, also debated ending slavery, in roughly the same period and with the same results; the measures failed. But unlike New York and New Jersey, they followed Virginia's example and made manumission easier than it had been, Delaware in 1787 and Maryland in 1790.

North Carolina had some difficulty making up its mind and adopted various pieces of contradictory legislation, but in all these states the free black population expanded considerably. North Carolina Quakers were particularly active in conveying the enslaved to freedom. They took advantage of every legal opportunity that was offered, including ensuring that slaves promised freedom in return for fighting were not reenslaved. They also bought bondsmen and let them pay off the debt and live as free people in all but name.

Yet there were distinct differences between the situation in New York and New Jersey and in the states south of Pennsylvania. African Americans were never more than about ten percent of the population of these Middle Atlantic states. They made up almost a third of Virginia and Maryland, and nearly as large a proportion in Delaware and North Carolina. Moreover, they were an important economic asset in the South. This was true equally in terms of their labor on farms and plantations, where they were a much higher percentage of the labor force than in the North, and in their value as property. If they were freed, their labor could continue, of course, on a different basis. They could be paid instead of forced to work. But such a transformation still required a radical social and economic reorganization. Equally important, it required a mental restructuring.

Complicating the social issue was the question of race. Many white people did not think that white and black people could live together in peace—or, if they did so, only if one race was subordinate to the other. A prominent spokesman for this view was Thomas Jefferson. "Nothing is more certainly written in the book of fate than that these [black] people are to be free," he wrote on one occasion. "Nor is it less certain that the two races, equally free, cannot live in the same government."

He felt that peaceful relations would be prevented by prejudices that white people held against blacks and by the memories that black people had of the past injustices suffered from whites. Nor could he ever get over his feeling that black people were inferior to white people. Unlike some people, who felt that the environment of slavery was responsible for whatever shortcomings blacks exhibited, Jefferson struggled unsuccessfully against the suspicion that Africans were inferior by nature. This did not mean, however, that he intended to exclude African

[he has incited treasonable insurrections of our fellow-citizens, with the allurements of forfeiture & confiscation of our property.
he has waged cruel war against human nature itself, violating it's most sa-
-cred rights of life & liberty in the persons of a distant people who never offended him, captivating & carrying them into slavery in another hemi-
-sphere, or to incur miserable death in their transportation thither. this
piratical warfare, the opprobrium of infidel powers, is the warfare of the
Christian king of Great Britain. determined to keep open a market
where MEN should be bought & sold: he has prostituted his negative
for suppressing every legislative attempt to prohibit or to restrain this
execrable commerce: and that this assemblage of horrors might want no fact
of distinguished die, he is now exciting those very people to rise in arms
among us, and to purchase that liberty of which he has deprived them,
by murdering the people upon whom he also obtruded them: thus paying
off former crimes committed against the liberties of one people, with crimes
which he urges them to commit against the lives of another.]
in every stage of these oppressions we have petitioned for redress in the most humble

This section from Jefferson's handwritten draft of the Declaration of Independence contains a passage condemning the slave trade. This clause was omitted because of objections from Georgia and South Carolina planters who needed slaves, and from New England shippers who sometimes engaged in slave trading.

Americans from the inalienable rights he declared all men to have. His charge in the Declaration of Independence that King George III had "waged cruel war against human nature itself" in his pursuit of the slave trade, and that the king had thereby violated Africans' "most sacred rights of life and liberty," indicates that Jefferson regarded Africans and African Americans as full members of the human community. Moreover, to underline the point, he would later say that "whatever be their [the blacks'] degree of talent it is no measure of their rights. Because Sir Isaac Newton was superior to others in understanding, he was not therefore lord of the person or property of others." But his reasoning could not withstand his emotion, and his was a perspective widely shared in Virginia and elsewhere in the country. When Jefferson spoke of abolition, therefore, he also talked of removing blacks from the continent.

There were elements of this outlook in the Middle Atlantic states, but because the black population there was smaller, opposition to emancipation focused around the issues of property and compensation rather than on the social consequences of freeing blacks. Here the relationship between human rights and property rights could be more easily discussed. The problem surfaced everywhere, but it could be more easily separated from other issues in the North than in the South. Moreover, in New York and New Jersey, where slavery was generally more important than in New England, the discussion had more resonance. It affected more people more closely. Everywhere the issue arose it involved the well-being of people. Part of this equation included money and wealth and comfort. Another part included public and private safety and peace of mind. The various factors had to be weighed practically as well as philosophically.

When New York's manumission law was finally passed, a legislator, blaming opposition mainly on the Dutch, commented they "raved and swore . . . that we were robbing them of their property. We told them they had none, and could hold none in human flesh . . . and we passed the law."

Nevertheless, the freeing of slaves in New York and other Middle Atlantic states took a long time to happen. Fifteen years after the end of the Revolutionary War and fourteen years after the final acts of liberation in New England, New York agreed to manumission. New Jersey did not do so until twenty years after the war. In the 1790s, while slavery was dead or dying in Philadelphia, it was still growing in New York City.

Slavery's usefulness and profitability in the 1780s and 1790s caused many to adopt it to their advantage. But also, in view of the undoubted anti-slavery sentiment of the time, many Northerners disassociated their institution from the horrors that were assumed to characterize slavery on Southern or Caribbean plantations. Slaves were "better off than the generality of the white poor," one New Jersey man argued, "who are obliged . . . to work harder than the slaves in general in this state." In this way slave owners could salve their consciences and at the same time attack slavery in the abstract. They could even work toward ending it locally, though they did so with no apparent urgency.

Several things countered this comfortable middle position among those inclined toward abolition in New York and meant that they would soon have to choose sides. One was the increasing numbers of free blacks, whose presence and activities weakened the institution. They served the slaves as examples of the possible. They were joined in their subversion by slaves themselves, who had a unique history in this region of being able to negotiate the conditions of their servitude. Black servitors had long been permitted to search for a new master if, for example, their current situation or location displeased them. A slaveholder's move from city to countryside might well prompt his servant to ask for permission to look for a new owner, so as to avoid exile to a rural location far from friends and family. Many did not stop at trying to better their terms of servitude, however; in a revolutionary age, bondsmen sought also to arrange their freedom. Their increased desire for personal liberty marred any assumption that they were satisfied with bondage.

The immigration of refugees from the slave uprising in Saint Domingue was another factor disturbing the presumption of a benign servitude. White refugees frequently brought slaves with them and their severe treatment of them, conditioned by the harsher environment of the West Indies, strikingly illustrated the disadvantages of slave life wherever it existed. It was difficult to maintain the myth of a mild slavery when some were so obviously, and sometimes publicly, mistreated. For their part, Saint Dominguan slaves contributed significantly to slave unrest, further corroding the feeling of ease. Finally there were the activities of kidnappers who stole free blacks and sold them outside the state. They exhibited the crass economic nature of the institution, the unpleasant underbelly that was better left unexposed.

The New York Manumission Society arose as an answer to the problem of slavery in New York State. Formed in January 1785 in response to "violent attempts lately made to seize and export for sale several free Negroes," the society also aimed to promote eventual abolition. Its moral outrage was strictly limited, however. It did not engage in a scathing critique of slavery or slaveholders as they existed in New York, nor did it exclude slaveholders from membership. John Jay, the society's first president, owned slaves. He explained his apparent inconsistency: "I purchase slaves and manumit them when their faithful services shall have afforded a reasonable retribution." Whether his was an act of charity or hypocrisy, the fact that he and other slaveholders joined an anti-slavery society was indicative of the trend of the times. Even though they sometimes seemed to devote more effort to humanizing slavery than to getting rid of it, they nevertheless introduced gradual emancipation legislation and other measures to free and protect blacks. But if even some slaveholders could envision and work toward emancipation, one could reasonably foresee its doom. The ending of slavery in New York was drawn out and complicated. Its last manumission law, adopted in 1817, granted freedom to slaves born before July 4, 1799, to be effective July 4, 1827. But most slaves came to an agreement that provided their freedom considerably earlier than that date. New Jersey moved more slowly, adopting comparable legislation in 1804 and 1846. It still had a few slaves at the time of the Civil War.

If abolition came slowly in the Middle Atlantic, it was indefinitely delayed farther south. The Upper South, the region north of South Carolina, was as much affected by the ideology of the Revolution as any area of the country. George Washington, Thomas Jefferson, and many other prominent leaders of America's struggle against Great Britain were Virginians. Nearly all of them expressed reservations about slavery. Many, including Washington and Jefferson, expressed a desire to see it end.

Besides, there were more reasons than philosophy to support that position. Evangelical Methodists and Baptists, quite active in the Chesapeake in the 1780s, carried out widespread religious revivals. They added Christian egalitarianism, or the belief that all men are equal in the sight of God, to the secular claims of equality advanced in the Revolution. Moreover, they were effective. Virginia's Robert Carter, one of the richest and most successful planters in the country, freed five hundred slaves beginning in 1791, at least partly from religious conviction. "I have for some time past," he wrote in his deed of manumission, "been convinced that to retain them in Slavery is contrary to the true Principles of Religion and Justice, and that therefor[e] it was my Duty to manumit them."

Finally, there were economic considerations. Many planters in Virginia, Maryland, and Delaware began to shift from tobacco to cereal crops, such as wheat, oats, barley, and corn, beginning in the mid-eighteenth century. They made this shift because of a fall in tobacco prices at the same time that the worldwide demand for food crops increased. They also moved to grains because tobacco so rapidly exhausts the soil. These new products did not require as much slave labor and many planters felt that they had a surplus of slaves. They were prepared to consider alternatives like the labor of free blacks. So for many reasons people in the Upper South could seriously consider manumission, and some moved from thought to action. Yet Southern revolutionaries ultimately contented themselves with making manumission a matter of personal conscience. Proposals for total abolition were considered but dismissed.

A major objection, as we have seen, had to do with race. One Southerner, still sensitive to the issue of bondage, tried in 1797 to put the best face on an obvious Revolutionary failure. "On inquiry," he explained, "it would not be found the fault of the southern states that slavery was tolerated, but their misfortune; but to liberate their slaves would be to act like madmen; it would be to injure all parts of the United States." He implied that Southerners were self-sacrificing statesmen for their willingness to keep black people in chains and under control, and he meant thereby to make slaveholding a patriotic duty. But by that time the economy had changed again. Slaveholders in the Upper South could now find a ready market for their slaves in the expanding cotton regions of the southwest. The momentum toward the abolition of slavery in the Upper South began to slip away.

The Lower South states of South Carolina and Georgia were largely exempt from the tenderness of conscience that afflicted the Upper South. They had a plantation economy that was starved for bound black labor. While the loss of slaves during the war had inconvenienced Virginia planters, it had devastated those in the Lower South, whose prime concern was how soon the slave trade could resume. Moreover, slaves were a much higher percentage of their population; therefore the social and economic effects of the abolition of slavery were more significant. The relatively liberal period that flowered in the Upper South, therefore, had no counterpart in the Lower South. Some emancipations occurred, but these were prompted more by blood ties than abstract philosophy. Lower South planters were more likely to free their sons and daughters by slave mistresses than anyone else, so the free colored population that grew here was lighter-skinned than that in the Chesapeake, where manumissions were more often motivated by conscience.

Abolitionist pressure could in some instances be more effectively brought to bear at the national level, but the government formed under the Articles of Confederation (which were finally adopted in 1781) did not have much power. Having rejected a strong centralized government in Europe, few Americans were disposed to create a new one in their midst. The new states were jealous of their prerogatives and reluctant to surrender any more than necessary to what amounted to little more than a wartime alliance against England. Consequently, most activities that affected African Americans occurred at the state and local levels.

There was one crucial exception to this rule, and it had to do with territories to the west, where Americans expected their growing population would settle. Indeed, a struggle over the status of these lands kept the Articles from going into effect for years. Maryland, a small state, wanted the issue solved in such a way as to guarantee equal access to the West for the citizens of all the states, rather than trying to sort out conflicting and overlapping claims. Only when Maryland secured agreement that western territories would be considered the common property of all the states would it assent to the compact. Congress, under the Articles, therefore had to consider some plan for orderly settlement.

Thomas Jefferson offered a solution in his proposal for the Land Ordinance of 1784. Under his proposed law, slavery would have been prohibited in all western lands after 1800. This would have meant that all territory west of the Alleghenies, north and south, would have prohibited slavery at the beginning of the nineteenth century. But the proposal would have allowed a sixteen-year period for slavery to become entrenched before the law took effect. Some historians think that had that happened, the prohibition would have been repealed and slavery would have been allowed in all these western territories.

In any case, it failed by one vote. The measure that was adopted, the Northwest Ordinance of 1787, forbade slavery only in the area east of the Mississippi and north of the Ohio River, which was called the Northwest Territory. The ordinance did not free slaves already there, and it provided that any fugitive slaves who fled there should be returned to their masters. Slavery continued to exist in Indiana until 1818 and in Illinois until the 1840s. Nonetheless, an important principle had been established and slavery's spread had been curbed.

In making the Constitution of 1789, however, the Founders did not find revolutionary idealism all that useful. They had to reconcile many differences to form a strong nation, and to come to a compromise between the conflicting principles of freedom and property. In effect, this meant that blacks had to be compromised. This was not difficult for the framers of the Constitution because at the time of the Constitutional Convention in 1787 most states were slave states. Only in Pennsylvania and New England was slavery on the road to extinction. This did not mean that there could be no sectional division between North and South over this issue, because slavery was not nearly as important in northern places where it remained, nor did Northerners generally associate their practice with the southern one. Most

Northerners expected its eventual end in their localities. In a real sense, slavery was already the South's "peculiar institution."

The process of compromise began as early as 1783, when Congress had to decide on a basis for raising national revenue. The states with the largest slave populations, Virginia and South Carolina, wanted land values to be the standard. Other states wanted to use population. Congress eventually settled on population but adopted a formula whereby a slave would count as three-fifths of a free person in the calculation. The measure never became part of the Articles of Confederation because it was not unanimously adopted by the individual states. Nonetheless, Congress had devised a workable formula and it was revived when delegates met at the Constitutional Convention in Philadelphia in 1787.

One of the first problems that had to be overcome at that convention involved representation in Congress. Edmund Randolph's Virginia Plan proposed altering the practice under the Articles whereby each state had one vote. Randolph proposed that a state's power in the national legislature be determined by its population. That proposal sparked sharp disagreement among the delegates, one usually described as along the lines of small states versus large ones. Yet the division was also between slave and free states, because obviously a state with a large slave population might turn into a small state if slaves were excluded. Southerners feared that in such a national union they would be consistently out voted by the larger free population of the North.

Many Northerners felt, however, that to count slaves equally with free people, or to count them at all, was ridiculous. Elbridge Gerry of Massachusetts, in protesting the three-fifths compromise eventually adopted (in which all slaves were counted as three-fifths of a free person to determine the number of representatives each state would be allowed in the House of Representatives), declared, "blacks are property, and are used to the southward as horses and cattle to the northward; and why should their representation be increased to the southward on account of the number of slaves, than horses or oxen to the north?" He did not argue the morality of keeping blacks as chattels in the same light as horses or oxen, nor did he dispute the assumption that there could be property in humankind. Yet such a criticism was implied, for no one would have suggested the representation of horses and oxen. Slave property was clearly of a different character than horses and oxen, at least in some respects. From the revolutionary perspective, that difference derived from the fact that they were human beings and as such deserved to be masters of their own destinies, but that attitude was of no use in an attempt to build a nation in association with those who insisted on the character of slaves as chattels. The revolutionaries had a choice: They could build two nations, based on opposing principles, or one nation, papering over contradictions and inconsistencies. They chose the latter course.

Northern delegates agreed to accept the principle that slaves would be counted for purposes of representation in Congress, and the South granted that they would not be counted as whole people. The sections settled upon the precedent-setting three-fifths compromise. Once that initial concession was made, other clauses respecting slave property could follow more easily. These included a fugitive slave provision, requiring runaway slaves to be returned to those who claimed them, and an agreement not to terminate the slave trade for twenty years. Northerners remained sensitive to the issue, however, and insisted that the word "slave" not appear in the Constitution. Slaves were instead referred to as "persons held to service or labor." Northerners even objected to placing the word "legal" before service, fearing that would suggest that black bondage was somehow legitimate, and disliked "servitude" as well as "slavery." Thus they could argue that they were being true to revolutionary principles at the same time that they denied them in practice.

The fact that the two sections were trying to reconcile opposites was no secret. This can be clearly seen in the way that Southerners defended, and felt that they had to defend, the new national compact in their arguments to convince their constituents to ratify it. Nor, in this instance, was there any difference between Upper and Lower South. "We have a security that the general government can never emancipate" the slaves, General Charles Cotesworth Pinckney of South Carolina argued, "for no such authority is granted; and it is admitted, on all hands, that the general government has no powers but what are expressly granted by the Constitution." He concluded, "In short, considering all circumstances, we have made the best terms for the security of this species of property it was in our power to make."

Moreover, the two foremost Virginians (George Washington and Thomas Jefferson), both of whom had expressed anti-slavery sentiments, decided that their political careers would be more secure if they ceased making public statements that might negatively affect their standing and influence. Consequently, when two British evangelists visited Washington in 1785 and asked him to sign a petition favoring emancipation, he refused. He said that it would not be appropriate. He indicated, however, that if the Virginia assembly agreed to consider the petition, he would give his opinion of it. The assembly refused and Washington remained silent.

Jefferson took no more public actions on emancipation, or at least no more favorable ones, after he drafted the Land Ordinance of 1784. His official actions thereafter were all supportive of slavery. He resisted publication of his *Notes on Virginia* (originally written as private answers to questions from a French friend) because in it he had expressed mild anti-slavery sentiments. His fears appeared to be justified. A South Carolinian wrote to tell him of "the general alarm" that a particular "passage in your Notes occasioned amongst us. It is not easy to get rid of old prejudices, and the word 'emancipation' operates like an apparition upon a South Carolina planter."

There was every reason for politicians to be careful when it came to slavery, for there was widespread Southern support for it. Simultaneously, Southerners were equally attached to liberty. But if Northerners had followed the logic of revolutionary ideology to the conclusion that there could be no right of property in men, Southerners had rejected that deduction. "By Liberty in general," a Charleston minister declaimed, "I understand [not just civil liberty but] the Right every man has to pursue the natural, reasonable and religious dictates of his own mind; to enjoy the fruits of his own labour," and "to live upon one's own terms." It meant to be able to dispose absolutely of one's "property, as may best contribute to the support, ease, and advantage of himself and his family," and that would include property in slaves. He and other Southerners were quite willing, therefore, to deny Enlightenment principles and qualify revolutionary declarations. Consequently, when Charles Cotesworth Pinckney recommended the Constitution to his constituents, despite its failure to include a bill of rights, he explained, "such bills generally begin with declaring that all men are by nature born free. Now, we should make that declaration with a very bad grace when a large part of our property consists in men who are actually born slaves."

Alternatively, Southerners defended themselves by disputing the assumption that blacks were fully men. It was true, as a South Carolinian wrote, that blacks had "human Forms," but, as another continued the argument, they were "beings of an inferior rank, and little exalted above brute creatures." They were thus fit objects as property. It followed that even as free people their defect of color, with all that it entailed, excluded them from citizenship. The revolution had been "a *family quarrel among equals*" in which "the Negroes had no concern."

Even in the North, where slavery was abolished, there was opposition to blacks as citizens equal to all others. This can be seen most clearly if one looks at the emancipation laws and controversies surrounding them. The Pennsylvania law (1780), the first to be passed, was also the most severe when compared to the emancipation acts of other Northern states passed between 1780 and 1804—this in a region dominated by Quakers and pretending to great liberality. No slave was immediately freed by it, and children born after March 1, 1780, had to serve until they were twenty-eight years old before their freedom was recognized. This represented a tightening of an earlier draft of the law that freed females at eighteen and males at twenty-one.

In Massachusetts, where there were fewer blacks than in Pennsylvania, the uneasy feelings directed toward blacks were somewhat greater. The first state constitution, passed by the legislature in 1778 but rejected by the people, denied African Americans the right to vote; Pennsylvania's did not. The constitution of 1780 that Massachusetts finally adopted removed that prohibition, but blacks were strictly limited in their possibilities of employment and singled out in newspaper editorials for their supposed inability to work. Nor could they attend the schools that their taxes supported.

These and other prejudicial actions on the part of white citizens in Massachusetts, Pennsylvania, and elsewhere forced black people even more than whites to reflect on the relationship between freedom, revolutionary principles, slavery, and race. Even many of their supporters did not expect African Americans to prosper, and their enemies occasionally sought to stand in their way.

Yet bad as the situation was, this antipathy between black and white people was not as great as it would later become. Indeed, one student of Northern working-class people in New York found them to be refreshingly free of the racial stereotypes that common white folks were supposed to have. Although jokes about black people were common, they suggested a sympathy for and an identification with blacks. Both blacks and working-class whites were pictured as underdogs. Even so, there was enough of an edge to the jokes and sufficient force behind some of the actions to convince a small group of blacks that they should seek their fortune elsewhere.

One of the first black organizations to advance this aim was the Free African Union Society. Founded in 1780 in Newport, Rhode Island, it was a benevolent and moral improvement society as well as an agency of black emigration. It, like white abolitionists, was concerned with the plight of blacks. Thus it encouraged its members to refrain from idleness and drunkenness, tried to ensure that they made their marriages legal, and promoted investment in real estate. The society provided death benefits for the wives and children of deceased members and furnished loans for those in need. It also had a religious mission and held weekly services. Most importantly, the society tried to convoke a consensus that a return to Africa was the best course of action.

In January 1787, the Free African Union Society decided that it would establish its own settlement in Africa. About seventy people agreed to participate in the venture. Although many were African-born, they did not wish to merge with the indigenous people but rather to found a new country of their own. They wanted to get clear title to land somewhere on the continent in order to avoid conflicts with local people.

To this end, they sought out a rather flamboyant anti-slavery Quaker, William Thornton of Antigua, who was visiting the United States. A wealthy man, he was also a philanthropist who had developed a scheme to free his own slaves and set them up on a self-sustaining plantation in the West Indies. When island authorities discouraged that plan as a threat to slavery, he envisioned colonizing his blacks somewhere in Africa. Advised that free Christian African Americans also wanted to emigrate, Thornton revised his plans. He believed that the literate blacks in New England would perfectly complement agriculturally sophisticated West Indian blacks, who together could secure the colony's survival. One group would bring morality and industry and the other technical expertise. In Africa they would grow tropical products, repay the cost of their passage, and show slaveholders how the institution might be brought profitably to an end. They would establish a trade in products grown as free men, the value of which would rapidly surpass that of slave-grown crops.

Though the plan was laudable, the details were not. The Free African Union Society soon made it clear to Thornton that its members had no interest in becoming part of any venture in which they would be subservient to whites. They wanted to go someplace where they would be their own rulers. Nor were they willing to let Thornton act as their agent. They did feel, though, that if he was a truly charitable person, he might be willing to finance an advance group of Newport blacks to search for a suitable location. They also made contact with seventy-five blacks in Boston who had recently petitioned the Massachusetts legislature to provide assistance for their removal to Africa.

The petitioners there were led by Prince Hall, founder of the first African-American lodge of Freemasons. The Masons were a fraternal organization of men who met to exchange news and ideas and occasionally to conduct religious services or discussions. They sought to overcome social and religious divisions among men and to create greater understanding based on Enlightenment principles. Hall described the "true spirit of Masonry" as "love to God and universal love to all mankind." In 1775 he and fourteen other blacks joined a lodge attached to a British regiment stationed in Boston. When the British left, they permitted the blacks to continue to meet as the African Lodge No. 1. Local Masons refused to recognize them, however, and they applied to England for a charter. Granted in 1784, the charter finally arrived in 1787. By that time, however, they were disillusioned—as individuals, if not as Masons—because, as they told Massachusetts's General Court, despite their freedom "we yet find ourselves, in many respects, in very disagreeable and disadvantageous circumstances; most of which must attend us, so long as we and our children live in America."

Having found kindred spirits in Boston, the Free African Union Society finally communicated with Granville Sharp in London, who was becoming involved with the settlement of Sierra Leone. But Sharp was not enthusiastic about American blacks coming over, especially if they insisted on acting independently. He made clear that if they came to Sierra Leone, they would have to act like English subjects and be bound by the common laws of England. The vision came to nought. Massachusetts was unwilling to put up any money to aid black emigration and Thornton, for all his planning, did not come through either. The blacks lacked the financial wherewithal to do it on their own.

Still, New England blacks would not give up. In 1789 the Free African Union Society addressed an appeal to compatriots in nearby Providence, Rhode Island, proposing a new plan of emigration. In this document they advanced an early black nationalistic concept of uniting blacks in Africa, the West Indies, and the United States. Because they were "attended with many disadvantages and evils with respect to living" in the new American nation, they sought a nationhood of their own. They suggested a return to "the natives in Africa from whom we sprang, [they] being in heathenish darkness and sunk down in barbarity"—to whom African Americans would bring light. The success of the project would benefit

Africans everywhere, for Africa's lack of civilization, as they saw it from a western point of view, was a source of shame. That lack was used to justify enslavement and the slave trade. If Africa were redeemed, the slave trade would cease, Africans overseas would be able to take pride in their homeland, the black man's humanity would be vindicated, and the link between blackness and slavery would be dissolved.

The Boston group invited the Providence blacks to join them in a united society that would meet every three months "to consider what can be done for our good, and for the good of all Affricans." "Now is the time," the Providence group would say in advancing yet another emigration plan in 1794, "if ever for us to try to Distinguish ourselves as the More remote we are situated from the white people the more we will be respected."

It is interesting to compare the plans developed by blacks (called "emigrationist") and those envisioned by whites (referred to as "colonizationist"). People like Jefferson who wanted blacks to depart were primarily concerned about the future and well-being of white people. Jefferson was not much interested in what happened to blacks, and his emancipation plans for Virginia would have compelled them to leave whether they wanted to or not.

People like Thornton, by contrast, had a religious and moral concern. They were interested in illustrating that blacks could progress in economic terms, both in America and Africa, because such advances would justify their struggles for black emancipation, validate their faith in the essential unity of humankind, and contribute to an end to black servitude worldwide. But they also adopted an attitude of paternalism: They doubted the ability of blacks and were sure that black people could make progress only under white direction. African Americans, believing as much in their capability as their equality, thought they could and had to develop themselves largely on their own. They could welcome white help but objected to white domination. They were cultural hybrids and appreciated their American identity. Having adopted western values, they intended to westernize Africa, but they also wanted to cultivate a pride in being black. Only a great black nation would prove without doubt that blacks were not born to be slaves. But, because of lack of financing from white Americans and those African Americans who did have money, these early emigrationist movements all failed. For this reason, revolution in Haiti, which was developing even as these projects vanished, was an event of crucial significance.

Despite the movements to return to Africa, the period before the turn of the nineteenth century was one of hopefulness. In half the nation slavery had ended. This occurred not because it was unprofitable, or because there had been no opposition, or because the climate was uncongenial. It had happened largely as a result of war and revolution. And the revolution was not just political but social as well, a revolution in thinking as well as in acting that caused a part of the nation to confront prejudice and injustice and put them partially to rout. It was true that slavery had never been as important in the places where it ended as in those where it remained, that people who opposed it often had practical reasons as well as philosophical reasons for doing it, that many of those who favored freedom often had little confidence in the capacity of blacks to handle it. But a start had been made, and African Americans moved swiftly to take advantage of their opportunities.

Richard Allen and the Promise of Freedom

On April 12, 1787, Absalom Jones and Richard Allen, "two men of the African race," as they described themselves in their Preamble and Articles of Association, "who, for their religious life and conversation have obtained a good report among men," met together with others in Philadelphia to form "some kind of religious society." Their Free African Society derived from "a love to the people of their complexion whom they beheld with sorrow, because of their irreligious and uncivilized state."

Jones and Allen's Free African Society was a mutual aid and moral improvement group that also had a religious bent. It was nonsectarian, in an attempt to attract African Americans of various Christian denominations, though it was closely associated with the Quakers. The society's rules specified that the clerk or treasurer should always be a Quaker, and eventually, meetings began with a period of silence in the Quaker fashion. The organization prohibited drunkenness among its members and provided death benefits.

Although it, like Newport's Free African Union Society, had been formed in the face of discrimination, and its assessment of the condition and immediate prospects of blacks in America was largely the same, its prescription was not. The Philadelphia group had none of the sense of mission or adventure evidenced in Newport. Or, rather, their sense of mission was distinctly different. They thought the solution to blacks' misfortune was self-improvement (with which New England blacks agreed), but otherwise they would depend on divine deliverance achieved through prayer and fasting. They rejected Newport's call for emigration. "This land," Richard Allen would later say about America, "which we have watered with our *tears* and *our blood* is now our *mother country*."

The different reactions of two African-American organizations who had basically the same diagnosis of the plight of black people in the United States is evidence of the "double consciousness" that the esteemed black scholar W. E. B. Du Bois wrote about at the turn of the twentieth century. The African American, he suggested, "ever feels his twoness—an American, a Negro; two souls, two thoughts, two unreconciled strivings; two warring ideals in one dark body, whose dogged strength alone keeps it from being torn asunder." The people in these organizations memorialized their background by calling themselves African. They acknowledged their American identity by clinging to and seeking to spread various forms of Christianity. They adopted religious and cultural ideas of morality, hard work, thrift, and accumulation of wealth, and favored individual initiative together with group solidarity.

Within this common outlook, whether one stressed the African side of the equation and embraced black nationalism and a return to Africa, or seized upon America and more limited forms of separatism, depended to a great extent upon circumstances and personal inclination. In periods and locales where there seemed to be a chance for black progress in America, fewer were attracted to emigration; when and where the situation appeared less hopeful, more were inclined to leave. A firm religious belief and a conviction that, as Philadelphia responded to Newport, "the race is not to the swift, nor the battle to the strong," motivated some blacks to cling to their American identity, no matter what.

This attitude can be clearly seen in the lives of Richard Allen and Absalom Jones. Jones stayed in Philadelphia throughout the British occupation and remained with his master even after the English left. Allen also failed to run away, to either British or American forces. Both chose to take their chances under existing conditions and trust the promise of America. They had several reasons to do so.

Born a slave in Sussex County, Delaware, in 1747, Jones was at a young age removed from the fields and made a house boy. In that situation he was able to obtain some learning. From money earned around the house, he "soon bought . . . a primer," he related in an autobiographical sketch, "and begged to be taught by any body that I found able and willing to give me the least instruction." When his master left Delaware for Pennsylvania in 1762, he sold Absalom's mother and brothers and sisters, having no need for a large slave family in Philadelphia. But he took the fifteen-year-old Absalom with him. Whatever distress the separation from family caused, the move nevertheless permitted Absalom to pursue an education. Philadelphia was the scene of much Quaker abolitionist sentiment, and people like Anthony Benezet had made some provision for black education. Despite having to work in his master's shop throughout the day, obliged "to store, pack up and carry out goods," a clerk taught him to write, and he secured his master's permission to attend school at night.

When he was twenty-three, he married Mary, a neighbor's slave, and they determined to get their freedom. It made sense to secure Mary's first because that would allow their children to be born free, since children legally followed the condition of the mother. Absalom drew up a plea for his wife's freedom and carried it to prominent Quakers, some of whom lent, and others donated, the required cash. Working at night for wages, he and his wife repaid their loans. And while he beseeched his master to permit him to purchase himself, the couple saved enough money to buy a large house in a substantial neighborhood in January 1779, a few months after the British evacuated the city. Absalom owned property, therefore, while still a slave. Several more years passed before his master consented (in 1784) to his self-purchase. Bearing no animosity and receiving none in return, he continued to work in the store. When Richard Allen arrived in Philadelphia in 1786, Jones was a prominent black member of the largely white St. George's Methodist Church.

Richard Allen was born a slave in Philadelphia in 1760, but his master maintained a plantation in Delaware where Allen may have been raised. He was sold to a small slaveholder who worked a farm outside of Dover, Delaware, and his owner, a fair man, permitted him to join the local Methodist Society and attend classes after he was converted by itinerant preachers in the 1770s. His conversion may have been spurred by the sale of his parents and younger brothers and sisters shortly before his turn to religion. His conversion was no less sincere for that fact, and when neighbors criticized his master for permitting his slaves to attend frequent religious meetings, Allen and a remaining brother "held a council together . . . so that it should not be said that religion made us worse servants; we would work night and day to get our crops forward."

This diligence enabled Allen's owner to confound his critics, and, as Allen reported in his autobiography, he "often boasted of his slaves for their honesty and industry." Perhaps the example of his slaves as well as the teachings of itinerant Methodists moved him, too, to religion. But Methodism at this point was opposed to slavery, and a minister told him that his slaves would keep him out of heaven. In 1780, therefore, he encouraged Allen and his brother to purchase their freedom.

Allen then became a traveling preacher himself, taking the Methodist gospel as far afield as New York and South Carolina and into the backcountry. He supported himself by doing odd jobs and he preached to white and black audiences alike. In Radnor, Pennsylvania, twelve miles outside Philadelphia, where he had "walked until my feet became so sore and blistered . . . that I scarcely could bear them to the ground," he was forced to rest. Taken in and cared for by strangers, he repaid them by preaching. The townspeople took to him and persuaded him to tarry. "There were but few colored people in the neighborhood," he recalled; "most of my congregation was white. Some said, 'this man must be a man of God; I never heard such preaching before.'"

From there, in 1786, Allen received a call from St. George's to preach to the black congregants at 5:00 A.M. in order not to disturb white services. His ministry caught on. He soon had a group of blacks meeting separately for prayer meetings, among whom was Absalom Jones. Allen felt cramped within the confines of his relationship with St. George's, however, and proposed founding a separate black congregation. Other blacks agreed, but the white clergy was opposed. The minister, according to Allen, "used very insulting language to us to prevent us from going on," and tried to bar their meetings altogether. It was at this point that Allen and Jones organized the Free African Society as a nonsectarian organization. They conceived a plan to build an independent African-American community church that could attract black people without regard to denomination.

When the African Church of Philadelphia was formally proposed in 1791, its plan of church government was described as "so general as to embrace all, and yet so orthodox in cardinal points as to offend none." The group's justification for going its separate way was that a black church was more likely to attract black people than a white one. They reasoned that "men are more influenced by their moral equals than by their superiors . . . and . . . are more easily governed by persons chosen by themselves for that purpose, than by persons who are placed over them by accidental circumstances." In this phrase, directed at wealthy white people from whom they hoped to gain financial support, they combined democratic principles with strategic modesty and self-effacement. At the same time, they boldly declared their independence of paternalism and their rejection of discrimination within white denominations. White religious leaders, Methodist, Episcopalian, and Quaker, were virtually unanimous in opposition to the plan, revealing a clear unwillingness to relinquish their direction of black religious life. Moreover, they stood to lose their African-American congregants, who, whatever their humble status, sometimes made significant contributions to church affairs.

Not long after this effort was set in motion, an event occurred that is often said to have prompted the move toward black religious separation. Jones and Allen still worshiped at St. George's Methodist Church. Blacks, like other members, contributed to the church's expansion, but when the addition was completed, blacks were asked to retire to newly installed galleries. Even so, when Jones and Allen arrived for services one Sunday morning and knelt to pray above the seats where they formerly sat, they were approached by a trustee and asked to move. Jones requested him to wait until the prayer ended but the trustee said, "No, you must get up now, or I will call for aid and force you away." Jones again asked for a delay, but the trustee motioned for another to come to his aid. Just as the two were about to act the prayer ended and the blacks got up and walked out together. "They were," said Allen, "no more plagued with us in the church." This affair occurred in 1792, after plans for the African church were already in motion. Nevertheless, it reinforced the need for African Americans to form their own religious community.

Several years passed before the African church came into being. The disapproval of white religious leaders slowed donations, though such prominent people as George Washington, Thomas Jefferson, and Granville Sharp, in England, sent small contributions. Newport's Free African Union Society also made a donation. Blacks engaged in various efforts to raise money—but they were hindered in early 1793 by an influx of refugees from Saint Domingue and later in the year by a yellow fever epidemic. The latter furnished them an opportunity to show their public spirit by volunteering to nurse the ill and bury the dead, while many of the white people fled. The reception of Saint Domingue's white refugees, however, provided evidence of the black community's relative standing among the whites. Philadelphia's white citizens raised twelve thousand dollars in a few days for displaced slave owners, but the church for former slaves, costing less than a third as much, was delayed for several years for lack of money.

In July 1794 the African church opened its doors. Its members had decided to affiliate with the Episcopal church, feeling that some denominational connection was important for the security of the congregation. Only Jones and Allen voted for the Methodists. Calling itself the African Episcopal Church of St. Thomas, the congregation chose Absalom Jones as minister. The members sought to guarantee their local control by providing that only African Americans could be elected to church offices, except the minister and assistant minister, and that the congregation chose all church officers, including the minister and his assistant. They would permit themselves the possibility of choosing a white minister if they ever so desired, but they wanted the church to remain firmly in black hands. They would not surrender the revolutionary principle of self-government.

There were several reasons why blacks such as Jones and Allen were attracted to Methodism. As a new evangelical denomination, it had few ties with colonial slavery, and its founder, John Wesley, adopted an anti-slavery stance. Their religious egalitarianism reinforced revolutionary principles of equality, but, ironically, the fact that many Methodists were loyal to the British during the Revolution set them apart from patriotic groups, which were often pro-slavery. To many African Americans, Methodists represented a strain of British anti-slavery in opposition to an increasingly pro-slavery American nation.

The itinerant nature of Methodist evangelicals increased their appeal to blacks (and poor white people), for they went out onto the roads and highways, into the fields and byways, to spread their message of salvation. They usually spoke in a direct, simple, emotional style and appealed to the heart rather than the intellect. Their methods had much in common with a traditional African religious outlook.

The emotional attraction is important because it is perhaps the one aspect of Methodism that made it more appealing than Quakerism, which shared many of Methodism's other attributes. Although Quakers held slaves, they were also among the earliest to express opposition to the practice and perhaps the first to act against it. They dominated early anti-slavery societies in Britain and America and were often loyal supporters of the English as well as pacifists during the years of revolutionary struggle. Their loyalism, however, seemed to discredit them more than it did the Methodists—perhaps because the Quakers were a more powerful group in colonial America—and it lessened the effectiveness of their anti-slavery efforts in the immediate postrevolutionary era. By contrast, the Methodists were less rigid about their abolitionst message and modified it in order to accommodate slaveholders in areas where slavery was legal. Despite their willingness to get along with slaveholders, the Methodists had an emotional appeal for blacks that the Quakers could not match.

Nevertheless, the African church affiliated with the Episcopalians. This probably had to do with what they perceived as Methodist shortcomings, for the Methodists, like other white people, often viewed blacks as childlike creatures who needed firm regulation. Blacks, they said, could not be trusted on their own. There was also at least occasional jealousy at the competition blacks offered. Thus one chronicler related that Richard Allen was encouraged to get off the circuit and remain in Philadelphia because a prominent white Methodist itinerant minister compared unfavorably.

By contrast, a black Methodist in New York, George White, was forced to preach outside the city for years because of the refusal of white Methodists in the urban area to accept him as an equal. These prejudicial attitudes encouraged black Methodists in New York City, led by James Varick, to leave the parent organization in 1796. They founded what later became the African Methodist Episcopal Zion Church, with Varick as its first bishop. Similar experiences in Baltimore and other cities provoked similar actions. Not merely prejudice but blacks' own religious and social outlooks encouraged black separatism. For blacks, slavery was a sin and America could never be a truly Christian nation so long as it condoned slavery. They could not, as their fellow white Baptist and Methodist believers did, relegate it to politics nor consider it beyond the scope of religion.

Despite the problems, Allen remained committed to Methodism. He refused to accept leadership of the African church once it allied with Episcopalians, allowing the position to go to Jones instead. Allen persisted in building his own Methodist church. Established in the same year, a few blocks away from the black Episcopalians, it became the foundation of an independent black denomination, the African Methodist Episcopal church. "Mother Bethel," as Allen's Bethel African Methodist congregation was called, also attempted to safeguard its rights of local autonomy. It was a fight over that issue, and over ownership of the congregation's property, that prompted African Americans to leave the white-dominated Methodist organization and form their own denomination in 1816.

Once the black churches were established, they became the centers of black settlement in Philadelphia. The surrounding neighborhoods did not become black ghettos, because blacks were frequently interspersed with working-class whites and were not in the majority. But community activities among blacks were of necessity stronger than among their white companions, because they had few alternative sources of support. Nor could they move out of the neighborhood as easily.

Blacks also lived in other sections of the city and their numbers gave them a sense of possibilities. Philadelphia at the time had the largest free black population in the United States and developed the most thriving free black community. It had grown to two thousand by 1790. At the same date, New York City, with as many blacks, was largely a slave city; indeed it possessed more bondspeople than any other American city except Charleston, South Carolina. Boston listed no slaves by that date but had a smaller black population. Because of its size and influence, Philadelphia is a good place to view the situation of blacks in the years immediately following the revolution. The stages of development there were paralleled in other Northern cities.

It was a relatively successful community, despite a postwar depression that

This watercolor from the early nineteenth century offers a stereotypical view of blacks attending a church service in Philadelphia.

affected large segments of the city. Newly freed blacks flocked to Philadelphia from rural Pennsylvania and neighboring areas of Delaware, Maryland, New Jersey, and even southern New England. They sought gainful employment and economic independence. Men were drawn to seafaring, serving on merchant ships or working around the docks. By the beginning of the nineteenth century, about twenty percent of Philadelphia's merchant seamen were black. Women, who outnumbered men, reversing a disproportion in favor of men during slavery, worked primarily as domestics. Although most blacks worked as common laborers of one sort or another, some set up small business enterprises or engaged in professional activities. The 1795 city directory listed black grocers, fruiterers, shopkeepers, and milkmen, among others. There were also a few artisans practicing shipbuilding, metalworking, leather working, and other crafts.

The black situation was not idyllic, however, for many worked as servants in white households, much as they had in slavery. This meant, as in slavery, a fractured family life, because few white owners or employers were prepared to keep a whole black family together under one roof. They might be spread throughout the city, or even outside it. Many black youths were indentured—bound by contract to serve others for a specified number of years. This was a practice common with white children as well, but white females normally served until age eighteen and white males until twenty-one, whereas blacks usually served until twenty-eight. These were their most productive years in a lifespan that did not usually extend much past forty.

One of the first tasks of freed blacks, therefore, was to claim an independent residence. In view of their economic circumstances, this was not always easy, and the move out of white households and into stable two-parent family groupings proceeded by stages. Along the way, blacks sometimes formed extended families, locating several generations under one roof, or made other creative household arrangements in order to remove themselves sooner from the constraints of life in white homes. In Boston, where slavery ended soonest, a majority of blacks lived in two-parent households as early as 1790, and the percentage increased in the nineteenth century. This was also true in New York City at the same date, but its proportion decreased in the following decades as a result of the expansion of slavery in the city in the 1790s. In Philadelphia, where the emancipation process was slower than in Boston, close to half of blacks lived in two-parent households in 1790 and the process of independent family formation speeded up thereafter. Blacks moved rapidly after slavery to secure a degree of social and cultural independence based on strong families and their own religious outlook.

Perhaps Philadelphia blacks developed confidence in America, despite discrimination, because of their large and growing community and because of significant support from whites. Their most dedicated supporter, Anthony Benezet, died in 1784. But his place was taken somewhat by the physician Benjamin Rush, who gave active backing to the African church project and to other issues of concern to blacks. In addition, the Pennsylvania Society for the Abolition of Slavery was revived in 1784. It found renewed work in preventing the sale or kidnapping of bondspeople to the South, in monitoring other evasions of the manumission law, and in aiding blacks to get employment. The aged Benjamin Franklin lent his prestige by becoming president of the society.

The smaller black population in New England, not quite submerged in a sea of whites, apparently lacked similar support and showed signs of having greater disappointment in their white neighbors. Certainly the nature of repressive laws there suggests that conclusion. The experience of Phillis Wheatley also supports it. Despite her celebrity status, she was never able to raise a sufficient number of subscriptions in Boston to permit publication of a second volume of her work. She was reduced, instead, to labor outside her home, doing the kind of difficult domestic work in freedom that she was spared in slavery.

The domestic chores of housecleaning, washing, sewing, and cooking, the common lot of black women of the era, were strenuous tasks in the eighteenth century, and overtaxing to someone of Wheatley's delicate physique. She was probably also undernourished, for her marriage to free black John Peters in 1778 was not entirely successful. He was apparently overproud and unable to provide for her as well as she could have wished. She was reported at one stage to be living in abject poverty. None of her three children survived. She was only thirty-one years old when she died at the end of 1784.

While Northern blacks moved toward greater self-definition, southern blacks did the same. They operated under greater restraints than simple racism, however, for most were still enslaved. Although the religious revivals of the Great Awakening left the mass of slaves unaffected, they appealed to blacks nevertheless. African Americans responded particularly to the doctrine resolved by a Baptist committee in 1789 that slavery was "a violent deprivation of the rights of nature, and inconsistent with a republican government." By the 1770s, a number of blacks had been converted by Baptist or Methodist preachers and felt the call to go out on their own. If they were slaves, they sometimes left without permission, as runaway ads in newspapers testify. Such men were involved in the first black Baptist church in America developed independently of a white one, in Silver Bluff, South Carolina, between 1773 and 1775. From this region, including nearby Savannah, Georgia, came a band of black Baptists who went on to found separate black churches in various parts of the world.

George Liele has been described as the Southern (and Baptist) counterpart of Richard Allen and as the energy behind the early black churches in Georgia and South Carolina. Born in Virginia, he accompanied his master to Savannah, Georgia. His master was a loyalist who freed Liele before his death in British service in 1778. Liele, meanwhile, preached to slaves on plantations along the Savannah River and moved into the city of Savannah after his master's demise. There he continued to preach to slaves and he brought the future preacher Andrew Bryan to the faith. Liele left with the British, however, unsure of his free status without their protection, and introduced the Baptist church to Jamaica.

Still a slave, Andrew Bryan refused to depart with the others who cast their lot with the English; he ministered to a small congregation in Savannah instead. In the period of unrest at the end of the war, however, they were persecuted by anxious whites and Bryan had to suffer for his faith. He and his brother "were twice imprisoned, and about fifty were severely whipped, particularly *Andrew, who was cut, and bled abundantly,*" a fellow minister revealed in a letter. In 1788 Bryan was formally licensed to preach, eventually gained his freedom, and by the turn of the century was able to report that the First African Baptist Church of Savannah met "with the approbation and encouragement of many of the white people." The response to his message was so great that two other black Baptist churches soon formed in the city. In 1793, meanwhile, the Silver Bluff church, having outgrown its location, moved twelve miles away to Augusta, Georgia, to form the First African Baptist Church under one of the original founders, Jesse Galpin.

Slaves who preached, and the bound congregations to whom they ministered, had to operate within limitations set by their masters. Like the Methodists, many early Baptist congregations were integrated, even though blacks were normally restricted to a section of their own in the back or balcony. In rural areas, slaves often accompanied their masters to church. Blacks could preach to whites, and vice versa, but blacks usually preached to their own. Though many black churches came into being as a result of independent black activity, others were offshoots of white congregations. Unlike in the North, the move had to be one with which white people agreed, for the activities of enslaved blacks were strictly controlled. Frequently the move to separate came from white people, once the black membership became too large. Blacks might continue to operate on their own, much as they had before, under either a black or white minister, though most preferred a person of their own color, for the message in its subtleties and the preaching style would differ. They would remain under the watchful eye of whites in any case.

Baptist principles of congregational independence made this arrangement easier. Unlike the Methodists, Baptist churches were less subject to the control of a national church organization. They seemed more willing to accept black preachers and allowed more individual freedom. Although they possessed the same beliefs in the equality of all persons as the Methodists did, their lack of structure before the nineteenth century permitted individuals to accommodate a pro-slavery message earlier than the Methodists, without it having the same import. While Methodist convocations adopted anti-slavery policies several times in the 1780s, they had to back off because of popular opposition. Baptist declarations of that kind had not the same organizational support because the congregations were not so tightly bound together or used to taking orders from a national authority. There was no organizational decision on the matter. This permitted individual congregations to adjust to local sentiment without compromising a national decision or obligating other localities. In any case, blacks were early attracted to the denomination, which seemed to have the greatest appeal.

Things changed in the nineteenth century, when the Baptists, too, desired greater conformity among their members, and, under pressure from secular authorities, withdrew the freedom granted Southern black Baptists. In the meantime, blacks often had significant leeway in choosing their ministers, church officers, and even in sending representatives to regional Baptist associations. The transition can be seen, particularly in the hardening of racial lines, in two decisions of the Baptist Association of Portsmouth, Virginia. In 1794 the association answered the question "Is it agreeable to the Word of God to send a free black man a delegate to the Ass'n?" in the affirmative: "We can see nothing wrong in this. A church may send any one it chooses." In 1828, it decided that "whereas the constitution of independent and colored churches, in this state, and their representation in this body, involves a point of great delicacy," black churches could only be represented by whites.

Southern (and Northern) black Methodists had to fight to obtain the sort of independence enjoyed by Southern black Baptists. The Methodists' personal slights pushed them toward it, however, and blacks in Baltimore, under Daniel Coker, in

Wilmington, Delaware, under Peter Spencer, and in other locations departed congregations dominated by white Methodists and eventually joined with Richard Allen to form the African Methodist denomination or made other provisions. A harbinger of more repressive times can be found in the special edition of the Church's *Discipline* for Southern states in 1804 and 1808 (containing religious doctrines and beliefs), which omitted any reference to resolutions on slavery. Even Methodist Bishop Francis Asbury, an early leader of the church who abhorred slavery, eventually gave way before pro-slavery forces and wrote in his journal that it was more important to save the African's soul than to free his body. But not many African Americans were prepared to accept that priority. Increasingly, in the nineteenth century, they decided to worship apart from their white brethren.

That was true, of course, when they engaged in Christian worship at all. For important as Christianity was in fostering a will toward independence among blacks, in providing a gauge and a focus for greater self-assertion and self-reliance, in providing solace during times of deprivation, the likelihood is that most blacks were barely touched by it. One historian argues, in fact, that the slaves' religious practices were overwhelmingly more African than Christian. If slave preachers could not relate to those in a plantation community who knew little or nothing about Christianity, he suggests, they could not minister to most of their people. He and other historians push this argument into the nineteenth century. But it has particular relevance for the eighteenth century, and especially in the postrevolutionary period, for the number of Africans imported into South Carolina and Georgia exceeded 100,000 before the overseas slave trade finally ended in 1808. These imports brought renewed contact with Africa. But coastal South Carolina and Georgia had maintained a greater African presence than the Chesapeake had anyway, and African-American Christianity, there and elsewhere, was greatly influenced by African beliefs and attitudes. Most prominent is the "ring shout," a counterclockwise circular dance motion accompanied by singing and hand clapping, which is a basic feature of low-country Christianity in South Carolina and Georgia and is argued by several scholars to be essentially African. Yet Christianity developed an increasing appeal to African Americans in the period just before and after the Revolution and its influence was to grow.

Paul Cuffee and the Failure of Freedom

Despite the religious and, in the Upper South, secular feeling of generosity on the part of whites that made life more tolerable for Southern blacks in the decade after the American Revolution, planters renewed their commitment to black bondage. In most cases, indeed, it scarcely slackened. Although the Lower South was not as affected by the abolitionist trend of the times as regions farther north, it was not completely exempt either. The military proposals of John Laurens, to arm slaves and free them at the war's conclusion, were just one example. A few

This 1812 engraving shows Captain Paul Cuffe, a New England merchant-sailor who developed trading interests in Africa and transported black colonists there in 1815.

slaveowners were even moved to manumission. South Carolinian John Peronneau freed his slave Romeo in 1781 "in consequence of my aversion to and abhorrence of Slavery which natural Religion and common sense do equally condemn."

But most Southern whites did not go that far. A Georgia planter readily admitted that racial slavery was "subversive of every idea of moral as well as political justice." He was not prepared to concede that emancipation was the answer, however; rather, he believed that American slaves were better off than European peasants. One historian of South Carolina argues, in fact, that low-country planters felt a need to justify slavery even before the Revolution, and that this need developed out of an increased recognition of their slaves' humanity. This realization arose partly from the slaves' development of a creole, or American, culture in the second half of the eighteenth century. "Creole" originally referred to Europeans born in the New World but now extends to other peoples and things brought to life in the Americas, including culture—for example, language, religion, and new tastes in food. Despite the continued importance of the slave trade to low-country planters, by 1760 less than half of South Carolina's slave population was African-born. Creole slaves were closer to their masters in culture and, unlike Africans, were better able to impress upon European-centered white people that they were human beings.

In both regions of the South, a relatively stable, family-based creole slave society had developed by 1770. In both regions, the slave population had begun to reproduce itself naturally, a clear advantage for planters who maintained family units on their estates. Natural reproduction was greater and more important in the larger and older slave society in the Chesapeake, but its value was also acknowledged farther south. War disrupted this not quite idyllic setting. Slaves were moved and families and communities torn asunder. This process continued in the war's aftermath and was accelerated by economic change.

Cotton was the crop that dominated the plantation economy of the nineteenth-century South—the South of myth and legend. Eli Whitney's improved cotton gin of 1793, which more easily separated the seeds from the strands of cotton, and is often blamed for perpetuating slavery in a region that expected rapidly to eradicate it, has been unfairly charged. The regions into which cotton expanded so quickly had been preparing for years, and frontier planters needed only the right circumstances to seize their expected promise. But Eli Whitney did make that expansion more certain. Slaves who could clean one pound of cotton in a day without Whitney's invention could prepare fifty pounds with it. The economic possibilities were obvious; production that had formerly been confined to home use could now be grown for commercial export.

In the Lower South, slaves produced cotton independently during the unrest and disorder of revolution and planters made concessions to ensure that they remained on the plantation. Both needed a domestic source of cloth, because imports of all kinds were cut off by British military activity. There was likewise more production of food crops for local consumption than before the war. For planters, the production of cotton and the wearing of local homespun woven from it became a patriotic duty, symbolic of their ability to do without British finery.

But slaves who did not leave the plantation had a personal interest in this cultivation, too, for their well-being, perhaps even more than their masters', depended upon it. Many simply produced food and cloth for their own use. Planters were happy to leave them to their own devices, so long as they remained on the land. If slaves could extract greater leeway from their owners to grow something they needed anyway, so much the better. But, as one historian keenly advises, there was a depressing irony in this situation of wartime independence. The crop that provided slaves a temporary liberation from the master's stern gaze during the Revolution formed the links of a chain that more tightly bound their children and grandchildren.

Low-country planters continued to grow rice, both during and after the Revolution, but the industry was undergoing a transition to a new method of cultivation using the tidal flow from rivers. This process required an initial output of tremendous labor to construct embankments, dig ditches, and build "trunks" or sluices to control the flow of water onto the rice fields. It saved labor in cultivation, particularly in terms of weeding, but required considerable maintenance.

Indigo, which had supplemented rice cultivation in the colonial period, was replaced after the Revolution by cotton. As with indigo, slaves attended to cotton during the periods when the rice fields needed less attention. A long-staple variety, called sea island cotton, suitable to warm, moist conditions, grew along the Georgia–South Carolina seacoast and on islands off the coast. Short-staple varieties spread inland into the piedmont and backcountry of South Carolina and Georgia, across the dark, fertile soils of Florida, Mississippi, Alabama, and Louisiana, and up over the Appalachians and Alleghenies into Kentucky and Tennessee. They penetrated the Virginia frontier and various locations in the Chesapeake. It was the spread of these short-staple varieties that Whitney's gin aided, for the seed separated more easily from long-staple cotton.

The spread of cotton affected African-American communities all along the eastern seaboard. The greater freedom that war had brought to slaves in most regions continued for some time thereafter, though more in some places than others. In the Chesapeake Bay area, slaves experienced more mobility, greater access to freedom, and more opportunity for employment and self-improvement once freedom came. Some planters, particularly in Maryland, freed their slaves and set them up as tenants. Other recently freed blacks began a slow process of setting themselves up independently.

However, as the Chesapeake area's major crop, tobacco, decreased in price, many slaveholders decided to sell their slaves to buyers in the booming markets of the southwest, or else move there themselves with their slaves. Between 1790 and 1810, one hundred thousand slaves were moved from the Chesapeake Bay area into newly opening cotton lands in the West and Southwest. Communities were ruptured and families dissolved as slaves accompanied masters toward a white man's opportunity. In their new locales, they had to begin the painful process of reconstructing family and community in a situation not as advantageous as the ones they had left. In the new regions there were more farms than plantations, few slaves on each unit, long distances between individual landholdings, hard labor in clearing fresh land, and little chance of finding a mate. The erosion of slavery continued in Maryland but, because of cotton, many blacks born there would not stay to see it. They went west to make their masters' fortune.

The frontier clamor for cotton slaves was also met by recourse to the slave trade. At least one hundred thousand slaves were imported from Africa between 1783 and 1807, and directed to developing cotton regions. This trade entered through Savannah in the 1790s, since South Carolina had suppressed the commerce. In view of the looming constitutional prohibition of the trade, which would take effect in 1808, however, South Carolina belatedly responded to inland settlers and reopened its ports in 1803. Slavers then shifted to Charleston and landed almost ten thousand Africans a year until the final termination of the trade.

Nearly half of these slaves came from the Congo-Angola region of Central Africa, reinforcing a strain of African culture that had predominated in the first decades of the eighteenth century. People from this region had led the largest slave revolt in colonial British North America and had a reputation for possessing an aptitude for mechanical skills. Another quarter left the Senegambia area of West Africa, fortifying a cultural tradition that had been influential throughout the period. People from this region contributed to the development of South Carolina's rice industry. These new imports were going mostly to different regions than their country people who preceded them, so the cultural effect may not have been as profound as it could have been. Indeed, these Africans were moving where they most likely encountered creole slaves from the Chesapeake. Culturally different, the two groups would have had to forge a common identity as they formed a new community.

Some blacks, who had developed maroon, or runaway, communities during the war refused to give up their freedom after it, and they continued to enjoy greater liberty than a slave society could possibly permit. Thus the *Charleston Morning Post* reported in October 1786 that a group of around one hundred African Americans had established an independent settlement on an island in the Savannah River, about eighteen miles from the coast. From there they conducted periodic foraging expeditions against neighboring plantations to supplement the supplies they grew. Aside from the threat to landowners in the vicinity, their message of self-assertion was not one that planters desired to see spread. Militia forces attacked the settlement, forced the blacks to retreat, and destroyed their homes, fields, and supplies.

Most African Americans, enslaved and free, found other ways to assert their autonomy. This is easiest seen in how they named themselves. Northern blacks who won their freedom frequently took a new name. The names their owners chose from Greek or Roman history or mythology, such as Caesar, Cato, Diana, or Daphne, or from European places such as London or Hanover, were gradually replaced by English or biblical names such as James, John, Elizabeth, or Sarah. Parents with these older names did not pass them along to their children. Commonly, they rejected their previous names themselves, choosing new ones soon after emancipation. The use even of African names diminished, indicating blacks' increasing American identification.

They also took surnames, seldom memorializing past masters. Neither Richard Allen nor Absalom Jones took the names of their former owners. Those who remained in bondage in Southern states claimed the right to name their offspring. They often called their children after relatives, particularly their fathers, from whom sons and daughters might be separated. Accordingly, Thomas Jefferson's slave woman Molly, wife of Phill Waggoner, named their first two children Phill and Phyllis. If their masters insisted on calling them one thing, they might still be known as something else in the quarters, among the common folk with whom they lived and worked. There was more than one way to insist upon their humanity.

While blacks struggled to define themselves, the nation also groped toward an identity. Free blacks in Southern slave society, even more than those in free-labor Northern ones, faced an uncertain situation in a nation in flux. Racial lines were drawn, but not as inflexibly as they would become. For instance, the situation of free colored people in Charleston, often of mixed blood and tied by interest and inclination to the planter class, was not the same as that of free blacks in the Chesapeake area, who were offered little protection by prominent whites and thus fended for themselves. The status of free blacks and coloreds, or mixed-race people, in New Orleans, when it became part of the United States in 1803, was different still. In 1790 Charleston's colored elite formed the Brown Fellowship Society, a mutual benefit organization similar to those formed by Northern blacks. However, it excluded people with darker skins. New Orleans had similar associations. The various regions of the nation and the variants of black culture would move toward greater uniformity in the nineteenth century. But it would be a mistake to read the present back into the past and to assume that race relations in the eighteenth century were always worse than in the twentieth. The careers of two men, both born free, one (Benjamin Banneker) in a slave society, the other (Paul Cuffe) in one of the earliest free societies that had once tolerated slavery, demonstrate the unformed and still flexible nature of the national atmosphere.

Born in 1731, Benjamin Banneker was the grandson of European and African immigrants, an Englishwoman named Molly Welsh and the African man she bought, freed, and married, called Bannaka. Interracial marriages were illegal in the Maryland of Molly Welsh's day, and she faced the enduring threat of punishment for her transgression. Yet in her life among her husband's people in the countryside outside Baltimore she apparently was not bothered.

Benjamin, whose mother was Molly's daughter and whose father was also a freed slave, grew up in a peaceful setting. He attended a one-room schoolhouse with several white and one or two colored youngsters, taught by a Quaker schoolmaster. The school was open only in the winter, and the rest of the year he had to help his family with the farmwork—raising tobacco and corn, caring for a few cattle and chickens, working in his mother's vegetable garden or his father's orchard, hunting and fishing in nearby woods and streams, and performing other chores that any farmboy who lived in a wilderness environment might have to do. He was more lucky than most, for his parents owned the land they worked and his name was on the deed. He would inherit it. Despite the necessity for physical labor, at an early age he developed an interest in mathematics and, in view of the limitations of his schooling, was largely self-taught.

He first came to local fame when in 1753, at twenty-two years of age, he built a clock. Modeled after a watch he had borrowed, it was painstakingly constructed nearly all of wood, and illustrated an unusual mechanical genius. It operated until his death more than fifty years later.

Late in life he added to his interest in horology, the science and art of measuring time and making timepieces, an interest in astronomy. He borrowed books and instruments from a neighbor and mastered a new science. He went on to publish several popular almanacs and was appointed by Secretary of State Thomas Jefferson to help survey the federal territory for the new national capital at Washington, D.C. He worked with Andrew Ellicott, the chief surveyor, from February to April 1791. He had never before been away from his birthplace. Excited about the project though he was, he was then an old man of sixty years and unaccustomed to

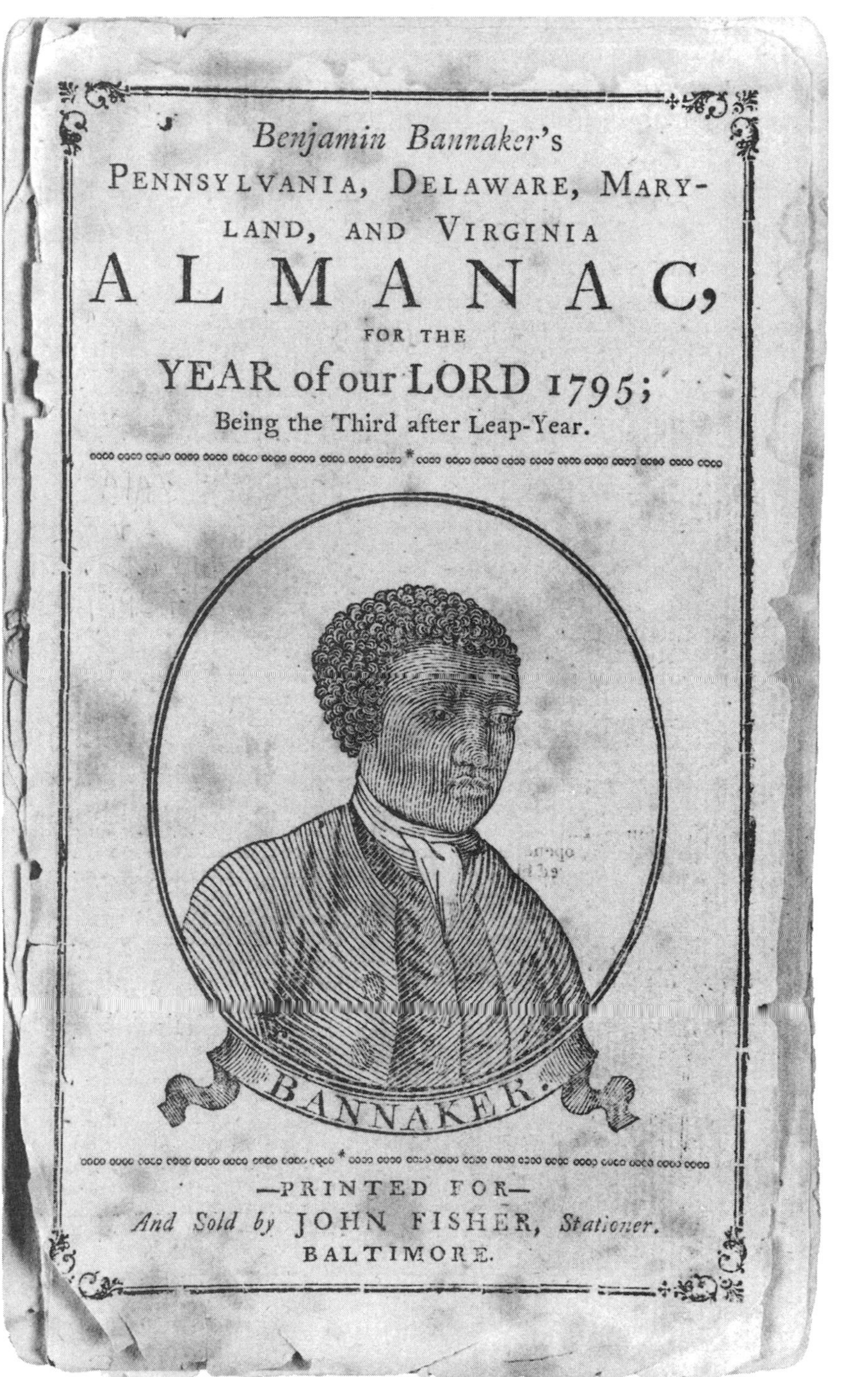
Benjamin Bannaker's
PENNSYLVANIA, DELAWARE, MARY-
LAND, AND VIRGINIA
ALMANAC,
FOR THE
YEAR of our LORD 1795;
Being the Third after Leap-Year.

BANNAKER.

—PRINTED FOR—
And Sold by JOHN FISHER, *Stationer.*
BALTIMORE.

The title page from Banneker's *Almanac*—on which his name was misspelled—from 1795. He sent a manuscript copy of his first almanac to Thomas Jefferson in 1791 in an attempt to discredit ideas about black inferiority.

the rugged discomfort of wilderness surveying. He was not unhappy to return to his farm when Ellicott secured other aid.

Born free, an owner of land, with a rudimentary education and gifted with uncommon mathematical and mechanical skill, Banneker experienced relatively little discrimination as far as we know. Nor was he much touched by the Revolutionary struggle. The region in which he lived largely escaped military conflict. His was not the typical eighteenth-century Maryland black experience any more than Phillis Wheatley represented the typical New England slave. This does not mean that he had no knowledge of America's racial divide, for he surely knew that the attention he received derived partly from his color and the assumptions people made about it. Moreover, when white engineers in the District of Columbia "overlooked" his color, as an early commentator described the scene, and invited him to eat with them, "his characteristic modesty" prompted him to decline the offer. He dined in the same tent but at a separate table. This surely tells much about developing racial customs.

Banneker, like Wheatley, was caught up in the abolitionist crusade through the continuing controversy over blacks' intellectual capacities. Accordingly, the *Georgetown Weekly Ledger* described him soon after his arrival in the Federal District as "an Ethiopian, whose abilities, as a surveyor, and an astronomer, clearly prove that Mr. Jefferson's concluding that race of men were void of mental endowments, was without foundation." If Wheatley was the rage of the pre–Revolutionary anti-slavery set, Banneker became almost as important for the post–Revolutionary generation. In some ways he was more important, for his achievements were scientific rather than literary. Of the latter there were several cases, but examples of the former were rare indeed. If blacks were to gain full rights of citizenship, it was clearly important that they exhibit a broad intellectual competence. With the coming of freedom to the North and the continuing struggle against the Atlantic traffic in slaves, postwar abolitionists sought as much evidence of black talent as they could muster.

Blacks also demonstrated organizational ability, or capabilities in financial management, but these were seldom brought forward for discussion in considering their intellect. Consequently, the business success of Paul Cuffe—a New England shipping entrepreneur—was not something that abolitionists immediately valued in championing blacks' mental equality. Indeed, if that were his only claim to fame, important though it was, he might be passed over quickly. Yet his career is a measure of what skill mixed with luck could bring about for a black man in early America and is an answer to American racism of that era. It is also a cautionary tale of how and why a black man of the time could become disillusioned with America's promise.

When Cuffe came to the attention of the Delaware Society for the Abolition of Slavery as a result of business connections, the society published a short biographical tract. The purpose of this pamphlet, which was published in 1807, was to prove that:

> with suitable culture and a fair opening for the exertion of talents, the NEGRO possesses a portion of intellect and energy by which he is enabled to form great designs, to adopt means to the end in the prosecution of them, to combat danger, to surmount difficulties; and thus to evince that, with equal advantages of education and circumstances, the Negro–race might fairly be compared with their white brethren on any part of the globe.

The society wanted Cuffe to work with Quaker-dominated international anti-slavery interests in securing black settlements in Africa and it was important for them to show that black people were capable of enterprise. People concerned in the Sierra Leone venture took especial note.

Cuffe's father, Kofi, lived in the Asante kingdom among Akan-speaking peoples on the western coast of Africa. He came to America as part of the slave traffic in 1728 when he was eleven or twelve years old. To his good fortune, he was purchased by a Quaker family, one that evidently had anti-slavery leanings, and his owner, John Slocum, freed him in 1740. In 1746 he married Ruth Moses, a Wampanoag, and eventually bought a farm on the Massachusetts coast near Martha's Vineyard. Paul was born in 1759, the seventh child and youngest son of ten children. As a farm boy, he, like Banneker, was brought up to hard work and his education was limited. He was largely self-taught but extremely shrewd. His natural charm and native intelligence made up for what he lacked in formal education.

Cuffe was thirteen years old when his father died, and he assumed part of the responsibility of supporting his mother and younger sisters. He did not see his future in farming, however, and like many New Englanders turned to the sea. His skill as a seaman together with his daring as an entrepreneur led eventually to his acquisition of a respectable fleet of ships. Some of these he built himself in his own shipyard. He achieved wealth and popularity and was the most successful black businessman in America at the turn of the nineteenth century.

Unlike Banneker, who spent most of his life near his birthplace and was consequently somewhat shielded from racial discrimination, Cuffe traveled widely, which brought him face to face with it. This was particularly the case since he frequently traveled to plantation regions. Many slave societies regarded free blacks with suspicion and unease, none more so than the United States. The divide between slave and free states, however, did not necessarily mark a division in the treatment of free blacks, and Cuffe occasionally experienced racial slights in restaurants or on public transportation in the North as well as the South. Both Maryland and Massachusetts had laws against interracial marriages in the latter half of the 1780s (though Pennsylvania did not). Both Maryland and Massachusetts had repressive legislation aimed at unfamiliar free blacks in the 1790s, though neither state strongly enforced it. Repressive laws, whether enforced or not, and racial discrimination, whether constant or not, created an environment that reminded Cuffe of his racial status.

Because of his mother and his wife, Cuffe remained aware of both his African and Native American heritages. In his protests against discriminatory taxation laws applied against him and his family in the 1770s and 1780s, therefore, he was prepared to use whatever facet of his background seemed the most favorable. In one petition he said that "we being chiefly of the African extraction" were subject to taxation without representation. In another he said that he and his brother were "Indian men and by law not subject of taxation." Increasingly, however, he identified himself with Africans, and as the nineteenth century dawned and racial attitudes hardened, his own attitudes hardened as well.

An acquaintance described Cuffe in 1806 as "averse to all mixtures," despite his own marriage across racial and ethnic lines. When his wealth and accomplishments brought white friends to his home, he served them at separate tables. He, like Banneker, "reluctantly partook of vituals with persons of other colors." The fact that this attitude developed as a result of unequal treatment is indicated by his observation to the acquaintance that "he would willingly consent to be skinned if his black could be replaced by white." He was increasingly drawn to the conclusion that black people might be better off in Africa, and he became a leading figure in nineteenth-century emigrationist projects. Although he carried a group of black people there in 1815, he never actually committed to moving to Africa himself. Certainly his wife had no interest in going, and perhaps his children did not either. Besides, whether they went there or not, many black Americans by that time looked with interest at the prospect of black nation-building much closer to home.

Haiti and the Image of Freedom

Prince Hall, the founder of African-American freemasonry, addressed his African Lodge in Cambridge, Massachusetts, in June 1797 concerning racial harassment directed at black Americans in public places in Boston. Ten years had passed since the arrival of the charter from England granting them formal recognition as a lodge, and various proposals for blacks to leave America to escape discrimination had failed. But the negative attitudes that had prevented black Masons from gaining a local charter, and caused some blacks to want to leave their homeland for an uncertain future overseas, were alive and well.

Indeed, in many areas of the United States they were stronger. The revolutionary current favorable to black freedom in the South had reversed itself and abolition had not yet succeeded in New York and New Jersey. Hall advised his brethren to be mindful of "these numerous sons and daughters of distress" yet enslaved and who, of all the downtrodden peoples on the earth, deserved their particular consideration. He also charged them to have patience and forbearance in face of the "daily insults we meet with in the streets of Boston," especially on "public days of recreation." He went on to describe vividly how envious white working men and women, some not long out of servitude themselves (for some had come indentured) and doubtless encouraged by alcoholic beverages imbibed to enliven the holiday, "shamefully abused" blacks who ventured upon the parks or public squares. "[A]t such times," he lamented, ". . . we may truly be said to carry our lives in our hands. . . . Helpless women have [had] their clothes torn from their backs." Nevertheless, Hall had hopes for change. He cast his eyes with expectation to the Caribbean where, a few years earlier, in response to revolution in France, enslaved men and women in the French Empire had staked their own claim to freedom. "[S]ix years ago, in the French West Indies," Hall related, "Nothing but the snap of the whip was heard, from morning to evening. . . . But, blessed be God, the scene is changed. They now confess that God hath no respect of persons."

At the time that Hall spoke, slavery had been abolished in the French colonies in the Caribbean, the most important of which were Saint Domingue, Guadaloupe, and Martinique. Moreover, under the French revolutionary slogan of "Liberty, Equality, and Fraternity," revolutionary patriots were attempting to construct interracial societies consistent with their beliefs. In Saint Domingue this process went farther and lasted longer than anyplace else. In 1797 the black liberator Toussaint L'Ouverture was well on the way to establishing his leadership over the colony. He had already made clear his disposition to build a society where people of all colors could live in peace and prosperity. Although his vision of interracial cooperation was ultimately to fade amid bloody strife, he led the only successful slave revolution in the history of the world. And the banner of black freedom he raised was to stand as a beacon to black men and women throughout the Americas. Its example would spur unrest and insurrection from Brazil to the United States. Its triumph would provide lingering inspiration.

Never before, not even in the ancient world, had slaves ever overthrown and restructured an entire slave society. The United States was the first nation in the Americas to achieve its independence, but Haiti was the second. And though the United States was the first to declare that all men were created equal, Haiti was the first to make that declaration a fact.

The Haitian Revolution was the third in a series of democratic revolutions that changed the way people in the Western world viewed government, society, politics, and individual freedom. The era is often called the Age of Revolution. Each was more radical and far-reaching than the previous one, and each expanded the limits of ideas expressed in the Enlightenment.

The American Revolution was the first of the three. It was conceived as a political rather than a social revolution (that is, it sought to change the government rather than the everyday lives of the people), although it laid the basis of a social revolution. Moreover, it had some immediate social consequences, including the Northern abolition of slavery.

The French Revolution was the second uprising in the Western world. It was a social as well as a political revolution, for it accomplished not just the displacement but the overturning and destruction of the French monarchy and much of the nobility and a reordering of French government and society. The most radical of its participants sought the absolute ruin of the former ruling classes. The shock waves of revolution in France extended to the colony on Saint Domingue. There it established principles of individual liberty beyond the dreams even of most of the revolutionary generation in North America, and of many in France itself.

The struggle in Saint Domingue was more bloody than even the French Revolution, because added to the conflicting outlooks and tangle of local interests was the complicating factor of race. Saint Domingue society was divided into three classes, consisting of whites, free people of color, and slaves. As in North America, and partly under American Revolutionary influence, white colonists wanted less restrictive trade regulations. They particularly wanted greater leeway to exchange their goods with New Englanders, on whom they depended for many of their supplies. They also wanted greater say in how they were governed. Revolution in France provided an opportunity to press these aims, but it also posed a threat. As much as they wanted greater freedom for themselves, they desired no change in island social structure, and in this regard, the most radical principles of the revolution stood against them. The first article of the French Declaration of the Rights of Man proclaims that "men are born and remain free and equal in their rights." This is a dangerous principle in a society based on the labor of slaves. Moreover, Saint Domingue's free people of color were subject to severe social and political discrimination and they wanted greater freedom of their own. They saw no problem with maintaining slavery so long as all free people, regardless of color, participated in the government.

The free people of color were supported in France by the Society of the Friends of the Blacks. Too many people in France and the West Indies had too great a stake in slavery and the slave trade for the Friends of the Blacks to stand much chance of succeeding immediately in abolishing these evils. They contented themselves with championing the claims to equality of colonial free people of color. Both they and their opponents saw this as the first step toward a more radical social reconstruction of the colonies. Whites in Saint Domingue therefore rejected the National Assembly's recommendation that a limited number of free coloreds be granted citizenship rights. Consequently, in 1790 the free colored people revolted. The free colored revolt was ruthlessly put down, but the whites also divided among themselves, some favoring a greater degree of local self-rule and separation from France than others. Besides, in the colony, as in France, a few people still preferred royal authority to government reform of any kind. These disputes also led to violence. The divisions among the free classes over the meaning of the revolution provided an opening for the slaves.

The slaves needed no formal declarations, either from Europe or America, to justify their claim to liberty. They greatly outnumbered the white people—indeed, all classes of free people—in Saint Domingue. The vast majority of Saint Dominguan slaves were African-born, had experienced freedom before their captivity, and knew that their subjugation rested on no firmer basis than superior arms.

Encouraged by the rumor that the king and National Assembly had decreed three days a week for them to work for themselves and the abolition of whippings, they rose up on August 22, 1791. They would not finally lay down their arms until they proclaimed Haiti an independent nation on January 1, 1804.

The man who soon came to dominate the revolution was Toussaint L'Ouverture. Born in 1744, he was forty-seven at the start of the rebellion. Of mild disposition, he had been fortunate in his master and had not suffered the severe mistreatment of some slaves. Indeed, by the time of the outbreak, he was free in all but name; aside from the duties of coachman, he lived pretty much on his own, with his wife and three boys. He was and remained a devout Catholic. He was also literate, enjoyed reading, and in letters of state composed later made frequent reference to ancient history and philosophy.

His fortunate experience was unusual for a region where the face of slavery was particularly harsh, and provided him with a distinctive outlook toward interracial cooperation that set him apart from most people on the island. As a military leader, he was beloved of his men, a strict disciplinarian but willing to share their hardships and to lead by example. Extremely brave in battle, he was wounded seventeen times. He was once struck in the mouth by a spent cannon ball but only suffered the loss of some teeth. He had a talent for organization and a genius for warfare. By 1795 he was the colony's leading general and by 1798, with the expulsion of interfering British forces, its effective leader. He defeated French, Spanish, British, and opposing local forces in their turn. He had two abiding aims: to maintain black freedom and to rebuild the island's economy. The first he could do by force of arms; the second with white expertise and cooperation and the controlled labor of free black peasants.

The United States and Great Britain viewed events in Saint Domingue with alarm. Both had slave regions to preserve from the contagion of liberty. The British attempt at conquest as part of its war against France came to naught and when they evacuated, they came to a trade arrangement with Toussaint under which they agreed to supply him in return for his promise not to spread revolution to their territories. The United States was also party to the agreement. President John Adams and the Federalist party he represented had always been pro-British in the wars between Britain and France that broke out in the wake of the French Revolution. In addition, there had always been strong commercial relations between the French West Indies and New England that continued during the slave rebellion. In the last two years before 1800 the United States and France had engaged in an unofficial naval war that prompted a momentary interruption of commerce with French colonies; but that conflict was soon settled and, in any case, the United States was unwilling to allow the British to monopolize Saint Domingue's trade.

The election of President Thomas Jefferson in 1800 changed the situation. Jefferson was a slaveholder and highly sensitive to the consequences of slave rebelliousness. Moreover, the Democratic-Republican party he led had taken the French

This picture of "Free Natives of Dominica" offers a glimpse of how some of the wealthy free people of color in St. Domingue may have looked before the Haitian Revolution.

side of the European conflict. Napoleon Bonaparte, who had come to power in France, and would soon destroy the First French Republic, wanted to end black rule in Saint Domingue. Having temporarily made peace with England in 1801, he had little difficulty convincing that nation and the United States that the eradication of black government was in their best interests. Jefferson was not convinced that Napoleon would succeed in his mission, however, and delayed withdrawing American material support from Toussaint. His decision was further slowed by the news or rumor that Louisiana, recently a colony of Spain, had been transferred to France. Jefferson, like many Americans, looked forward to American expansion into the Louisiana Territory and was convinced that no nation who held that region could long be friends with the United States. He would hedge his bets until he was sure of French intentions. Not until after France agreed to sell Louisiana to the United States in 1803 did Jefferson cease to trade with Saint Domingue.

Part of the reason for Napoleon's decision to sell had to do with the outbreak of war with Britain again and his failure, as Jefferson suspected, to succeed in his conquest of Saint Domingue. Napoleon wanted to rebuild the French Empire, which, under his plan, included restoring slavery. Saint Domingue, once the jewel of French Caribbean possessions, would be restored to its original splendor, and French Louisiana would replace the United States as a supplier of foodstuffs not grown on the island. But he calculated without taking into account the blacks' attachment to their hard-won freedom.

Although he was virtually an independent ruler, Toussaint posed as a defender of the French Republic. The National Convention's law of February 1794 that abolished slavery also made the former slaves French citizens. Toussaint was always careful in his dealings with France to operate as if under the authority of the Republic. He had even resisted British and American pressure to declare Saint Domingue independent in 1798–99 when both nations, one officially, the other unofficially, were at war with France. Conditions changed when France made peace with these English-speaking nations. Under Napoleon's leadership, France now felt strong enough to reassert its control.

Napoleon sent his brother-in-law Charles Leclerc with sixteen thousand troops in 1802 to "rid us of these gilded Africans," as he ordered, referring to Toussaint and his black generals. Once he reasserted French authority, Napoleon planned to remove and banish all black or mulatto officers over the rank of captain in order to put his colonial plan into operation more safely. He thought the colony, deprived of leadership, would keep quiet. Hoping to prevent fanatical resistance at the outset, however, he resorted to deceit and denied any intention of bringing back slavery. Toussaint was not convinced, and he and his most trusted generals Henri Christophe and Jean Jacques Dessalines resisted.

So long as he posed as a champion of the French promise of liberty, Leclerc had some success. Christophe and Dessalines defected to the French and Toussaint agreed to lay down his arms. But not all rebels surrendered and the colony was still unpacified.

In April 1802 Napoleon reopened the slave trade and nullified the decree abolishing slavery. In June he ordered Leclerc to restore slavery at his discretion. Guadaloupe's governor acted before Leclerc, and the arrival of news that slavery had been restored in Guadaloupe and Leclerc's tentative moves in that direction in Saint Domingue aroused the suspicions of more blacks about their future, and more left to join rebel bands. At the same time, Dessalines, in particular, began to play both ends against the middle and lent the rebels secret support. The betrayal of Toussaint, whom the French lured to a June meeting on the promise of protection and then arrested and sent to France, caused outrage. He was to die in prison the next year (April 7, 1803) of suffering from frigid temperatures, bad treatment, and little food. Finally, the increasing brutality of the French spurred resistance. Leclerc decided, in fact, that French control of the island would never be secure until he had destroyed all black men and women over twelve years of age.

But Leclerc, like many of his men, died of yellow fever and was succeeded in November by Count Rochambeau. He was not the best choice. For as Leclerc warned Napoleon, "Rochambeau [is] a brave soldier and a good fighter, [but he] has not an ounce of tact or policy. Furthermore, he has no moral character and is easily led." It was Rochambeau who stood with Washington at the Battle of Yorktown to receive the British surrender. The hero of white revolutionaries in America, however, was the scourge of black revolutionaries in Haiti, and if Dessalines eventually chose to ensure Haiti's future by exterminating the whites, Rochambeau led the way when he tried to ensure France's future there by exterminating the blacks.

By August 1802 the black generals who had gone over to the French began to desert. In November they held a conference, supported independence, and recognized Dessalines as leader of the resistance. According to legend, Dessalines took the French flag, ripped out the white band, and left a flag of blue and red as the national banner. In 1804, after more months of struggle, the French evacuated and the Republic of Haiti, a name derived from a Native American word for a mountainous place, was proclaimed.

From Venezuela to Virginia slaves were encouraged anew to reclaim their natural rights. The Spanish governor of Cuba informed his superiors in 1794, at the height of Jacobin radicalism, that "the rumor is too widespread that the French desire that there be no slaves" and were determined to free them. In 1795 slaves mounted uprisings under French revolutionary influence, reminiscent of Saint Domingue, in Dutch Curaçao; Coro, Venezuela; and Pointe Coupee, Louisiana.

In the United States plots and rebellions or rumors of plots and rebellions occurred along the eastern seaboard during the 1790s and later. Whites in Charleston, South Carolina, blamed a series of fires in the city on a group of "French Negroes" who "intended to make a St. Domingo business of it." The most serious

An 1805 account of the Haitian Revolution included this gruesome illustration with the caption: "Revenge taken by the black army for the cruelties practised on them by the French."

threat occurred in Richmond, Virginia, where, in 1800, the slave Gabriel planned a large-scale uprising. Born on a plantation outside the city in 1776, Gabriel was raised as a blacksmith and taught to read. He grew up in a period of revolutionary ferment and could not avoid being influenced by talk about the rights of man. As a skilled worker he was often hired out and spent much time among working-class people where blacks and whites mixed freely. He, like others, learned about the events in Saint Domingue and that was clearly one source of stimulation. He planned not a war against the whites but a war against the merchants. He expected working-class whites as well as slaves to join his rebellion and warned his followers to spare all "Quakers, the Methodists, and Frenchmen" because of "their being friendly to liberty." He planned to take Richmond and set up a new social and political order, though precisely what kind he did not say. However, he clearly envisioned personal freedom and racial and social equality.

Gabriel's conspiracy was widespread, including people in ten counties, a few whites among them. He estimated "his associates to the number of five–six hundred." While not all of these were people he could count on, at least 150 gathered for word of the outbreak. Torrential rains prevented the plan from going into effect on the night it was scheduled and the plot was discovered before it could be reorganized. Gabriel and scores of slaves were hanged and others were sold out of the state. But the governor of Virginia, James Monroe, and the vice president of the United States, Thomas Jefferson, could take little comfort in hanging revolutionaries, even black ones. "The other states and the world at large will forever condemn us," Jefferson wrote Monroe, "if we indulge a principle of revenge, or go one step beyond absolute necessity. They cannot lose sight of the rights of the two parties, and the object of the unsuccessful one."

Free blacks as well as slaves were attracted by French principles and the Haitian example of equality. Free African Americans lived in a country that boasted of its freedoms but increasingly denied them to former slaves. By the date of Haiti's independence in 1804, slavery was finally on the road to extinction in all the Northern states. At the same time, probably a larger number of slaves had been freed in the South by a master's personal act of conscience than by Northern legislative acts of emancipation. But also by that date racial lines had hardened.

In Virginia, for example, the legislature had once supported education for free blacks; in 1806 it reversed that decision and also denied them the right to carry firearms. Maryland's constitution of 1776 had made the possession of property rather than white skin the requirement for voting. In 1783 the state decided that no blacks freed after that date could vote, hold office, or testify against white people in a court of law, nor could any of their descendants. In 1810 it limited the vote to white men. In Philadelphia it had been customary for many years for black and white people to gather before Independence Hall on the Fourth of July to celebrate the birth of a new nation dedicated to freedom and opportunity. In 1805 the white people drove the black people away. Thereafter blacks approached the festival only at the risk of their lives. Throughout the nation similar events heralded a new birth of intolerance. American democracy, they said, would be limited to white people. In these circumstances Haiti stood out as a beacon of liberty to oppressed people of color all over the New World.

CHAPTER 4

Let My People Go

1804–1860

Deborah Gray White

On August 30 in the year 1800, a chilling fear spread among the white people of Henrico County, Virginia. Within a few days the fear had gripped the minds of most white Virginians. Within weeks, slaveholders as far west and south as what was then the Mississippi Territory were cautioning each other to beware of suspicious behavior on the part of blacks. On their tongues was the name Gabriel Prosser; in their minds were thoughts of what might have happened if Prosser had succeeded in leading Virginia slaves in revolt against slavery.

Prosser, his wife, Nanny, and his two brothers, Martin and Solomon, were a slaveholder's nightmare. Born into slavery, they declared themselves fit for freedom. They decided not only that they would be free but that all slaves should be free. Together they plotted to lead the slaves of the Richmond area in revolt against the city. Their plan was to capture the arsenal and, once supplied with weapons, to take over Richmond and then other cities in the state. Virginia, it was planned, would become a free state, a black state, a homeland for those unfit for slavery.

But Prosser never got a chance to put his plan into action. On the night of the scheduled attack on Richmond, a terrible storm washed out the bridges and roads to the city. Prosser had to postpone his rebellion, and the delay gave someone time to betray him and expose the plan. All who conspired in the revolt were captured and put to death. Gabriel was among the last to be captured, tried, and hanged.

He was, however, one of the first people in the nineteenth century to struggle in the name of freedom. And this is really the theme of this period of African-American history: the fight against slavery, the struggle to be free American citizens, and resistance, despite incredible odds, to maintain human dignity in the face of overwhelming inhumanity. The chance that the African Americans would succeed was small. The odds against it being a bloodless struggle were overwhelming. And those odds increased when cotton became this country's principal export crop, after Eli Whitney's cotton gin made the production of hearty short-staple cotton profitable.

By making cotton a profitable crop for Southern farmers, the cotton gin increased the demand for slaves and changed the course of history for black Americans.

Short-staple cotton was in demand throughout the world, especially in England, where textile manufacturers never seemed to get enough. It was not long before cotton became the principal cash crop of the South and of the nation. In 1790 the South produced only 3,135 bales of cotton. By 1800 this figure had grown to 73,145 bales; by 1820 output amounted to 334,378 bales, accounting for more than half of the nation's agricultural exports. On the eve of the Civil War, production peaked at

4.8 million bales. If ever circumstances conspired against a people, it was the coming together of the cotton gin, short-staple cotton, fertile lands, and world demand. Once this happened, slaves who might have been set free by debt and conscience-ridden Chesapeake planters were instead sold to the planters of the cotton-growing states of the Lower South. Cotton sealed the fate of slaves and slavery.

It seemed as though Gabriel Prosser knew this. Like so many other blacks, he probably saw slaveholders close down their Virginia tobacco farms and plantations and head with their slaves south and west toward the fertile black soil of the soon-to-be cotton belt. Like others, he no doubt winced at the sight of chained slaves heading out of the declining economies of Virginia, Maryland, and South Carolina to the booming areas of Alabama, Mississippi, Louisiana, Arkansas, and Texas. In 1800 these areas were not even states. Texas, in fact, was still part of Mexico. These places were not uninhabited, but were home to five Native American tribes, the Creeks, Choctaws, Seminoles, Chickasaws, and Cherokees. No matter, though. The certain wealth that cotton brought ensured that these areas would soon be flooded with white settlers who would see to it that the land became theirs. They would turn the territories into states and in the process transform the very nature of slavery.

Essential to the transformation was the domestic slave trade. Before 1800 a slave stood some chance of obtaining his or her freedom, either through self-purchase, meritorious service, or simply through the good will of a master or mistress; after 1800 the increased profitability of slavery made manumission for an individual slave less likely. Once cotton gave slavery a new lease on life, slaves who were of no use in the Upper South were not set free, but sold to the Lower South. This meant that a good many of the slaves born in Virginia, Maryland, or South Carolina were likely to die in Mississippi, Alabama, or Louisiana. The domestic trade established the means of getting them there. At the same time that slaves lived in fear of having their families torn apart and being "sold down the river," domestic slave traders calculated just how much able-bodied field hands, especially those between the ages of fifteen and twenty-five, sold for in the new markets.

The sale and transportation of black people within the United States thus became big business. What had once taken place mostly on the African continent—the theft of people, the rending of families—now took place with vulgar regularity before the eyes and ears of American whites and blacks. From Virginia alone, an estimated three hundred thousand slaves were transported south for sale between 1830 and 1860. As the slave pens sprung up, so too did the sights and sounds of human misery. Within view of the nation's capitol were slave pens that, as kidnapped slave Solomon Northup described them, were constructed so that "the outside world could never see the human cattle that were herded there." Within the walls of the pens, in open-air dirt yards, and on the auction blocks, slave husbands and wives were separated from each other, parents were parted from their children, and infants were torn from their mothers' breasts. Free blacks, too, feared the trade, for like Northup they could be, and were, stolen by unscrupulous traders anxious to make money by any means. Blacks, who once had hoped that the constitutional provision for the ending of the slave trade in 1808 would put slavery on the road to extinction, now knew that slavery was not about to die.

Free black men and women, like Philadelphia sailmaker James Forten or abolitionist Maria Stewart, were always an anomaly in a society where dark skin color was a badge of bondage, but they became even more insecure with the transformation of slavery. First and foremost, the newly revitalized institution of slavery decreased their numbers. This meant that the free black population would always remain small, with limited ability to affect the course of slavery. Free blacks always had to protect themselves against kidnappers. Those who made up the small communities of southern free blacks had to keep their free papers close or else be mistaken for slaves. In both the North and South free blacks found it beneficial to have white friends who could testify on their behalf should they be mistaken as slaves. The long and the short of it was that the transformation of slavery put free blacks at risk.

What it did to those in bondage was much worse. Their loss was very personal, because throughout the Upper South their families were torn apart. Whites who migrated to the Lower South went in family groups. Those who did not were usually single men who chose to seek their fortune in the new area. Slaves had no choice. They were taken or sold against their will, forced to leave family, friends, and all that was familiar. Lost to each other forever, family members separated by hundreds of miles suffered tremendous grief.

By the time cotton production began to soar in the states of the Lower South, Virginia, Maryland, North Carolina, and South Carolina were considered "old" states. The land had long been cleared of brush and trees, farms and plantations had already been built, and fields had been readied for crops. Roads made transportation and communication easy, and cities made commercial and cultural exchange possible.

The Lower South was not so "civilized." All the work that had been done in the Upper South had to be repeated here. It was the new frontier, and as on all frontiers the work was more backbreaking. To Adeline Cunningham, an ex-slave from Texas, everything was hard. As she put it: "Dey was rough people and dey treat ev'ry body rough." Evidence of rough treatment could be found in the slaves' birth and death rates. Compared with African Americans in other regions in the United States, blacks in the Lower South did not live as long nor have as many children.

And yet, for all of the terrible changes that took place in the first few decades of the nineteenth century, the overall condition of the average slave actually improved. This is one of the great paradoxes of the history of bondage in America. As slavery became more entrenched, as more families were separated and freedom became less attainable, it actually got better in terms of physical treatment. In the nineteenth century there were far less brandings that marked slaves as personal property. Limb amputations for theft and running away were curtailed and disabling whippings and murder occurred less frequently. Work was still backbreaking and endless, punishment was still certain, but more attention was paid to diet, slaves were given more personal time, and marital life was encouraged.

The reasons for these seemingly contrary occurrences are easy to understand. They were the consequence of the closing of the international slave trade at the very time that cotton made slavery profitable. Once it was no longer possible to bring slaves from Africa, slaveholders were forced to treat the slaves they had better. They needed slaves for work, and so they needed to keep the slaves they had healthy and productive—and they needed those slaves to reproduce.

This need resulted in better material conditions for African Americans held in bondage. Even given the severe conditions on the frontier, in comparison with Africans held in slavery in Brazil, Cuba, and Puerto Rico, American slaves lived longer. Of critical importance was the high birthrate in the United States. The better living conditions that caused the higher fertility rates developed out of white greed and intense disregard for African-American humanity—negative qualities, but ones that helped the African-American community grow. Only here was the ratio of slave men to women relatively equal, and only here did families develop. Only here did this result in the creation of what has been termed "the slave community."

The lives of black Americans, however, compared to that of other Americans, was hard, intolerable, and unprotected. Everything about slavery went against every principle upon which the nation was founded. In slavery there was no liberty, no equality, no democracy. It therefore needed justification. A reason had to be found to explain why slavery existed in the nation that was the most free in the world. A reason was needed to excuse the South and ease the conscience of the individual slaveholder.

In the pro-slavery argument was every excuse upon which the South built its institution. At its center was denial of the worth of the African American. Blacks, the argument went, were not prepared for freedom. They were childlike, in need of direction. They were lazy people who would not work unless forced to. They were cursed by God, and slavery was God's punishment. They were, some insisted, so unlike whites that they were a different species. In short, the pro-slavery argument turned slavery into something that at its worst was a necessary evil, and at its best a positive good.

Slavery was good for the South, good for black people, and good for the nation, or so the argument went. William Harper, chancellor of the University of South Carolina, declared that blacks "are undergoing the very best education which it is possible to give. They are in the course of being taught habits of regular and patient industry, and this is the first lesson that is required."

Like Harper, pro-slavery writers generally overlooked or denied the brutality of slavery. Most insisted that cruelty occurred only in the rarest of instances. Most

THE NEGRO IN HIS OWN COUNTRY.

THE NEGRO IN AMERICA.

Two engravings from the *Bible Defence of Slavery* (1853). Many Southern slave owners believed that blacks benefited from slavery.

also believed that their slaves lived better than the average industrial worker, including those in the Northern United States. Factory owners, it was argued, cared nothing for their laborers. In contrast to Northern and European "wage slaves" who were worked until they were of no use to the company, after which they were fired to fend for themselves, Southern slaves received free food, clothing, housing, and medical care for life. A typical opinion on this matter was expressed by

Virginia Baptist minister Thorton Springfellow. Like most slaveholders, he believed that the slaves' "condition . . . is now better than that of any equal number of laborers on earth, and is daily improving."

Obviously, Gabriel Prosser and his followers thought differently. To them slavery was not a kind and caring institution but a malicious one that robbed them of their freedom. Their feelings were shared by both free and enslaved African Americans, all of whom struggled in one way or another against slavery, all of whom at one time or another raised the plaintive cry: "Let my people go."

What Slavery Was

In the South, before the Civil War, the year began the same way as it ended—with work in cotton. During January and February slaves finished ginning and pressing cotton, and hauled it in wagons to the point of shipment. In March and April they were ready to start planting again. It took at least three slaves to plant a row of cotton. One slave drove a mule and plowed through the dirt to break the land into a row. A young slave came behind dropping the seed into the ground, followed by another slave with another mule-drawn plow, covering up the seed. Between April and August, the cotton was plowed and hoed by slaves, first to make sure that there was only one stalk of cotton to what was called a hill, then to keep the land free of weeds and grass. In late August, slaves began the cotton-picking season. Unmercifully long, it lasted through January of the next year.

Slaves who cultivated rice, tobacco, hemp, or sugar had a similar year-round routine, and like those who worked in cotton, their work did not end with the sale of the crop. There were hogs to kill, and then the meat had to be cut and salted. New land was cleared. Ditches were dug, cleaned, and repaired. Fences were built and under constant repair, wood was cut and hauled, and vegetable gardens were cultivated. On top of all this was the cultivation of corn, a crop that needed extensive hoeing, plowing, and harvesting just like the cash crop.

The slaves' day did not end when fieldwork was done. At night men cut wood while women prepared meals, spun thread, wove cloth, and made clothes. On Saturday afternoons men often trapped while women washed clothes, made candles and soap, and helped the men tend the garden plots where they grew the few vegetables they ate.

Slaves whose chores were in the master's house worked as much as field hands. Besides taking care of their own families, and doing their cooking, cleaning, sewing, and washing, they did all of the domestic tasks, day and night, for the slave master's family.

For the slave this added up to endless work. But that is what slavery was, a system of forced labor in which the African American worked without pay for someone else's profit. Everything else derived from slavery was secondary to this central point. For instance, this system of forced labor provided slaveholders with the wealth and prestige that they needed to dominate southern politics and social relations. Further, slavery organized the races not only to separate blacks and whites, but to give all whites status simply because they were white, and to deny status to all blacks simply because they were black. An example of how inhumane one group of people could be to another, slavery was also one of the main causes of the Civil War, the bloodiest conflict ever fought on American soil.

As a system of labor that exploited black work, slavery usually benefited a white man, but sometimes the slave master was a white woman, a Native American, or rarely, a black man or woman. Ultimately, the nation prospered from this exploitation, because as the South grew rich off the cultivation of cash crops, so did the country as a whole. The losers were the African Americans whose lives were organized around endless work; the rewards always went to someone else.

Wherever one went in the South between 1800 and 1860 one could expect to see slaves doing some kind of work. They worked as lumberjacks and turpentine producers in the forests of the Carolinas and Georgia. In Virginia and Kentucky, slaves worked in the gold, coal, and salt mines. On the Mississippi River steamboats, they worked as deckhands and boiler stokers. In Georgia and Louisiana, they worked as textile laborers. Slave labor was so profitable that in 1847 the owners of the Tredegar Iron Works in Richmond, Virginia, shifted from using white laborers to slave labor. In addition to serving as factory laborers, slaves also made up a significant portion of the South's skilled artisans—carpenters, coopers, blacksmiths, silversmiths, and the like.

However, most of the four million African Americans who were enslaved in 1860 worked in the fields of the farms and plantations of the South. They worked on an average day fourteen hours in the summer and ten hours in the winter. During harvest time slaves often worked eighteen-hour days in sun that was piercing, heat that was sweltering.

Needless to say, their work was backbreaking. The average slave worked in cotton production, and during harvest season was expected to pick about 130 to 150 pounds of cotton per day. Work in sugar and rice was equally hard, if not harder. Both crops demanded constant cultivation and the digging of drainage ditches in snake-infested fields. At harvest time on the sugar plantations, slaves had to cut, strip, and carry cane to the sugar house for boiling. This was extremely strenuous work. Rice cultivation was even more miserable. Since rice is grown under water, slaves spent long hours standing in water up to their knees.

With so much wealth riding on it, slave work was hardly done haphazardly. On the contrary, it was carefully organized so that slaves worked either in gangs or according to tasks. Slave work gangs usually did as much work as the fastest worker could do. The task system provided greater flexibility, and although assignments were as taxing as those done by gangs, when a slave or a group of slaves finished the assigned task, they could quit work for the day. Unlike the gang system, in which men and women usually worked in separate groups, tasks were often assigned to a family.

A white woman whips a slave, probably a house servant. For slaves, violent attacks could come from any direction, and at any time.

Slaves who worked in the house had a totally different regimen, one that was physically easier but mentally taxing. Women predominated in the house, and like male slave artisans, they did work that allowed for more creativity and self-direction than the work done by field hands. Working indoors, they cooked, cleaned, did laundry, sewed, and cared for infants. Although they could count on better food and clothing than their counterparts in the field, they were under closer supervision, were on call both day and night, and were more often involved in personality conflicts with the white family. As put by one house servant, "We were constantly exposed to the whims and passions of every member of the family." This meant everything from assignment to petty jobs to insults, spontaneous angry whippings, and sexual assaults.

Although house servants were under the closest surveillance, compared to slaves in other parts of the Americas all slaves in the United States were relatively closely supervised. Unlike in Caribbean slave societies or in Latin America, slaves, slaveholders, and overseers in the United States lived in very close proximity to each other. In Jamaica, for instance, one-third of all slaves lived on estates with two hundred slaves or more, and three-quarters of all slaves lived on holdings of at least fifty. Such large numbers of bondsmen made close supervision of slave life and work impossible.

In the United States, by contrast, such large plantations were rare. Only one-quarter of all slaves lived on plantations with more than fifty slaves. Since most lived on holdings of ten to forty-nine slaves, and about one-quarter lived on very small holdings of one to nine slaves, slave work and life was constantly monitored and supervised so that masters could reap every bit of profit to which they thought they were entitled.

Of course, slave masters like to think that slaves were happiest when they were at work. Some even made this claim as part of the pro-slavery argument. But most slaveholders understood that it was the threat of physical punishment that kept slaves hard at their jobs. In fact, the submission of most slaves was never perfect, and they could seldom do as much work as fast as the owners demanded. This is one reason why slaves were whipped: to get them to work harder, faster. This was certainly the case on Edwin Eppes's Louisiana plantation, where the end of the cotton-picking day brought fear instead of relief. At sundown the cotton was weighed, and no matter how much cotton they had picked, the slaves carried their cotton to the gin house in fear. As told by kidnapped slave Solomon Northup, "If it falls short in weight—if he has not performed the full task appointed him, he knows that he must suffer. And if he has exceeded it by ten or twenty pounds, in all probability his master will measure the next day's task accordingly. So whether he has too little or too much, his approach to the gin-house is always with fear and trembling. . . . After weighing, follow the whippings."

On antebellum Southern plantations whipping and work went hand in hand. For instance, on one Alabama estate, women who had just given birth to infants and were still confined to the slave cabins had to spin thread. According to an ex-slave named Cato, "If they did not spin seven or eight cuts a day they got a whipping."

Overseers' and drivers' reports tell the same gruesome story. These black and white men who worked for slaveholders had the prime responsibility for the production of the crop. White overseers attended to the overall day-to-day and season-to-season strategy of plantation work, and black drivers were on-the-spot disciplinarians who made sure the work got done. Charged with managing slaves to ensure that the plantation turned a profit, and faced with the loss of their position if it did not, both overseer and driver used any means necessary to make slaves work as hard as possible. This was especially true on plantations where the owners were absent. Without the supervision of slaveholders, who were obviously more interested than their managers in protecting their investment in the slaves, overseers and drivers could and often did use as much force as they wanted. This disturbed those who were vigorous supporters of slavery. Pro-slavery Southerner Daniel R. Hundley admired and defended the South's institutions. Nevertheless, he admitted that "the overseers on many southern plantations are cruel and unmercifully severe."

Even those overseers and drivers not considered especially brutal revealed the inherent violence of the system. For instance, in one of his weekly reports Robert Allston's overseer casually noted that he had "flogged for hoeing corn bad Fanny twelve lashes, Sylvia twelve, Monday twelve, Phoebee twelve, Susanna twelve, Salina twelve, Celia twelve, Iris twelve." George Skipwith, a black driver for John Hartwell Cocke, a Virginia planter, was equally liberal with the whip. In 1847 he reported to his master that several slaves who worked under him "at a reasonable days work" should have plowed seven acres apiece but had only done one and a half. Therefore, without a thought of the unreasonableness of his demands, and without sympathy for those of his own race, Skipwith reported, "I gave then ten lick a peace upon their skins [and] I gave Julyann eight or ten licks for misplacing her hoe."

That Skipwith was black and that he wielded the whip as readily as any white man should come as no surprise. It was to the slaveholders' advantage to allow blacks a measure of supervision over some of the day-to-day work. Not only could overseers not be everywhere at once, but their tenure on a particular plantation was often short-term. In contrast, as a slave, and a valued one at that, the driver's service was perpetual, and because it was, he provided continuity that made for the smooth running of the plantation. Since drivers lived with the slaves, their supervisory role extended into the after-work hours, which were spent away from white overseers. In fact, it was this familiarity with the slaves that made the drivers so necessary. Although it was illegal, some masters never even hired white overseers, but relied on the driver, a man who usually knew as much, if not more, about the daily management of a plantation.

Like overseers, drivers came with all kinds of temperaments and skills. Some were particularly cruel and mean. They raped women and used their power to prey on their fellow bondsmen. Such was the driver remembered by Jane Johnson, a former South Carolina slave. According to her, the driver was "de meanest man, white or black." Other drivers, though, used skillful methods of leadership to get their way. They used the whip only when necessary. They mediated disputes between slaves and acted as their representative to the master. They earned the respect of their fellow slaves and therefore their compliance. Such was the driver remembered by West Turner of Virginia. This driver whipped hard only when the master was looking. At other times "he never would beat dem slaves," but tie them up and pretend to beat them.

However they accomplished their jobs, drivers were part and parcel of the system that not only got maximum work out of the slave but also ensured "perfect submission." Indeed, slaveholders could command a slave's labor only if they could minimize the slave's resistance to their authority. Resistance, no matter how slight, was rightfully perceived as a reflection of independence. Since independence was clearly incompatible with slavery, all behavior on the part of the slave that suggested even a hint of self-determination had to be squelched. Dependence had to be instilled. Slaves who showed too much self-direction were deemed rebellious and judged dangerous. Punishment, therefore, served the purpose of making slaves work, but it also functioned to awe the slave with a sense of the master's power. And power is what the master used to make the slave stand in fear.

The slaveholder and his family demonstrated their power in a variety of ways. To begin with, they always made the slave show deference, not just to them but to all white people. Slaves had to bow in the presence of whites, they had to give way to whites walking in their path, and they were subject to whippings given by white children. When they approached the overseer or the master they had to show humility. On Charles Ball's plantation the slaves, according to one of Ball's former slaves, "were always obliged to approach the door of the mansion, in the most humble and supplicating manner, with our hats in our hands, and the most subdued and beseeching language in our mouths."

Hand in hand with humility went cheerfulness. Slaveholders feared the rebelliousness of slaves who showed dissatisfaction, and therefore did not tolerate sullen or sorrowful moods. Former slave Henry Watson noted that "the slaveholder watches every move of the slave, and if he is downcast or sad,—in fact, if they are in any mood but laughing and singing, and manifesting symptoms of perfect content at heart,—they are said to have the devil in them."

The power to make slaves work and to show deference and false happiness was granted to slaveholders by state and city legislatures through statutes called slave codes. Historians debate the protections afforded blacks by slave laws, but it is clear that throughout the South the legal system was designed to protect the interests of white slave owners. Slavery differed as one went from one region of the South to another, from one crop to another, even from one master to another. What gave the system its uniformity, however, was the consistency of social thought on the matter of slaveholder power. Manifested throughout the South in the slave codes, the white South's thinking about slavery left the enslaved no legal means to challenge actions committed against them in violation of the law.

The Louisiana slave code was typical of other state and city codes. The very first provision stated that the slave "owes to his master, and to his family, a respect without bounds, and an absolute obedience." The code defined slaves as property that could be "seized and sold as real estate." Most of the provisions stated what slaves were prohibited from doing. For instance, slaves could not travel without a pass, nor assemble in groups. They were prohibited from buying and selling any kind of goods and they could not carry arms, nor ride horses without the permission of their master. Besides dictating the behavior of blacks, the codes also restricted the actions of whites. Whites could not sell to, or buy anything from, slaves. Whites could not teach slaves to read or write, and a slaveholder could not free a slave without posting a thousand dollar bond guaranteeing that the freed slave would leave the state. The code also made death the penalty a slave suffered if he or she willfully harmed the master, mistress, their children, or the overseer. If a slave set fire to the crop or any part of the owner's property, if a slave raped any white female or assaulted any white person in an attempt to escape from slavery, the code also made death the punishment.

Whether or not the slave codes were enforced, the stories told by ex-slaves reveal this system of forced labor to be just as cruel and inhumane as the statutes suggest it was. Even the "kindest" masters kept their slaves illiterate, broke up families through sale, gave them too much work, and fed their slaves a diet that lacked fresh meat, dairy products, and vegetables. Throughout the South slave children were denied proper physical care and emotional support, and adult slaves were stripped naked and whipped in front of family and friends for the slightest infractions. Sadly, too, the presence of thousands of mulatto children gave undeniable testimony to the frequency of the sexual abuse of black women.

And yet, African Americans survived this barbarity better than any enslaved black people in the Western Hemisphere. Survival was a tribute to the North American slave's ability to adapt and resist, and to create communities that nourished the strength it took to resist some of the most inhumane aspects of the system.

Slave Communities

In the slave quarters, far removed from the eyes and ears of the slave master and his family, slave parents told their children the now-classic story of Br'er Rabbit, the Wolf, and Tar Baby. The story begins when the strong and powerful Wolf creates a sticky doll, or Tar Baby, to trap Rabbit, who is inquisitive and sly. While walking through the woods one day, Rabbit comes upon Tar Baby sitting by the side of the road, where it has been placed by Wolf. Being a friendly sort, Rabbit greets it with a "Hello, howdy do." When Tar Baby does not reply, the angry Rabbit hits the baby doll. First one hand gets stuck, then the other. Losing his temper even further, Rabbit kicks Tar Baby and butts it with his head, only to get his entire body stuck to Tar Baby.

When Wolf arrives to collect Rabbit, he decides to kill him by burning him in the brush. Instead of cringing in fear, Rabbit's clever response is to pretend that he wants to feel the warmth of fire on his coat. Wolf falls for Rabbit's deception and decides that the thorny briar patch might be a more suitable punishment. Rabbit, however, knows that if he gets thrown in the briar patch he can work his way loose from Tar Baby and escape. He therefore pretends to cringe at Wolf's threat: "Mercy, mercy, whatever you do, please don't throw me in the briar patch." Wolf falls for Rabbit's feigned terror and throws him in the briar patch, whereupon Rabbit makes a quick escape.

In the assortment of tales told by adult slaves to the young was another about a very talkative slave. In this tale, the slave comes across a frog who can speak. Amazed at such a wonder, the slave runs and tells his master of this miracle. The master does not believe the slave and threatens to punish him if he is lying. When the frog refuses to talk for the master, the slave is beaten severely. Only when the master leaves does the frog speak, saying, "A tol' yuh 'de othah day, yuh talk too much."

These are only two of the hundreds of tales that were told in the slave quarters, but if we use these tales to represent plantation life, they tell us a great deal about the relationship between slaves and masters. One thing they tell us is that masters did not always have their way. Wolf had Rabbit in his control, at his mercy, but he was still unable to conquer him. Slaves learned from this. They learned that quick-wittedness was an essential survival trait, and that deception could give the weak some control over the strong, allowing the powerless to survive with a minimal amount of physical or emotional assault. The story also laid bare the concepts that might did not always make for right, and that rash behavior, like that indulged in by Rabbit, seldom yielded rewards. These were important lessons for the slave child. They were lessons about life—not a life that was distant and abstract, but one the slave had to live every day.

The same was true of the second story. Though simpler than the first, it taught young blacks important lessons about survival. First, it showed the slave's world to be unpredictable. Where else but in a world filled with uncertainty would a frog speak, and speak to a powerless slave, at that? In the slave's real world, masters, angry at God knows what, might lash out at a slave at any moment. A mistress might all of a sudden find fault with her housemaid and strike out with a fist or a foot. A year or two of bad harvests might lead to a slaveholder's financial ruin, forcing him to sell some of his slaves. This might separate parent from child, husband from wife, brother from sister.

What the slave learned from the story of the talking frog was that the best defense against unpredictability was silence, the key to secrecy. Silence kept masters ignorant of everything that went on behind their backs: the food slaves stole, the religious services held in secret, the escapes made by the boldest of slaves, the anger and hatred that blacks felt toward whites. Silence protected the slave quarters. It kept the slave family and the slave's religious life removed from white invasion. In other words, the story taught the slave child how to protect African-American plantation communities.

If masters could have survived without the slave community they no doubt would have. Work, not community, was what they wanted most from slaves. Relationships that gave the slave points of reference outside of their influence were not as important as those that put the slave under their control. They did not want bonded men and women to have too many roles that were independent of that assigned to them. Therefore, to the master, the fact that African Americans were parents, preachers, or anything other than laborers was immaterial. They demanded, and usually got, obedient workers.

And yet, because masters and slaves were locked in a cycle of mutual dependency that both understood, their demands aided the development of the slave community. Slaves knew that the laws of slavery gave the master the power of life and death; and that these laws in turn made them dependent on their master's good will. But they also knew that as long as slave owners relied on them for their wealth there were limits to the slaveholder's power. Masters understood this too. They had the power of life and death over the slave, but dead slaves could not cultivate crops, and injured or rebellious slaves could not work. In the end both master and slave settled on an arrangement that took into account this mutual dependence. Though complex in its workings, the relationship that developed was really quite simple. In general, as long as slaves did their work with diligence, deference, and obedience, masters allowed them some discretion over how they spent their non-work time.

The slave family was at the center of life on the plantation, but was viewed in different ways by the master and his enslaved workers. For the master, slave families provided a means of organizing the plantation. Rather than the barrack-style living that one found in the Caribbean and Latin America, slaves in the American South lived in quarters with their families. These living arrangements made for less rebelliousness among the slaves, a fact of which masters took advantage.

Although slave owners used the slave family to maintain control over bonded men and women, their most obvious use for the family was to reproduce the slave population. This was especially so after the foreign slave trade became illegal in 1807. After that the only legal way for a master to increase his holdings in slaves was to purchase them from another slaveholder or a slave trader, or to encourage his own slaves to have children. The latter means was preferred because it was cheaper, easier, and the most natural—natural because slaves had their own reasons for wanting to have children, and easier because it usually did not require forceful intervention by the master.

Families therefore were in the master's best interest and fertility statistics prove it. In each year between 1800 and the Civil War more than one-fifth of the black women between the ages of fifteen and forty-four years of age bore a child. On average female slaves had their first child at age nineteen, two years before the average Southern white woman had hers. Slave women continued having children at two-and-a-half-year intervals until they reached the age of thirty-nine or forty. It bears repeating that this level of fertility is what made North American slavery unique in the Western Hemisphere. In most other places slave owners relied heavily on purchasing new slaves from Africa.

To say that slave owners depended on natural increase is not to say that they did not try hard to manipulate family formation. In addition to the verbal prodding to encourage young women to reproduce, slave owners used more subtle techniques

Children were given chores at an early age. Here, women and children work and play in front of their cabins during a break.

as part of the management of their plantations. For example, most, though by no means all, pregnant and nursing women did less work and received more food than non-pregnant women. Frances Kemble reported that on her husband's Georgia and South Carolina rice plantations, when children were born "certain additions of clothing and an additional weekly ration were bestowed upon the family." If inducements such as these were not sufficient to secure the cooperation of the slave of childbearing age, the master always had recourse to punishment. According to ex-slave Berry Clay, "a barren women was separated from her husband and usually sold." And it was not uncommon for slaveholders to demand their money back for female slaves they had purchased who later proved incapable of giving birth.

Because most slaves themselves wanted a family life, they actively sought out their own mates and did what they could to make the family a stable unit. It was hard, of course. The slave master's power was disruptive. But it was the family that softened the impact of that power. The family was the buffer that stood between the master and the individual slave.

Only in the eyes of the law and the master were slave marriages not binding. For slaves who had chosen their own spouses, marriage vows were sacred. It did not matter that the ceremony was often a simple ritual, sometimes accompanied by the act of jumping over a broom to symbolize the beginning of domestic living together. For slaves, it was attended with reverence.

And for good reason. The family gave the slave a point of reference that did not begin and end with the master. It gave bonded men and women the role of parent. It gave their children the sibling role, which evolved into the roles of aunt and uncle. With the family, slaves became providers and protectors for their spouses and their children. If parents were lucky enough to survive into old age without being separated, and usually it was a mother surviving with a daughter, then the mother could count on her daughter's care. Clearly, family life happened within the constraints of slavery, but the little room left by the master's dependence on the slave allowed it to happen nevertheless.

Courtship patterns show how the slave community and the family absorbed so much of the pain and desperation of slavery. For instance, during the week the clothes of field workers were tattered and dirty, but on Sundays slaves wore their best clothing. This made a real difference in their otherwise dreary lives, especially the lives of slave women. On Sundays they wore dresses that had been packed all week in sweet-smelling flowers and herbs, dresses perfumed to attract the opposite sex. Ex-slave Gus Feaster had pleasant remembrances of the women who "took their hair down outen the strings," who charmed the men "wid honeysuckle and rose petals hid in dere bosoms," and who "dried chennyberries and painted dem and wo'em on a string around dere necks." If courtship allowed for feminine expression, it also gave men the opportunity to demonstrate masculinity in a domain not controlled by the master. When these courtship rituals resulted in marriage, the slave could count on an even greater variety of roles, not to mention a new kind of companionship. From each other, slave husbands and wives could count on compassion.

In what was, by necessity, an egalitarian marital relationship, both parents provided what extras they could for each other, their children, and other relatives. As parents, slaves also educated their children. Part of that education included teaching the children how to become good parents and providers when they grew older. Fathers took pride in teaching their sons how to trap wild turkeys and rabbits, how to run down and catch raccoons, how to build canoes out of great oak logs. Mothers taught their daughters how to quilt and sew, and hunt and fish, too. Both parents told their kids the animal stories that taught so many lessons about how to live in a cruel and uncertain world. And usually, at their own peril, both parents did what they could to show their children how to protect their own. A case in point involved the mother of Fannie Moore. With pride, Moore recalled that in the face of hatred from "de old overseer," her mother stood up for her children and would not let them be beaten. For that "she get more whippin . . . dan anythin' else."

Lest we err on the side of idealism, it should be remembered that for all the good the family could do for the slave it could also be a source of heartbreak and did in

BY

HEWLETT & BRIGHT.

SALE OF

VALUABLE

SLAVES,

(On account of departure)

The Owner of the following named and valuable Slaves, being on the eve of departure for Europe, will cause the same to be offered for sale, at the NEW EXCHANGE, corner of St. Louis and Chartres streets, on *Saturday,* May 16, at Twelve o'Clock, *viz.*

1. SARAH, a mulatress, aged 45 years, a good cook and accustomed to house work in general, is an excellent and faithful nurse for sick persons, and in every respect a first rate character.

2. DENNIS, her son, a mulatto, aged 24 years, a first rate cook and steward for a vessel, having been in that capacity for many years on board one of the Mobile packets; is strictly honest, temperate, and a first rate subject.

3. CHOLE, a mulatress, aged 36 years, she is, without exeception, one of the most competent servants in the country, a first rate washer and ironer, does up lace, a good cook, and for a bachelor who wishes a house-keeper she would be invaluable: she is also a good ladies' maid, having travelled to the North in that capacity.

4. FANNY, her daughter, a mulatress, aged 16 years, speaks French and English, is a superior hair-dresser, (pupil of Guilliac,) a good seamstress and ladies' maid, is smart, intelligent, and a first rate character.

5. DANDRIDGE, a mulatoo, aged 26 years, a first rate dining-room servant, a good painter and rough carpenter, and has but few equals for honesty and sobriety.

6. NANCY, his wife, aged about 24 years, a confidential house servant, good seamstress, mantuamaker and tailoress, a good cook, washer and ironer, etc.

7. MARY ANN, her child, a creole, aged 7 years, speaks French and English, is smart, active and intelligent.

8. FANNY or FRANCES, a mulatress, aged 22 years, is a first rate washer and ironer, good cook and house servant, and has an excellent character.

9. EMMA, an orphan, aged 10 or 11 years, speaks French and English, has been in the country 7 years, has been accustomed to waiting on table, sewing etc.; is intelligent and active.

10. FRANK, a mulatto, aged about 32 years speaks French and English, is a first rate hostler and coachman, understands perfectly well the management of horses, and is, in every respect, a first rate character, with the exception that he will occasionally drink, though not an habitual drunkard.

☞ All the above named Slaves are acclimated and excellent subjects; they were purchased by their present vendor many years ago, and will, therefore, be severally warranted against all vices and maladies prescribed by law, save and except FRANK, who is fully guaranteed in every other respect but the one above mentioned.

TERMS:—One-half Cash, and the other half in notes at Six months, drawn and endorsed to the satisfaction of the Vendor, with special mortgage on the Slaves until final payment. The Acts of Sale to be passed before WILLIAM BOSWELL, *Notary Public*, at the expense of the Purchaser.

***New-Orleans, May* 13, 1835.**

PRINTED BY BENJAMIN LEVY.

When the owner of these slaves moved to Europe, he auctioned off his slaves individually. Slave families lived with the constant fear that they could be torn apart or sold away from one another at any moment.

fact lessen resistance to the master. Few men who had romantic relationships with women escaped without wounded pride, enduring anger, and a diminished sense of manhood. Louis Hughes stood stark still, blood boiling, as his master choked his wife for talking back to the mistress. His wife was subsequently tied to a joist in a barn and beaten while he stood powerless to do anything for her. The family was also the scene of domestic violence. When Ellen Botts's mother showed up in the kitchen of a sugar plantation with a lump on her head it was because her hot-tempered husband had put it there. And for all that parents could do for their off-spring, they could not shield them from the painful realities of perpetual servitude, from the whip, or from the knowledge that whatever instructions they gave them, masters and mistresses had the ultimate authority.

And yet in the slave's view, the family, with all that could go wrong with it, was the most important unit on the plantation. So much so that when family members were separated by sale or death, unrelated members of the slave community filled in as kin. If a child was left motherless or fatherless an aunt or uncle or close friend "adopted" the child and became its mother or father. Older community members became grandparents to children who had none. When men from Upper South slave states like Virginia and North Carolina were sold to the new Lower South states of Mississippi, Alabama, and Arkansas they created brothers and sisters of slaves who, like themselves, had been separated from their real family. Always there was this familial bonding, always the search for an identity that made the slave more than a beast of burden.

The slave's sacred world, reflected in song, music, religion, and folk beliefs, was another space African Americans created apart from the realm of the slave master. Like the family, the sacred world put distance between the master and the slave. It prevented legal slavery from taking over the soul. Even more than the family, which could after all be split apart and affected in other ways by whites, the sacred world, the world that grew from the spirit, inhabited an untouchable sphere.

But as they did with the slave's family, slaveholders tried to control it and use it to their advantage. They especially tried to use religion as a means of social control. "You will find," wrote Thomas Affleck in his instructions to overseers, "that an hour devoted every Sabbath morning to [slaves'] moral and religious instruction would prove a great aid to you in bringing about a better state of things amongst the Negroes." From the slaveholder's point of view a better state of things meant more obedience, less stealing, more hard work. Slave testimony reveals that white preachers always stressed these points. Hannah Scott resented it: "All he say is 'bedience to de white folks, and we hears 'nough of dat without him tellin' us." The religion the masters ordered for the slave was not only meant to directly control the slave; it was also an attempt to make slavery safer and legitimate. It was no mere coincidence that masters began hiring preachers in great numbers around 1830, the same time that the pro-slavery argument was pushed with greater intensity. Both eased the sometimes troubled mind of the slave master. Religious instruction

A plantation owner and his family attend church services with their slaves. Slaveholders tried to use religion as a tool to more fully dominate the lives of their slaves.

gave slaveholders the means of imparting their own code of morality, while it also gave them a way to prove to themselves that they were really trying to uplift those they had declared barbaric heathens. The thought that religion could make slavery safer by making slaves less rebellious was an additional source of psychic comfort. For masters who feared that slave ownership dammed their own souls, the religious instruction they gave their slaves was the means by which they hoped to redeem themselves.

Masters made similar use of other aspects of the slave's sacred world. Slave song, for instance, was taken by them and their families as evidence of the slaves' happiness. On some plantations the slave's music even became the centerpiece of entertainment, with blacks asked to perform their spirituals and play their instruments before invited white guests. These performances lent the appearance of master and slave locked in harmonious bliss, each content with their status and rank, each satisfied with their particular "place."

Appearances, though, were deceiving, especially to the master. Slave religion, and the song that was an integral part of it, reflected a world the master could not see. They were the outward manifestation of a worldview possessed by black people. Together with folk beliefs and slave tales, religion and music demonstrated not that slaves were content, nor that slavery was safe. The sacred world of black people demonstrated the indomitable strength of the spirit.

Christianity is a prime example. It was given to slaves one way, but digested another. African Americans took at face value the idea that all men were equal in the sight of God. Because they did, they could not take seriously the white preacher's text "slaves obey your masters." If God was the all-powerful Master with no one, not even the slave master, above Him, and if all men and women were God's children, without regard to rank and station in life, then all God's children were equal, white and black alike. All, including the slave owner, had to answer to a higher authority.

Slaves believed that the slaveholder, not the slave, was the sinner, and the Bible gave them the evidence that they were right. Hadn't God sent Moses to deliver the Israelites out of bondage? Had he not punished the Egyptians for enslaving his chosen people? Had he not sent his son, Jesus, to redeem the world, and was not Jesus, like the slave, a humble sufferer, a servant? By identifying with the Israelites and with Jesus, the slave turned the master into the sinner and gave himself the inner strength that flowed from the belief in his own salvation in the next world. In his everyday world, this inner strength gave the slave enough psychic freedom to resist becoming completely subservient to white people.

The deliverance slaves prayed for was not just for the next world. They wanted to be free in this world, and many of the sacred songs contained elements of protest and messages of liberation. For example, when Frederick Douglass, and many of his fellow slaves, sang "O Canaan, sweet Canaan, / I am bound for the land of Canaan," they were singing not only about someday going to heaven, but about reaching the North. The North was also the implied destination in the song "Run to Jesus, shun the danger, / I don't expect to stay much longer here." In the same vein, when slaves sang "Steal Away to Jesus," they were just as likely to be announcing a secret worship service as they were to be talking about salvation. The service, under the direction of preachers African Americans themselves chose, gave slaves a sense of independence, a kind of freedom, and the courage to resist and escape slavery altogether.

Folk beliefs, another crucial part of the slaves' sacred world, also instilled this sense of freedom and resistance. Although most whites, and some slaves, generally found beliefs in fortune tellers, witches, magic signs, and conjurers to be at odds with Christianity, for most slaves there was no gap between the two. The same slave who believed fervently in Jesus Christ could also believe that the dead returned to the living in spiritual visitations, that children born with teeth or as twins came under an ominous sign, that conjuring caused insanity and other illness.

In slave folk religion signs were important. A screech owl's cry was a sign of death that could be countered by turning shoes upside down at a door, or turning one's pockets inside out; a black cat crossing one's path was bad luck unless one spit on the spot where the paths met. Many slaves believed that a cross-eyed person could bring on a spell unless one crossed one's fingers and spat on them.

Dreams were also taken seriously. A former South Carolina slave reported that he dreamed he saw his three uncles skinning a cow and cutting it open while women and children sat around crying. When he told his mother about the dream she told him that fresh meat in a dream was a sign of death. "Sure enough that very evening Uncle Peter Price died." According to the former slave, his dreams came true so often that the older people on his plantation used his dreams as a way of predicting the future.

And in a way predicting was what folk beliefs were all about. Slaves lived in a world over which they had little control. For them, life held so many uncertainties, so little that was predictable. Folk beliefs provided a way of imposing order on an unstable environment. Like Christianity, slave folk beliefs could not be controlled by whites and therefore became another source of strength.

Although all slaves could make use of this power, conjurers were the people believed to have a special gift for reading signs and dreams, at effecting change through the use of spells, herb mixtures, and charms. African in origin, conjuring survived white attempts to eliminate it. Most slaves feared conjurers as much as they feared the master because they believed that these men and women could bring about all manner of bad or good luck. They could make mean masters kind and kind masters mean, prevent or cause whippings, separations, illness, or death, ensure love and happiness or friction and hate. They were especially known for the evil they could do.

Rather than submit to the cures of white medical doctors brought in by masters, African Americans usually preferred to treat their own illnesses and make their own medicines. They had good reason. Because early nineteenth-century medicine was hardly an exact science, the medical practitioners' treatment was likely to be as successful as that applied by black root and herb doctors. Slaves looked to their own when they were sick or in need of spiritual guidance. Because they did, they strengthened their own community and gave men and women a chance to gain status in their own group.

Without their community to confirm and reinforce their families, religion, and folk beliefs, the individual slaves would have had only the master's definition of their existence. As it was, slave children did learn at an early age that they were among the world's weak and powerless. But through the slave tales they learned how to survive and circumvent the powerful. They belonged to a community that, though powerless, put psychological space between themselves and the whites around them.

Fit for Freedom

Sometime around 1833, Frederick Douglass looked out across the Chesapeake Bay with his mind bent on freedom. He asked himself, "O why was I born a man, of whom to make a brute!" The more he thought, the more he knew he wanted his freedom:

The Fugitive's Song was composed in 1845 as a tribute to Frederick Douglass, who had escaped from slavery in 1833 to become a revered abolitionist, newspaper editor, and lecturer.

> Why am I a slave? I will run away. I will not stand it. Get caught or get clear. I'll try it. . . . I have only one life to lose. I had as well be killed running as die standing. . . . It cannot be that I shall live and die a slave.

For all the millions of slaves who at one time or another had these thoughts, only about a thousand a year actually acted on them. This is because escape was incredibly difficult. Slaves like Douglass, who were in the Upper South, close to free states, stood the best chance of success. Those close to southern cities also had a good chance, for if they escaped to an urban area they could become lost in its hustle and bustle, as well as in its free black community. Slaves who accompanied their masters and mistresses on northern trips were also likely runaways, but like any slave they had to have the will to run. This will had to be more powerful than the fear of a brutal whipping or sale away from family and loved ones, more powerful even than the fear of death.

Douglass found he had the needed will when one day he refused to be whipped. His master had hired him out for a year to a man named Edward Covey, who was widely known for his ability to break the spirit of unruly slaves. Covey had almost succeeded in working and beating Douglass into the most abject obedience when Douglass by chance visited a conjurer, who gave him a root reputed to prevent whippings. As he was told to do, Douglass kept the root in his right pocket. The next time Covey tried to beat him he seized Covey around the throat, flung him to the ground, declared that he would no longer be treated as a brute, and fought off the other slaves Covey got to assist him. The fight continued for two hours, but in the end Douglass won out over Covey, and he was never again whipped by him or any other white man.

The victory Douglass won over Covey was small compared to the one he had won over his own fear. As he put it, "I felt as I never felt before. . . . My long crushed spirit rose, cowardice departed, bold defiance took its place; and I now resolved that, however long I might remain a slave in form, the day had passed forever when I could be a slave in fact." Four years later, Douglass escaped from slavery and found his way to New York.

But the records of slavery show that few fled slavery as Douglass did. Fewer still participated in large-scale rebellions aimed at overthrowing the institution. There were, however, many slaves who took a stand against their servitude, who somehow managed to be slaves in form but not in fact. These were men and women who resisted the worst aspects of slavery. Some, like Douglass, refused to be whipped; some ran away for short periods of time. Some feigned ignorance of how to do a particular chore and others feigned illness rather than work to the limits that the master wanted. Still others used individual acts of violence to counter the authority of the master.

Unlike running away, this kind of resistance only separated the slave from the worst aspects of slavery. Its end was not liberty, just release from some of slavery's misery. However, like the slave family, slave Christianity, and folk religion, it nevertheless helped African Americans survive this most inhuman institution. Resistance of all types proved that black people were fit for freedom.

Whatever other circumstance came together in the life of a slave to make him or her commit an act of individual resistance, one thing is for sure: The slave who resisted did not stand in perpetual abject fear of their master, nor did the slave completely lose those qualities that made him or her a whole human being. Slaves who stole extra food, for example, cared enough about their own well-being to defy the slaveholders' rationing system. Slaves who risked their lives in their struggle not to be whipped were making a personal statement about their self-esteem and individual honor. Women who kicked and clawed their sexual abusers made eloquent statements about their personal dignity. These individual acts of resistance were attempts to retain or take back some control over lives that were by law assigned to someone else.

Nowhere is this more apparent than the attempts by some slaves to get enough to eat. The usual fare on most farms and plantations from Virginia to Mississippi was salt pork and cornmeal. When they could, slaves supplemented this with vegetables grown in their own gardens, and meat and fish they caught. Most slaves needed more and most stole what they needed. Many did not view stealing from the master as something sinful. Whether they stole clothing, money, crops, or food, slaves often justified their actions with the argument that not only had they worked for the goods, but they were simply moving them from one part of the master's property to another.

This thinking was especially obvious during the Civil War. Those who fled to Union troops taking their master's goods with them felt that the promised time of retribution had arrived. Southern mistress Adele Pettigru Allston probably made an accurate assessment of the slave's attitude when she complained: "The conduct of the negroes in robbing our house, store room, meat house, etc., and refusing to restore anything shows you they *think it right* to steal from us, to spoil us, as the Israelites did the Egyptians."

Many slaves did not wait until the Civil War to act this way. Besides stealing, they burned gin houses, barns, corncribs, and smokehouses. Some slaves used poison or outright physical force to kill their masters. Capture always meant certain death, but they did it nonetheless.

To guard against violence, especially that which could lead to large-scale rebellions, slaveholders created the slave patrols. These were groups of white males, usually of the lower classes, called together to look for runaways, to prevent slave gatherings, and generally ensure the safety of the white community. Since slaves were not allowed to travel the countryside without a pass from their master, a principal task of the patrols was to enforce the pass system. This they often did with excessive brutality, administering beatings on the authority given them by slaveholders who used the patrol system as a way of binding all whites together against all blacks.

Despite the patrol system slaves resisted. They used passes written by the few in their own group who could read and write. They sheltered runaways in their cabins, and they laid traps that tripped up patrollers' horses.

Some slaves just stood and fought. Some found the courage to escape, and many more found the will to try. Georgia slave John Brown ran away several times before he finally succeeded. One time he got as far as Tennessee; another time, thinking he was going north, he traveled almost all of the way on foot to New Orleans. Each time he was captured he was whipped, chained, and had bells attached to him. Over and over again he escaped until he finally reached Indiana. Aunt Cheyney of the Kilpatrick cotton plantation in Mississippi was not so fortunate, however. She was one of her master's mistresses and had recently given birth to the fourth of her master's children when she ran away. Kilpatrick set his dogs on her trail. When they caught up with her he ordered them to attack. According to her friend Mary Reynolds, "The dogs tore her naked and et the breasts plumb off her body." This served as a punishment for Cheyney, but it was also Kilpatrick's way of warning all slaves, especially women, against running away.

However much African Americans were haunted by these kinds of horrors, there were still those who would not be stopped. The stories of escape reveal as much relentless perseverance as they do ingenuity. Henry "Box" Brown, for example, was carried for twenty-seven hours from Richmond to Philadelphia by Adams Express in a box three feet long and two feet deep. He literally mailed himself to freedom. The light-skinned Ellen Craft escaped by pretending to be a sickly white man traveling in the company of his slave. The slave in attendance was in fact her darker-skinned husband William. Together the two traveled by stagecoach, boat, and train from Georgia to Philadelphia. They stopped at some of the best hotels along the way, and Ellen even conversed with slaveholders about the trouble of runaway slaves.

The person who seemed to give the South the most runaway trouble, though, was Harriet Tubman. She was born a slave some time around 1821 on Maryland's Eastern Shore and lived in slavery for twenty-eight years. Like most slaves in this Upper South region, Tubman lived in dread of being sold to the Deep South. In 1849, when she learned that she was indeed going to be sold, she joined the thousands of others who took to the woods and stole themselves.

What made her unique is that she returned, not once but many times, to rescue others, including her sister, her sister's two children, and her parents. Given the identification of African Americans with the Israelites it should come as no surprise that Tubman was called "Moses." And given the way African Americans used their religion to speak about freedom, it is also not surprising that when Tubman said, "Tell my brothers to be always *watching unto prayer,* and *when the good ship Zion comes along, to be ready to step on board,*" this was her signal to leave, not for heaven, but for freedom. It is said that she returned nineteen times and rescued more than three hundred slaves. She was so good at what she did that Maryland planters offered a forty-thousand-dollar bounty for her capture.

Slaveholders wanted to catch Tubman about as much as they wanted to put an end to the Underground Railroad. This network of hiding places run by opponents of slavery provided the slaves fortunate enough to use it with food, shelter, money, clothing, and disguises. A black man, William Still, an officer of the Philadelphia Vigilance Committee, was the moving force behind the Underground Railroad. He wrote of Harriet Tubman that she was "a woman of no pretensions," and "in point of courage, shrewdness, and disinterested exertions to rescue her fellowman, she was without equal."

In general women had a harder time escaping than men because they were more reluctant to leave without their children. At the same time, it was the fear of losing them that often provided the incentive to flee. Escaping alone was difficult enough; escaping with children was close to impossible. There is no question that male runaways regretted leaving their wives and children behind, but women, it seems, suffered a special agony when faced with such a decision.

Truancy seems to have been the way many slave women reconciled their desire to flee with their need to stay. Men too practiced truancy, but women made the most likely truants because they nursed and were directly responsible for their children. Former slave Benjamin Johnson remembered that sometimes when women would not take a whipping they "would run away an' hide in de woods. Sometimes dey would come back after a short stay an' den dey would have to put de hounds on dere trail to bring dem back home."

Women's short-term flight was by no means a reflection of their lesser courage or greater accommodation to slavery. Truants faced punishment when they returned, punishment many braved over and over again. Moreover, truancy involved as much danger as running away. As Johnson's comment indicates, dogs hunted them down, and the woods and swamps they hid in held all kinds of dangers.

Rather than reflecting a lesser danger, or level of courage, what truancy mirrored was the different slave experiences of men and women, and therefore their different ways of resisting. For example, the division of labor on most farms and plantations conferred greater mobility on males than on female slaves. Few of the chores performed by female slaves took them off the plantation. Usually masters chose their male slaves to assist in the transportation of crops to market, and the transport of supplies and other materials to the plantation. More male than female slaves were artisans and craftsmen, and this made it more difficult to hire out a female slave than a male slave. Fewer female slaves therefore had a chance to vary their work experience. As a consequence, more men than women were able to test their survival skills under different circumstances.

Another factor affecting slave mobility was the "abroad marriage," a union between slaves who resided at different locations. When "abroad" spouses visited each other, usually once a week, it was most often the husband who traveled to the wife. All in all, it was female bondage, more than male bondage, that meant being tied to the immediate environment of the plantation or farm. For these reasons, female slaves much more than male slaves just "stayed put."

By and large, though, women did resist in subtle ways. For instance, they "played the fool" more than men. In other words, in order to avoid doing some onerous chore, they would smile humbly and pretend to misunderstand instructions given by the master, mistress, or overseer. The use of poison also suited women because they officiated as cooks and nurses on the plantation. As early as 1755 a Charleston slave woman was burned at the stake for poisoning her master, and in 1769 a special issue of the *South Carolina Gazette* carried the story of a slave woman who had poisoned her master's infant child. Since the slave's objective was not to get caught we will never really know just how many whites were ushered by slave women to an early grave.

We also will never know how many instances of illness were actually ruses to escape backbreaking labor. Women had an advantage over men in this realm because childbearing was a primary expectation that slave owners had of slave women. In an age where women's diseases were still shrouded in mystery, getting the maximum amount of work from women of childbearing age while remaining confident that no damage was done to their reproductive organs was a guessing game that few white slave owners wanted to play or could afford to lose. In deference to their "mysterious" conditions, women, especially those of childbearing age, were seldom designated as able-bodied workers. Unlike healthy young and middle-aged men who were considered full hands, women, depending on their stage of pregnancy and their frequency of nursing, were labeled three-quarter hands, half hands, or quarter hands. Men could and did feign illness. But since women did, in fact, have more sickness because of menstruation and childbirth, they were more likely to get away with it.

Whether they also got away with birth control and abortion is something we will never know. Few nineteenth-century women, white or black, were ignorant of the ways and means of avoiding pregnancy. The decline in the birthrate among white Americans from 7.04 in 1800 to 3.56 by the eve of the twentieth century is evidence of the use of birth control, including abortion. For white women, particularly those of the urban middle classes, a small family had its benefits, not the least of which was the lower risk of dying in childbirth and the ability to spend more time with an individual child.

The slave woman, however, had no such benefit. In fact, though she, like other nineteenth-century women, approached pregnancy with fear and never had enough time to spend with any of her children, she risked sale if she remained childless. The risk notwithstanding, some women just refused to have children. How they managed to stay childless, what methods of birth control they used, and the frequency of abortion, remained secrets that were virtually exclusive to the female world of the slave quarters.

Though few slave women divulged these secrets, slaveholders were convinced that black women knew how to avoid pregnancy and also how to bring on a miscarriage. A Tennessee physician, Dr. John H. Morgan, wrote that slave women used the herbs of tansy and rue, the roots and seeds of the cotton plant, cedar berries, and camphor to bring about miscarriage, and Dr. E. M. Pendleton claimed that planters regularly complained of whole families of women who fail to have any children.

More serious were the infrequent cases of infanticide. Women who chose to kill children they had risked their life having were clearly desperate. Yet they struck out at the system where they knew it would hurt, where they knew they had real impact—in the increase of the slave population. That they hurt themselves more than they hurt the master can be assumed, for they were either prosecuted and hanged, or they suffered emotional distress forever.

If African Americans could have overthrown the system that forced such tragic decisions, they would have. But black people faced hopeless odds. Unlike other slaves in other nations in the Americas, black people in the United States were overwhelmingly outnumbered by whites and grouped in small numbers on plantations that were miles apart. Whites had the guns, the ammunition, the horses, the dogs, and the law. They had the resources to crush any revolt by slaves, and the slaves knew it. Resistance, therefore, was individual because it had to be; whites put down the few large-scale rebellions and planned revolts with a viciousness that served notice that revolt was futile.

In spite of the odds and the repression, rebellions did occur, and conspiracies abounded. Among the first was the largest—an uprising in 1811 of close to four hundred slaves in St. Charles and St. John the Baptist parishes in Louisiana. Led by a slave named Charles Deslondes, the slaves sent whites fleeing their plantations for safety in New Orleans. Further east, in 1817 and 1818 blacks joined the Seminole Indians in their fight to keep their Florida homelands. To defend themselves, units of blacks and Indians raided plantations in Georgia, killing whites and carrying off slaves. Again in 1835 blacks joined the Seminoles in their unsuccessful fight against the militias of Florida, Georgia, and Tennessee. Seminole lands had continued to be havens for runaway slaves, and by the 1830s President Andrew Jackson was determined to eliminate these independent communities and seize all Indian lands for white slaveholders. By that time, though, it was hard to call Seminole land Indian territory because blacks and Indians had intermarried to the extent that they were indistinguishable. Indeed, so many hundreds of blacks fought on the side of the Seminoles that United States General Thomas Jesup declared: "This, you may be assured, is a negro, not an Indian war."

General Jesup understood what all slaveholders knew—that resistance had always gone hand in hand with slavery. The century had begun with Gabriel Prosser's attempt to seize Richmond, and the year he died, 1800, was the year that Denmark Vesey bought his freedom from his master and began his life as a free man. That same year Nat Turner was born. Both men were to become the slaveholder's worst nightmare.

Vesey was a free African-American carpenter who worked hard enough to become not just self-supporting but relatively wealthy by the standards of the day. He was a proud, literate, free black man who hated slavery and hated to see his people bowing and scraping to whites. At age fifty-three he gathered around him trusted black men, both free and slave, and planned to capture the city of Charleston. His followers were church leaders and craftsmen. One of them, Gullah Jack, was a conjurer. For months they planned their attack on the arsenal at Charleston and on plantations surrounding the city. During this time they recruited slaves and free men who had the steady nerves to carry out the plan. Then, on a fateful day in 1822, they were betrayed. Betrayal meant capture, and capture meant death. Peter Poyas, one of Vesey's lieutenants, went to the galleys with the words of the spirituals on his lips. "Fear not," he told the blacks of Charleston, "the Lord God that delivered Daniel is able to deliver us."

Nat Turner believed himself to be the deliverer. He carried himself in the manner of a messiah. Proud and self-confident, literate and articulate, he saw visions of God's deliverance of black people from bondage. He felt himself to be the Moses who would lead his people out of bondage. Acting on that feeling, Turner led about seventy slaves in an assault on the whites of Southampton, Virginia. In one of the most clear-cut cases of slave rebellion that occurred in this country, Nat Turner went from one plantation to the next killing whites. His instructions to his fellow insurrectionists were followed to the letter. They spared no one. Age and sex made no difference.

In the end Nat Turner was caught. By the time his murder count reached around sixty, bands of white men caught up with his men and put down the revolt. Turner took to the woods and managed to evade capture until most of his men had been put to death. As had happened in the Prosser and Vesey conspiracies, the fear of insurrection spread across the South with alarming speed, and whites lashed out mercilessly at blacks, especially those in the vicinity of the rebellion. Anyone suspected of aiding Turner was put to death. All acts of disrespect were taken as a direct challenge to white authority, and slaves who did not act in the most humble manner were punished severely, even killed. Blacks were not allowed to hold religious services or gather in groups at all. All blacks, slave and free, were watched by patrols who had their numbers increased and firearms ready. The message was clear. America was home to the free and the brave, but only for those who were white.

Somewhere though, deep down, slaveholders understood that as long as slavery existed so too would resistance. This is one of the reasons why nineteenth-century slaveholders tried to improve the material conditions of the slaves. They thought that more food, better living quarters, and fewer whippings would make slaves less rebellious and more content and willing to bear all of slavery's burdens.

African Americans did bear slavery's burdens, but not without resistance. The continuing struggle against slavery created the psychic space black people needed to survive, and it proved to contemporary and future generations that though enslaved, African Americans were fit for freedom.

A Different Kind of Freedom

On April 8, 1816, April Ellison, a mulatto expert cotton gin maker, stood with his white master, William Ellison, before a magistrate and five freeholders of the Fairfield District of South Carolina. It was a solemn occasion. No doubt every word, every movement became indelibly etched in April's mind, because it was the day of his manumission, the day that he bought himself out of slavery. At that time, April was twenty-six years old. By the time he was thirty he had legally changed his name to William, had bought his wife, Matilda, and his daughter, Eliza Ann, out of slavery, and had freed them. He had moved out of the district of his slave youth and established himself as a free person of color in Stateburg, in the Sumpter District. And he had bought two adult male slaves to help him in his business. Two years later, in 1822, he bought an acre of land, and two years after this he petitioned and received permission from the white members of Holy Cross Episcopal Church to worship with them on the main floor of the vestry, away from the slaves and free blacks who were confined to the balcony.

Elizabeth Hobbs, an attractive mulatto, was born into slavery in 1818, a year after Frederick Douglass's birth. She was born in Virginia, but in her teenage years she was sold further south to a North Carolina master by whom she had a son. Repurchased by a member of the family that had sold her to begin with, she was taken to St. Louis, Missouri, where she met and married a black man named James Keckley. Though Keckley told her that he was free, he was in fact a slave, and their life together was a short one. Far more long-term in its consequences were Elizabeth Keckley's abilities as a seamstress, skills perfected at her mother's instruction when she was just a child. As a dressmaker in St. Louis, she was so good, and so popular, that her customers offered to lend her the money to buy herself and her son out of slavery. In 1855, when she was thirty-seven years old, Keckley and her son became free persons of color. After she learned to read and write and paid off her loan, she returned east, first to Baltimore then to Washington, D.C. In Washington, her clients were among the city's elite, the most notable being President Lincoln's wife, Mary Todd, to whom she became a companion and friend.

While Keckley was keeping the company of the First Lady, Sojourner Truth was aiding and nursing refugee slaves fleeing the carnage of the Civil War. At the war's beginning she was sixty-one years old and had in her lifetime been a housekeeper, a preacher, an abolitionist, and a public speaker for women's rights. A dark-skinned woman, she had been born Isabella Bomefree about 1799, and was freed in 1827 by New York State law. Unlike Keckley or Ellison, Truth never learned to read or write, nor did the South ever hold her as a slave. Nonetheless she was eloquent in her attacks against slavery, and more than anyone else of her time, she was steadfast in her public defense of black women.

The lives of William Ellison, Elizabeth Keckley, and Sojourner Truth tell us a lot

Printed at the "TELEGRAPH"—ALTON.

UNITED STATES OF AMERICA,

STATE OF ILLINOIS, *Madison County,* } ss. { To all to whom these Presents may come—GREETING:

Know Ye, *That* Mary Jane Jones wife of John Jones *a person of Color, about* twenty four *years of age,* five *feet* Three & 1/2 *inches high,* Molatto *complexion,* has two small pitts on each side of her fore head Daughter of Elijah & Dicey Richardson

has exhibited, presented and filed, in the Office of the Clerk of the Circuit Court of the County and State aforesaid, a **CERTIFICATE,** *duly authenticated, of* **FREEDOM,** *as such person of Color.*

Now, therefore, I, WM. TYLER BROWN, *Clerk of the Circuit Court of Madison County, State of Illinois,* **CERTIFY,** *That said* Mary Jane Jones *is a* FREE PERSON OF COLOR, *a resident or citizen of the State of Illinois, and entitled to be respected accordingly, in Person and Property, at all times and places, in the due prosecution of* her *Lawful concerns.*

In Testimony whereof, I have, to these Presents, signed my name, and affixed the Seal of said Court, at Edwardsville, this 28th *day of* November *in the year of our Lord one thousand eight hundred and* forty-four

Wm. T. Brown Clerk.

A certificate signed by an Illinois county clerk was granted to a free black woman to certify her claim to freedom. Free blacks always had to keep such documents close by to avoid being sold into slavery by unscrupulous slave traders.

about the lives of all blacks who were free during the time of slavery. More than anything else, their lives, and those of all free African Americans, reveal that black freedom and white freedom were always very different.

The reason for the different realities of black and white freedom was white prejudice. It was strong in the South, where ninety percent of all blacks were slaves and a dark skin was a presumption of bondage. It was equally strong in the North and West where there was an abiding sentiment against both blacks and slavery. What

Fanny Kemble, a well-traveled white woman, said of free blacks in the North held true all over the country. "They are not slaves indeed, but they are pariahs, debarred from every fellowship save with their own despised race. . . . All hands are extended to thrust them out, all fingers point at their dusky skin, all tongues . . . have learned to turn the very name of their race into an insult and a reproach."

That some African Americans had a heritage of freedom that predated the American Revolution was of far less significance to whites than the fact that they were black. As the nineteenth century progressed and the country moved closer and closer to the Civil War, a dark skin carried the presumption of slavery in both the North and the South. More and more, free blacks had to prove that they were not slaves. This was a burden that no white person carried, because white skin color carried with it the presumption of freedom.

After the American Revolution, the free black population numbered 59,000 in 1790 and grew to 488,000 by the eve of the Civil War. These numbers were increased by blacks born of free mothers, including those of white women with black partners, and free mulatto immigrants from the West Indies, especially those who fled Haiti after the 1790 slave revolt led by Toussaint L'Ouverture. Every year natural increase added to their numbers.

When newly freed blacks chose their new names, they sometimes picked those that reflected their complexion. There were thus many Browns and Blacks among the freed population. Sometimes the name reflected their occupation. For example, the literal meaning of Sojourner Truth is traveling preacher. Indeed, Truth's oratorical skills were renowned and she used them in the cause of Christianity as well as abolitionism and women's rights. Henry Mason, for example, was a bricklayer, Charles Green was a gardener, and Thomas Smith could have been a blacksmith or a silversmith. Other former slaves chose the names of liberty. There were names like Justice, and many chose the name Freeman as a mark of their new identity.

In addition to signifying a new identity, the name chosen by these free men and women reflected their evaluation of their chances of success. Those who took the name of their craft, for instance, probably felt good about prospering economically. The few like William Ellison, who took their master's name, no doubt saw advantages in their choices, too. In a world where black skin was inhibiting, white men could ease the way to economic independence. Ellison knew this. His business making cotton gins was built as much on his own skills as on the Ellison name, a name associated with one of the wealthiest planters in a region where such wealthy planters had a need for his skill and product.

More than keeping his master's name, Ellison also kept his attachment to his master by staying fairly close to him, something most freed slaves avoided. Ellison's choice no doubt had a lot to do with the fact that his master was probably also his father. Though he did move about fifty miles to another town, this was far less of a move than that made by many freed people. Of course, runaways had to flee because their lives depended on it. But legally emancipated slaves also left the

A badge issued to a freed black living in Charleston, South Carolina. Both freed blacks and slaves were required to wear these identification badges.

area where they had been enslaved. Some just needed to test their mobility as a way of demonstrating their liberty. Others migrated to areas where they knew they had friends and family. Still others left for only a short while, returning *because* of the familiarity they had with the area and the people. Above all, they tried to get out from under their former master's supervision. The best way to do that was to move.

And yet, for black Americans freedom did not mean total liberty. Those who moved to rural areas found it difficult to make freedom work for them. In the South, rural free blacks who were not attached to plantations as carpenters, blacksmiths, coopers, and the like, rented land, equipment, and supplies and tried to eke out a living by growing and selling their crops. Very few were successful. White landowners charged exorbitant rates for the rental of land and just one mediocre harvest could put a free black family far into debt. African Americans in this situation were forced to go to prison or, to meet their debts, sign over their future crops to the landowner. In either case they became peons, people tied to the land. They either had to work forever for the person whose land they rented or be imprisoned. If they went to jail they were subsequently hired out and forced to work for the person the authorities had sold their labor to, to persons willing to pay their debts. Either way many rural free blacks found themselves in virtual servitude.

Faced with the choice of renting land under such unfavorable circumstances or signing labor contracts, most rural free blacks opted for the latter. But this too put them in slavelike circumstances. Most contracts specified that free Negroes work according to the same rules governing slave hands. Thus when Aaron Griggs hired himself to a Louisiana planter he pledged "to work as one of the hands of the plantation." He pledged also not to leave the plantation during his term of service, "to go out to the fields at the same hours with the people of the plantation & to work with the plantation overseer." In all likelihood Griggs got the same amount of food and clothing as the slaves, but since he had to pay for them at prices set by his employer he found himself at the end of the year in debt to the very person who he had worked for like a slave.

Free blacks who succeeded in the rural South were the rare exception. William Ellison falls into this category. His skill as a gin maker made him indispensable to white planters. He was therefore able to make freedom work for him. But Ellison also had other advantages. He was light skinned, and whites, especially those in the Lower South, showed a definite tolerance for blacks who were close to them in skin color.

It was not just a matter of standards of beauty. A light color signified a birth connection to a white person. Although there were enough whites who believed that one drop of Negro blood made one a Negro, there were also many white men who had fathered mulattoes, and some white women who had given birth to them. These white parents were often reluctant to leave their children totally exposed to racist hostility. They thus protected them by providing for some education or training in a trade. The industriousness of these free persons of color made some white South Carolinians feel safe in their presence. As a group of white men who signed an 1822 Charleston petition put it, mulattoes were "a barrier between our own color and that of the black."

For sure, Ellison made the most of this sentiment. Records show, for instance, that he was probably the son either of his master or of his master's father. It was this blood connection that saved him from becoming an ordinary field hand on the cotton plantations owned by his relatives. That he took the name of his masters, and identified with them in every way, even to the extent of holding slaves, is quite understandable.

Since most free blacks lacked Ellison's advantages, they had to find other ways of surviving. In both the North and the South the cities held more opportunities for African Americans than rural areas did. This is where most of the unskilled jobs were, and since, unlike Keckley or Ellison, most free African Americans were unskilled laborers, the city was the place to find work.

It was also a place to find other free blacks and begin the task of making new friends and building a new life. In the cities free blacks had more choices than they had in rural areas. There they could join a black church and worship the way they wanted. They could send their children to a school set up by that church or the school established by the benevolent society to which they might also belong. In the city they could hold celebrations. They could go to the grog shops or bars, or attend a show, or even bury their dead in a service under their own direction. They could do so, moreover, away from the constant supervising eyes of white slaveholders.

Small wonder then that by 1860, on the eve of the Civil War, free blacks could be described as the most urban of all of America's people. In the South more than a third of the free black population dwelled in cities or towns, although only fifteen percent of the whites and about five percent of the slaves lived in cities. In the North, Boston, New York, Cincinnati, and Philadelphia held the bulk of the free black population.

Opportunities prevailed in antebellum urban America but not without struggle. As in rural areas, blacks faced obstacles. Everywhere they turned they encountered white suspicion, competition, and hostility. Opposition to them was so fierce, and their freedom was so restricted, that like free rural African Americans it is more apt to describe their condition not as free but as quasi-free.

Most cities and states, in fact, tried hard to limit the size of the free black population, and where possible, to eliminate it. This effort began early in the 1800s and could be traced to the waning of the revolutionary fervor over liberty, the rise of cotton, and the resulting demand for slaves. Specifically, as the nation settled into its growing-up stage, and as its economy became more and more fueled by the money made from cotton production, anything that threatened slavery, the institution upon which cotton production was based, was perceived as dangerous.

By white standards, therefore, free blacks were dangerous. They threatened to disrupt the existing order because they contradicted the pro-slavery argument that Negroes could not survive without white supervision. They also threatened slavery because they had a vested interest in slavery's elimination. Not only did most have bitter memories of their time in slavery, but most had relatives or friends still in bondage. Moreover, as long as slavery existed, and as long as most blacks were slaves, all blacks were presumed slaves, even free blacks. Free African Americans therefore had every reason to want—and work toward—slavery's elimination.

Antebellum whites had a totally different mindset. In the North, South, and West, whites who were skilled artisans and common workers feared free African Americans. Thanks to the 1820 Missouri Compromise, slavery was outlawed north of the 36th parallel. Northern and western white laborers, therefore, did not have to compete against slave labor, a competition they could never win because they could not sell their labor as cheaply as the slave who, of course, worked for nothing. The free black, though, was a formidable competitor because discrimination forced African Americans to sell their labor for less than it was worth. It was in the white laborer's interest, therefore, to eliminate all black competition however he could.

One way he did this was by refusing to work alongside blacks. Frederick Douglass ran into this problem when, as a fugitive from slavery, he moved to New Bedford, Massachusetts, and sought work as a caulker. Employers would not hire him because they risked losing all their white employees. As Douglass explained, "I was told by an anti-slavery shipbuilder there, who had a vessel on the stocks to be caulked, that if he should even venture to send me on that ship, every white man would leave him, and he could not get her ready for sea. Go where I would, I could not get employment at my trade." Ex-slave carpenter Henry Boyd had a similar experience in Cincinnati. After days of unsuccessful job hunting, he finally found an Englishman who would hire him. When he entered the shop, though, "the workmen threw down their tools, and declared that he should leave or they would. 'They would never work with a nigger.'"

Laws restricting the movement and rights of free blacks were as effective as such impromptu attempts to limit the freedom of African Americans. In the South free blacks were forced to carry certificates of freedom on their person. If caught without one there was the danger of being claimed as a slave. In many places free blacks had to register with the police or court authorities. South Carolina, for instance, required free people of color between the ages of sixteen and sixty to pay a two-dollar tax each year. The tax enabled whites to know who was free and where free blacks lived. Like other Southern states, South Carolina also prohibited the migration of free blacks into the state, as well as the emancipation of slaves. These laws aimed to reduce the number of free blacks, and they did so very effectively.

A host of other laws were passed to curtail the rights of Southern free blacks. When free African Americans met in any numbers, even in church, they were required to have a white person in attendance. Southern laws also set curfews for black gatherings. Blacks were widely excluded from public parks and burial grounds, relegated to the balconies of theaters and opera houses, and barred from hotels and restaurants. Of all the Southern states only Maryland, Tennessee, and North Carolina gave free blacks the vote, but by 1835 all had repealed this right. To add insult to injury, no Southern court allowed them to serve on juries or give testimony in court against whites. And, if convicted of any crime, the punishment meted out to them was always more severe than that given to whites convicted of the same crime. Free blacks faced public whippings and, most ominous of all, enslavement, a fate whites never suffered.

Conditions in the non-slaveholding states were slightly better but got worse as one traveled from the Northeast to the Northwest. Slavery had been outlawed in the states of Ohio, Indiana, Illinois, Wisconsin, and Michigan by the Northwest Ordinance of 1787, but whites there were still prejudiced against blacks. As in the South, skilled laborers were especially fearful of black competition. To discourage black migration, Northwestern and Western states alike passed black codes that resembled the restrictive laws of slavery. Like Southern states they also required blacks to register their certificates of freedom at a county clerk's office, but here free blacks had to pay a bond of five hundred or one thousand dollars guaranteeing that they would not disturb the peace or become a public charge. Illinois, Indiana, and Oregon actually excluded black migrants altogether.

Conditions for free blacks were probably the best in the Northeast, but even in these states restrictions were intolerable. Most qualified black voters lost the vote and social custom kept them off juries. What the law did not do, mob violence did. Blacks in Philadelphia suffered the fury of the mob as early as 1805, when dozens of white citizens turned on those gathered for a Fourth of July ceremony and drove them away from the festivities with a torrent of curses. During the 1830s and 1840s, riots occurred again in Philadelphia, and also in New York, Pittsburgh, Cincinnati, and Providence. In each case white mobs burned and looted black churches, meeting halls, and homes, and beat, stoned, and even murdered black citizens.

To survive, most African Americans found a way to work around white prejudice. Nowhere in the United States was this easy. In the Northeast, employment opportunities in the emerging industries went almost entirely to whites who used every means, including violence, to keep their economic advantage. Blacks could find jobs only at the bottom of the job ladder as common laborers. They loaded ships, dug wells, graves, and house foundations, and toiled as sweepers, porters, ashmen, chimney sweeps, and bootblacks.

Paradoxically, economic opportunities increased for free blacks the further south one went into slave country. Not only were there fewer skilled and unskilled white immigrant laborers in the South, but white employers were accustomed to hiring blacks to do work that white men would not do. Free blacks, therefore, were able to eke out a living even though they faced competition from both slaves and native-born whites. For example, nowhere in the South would white men cut hair. Free blacks therefore acquired a monopoly on the barbering trade. In Charleston, skilled white carpenters, tailors, and millwrights were scarce, leaving these occupations to be filled by free blacks. Blacks also found employment in Southern industries, usually in the least-skilled positions. In Richmond, for instance, half the employed Negro men labored in tobacco factories, paper mills, and iron foundries.

Free black urban women did not have as many opportunities as their male counterparts. Elizabeth Keckley was exceptional. Both North and South, few blacks owned their own businesses or commanded their own time. Most worked in the service trades as laundresses, cooks, and maids. Even in this kind of work they faced competition from native-born white women of the poorer classes, and as the period progressed, from immigrant women, especially those from Ireland. Like free black men, though, they worked longer hours than the average white person, and longer hours than the average white woman, who often did not work at all. With some luck they managed to survive on their own.

Whether male or female, surviving in the city and surviving well meant being blessed with some amount of luck. Luck had different meanings for whites and free blacks. For the latter luck meant having a trade that was not taken over by white laborers. Luck also meant being able to support one's children so that officials could not force them into legal apprenticeships. Thousands of black parents in both the North and South had their children taken away and forced into eighteen or twenty years of service because state or city officials deemed them unable or unfit to care for them. In Philadelphia, apprenticeship periods for blacks were sometimes as long as twenty-eight years. Once in an apprenticeship black children seldom received the education or the training in a trade that white children received.

In light of all the restrictions on free blacks and the discrimination and prejudice they faced, it is worth remembering that they were not slaves. Although they were only semi-free, they were not in bondage. This status had real significance, significance a slave could appreciate. For, after all, free blacks could legally rename themselves. They could marry legally, and free women gave birth to free children. They had more opportunities to learn to read and write. For instance, although only one of Sojourner Truth's five children obtained any education, at least two of her grandchildren obtained literacy during the days of slavery. William Ellison's children were more fortunate than Truth's. He sent them to Philadelphia to be educated at the Lombard Street Primary School, a school run by Margaretta Forten, a free black teacher.

Free blacks could also make their lives meaningful in ways slaves could not. Throughout the country free African Americans had more control over their religious practices. Shortly after Sojourner Truth was freed, she joined a Methodist congregation in Ulster, New York. Like thousands of free blacks, Truth found the more participatory, unconstrained emotional services of the Methodists more to her liking than the quiet, solemn services of other denominations.

For free blacks, though, it was not enough to be accepted in a white congregation. Whites, however, protested independent black organizing, such as that conducted by Absalom Jones's Free African Society in Philadelphia. Especially in the South blacks encountered strenuous white resistance to black churches.

In the end, however, white prejudice worked *for* African Americans. In the South, where laws prohibited black assembly, whites nevertheless shunned integrated worship with free African Americans. Yet, adopting the same reasoning they employed regarding slaves, whites believed that Christianity would make free blacks more controllable and less dangerous. Therefore, even though black churches were often raided and shut down by suspicious whites, between 1800 and 1860, and especially after 1840, independent African-American churches grew and thrived.

To the extent that the churches survived and prospered, so too did African-American communities. Like slaves, free blacks identified with the Jews of the Old Testament and believed that God would deliver them in this world and the next.

For free blacks, however, the church was a structure—an institution—in a way it was not for the slave. Besides being the one corner of the world where blacks went unhindered by whites, the church was the center of black life. Most black schools were founded by the black church. Most self-help activities were conducted through the church, and most positions of leadership in the community were held in the church. Not surprisingly, it was often the church's struggle for survival against white efforts to shut its doors that lent unity and solidarity to many African-American communities.

So much was dependent on the survival of the black church. Black schools offer a good example. In antebellum America in both the North and the South adult education was almost nonexistent, and black children were either given substandard education or were barred from public and private schools altogether. It was usually the church that took up this burden. In the North and the upper and border Southern states, African churches ran Sunday schools where children were encouraged to read the Bible. Most churches in these areas had day schools that children attended for free or for a small fee.

In addition to the church, benevolent societies were a unifying element in free African-American society. One of the first was founded in Boston by Prince Hall, who before the American Revolution was granted a charter from England to establish a Masonic lodge. In 1797 Hall presided over the installation of the first officers in Philadelphia's African Lodge of Pennsylvania. By 1815 there were four lodges in Philadelphia that had pooled their resources to build a black Masonic Hall.

Like benevolent societies in other cities in both North and South, these organizations provided services to their members as well as to the larger black community. For example, they provided disabled members with "sick dues" to assure them an income when they could not work, and they also gave elderly members money to live on. They organized the burial of their members, providing plots, headstones, and ceremonies for the departed. Some of the associations ran schools for orphan children and provided for companionship for the sick and disabled. Some workingmen's associations tried to secure better wages and job security, and still others functioned like Baltimore's Society for Relief in Case of Seizure, an organization that guarded against the kidnapping of free blacks into slavery.

These benevolent societies not only provide an excellent example of African-American self-help but also give us insight into the social organization of most African-American communities. In 1790 the Brown Fellowship Society of Charleston, South Carolina, was formed by five free men of color. Membership was limited to fifty persons, who had to pay an initial membership fee of fifty dollars plus monthly dues. The fellowship used this money to provide for the funeral and burial expenses of its members and monthly stipends for the widows and orphans of members. The society also provided for the care of some of the poor among Charleston's free black population. Another society, also of Charleston, the Friendly Moralist Society, founded in 1838, functioned similarly. Yet another Charleston organization, the Humane Brotherhood, was formed in 1843, and it too provided sick benefits, burial expenses, and a fixed yearly income for widows and orphans of deceased members.

What makes these associations interesting is their organization around wealth and complexion. Obviously any free black who could afford the membership dues of these societies belonged to the exceptional class of free African Americans—people who, like William Ellison, had distinguished themselves from the masses of illiterate and unskilled free blacks. They owned property, were educated, and could provide for the education of their children, even if it meant sending them out of the state or even out of the country.

In every city, whether New York or New Orleans, there were classes of African Americans who were distinguished this way. They were the elite who succeeded despite all the obstacles placed in their way. In city after city they formed musical and literary societies. They preached a gospel of moral purity, and their social events were reported in black newspapers such as *Freedom's Journal,* first published by John Russwurm and Samuel Cornish in 1827 in New York City. They held themselves up to blacks and whites alike as the moral guardians of the race, the standard of excellence that all blacks could achieve if white prejudice disappeared.

These societies in Charleston were also notable because they were organized around color. Specifically, the Brown Fellowship and Friendly Moralist societies were exclusively for mulattoes, while the Humane Brotherhood was limited to no more than thirty-five "respectable Free Dark Men." This division of benevolent societies along color lines could be found everywhere in the United States, but it was especially pronounced in the Lower South, from South Carolina to Louisiana. It was in these states, where slavery was most entrenched, that the free black population was the smallest and most restricted. Manumissions, even during the Revolution, were never numerous, and slaves who were emancipated were very likely blood relatives of their master. In these states, mulattoes, usually called free people of color, were presumed by authorities to be free, and dark-skinned blacks, even those who were free, were presumed to be slaves.

In practical terms this meant that mulattoes had a better chance of surviving and succeeding than dark-complexioned blacks did. Often it was because their white relative gave them some advantage over other African Americans. In William Ellison's case it was an education and training as a cotton gin maker; for others it included a ticket out of the South. The fact that whites were not as threatened by mulattoes as they were by the darker skinned worked in the former's favor as well. Upper-class African-American society therefore was generally lighter than the poor, working, and middle classes.

And yet, the existence of the dark-skinned, upper-class Humane Brotherhood is evidence that wealth and good fortune were not always synonymous with light skin. At the same time that many dark-skinned blacks excelled, southern plantations held many mulattoes in slavery. Some were so white that their African heritage was not obvious. For African-American women, light skin could bring dubious advantages. White men often found them desirable and this sometimes had its end in freedom for the mulatto woman, but more often than not, the result could be a lifetime of sexual exploitation. Mulatto women probably saw more house service than did their darker sisters, but house service was not always a blessing.

A light skin could help with success, but other factors such as literacy, a trade or profession, and white connections helped structure free black antebellum society. And structured it was. Differences in wealth, literacy, complexion, and occupation made for different social connections and classes within black society. It was not unusual for wealthier African Americans to attend a different church from those of the middle and lower classes. Usually the wealthier the free black, the less emotional his religious denomination. Methodists and Baptists attracted the African-American masses, and those with skills, literacy, and wealth usually joined or formed their own more reserved Episcopal or Presbyterian church.

Despite the differences and varied occupations and chances for success, freedom for African Americans was always and everywhere limited. White freedom and black freedom were never the same, and although there were many things to divide blacks from each other, their partial freedom brought them all together. As the nation moved closer to the Civil War, the more similar all black life became. In the South, where by 1860 the color line was drawn fast and tight, all free African Americans—the light skinned and the dark, the skilled and the unskilled, the literate and the illiterate, the Episcopalian and the Baptist—faced the same hostile whites. As they raised their voices in protest in the years immediately preceding the Civil War they struck a chord of unity—unity with each other, and unity with the slave.

Let My People Go

In 1847 the first edition of Frederick Douglass's newspaper, the *North Star,* rolled off the presses. It was not the first African-American newspaper nor would it be the last. And like the names of many other African-American publications, *North Star* signified black aspirations, because the North Star, the light that guided so many runaways out of the South, symbolized freedom.

In his dedication Douglass tied the fate of all blacks together, the free and enslaved, those north and those south. "We are one," he declared, "our cause is one" and "we must help each other." Douglass went on to declare the unity of the free black with the slave. "What you suffer, we suffer; what you endure, we endure. We are indissolubly united, and must fall or flourish together."

Douglass's words were prophetic, but it did not take a prophet to see the wisdom of his remarks. The nation was just thirteen years from the Civil War. Already the ferment was rising. The American Anti-slavery Society was fourteen years old. Founded by blacks and whites, the society held religious revival-style meetings where abolitionists made stirring speeches condemning slavery as a moral wrong. They urged their listeners to put pressure on state legislatures to end slavery. The abolitionist movement spawned the Liberty party, and in 1840 and 1844 it ran anti-slavery presidential candidates. Although the Liberty party did not attract a significant following, it did plant the seed of fear of "slave power." The admittance of Texas into the Union as a slave state in 1845 and the promised addition of slave states from the territories taken by the United States as a result of the Mexican War in 1846 did in fact convince many Northerners that slaveholders would use their political and economic power to make slavery legal everywhere. More and more, Northern whites wondered whether slavery would or could be confined only to the South; more and more they wondered about the fate of white laborers in a slave labor economy.

Blacks, too, pondered their fate. But for them, the issues were different. Most important, the concerns of African Americans did not divide them as much as the debate over slavery divided whites. They had much to gain from white conflict over slavery, and they understood that they would not benefit at all if they were not united. And for the most part they spoke with one voice. Free blacks, those who could speak out against injustice, all wanted freedom for the enslaved and justice for the free. All wanted blacks to have the rights that were accorded by the Constitution

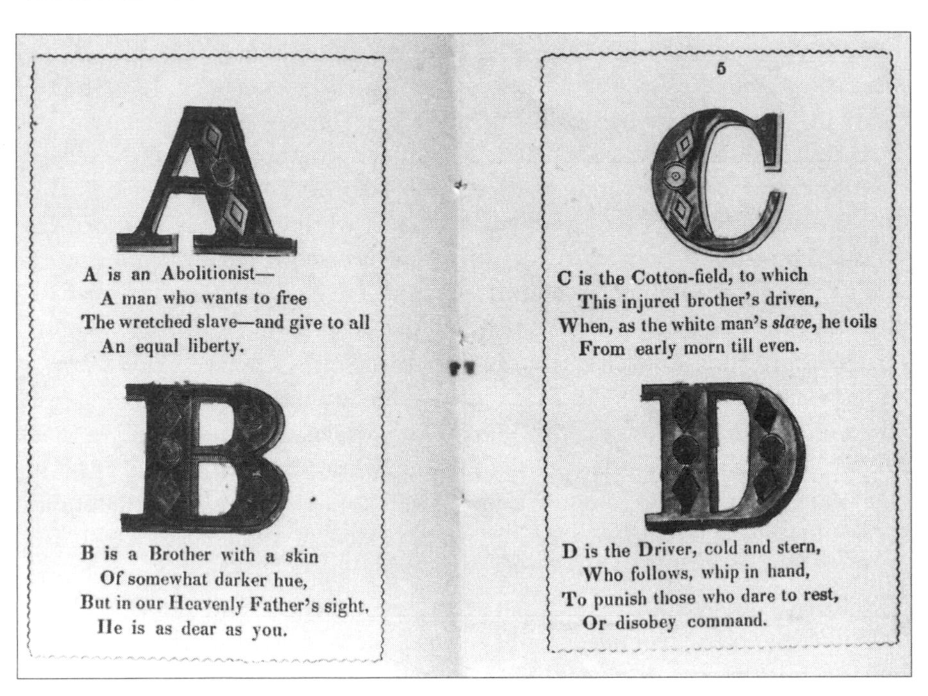
5

A

A is an Abolitionist—
A man who wants to free
The wretched slave—and give to all
An equal liberty.

B

B is a Brother with a skin
Of somewhat darker hue,
But in our Heavenly Father's sight,
He is as dear as you.

C

C is the Cotton-field, to which
This injured brother's driven,
When, as the white man's *slave*, he toils
From early morn till even.

D

D is the Driver, cold and stern,
Who follows, whip in hand,
To punish those who dare to rest,
Or disobey command.

The Anti-Slavery Alphabet, published in 1847 for an anti-slavery fair in Philadelphia, used simple rhymes to expose children to the horrors of slavery.

to all Americans. They differed, however, on the means to achieve these ends. The story of black protest in the years before the Civil War is one of unity on the large issues of rights and debate about the way to achieve them.

Black protest against slavery began long before the 1833 formation of the predominantly white American Anti-slavery Society. During the Revolution the Continental Congress was bombarded with petitions from Northern slaves who used the "all men are created equal" clause of the Declaration of Independence to claim their freedom. Protest against slavery continued through the Confederation period, and at the beginning of the nineteenth century the African Methodist Episcopal minister Absalom Jones walked the streets of Philadelphia carrying a petition that protested the renewal of the slave trade in Maryland, the birthplace of many Philadelphia blacks. In their churches and benevolent societies African Americans raised money to help runaways, wrote petitions protesting slavery, and spoke against black bondage whenever and wherever the opportunity arose.

On a more subtle level, blacks celebrated New Year's Day as their Independence Day. As Frederick Douglass noted, to the slave the national Fourth of July celebration was a day that revealed "the gross injustice and cruelty to which he is the constant victim." To the slave, the shouts of liberty and equality, the prayers, hymns, sermons, and thanksgivings were "hollow mockery ... mere bombast, fraud, deception, impiety, and hypocrisy—a thin veil to cover up crimes which would disgrace a nation of savages." New Year's Day, in contrast, had real meaning for African Americans. It was the anniversary of Haitian independence in 1804 and the end of the foreign slave trade with the United States in 1808.

As each New Year's Day passed, free blacks increasingly condemned the federal government for its perpetuation of slavery. They did not have to go much further than the Constitution to find a federal document worthy of condemnation. The Constitution allowed the foreign slave trade to persist for twenty years after its signing. For purposes of representation, it counted enslaved African Americans as three-fifths of a person. It also promised to put down slave insurrections and to track down fugitives from slavery and return them to their owners. This last provision, which put the federal government in the business of slave catching, was reinforced by a fugitive slave law in 1793 and by a particularly harsh one in 1850. African Americans vigorously opposed these laws, but between 1836 and 1844 the House of Representatives adopted a "gag rule" against all anti-slavery petitions. Under this rule all abolitionist petitions were automatically tabled so that they could not even be discussed on the floor of the House.

Still blacks protested. They took particular aim at the program of the American Colonization Society. Founded in 1816, this society counted some of America's most notable citizens among its members. Presidents James Madison and Andrew Jackson, Senator Daniel Webster, and Francis Scott Key, author of "The Star-Spangled Banner," all argued that blacks should be returned to Africa because it was the only natural home of black people. Central to their argument was their belief that blacks would never be accepted in America. According to national leader and presidential-hopeful Henry Clay, the "Great Compromiser," blacks would ever inhabit "the lowest strata of social gradation." In his opinion blacks were "aliens—political-moral-social aliens, strangers, though native." Africa, on the other hand, held hope for blacks. It was a place where they would not be degraded and debased. Moreover, advocates of colonization believed that American Negroes, having come under the civilizing influence of Christianity and having observed the benefits of democracy and capitalism, would redeem Africa. They argued that African Americans would transform Africa into prosperous mini-American black republics. Colonization would open up new commercial routes between Africa and America. In short, what blacks could not do here in America, they could and would do in Africa. In their minds, the end result of colonization would benefit both blacks and whites, America and Africa.

Colonizationists tried to recruit well-known, successful blacks to lead the exodus to Africa. The most common strategy was to lure influential black leaders with the prospect of power, wealth, and prestige. For example, they offered James Forten, a wealthy sailmaker, commercial advantages if he would lead blacks back to West Africa. He refused, but it did not stop colonizationists from sensationalizing the advantages of going to Africa.

All but a few declined the opportunity to return. Those who did leave settled on land near the British colony of Sierra Leone. Located on land purchased by the American Colonization Society in 1822, the colony was named Liberia, the "land of freedom." Settlers hoped that this small country would fulfill the promise of its name and provide the liberty that America withheld. Certainly this was the hope of two of its most renowned settlers, the black sea captain and shipowner Paul Cuffee and John Russwurm, an educator and the editor of *Freedom's Journal.* Both men endorsed colonization because they felt America would never treat its black citizens fairly. "If the slaves of our country with one accord were delivered from bondage," Russwurm asked, "can they be elevated to an equality with the whites? Can they while in this country be divested of the odium of inferior and degraded caste?" Russwurm's answer to his own question was "No!" For him and his small following, Liberia would provide the liberty denied by America.

But only a few people were willing to follow him. News of the troubled relationships that the settlers had with surrounding African tribes and the difficulty American blacks had with African diseases thwarted settlement. However, the most important reason why African Americans refused to return to Africa was their feeling that America was their country. Africa was indeed their *ancestral* homeland, but America was their birthplace and from it they drew their identity. They had fought and died in America's wars, had cleared this country's land and swamps, had helped build up its towns. The world, not just America, grew rich off the cotton, rice, and sugar grown by black people. They believed they had proved themselves productive, self-sufficient citizens, more so than even the slaveholder who had fewer skills, and who lived off the labor of others. To be asked to leave after such sacrifice to America was sheer injustice.

Many African Americans also believed that this push by whites exposed unadulterated white racism. African Americans asked that they be allowed to live free in this land that was the beacon of liberty. They protested the colonizationists' claim that blacks were incapable of living in freedom. They challenged America to stand by its principles of democracy and liberty.

Free blacks understood that it was their organized opposition to slavery that was threatening. Prominent among the leaders and members of colonization societies were slaveholders, none of whom supported the emancipation of slaves and their return to Africa, but all of whom argued that blacks were unprepared for freedom. In the opinion of most African-American leaders, colonization was a scheme to protect slavery and preserve freedom for whites only. Their fight against colonization, therefore, was a fight for themselves but also for their brothers and sisters in slavery. As they saw things, they were the slave's best hope, and the slave was their best ally in the cause of black rights.

Not that they did not want to forge alliances with white Americans, too. These were more problematic, however. For one thing, most prominent African-

American leaders were dismayed by the widespread support given to colonization societies. Before the 1830s men like William Lloyd Garrison, Gerrit Smith, Arthur and Lewis Tappan, and Benjamin Lundy—whites who actively opposed slavery—also supported colonization. They did not see how colonization helped preserve slavery, or how the scheme exposed free blacks to the rage of anti-black mobs.

Such a mob let loose its venom in Cincinnati in 1829. Tension in the city had been growing throughout the 1820s. As the free black population increased and competed for jobs, whites demanded their expulsion. They were encouraged by the leaders of the Cincinnati Colonization Society. Since its founding in 1826, it had prompted ministers and local newspapers to agitate against the city's blacks. Its propaganda provided the justification for driving them from the city. In the summer of 1829 city officials tried to push African Americans out by enforcing the Ohio Black Laws, which required blacks to post bonds guaranteeing "good behavior." Before black leaders could get a reprieve from the city legislature, white mobs attacked defenseless blacks. More than half the black population fled to Canada and other parts of the United States.

Although this and similar incidents convinced some sympathetic whites that colonization was inherently evil, it did not alter their prejudice toward blacks. This was another reason that African-American leaders found alliances with whites problematic. For example, even though black abolitionists like Peter Williams and William Watkins coaxed white men like William Lloyd Garrison and Gerrit Smith away from colonization, when Garrison and a small group of white friends met to organize the New England Antislavery Society in 1832, they invited blacks to join them only after all their plans had been formulated. Similarly, only three blacks were among the sixty-two signers of the American Antislavery Society's Declaration of Sentiments. Though it had twenty-six vice presidents and a nine-member executive committee, the society had no black officers.

African-American leaders were further disturbed by the limited perspectives and goals of white abolitionists. As free blacks they spoke against slavery as well as blanket discrimination against all blacks. White abolitionists, they found, were not much concerned with racism. Many black abolitionists shared the reaction of Theodore Wright, who criticized the "constitutions of abolition societies, where nothing was said about the improvement of the man of color!" Speaking before the New York Antislavery Society in 1837, Wright complained that "they have overlooked the giant sin of prejudice. They have passed by this foul monster, which is at once the parent and offspring of slavery."

Black abolitionists further noted that many white abolitionists refused to admit black children to their schools, would not hire black workers for anything but menial jobs, and even failed to hire blacks to work in anti-slavery offices. They also observed that in the early stages of their efforts, white abolitionists did not hire black lecturers, and when they eventually did they tried to control every aspect of their language and message.

A case in point involved Frederick Douglass. When Douglass first began lecturing in 1841 he related the trials of his slavery and the terrors of the institution. Garrison and others were pleased. They encouraged Douglass to repeat his performance over and over. As Douglass matured as a speaker, and as he pondered the meaning of freedom for himself and the nation, he grew more philosophical and learned in his talks. White abolitionists found Douglass the philosopher to be less "authentic" than Douglass the ex-slave. They did not want him to grow. Instead they repeatedly criticized him for appearing too smart. At one point he was told, "People won't believe you ever were a slave, Frederick, if you keep on this way. . . . Better have a *little* of the plantation manner of speech than not."

But Douglass, like other African-American leaders, listened to his own voice, and his own people, and in a very short time went his own way. Blacks continued to build their own movement, and central to it was the black press. Newspapers founded by leading personalities reminded black Americans of their role in the development of the American nation. There was no lack of articles on the role black soldiers played in the American Revolution and the War of 1812.

At the same time that newspapers confirmed the black's identity as an American, they also grounded that identity in the common black experience. Thus in their reporting of slave resistance, the terrors of slavery, and the free black communities' assistance to fugitive slaves, newspapers made it difficult for free blacks to forget their relatively privileged status in relation to the slave. Just as important, these accounts helped cement the bond between slave and free.

Newspapers with such names as *The Colored American*, the *Weekly Advocate*, the *New Era*, and the *Weekly Anglo-African* helped unify African Americans by keeping them informed of happenings in their own community and the nation. Articles and advertisements covering their various concerts, lectures, church events, educational opportunities, and school programs were regular features of black newspapers. By reporting national events from a black perspective and accepting editorials from ordinary African Americans, these newspapers allowed blacks to express their ideas on a variety of subjects and vent frustrations that had no other outlet. Since only a small percentage of the African-American population was literate, and these privileged few had to read or otherwise communicate the newspaper's contents to those who could not read, newspapers helped forge the bonds of community. They bridged the gap between the educated and the illiterate.

Through their own newspapers and a few edited by white abolitionists, ordinary African Americans learned of the protest activity of their leaders—men and women such as Douglass, Martin Delany, Henry Highland Garnet, William Wells Brown, William Whipper, and Maria Stewart. The question was how blacks should obtain their freedom. The decision was not an easy one. Would armed rebellion succeed? From their relatively safe surroundings, should they encourage the slaves to risk everything in a break for freedom? How far should free blacks go in opposing the fugitive slave laws? Should they hold off slave catchers with guns or would civil disobedience be enough? How would they achieve their rights of full citizenship?

Answers to these questions came from many quarters. In his speeches and in a pamphlet entitled *Walker's Appeal . . . to the Colored Citizens of the World But in Particular and Very Expressly to those of the United States of America,* David Walker urged African Americans to meet the slaveholders' violence with violence of their own. He blamed the oppression of blacks on white greed for money and power. In the by-now-typical African-American tradition of blending the secular with the sacred, of using religion to help solve life's problems, Walker urged black people to rise up and wage a holy war against whites, who had by their sin against African Americans sinned against God. "They want us for their slaves," he wrote. They "think nothing of murdering us in order to subject us to that wretched condition." In his justification of armed resistance, Walker wrote, "It is no more harm for you to kill a man who is trying to kill you, than it is for you to take a drink of water when thirsty: in fact the man who will stand still and let another man murder him is worse than an infidel."

No doubt many African Americans felt the same way Walker did, but most spoke with more moderate voices. Although they did not lose sight of the role played by whites in black oppression, many leaders urged African Americans to take an active role in liberation by uplifting themselves. Maria Stewart, one of the few African-American female public lecturers, urged blacks to give up drinking and invest in schools and seminaries. An admirer and follower of Walker, Stewart nevertheless believed that "nothing would raise our respectability, add to our peace and happiness, and reflect so much honor upon us, as to be ourselves the promoters of temperance, and the supporters . . . of useful and scientific knowledge." An advocate of female education during a time when it was thought that women best served the race by serving their husbands, brothers, and fathers, Stewart argued that the race needed both men and women in public roles. "Daughters of Africa" needed to unite. They could raise money to build schools to educate black youth, they could own stores that would service their community, they could educate themselves and through them the race would be uplifted.

As despairing as Stewart sometimes was when she looked at the plight of African Americans, she, like many others, was still more optimistic about the future than was David Walker. The goal of uplift was, after all, eventual integration into American life. Blacks were behind not because of natural inferiority but because of prejudice and slavery. Once these impediments were abolished, education and opportunity would remedy the situation.

Throughout the 1830s and 1840s Frederick Douglass shared Stewart's optimism. He did not support armed resistance or programs to go back to Africa. He believed that through constant preaching, political lobbying, and hard struggle blacks would eventually find liberty in America. "You must be a man here," he insisted, "and force your way to intelligence, wealth and respectability. If you can't do that here, you can't do it there."

But there were many who disagreed. Martin Delany, a Harvard-educated physician, was the most articulate spokesman against the views Douglass and others expressed. "No people can be free who themselves do not constitute an essential part of the *ruling element* of the country in which they live." These words, published in his 1852 book entitled *The Condition, Elevation, Emigration, and Destiny of the Colored People of the United States,* were part of his argument for emigrating from the eastern United States to Central or South America or to some nonsettled area in the American West. He did not share with Douglass the belief that America would allow blacks to become citizens. Much like Native Americans, blacks, he wrote, were "a nation within a nation." Blacks and whites shared a common country. But whites were an oppressor nation and blacks the oppressed nation. Black people, he claimed, loved America, but because that love was met with only belittlement and degradation, black people were "politically not of them, but aliens to the laws and privileges of the country." Thus separated, African Americans had a duty to establish a black society where they would be free to enjoy the privileges of citizenship.

These, then, were the lines of protest in African-American communities before 1850. Despite their different levels of optimism and different strategies of resistance, antebellum black leaders were united in their good feelings about themselves. Never did they give in to self-hatred, nor did they ever believe the proslavery arguments that held that they were naturally inferior to whites. Before America they stood tall and proud.

It was this black pride that eventually drove all black abolitionist leaders to advocate some degree of black separatism. In their minds, blacks, as a people, had to do for themselves; self-improvement had to be based on self-reliance. Said Phillip A. Bell, in the *Weekly Advocate,* whites may make "OUR CAUSE" their cause all they want, but their efforts will be unavailing "without our thinking and acting, as a body, for ourselves."

In thinking and acting for themselves blacks met during the 1830s through the 1850s in black-only national conventions. Northern cities such as Albany, Rochester, Cincinnati, Philadelphia, Buffalo, and Cleveland were the sites of some of the meetings where the means of uplift and strategies of resistance were debated. Although those who attended these conventions realized that some might think that all-black meetings worked against the goal of integration of blacks into the American mainstream, most concluded that racial solidarity was necessary to secure their status as full-fledged Americans. Separatism, whether in conventions, schools, or churches, was not the end in itself, but the means to the end.

For all of their work, it was, in the end, not black or even white abolitionists who struck the fatal blow against slavery. The institution proved so entrenched that it took a civil war to end it. Black protesters, however, could be proud of the work they did in unifying the spirits of free blacks and in forging the bond between free and enslaved African Americans. In so doing, they laid the intellectual foundation on which the protest of future generations of blacks and whites was built.

From Desperation to Hope

At the end of 1850 African Americans did not know that the nation was just a decade away from civil war, that slavery would be its cause, or that the war would end slavery for good. They could not know that it would be the bloodiest war ever fought on America's soil or that their citizenship and voting rights would hang in the balance.

However, black people could not help but sense that something out of the ordinary was happening. Slavery was at the heart of heated discussions about the nation's future, and the Compromise of 1850, meant to quell anxiety about the slavery question, actually fanned its flames. The Compromise brought California into the nation as a free state, eliminated the slave trade in the District of Columbia, and organized the territories of Utah and Mexico. Its most obnoxious part was the Fugitive Slave Law. Under its harsh provisions, the law forced blacks accused of being fugitives to prove their free status, not to a jury, but to a special commissioner who was paid more (ten dollars) for returning a slave to his owner than for setting him or her free (five dollars). The law also compelled Northerners to hunt down and turn in runaway slaves.

As slave hunters known as "kidnappers" flooded the North seizing fugitives, blacks had to decide what to do. They had always resisted fugitive slave laws, but by putting a bounty on every runaway's head, and making every white person a potential slave catcher, this latest fugitive law made resistance more risky and life for free blacks terribly insecure—so insecure that many free blacks took one last stride toward freedom by fleeing across the Canadian border.

The vast majority who remained faced a nation racked with conflict that did not lessen. Abraham Lincoln's election to the presidency in 1860 brought some hope that liberation was on the horizon. Mostly though, there was despair over the way the decade had proceeded and wretched bitterness over the country's betrayal of blacks.

Ironically, the 1850s was a decade of prosperity. Not only whites but blacks, too, did relatively well. This was indicated by the steady increase in black land and property ownership all over the country. In Nashville, for example, in 1860 there were twenty-six free blacks who were worth more than a thousand dollars who had owned no property ten years earlier. Charleston had always had a wealthy colored elite, but during the 1850s as many as seventy-five whites rented their homes from freemen. In Baltimore free blacks monopolized the caulking trade, and throughout the Upper South free black agricultural laborers took advantage of the movement of slaves south by demanding and receiving higher wages.

Economic success generated confidence. This confidence was visible in the new churches being built by larger and wealthier black congregations in the North and the South. It was also shown by the increased audacity of free blacks. In Petersburg, Virginia, for example, whites complained that blacks were slow to give way to whites on walkways.

Blacks also exuded more confidence in the way they responded to oppression. In Richmond, for instance, free blacks petitioned the city council to repeal the city's repressive Black Code, and in New York City there was the stunning behavior of Elizabeth Jennings. On a Sunday morning in 1854 she was pulled out of a horse-drawn trolley car and wrestled to the ground by a white conductor and driver who sought to keep her from sitting in the white section. With the same conviction and audacity shown by the free blacks of Richmond, Jennings took her case to court. Her victory there broke the back of segregation on public conveyances in New York.

All over the country blacks tried to do the same to the Fugitive Slave Law. Twice in Boston, blacks and whites stormed a courthouse in failed attempts to rescue Thomas Sims in 1851 and Anthony Burns in 1854. Others, such as Elijah Anderson, John Mason, and of course, Harriet Tubman, continued to risk life and limb going into the South and delivering African Americans from slavery. Frederick Douglass also risked harm by his resistance to the law. Though very much in the public eye, he, like countless others, raised money for fugitives, hid them in his Rochester home, and helped hundreds escape to Canada.

And, like others, he had to struggle with the meaning of the Fugitive Slave Law. In Rochester, New York, in 1853 Douglass and other black abolitionists held one of their largest conventions to try to decide what to do about resisting the law. Reluctant though they were to call for the creation of separate black institutions, they felt the Fugitive Slave Law left them no choice. America seemed determined to cast them aside and destroy their rights as citizens. Somehow, they had to salvage them. In their attempt to do this, black abolitionists called for the creation of a national council to oversee black improvement and a manual labor school for the education of black children in science, literature, and the mechanical arts. They did this, they said, not to "build ourselves up as a distinct and separate class in this country but as a means to . . . equality in political rights, and in civil rights, and in civil and social privileges with the rest of the American people."

Although black abolitionists as a group took larger strides toward separatism, some individuals spoke out in favor of armed resistance. Douglass was among them. He not only increased his aid to fugitive slaves but he became decidedly more militant: "The only way to make the Fugitive Slave Law a dead letter is to make a half dozen or more dead kidnappers."

For Martin Delany, Douglass's response fell short of a remedy. It was not enough to challenge the individual kidnapper when the source of the problem was the prejudice that permeated all American institutions, including the government.

Shoot one kidnapper, and another would take his place. The law was a reflection of government policy, and in Delany's opinion even the call for separate black institutions did not go far enough to counter white racism. When Delany pondered institutional discrimination and the Fugitive Slave Law, he concluded that "a people capable of originating and sustaining such a law as this are not people to whom we are willing to entrust our liberty at discretion." His advice was to "go to whatever parts of Central and South America" and "make common cause with the people." For Delany, emigration was still the only answer.

Delany found support at conventions held in Maryland in 1852 and Cleveland in 1854. Unlike the delegates to the Rochester convention, those who attended the Cleveland meeting were not reluctant supporters of black separatism, nor did they see the point in arguing for separation as a means to American citizenship. As Delany put it, it was time for black people to look outside of America, to grab hold of those places in the world where chance was in their favor and where the rights and power of the colored race could be established.

Although more blacks than ever took up this position in the 1850s, most African Americans remained hopeful of change within the United States. They could not abandon the land of their birth, give up the dream for which their forefathers had sacrificed so much, nor leave their enslaved brethren with no black advocates for freedom. Delegates to the Baltimore convention found this out when the meeting they called to discuss emigration was broken up by angry black crowds who wanted no part of Africa, Haiti, Mexico, or Canada. They did not disagree with the delegates' demand to be treated like men. Nor did they take issue with the convention's general sentiment that in Maryland swine were treated better than free Negroes. Clearly though, they, like most free blacks, wanted to make their stand here in America.

In the first few years of the decade it seemed that they had support. In fact, white Northerners did grow more sympathetic. This was in part because the Fugitive Slave Law brought the issue of slavery to their doorstep. Whites who witnessed slaves being dragged unwillingly back South found it difficult to remain detached from the issue. They could no longer treat it as something that just happened "down there."

And what was happening "down there" was made even more real by the publication in magazine installments, and then as a book in 1852, of Harriet Beecher Stowe's *Uncle Tom's Cabin.* In a brilliant manipulation of public sentiment, Stowe raised public consciousness about the evils of slavery. She did this by making her slaves people with whom almost all whites could identify. There were few Northern mothers who did not hail Eliza's courageous escape across the floes of the Ohio River, or cry over Little Eva's death. Only the meanest could side with the wicked Yankee slaveholder Simon Legree, and all could see the Christlike goodness of the beloved Uncle Tom. So large and so stirred was the Northern readership that when Lincoln met Stowe in 1863 he is supposed to have said, "So you're the little woman who wrote the book that made this great war!"

If African Americans had reason to be buoyed by this new awareness on the part of the Northern public, they surely had reason to be wary of the response it drew from Southerners. Already unnerved by the steady economic progress and increasing boldness of free blacks, Southern whites' anxiety only increased in the face of Northern anti-slavery activity. In particular, slaveholders were sure that free blacks and increased anti-slavery activity had something to do with the increase in the number of runaway slaves and incidents of overt resistance.

And to Southerners it seemed as though every day brought news of some other violent incident involving slaves. It was said that overseers in the Mississippi Valley so feared for their lives that they were never caught without their guns. In Tennessee four slaves were put to death for attempting to attack the iron mills where they worked.

Some blacks in Texas also seemed ready. From that state came news of an alleged plot that was to bring blacks and Mexicans together in an attempt to rid the state of its white population. Although whites killed five blacks suspected of fomenting the insurrection, they could not quell black discontent, nor white fear of it.

They tried to, though. Because they felt that the ever-growing free black population was inciting slaves to flee and rebel, Southerners tried to get rid of them. With the exception of Delaware and North Carolina, every Upper South state instituted a colonization plan. Virginia's was typical. In 1850 it appropriated thirty thousand dollars annually for five years to send free blacks and emancipated slaves to the West African nation of Liberia. A tax placed on free blacks added an additional ten thousand dollars. Maryland passed a similar law in 1852, Tennessee in 1853, and Missouri and Kentucky in 1855.

These plans failed for two reasons. To begin with, not enough money was appropriated for such a massive removal of people. But even had there been enough funds, there were few people who wanted to go. African Americans were already opposed to the emigration plans proposed by their own leaders. They were hardly more disposed to leaving under a program arranged by their oppressors. John Rapier said what most blacks believed: "They [colonizationists] would not care if all the free negroes in the United States was at the Botom of the Sea so they was out of the United States."

Not only was Rapier right, he caught what was fast becoming the temper of the nation. Everywhere, not just in the South, anti-black sentiment was rising. Indiana offers a good example of this mood. In 1851 state legislators rewrote the state constitution with provisions that deprived blacks of the rights to vote, attend white schools, and make contracts. African Americans who could not post a five hundred dollar bond were expelled from the state, and an 1852 law made it a crime for blacks to settle in Indiana.

If nothing else these state laws demonstrated that anti-slavery sentiment easily coexisted with hostility toward African Americans. Most white citizens did not want *any* blacks in their midst, slave or free. This sentiment found national expression in

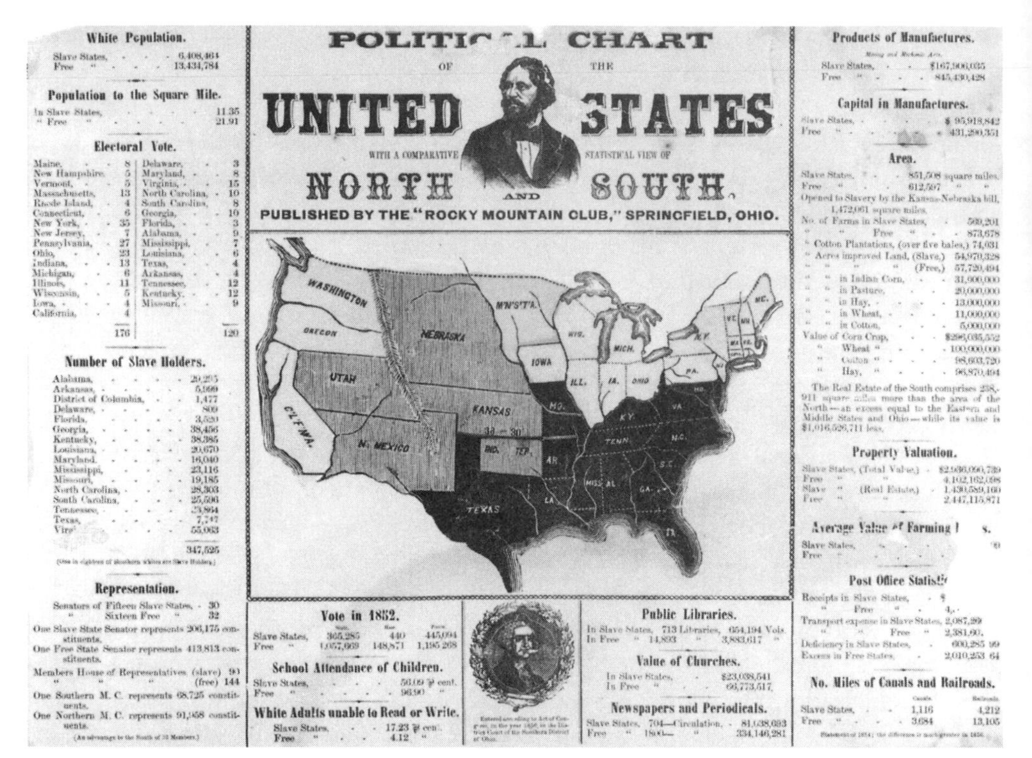

This 1856 chart of the United States shows the division between free and slave states. The chart also offers a statistical comparison between the North and the South, with figures for the number of public libraries, the number of children who attend school, and other categories.

the new Republican party, which was founded in 1854. The principal platform of this mostly Northern party was "no slavery in the territories." By this Republicans meant that they wanted to keep the new western territories as "free soil," meaning free of slavery. Slavery, they believed, retarded upward mobility and economic growth. From their point of view the South was stagnant and backward, while the North and Upper Midwest were energetic and progressive. Republicans promised not to oppose slavery where it already was. But inasmuch as America's democracy and its institutions depended on the ability of men to move and work in a free labor market, they argued that the future greatness of the American nation depended on the confinement of slavery and the expansion of free soil.

For African Americans the Republican party was both good and bad news. The good news was that many Republicans were abolitionists who opposed not just the expansion of slavery but also slavery where it existed. Senator William Seward of New York and Senators Charles Sumner of Massachusetts and George Julian of Ohio were ardent abolitionists who sought to divorce the federal government from the support of slavery by freeing slaves in the District of Columbia, repealing the Fugitive Slave Law, and eliminating the domestic slave trade.

There was good news too in even the limited goal of keeping slavery out of the territories. The rival party, the Democrats, had already gone on record as supporting popular sovereignty, the settler's right to decide whether slavery should exist in the territories. Its leading politician, Stephen A. Douglas, had pushed the Kansas-Nebraska Act through Congress early in 1854. This act allowed the people who settled in the newly organized Kansas and Nebraska regions to decide for themselves whether they wanted slavery. In allowing for the possibility of slavery in these territories the act overturned the 1820 Missouri Compromise, which had outlawed slavery in regions north of Missouri. The Republicans thus offered a much-needed counter to what was without a doubt a major threat from the power of the slave owners.

The bad news, though, was that the bulk of the party's support came from whites who were as much anti-black as they were anti-slavery. From the African American's point of view this made the party suspect. Republicans did not directly oppose slavery where it was, nor did they tackle issues like the domestic slave trade or the Fugitive Slave Law. Furthermore, the party's supporters and its prominent leader, Abraham Lincoln, did not favor equal rights for African Americans. In opposing the vote, jury service, and intermarriage, Republicans made clear their belief that whites were superior to blacks, and that the two races could not live together on terms of social and political equality.

The formation of the Republican party, therefore, left blacks with a lot to think about. They took heart that there was, for the first time, a political force opposing slavery, but they worried about the limits of that opposition and the extent to which the Republicans would go to keep blacks from exercising civil and political rights. That they were still without effective national allies in an increasingly hostile environment was a fact that did not escape them.

The depth of the nation's hostility to blacks was revealed by the Supreme Court's 1857 decision in *Scott* v. *Sandford* (the "Dred Scott case"), a ruling that sent shivers down the spine of black America. In 1846 Dred and Harriet Scott had filed suit in Missouri for their freedom. They argued that because their master had taken them into Minnesota, Wisconsin, and other territories where slavery had been outlawed by the Missouri Compromise, they were by right free. Chief Justice Roger B. Taney, writing for the court, disagreed. Dred and Harriet Scott were not free. Taney stated that blacks were "beings of an inferior order" and therefore "had no rights which white men were bound to respect." Justice Peter V. Daniel, of Virginia, added insult to injury by his claim that "the African Negro race" did not belong "to the family of nations" but rather was only a subject for "commerce or traffic," "slaves," "property."

If this part of the ruling fell like a dead weight on free blacks, the court's decision regarding the Missouri Compromise was a death sentence. In stating that the 1820 law was unconstitutional because Congress did not have the right to ban slavery in a territory, the court opened the entire country to slavery. If Congress could not ban slavery in the territories then it could not keep it out of Northern states.

Slaveholders could take their slaves north, settle wherever they wanted, and according to the logic of the Dred Scott decision, there was nothing that could be done about it. When put together with the Fugitive Slave Law, the Dred Scott decision left nowhere for the fugitive to run. Questionable as the North was as a haven for free blacks, these two measures eliminated it as a haven of any sort.

Events in Kansas between 1854 and John Brown's raid at Harpers Ferry, Virginia, in 1859, literally left free blacks nationless. After the Kansas-Nebraska Act was passed both pro- and anti-slavery forces rushed into Kansas, each group attempting to make sure that the territory was settled according to its wishes. At stake was whether the territories would be slave or free. With both forces willing to die for their cause, violence was inevitable. As the forces clashed in guerrilla-style warfare, only the free blacks' future there was certain: Slaveholders did not want them in their midst, and free-soilers wrote a constitution that forbade them from entering the state.

John Brown's raid only made the situation of free blacks more precarious. When the dust settled after the band of twenty-two men tried to take the federal arsenal at Harpers Ferry, free blacks were found to be among the conspirators. Slaveholders cringed when they thought about what might have happened had Brown's plan to seize and distribute weapons to slaves succeeded. They could and did hang John Brown for treason, but many thousands of free blacks who stood ready to take up Brown's mantle remained among the population. Having always viewed the free black as out of place in the South, white Southerners now saw an opportunity to eliminate this group for good.

Life for Southern free blacks had grown harder and more dangerous. States that had already made efforts to force them to leave through colonization renewed their efforts to eliminate them—this time through outright expulsion. Events in South Carolina, the home of William Ellison, were typical. On the urging of Charleston's white mechanics, city officials cracked down on free people of color. In October 1858 they began arresting those who had failed to pay the capitation (literally, "per head") tax, the tax free persons of color had to pay to attest to their freedom. In December of the following year, white Charlestonians formed a Committee of Safety to search out and arrest anyone with abolitionist sympathies. These included whites who ran black schools and blacks who received abolitionist newspapers or otherwise engaged in suspicious behavior. A similar committee was formed by Ellison's neighbors in Stateburg.

Meanwhile, as the state legislature debated reenslavement bills, South Carolina's newspapers carried articles assailing the free African American at every turn. One contributor asked why free blacks were allowed to attend balls, churches, and funerals in carriages; why they were allowed to assume the prerogatives and distinctions that "ought to be, among the landmarks separating the classes." "Shall they," he continued, "in silks and laces, promenade our principal thoroughfares, with the arrogance of equals."

If the white slaveholders who were the guardians of free blacks were willing to put up with such behavior, white workingmen made it clear that they were not. In the South Carolina state legislature their leaders introduced a bill that prohibited all free persons of color from "entering into contracts on any mechanical business on their own account." With a call to "MECHANICS, WORKING MEN AND ALL WHITE MEN WHO LIVE BY THE SWEAT OF THEIR BROW," white workers urged solidarity against free blacks.

Along with thousands of other free blacks throughout the South, most of whom were not nearly as wealthy, William Ellison and his family made plans to emigrate. Between 1858 and the election of Lincoln in 1860, the stream of free blacks heading out of the South became a river. As in South Carolina, every Southern legislature debated expulsion and reenslavement, and like Ellison, free blacks considered moving either north to Canada or south to Haiti or Central America. It did not matter that by the Civil War only Arkansas had actually expelled free blacks, ordering them to leave the state by January 1, 1860, or be enslaved. The fury with which expulsion and enslavement were being debated scared African Americans.

African-American leaders could not help but be disturbed. Everywhere they looked forces seemed arrayed against their people. Events in Kansas, the Dred Scott decision, the Fugitive Slave Law, expulsion and reenslavement bills all made for despair. The nation was moving toward dissolution with a certainty that was frightening. While free African Americans were being sacrificed, Southern calls for secession threatened to tighten the noose of slavery around blacks forever. So depressed was the ever-optimistic Frederick Douglass that he, like Ellison, began looking toward Haiti as a possible homeland for black people. Martin Delany, who had by Lincoln's election already moved himself, his wife, and his five children to Canada, traveled to West Africa in search of a place for his people to settle.

Amazingly, but understandably, the same events that caused so much despair for free blacks and their leaders seemed to inspire slaves. As they had done during the American Revolution and the War of 1812, slaves turned the nation's turmoil to their advantage. That they were at the center of the nation's divisions did not escape them, because by 1860 the future of slavery was on everyone's mind and lips. The slaves' knowledge was manifested by acts meant to subvert the system. From Austin, Texas, came reports of slaves' attempts to repeat "the horrors enacted at Harpers Ferry." In Montgomery, Alabama, it was reported that Negroes had plotted to divide up the estates, mules, lands, and household furniture of their white masters. The more conversations they overheard, the more newspaper articles that literate blacks read, the clearer it became that there were forces beyond the South lining up against slavery.

What was not clear though was the nature and the strength of these forces. The Republicans opposed slavery in the territories, but they also opposed black rights. Abraham Lincoln wavered when it came to African Americans. At one point he spoke in favor of black rights. Blacks, he said are "my equal and ... the equal of every living man." The Negro man, he declared, is "entitled to all the natural rights . . . in the Declaration of Independence" and had the right also to "put into his mouth the bread that his own hands have earned." At another point, though, Lincoln spoke words that were more in line with most of his generation. He claimed that he was against "the social and political equality of the white and black races," that he did not "favor making voters or jurors of negroes, nor of qualifying them to hold office, nor to intermarry with white people." Since, he said, there was a "physical difference between the white and black races which . . . will for ever forbid the two races living together on terms of social and political equality," Lincoln went on record as favoring whites over blacks. "There must be," he said during his campaign for the Senate in 1858, "the position of superior and inferior, and I as much as any other man am in favor of having the superior position assigned to the white race."

Expressions such as these inspired increasing despair. To Southerners, Abraham Lincoln was the devil incarnate, ready and willing to snatch their slaves from them at whatever cost. Upon his election to the presidency, legislatures of states in the South seceded from the United States by declaring that the states were no longer part of the Union. First, South Carolina seceded on December 24, 1860, followed by Mississippi, Florida, Alabama, Georgia, Louisiana, Texas, Virginia, North Carolina, Arkansas, and Tennessee. These eleven states joined together to form the Confederate States of America. They elected their own president, Jefferson Davis, and after initial debate established a capital in Richmond, Virginia.

Like Douglass, blacks wanted "the complete and universal *abolition* of the whole slave system," as well as equal suffrage and other rights for free blacks. In early 1861 Lincoln was still promising not to touch slavery where it was and not to repeal the Fugitive Slave Law. Small wonder then that African Americans hardly celebrated his inauguration.

The firing on Fort Sumter, South Carolina, on April 12, 1861 did, however, bring celebration. These first shots of the Civil War stirred real hope that slavery would soon end. It all happened so suddenly, soon after the officer in charge of the fort, Major Robert Anderson, informed Lincoln that he needed men, arms, and supplies to maintain the federal presence in Charleston harbor. Lincoln's dilemma was obvious. If he did nothing, he would appear weak and Sumter would fall to the Confederacy, as had other federal forts, custom houses, and post offices. On the other hand, if he sent forces this would no doubt be taken by the Confederacy as an act of war. Lincoln's choice—to send supplies but no troops or arms—shifted the burden of war to the Confederacy, which itself stood to lose credibility as a sovereign nation if it allowed Lincoln to maintain the fort within its borders. It was hardly their intention, but the shots Confederate generals fired on the ships sent to resupply Anderson were shots that put slavery on the road to extinction.

CHAPTER 5

Breaking the Chains

1860–1880

Noralee Frankel

In 1898, years after the Civil War, Alfred Thomas, an African-American soldier in the Union army, explained his decision to enlist. He was a slave in Mississippi when he first encountered the Yankees. After the Union soldiers rescued a slave from the plantation where Thomas lived, he and his companions became convinced that they should escape slavery themselves by going with the Union soldiers. As he recalled, "Well we had been hearing the guns at Natchez and all over the country and everybody was scared and kept hearing people say the negroes would be free and we heard of colored people running off to the Yankees. . . ." Alfred Thomas was one of eighteen hundred thousand African Americans who served in the Union army during the Civil War. There were also some twenty-nine thousand African Americans who fought in the Union navy. African Americans participated in fifty-two military engagements, and thirty-seven thousand died.

As the United States became increasingly polarized over slavery in the 1850s, the North and South became suspicious of each other's political power. Slavery was tied to the fight over states' rights—the doctrine that all rights not reserved to the federal government by the U.S. Constitution are granted to the states. Disputes between the supporters of slavery and the proponents of free labor were responsible for many of the political, economic, cultural, and ideological differences that divided the country during the war.

After Fort Sumter surrendered to the Confederacy on April 14, 1861, the southern states proceeded to organize an army under the leadership of Robert E. Lee. A West Point graduate and trained officer, Lee had turned down President Lincoln's offer to command the Union troops. Failing to obtain Lee, Lincoln named George McClellan general of the Union forces. But Lincoln grew frustrated by McClellan's cautiousness and failure to pursue the enemy. He replaced McClellan with a succession of generals to head the Union forces but found them all unsatisfactory. Lincoln finally selected General Ulysses S. Grant to head the Union's forces because he had proved to be an aggressive, tenacious fighter. Grant's fearlessness ultimately resulted in far greater casualties than would have occurred under McClellan, but under Grant's leadership the Union army won the war.

For the first two years of the war, Lincoln justified the fighting only as necessary to save the United States from becoming two separate countries. Not wanting to antagonize the border states like Kentucky and Missouri, which were slave states that had stayed in the Union, Lincoln refused to deal with the slave issue in any systematic manner. As the war progressed, however, African Americans and white abolitionists pushed Lincoln to change his mind and add the elimination of slavery to the reasons the Union was fighting the Civil War.

Free African Americans as well as slaves were convinced much earlier than Lincoln that a Northern victory would end slavery, even though the stated purpose of the war was to save the Union. As Frederick Douglass explained, "The American people and the Government at Washington may refuse to recognize it for a time but the 'inexorable logic of events' will force it upon them in the end; that the war now being waged in this land is a war for and against slavery." One African American complained, "Our union friends says the[y] are not fighting to free the negroes . . . we are fighting for the union . . . very well let the white fight for what the[y] want and we negroes fight for what we want . . . liberty must take the day."

During the war, some slaves remained on the plantation while others, often seeking liberty, escaped to the Union lines. Some planters fled to Texas and other states to keep their slaves away from the Union army. These flights made slave escapes almost impossible. When the soldiers were nearby, male slaves could escape but elderly slaves and women with small children often found it difficult to run to Union lines. As slaves fled, the work of those who remained on the plantation expanded. As one man recalled, during the war, slave owners made slave children "do a man's work."

Raids on a plantation by soldiers—of both armies—increased the difficulty of the slaves' work. Soldiers also raided the slaves' quarters, taking their few possessions. Deprivations caused by the war affected both the Southern whites and the African Americans on plantations.

Harsh treatment by Union soldiers made some slaves wary of them. Moreover, if slaves helped the Northern soldiers, they could be punished by their masters once the soldiers left. Some slaves therefore failed to cooperate, to protect themselves. Once when a Union soldier confronted a slave woman and demanded to know where the silverware was hidden, she told him that her owners were too cheap to buy anything that nice. (She had earlier helped bury the silver near the very spot where she was speaking to the soldier.) However, many other slaves did not protect their masters' property from soldiers.

The taking of food by Union soldiers and their destruction of plantation property confused some slaves, especially children. They developed an ambivalence toward the Union soldiers, unable to decide if the Yankees were their liberators or merely new enslavers. Even before having contact with them, slave children were predisposed to be afraid of Yankee soldiers because they had heard Southern whites refer to them as devils and monsters. Some slave children interpreted these words literally. Mollie Williams later recalled, "Us all thought de Yankees was some kin' of debils an' we was skeered to death of 'em."

Fear of the Union soldiers did not mean, however, that the slaves who remained on the plantations supported slavery or continued to work and act as they had under slavery. The Civil War and the general turmoil it brought destroyed the customary white authority on most plantations and small farms. As a result, slaves often refused to do certain kinds of work and argued over matters of discipline and the management of the plantation. Even before emancipation, they began to assert their rights as freed people. Before the close of the war, one slave owner greeted one of his workers with "Howdy, Uncle," but the slave responded with a demand for proper respect: "Call me Mister." On a minority of plantations, the freed slaves became violent, burning property and looting from their previous owners. Because of the war, some owners simply abandoned their plantations. The slaves who stayed behind divided the land and property among themselves. They planted food crops and sometimes cotton to sell.

Other slaves left their plantations to escape slavery. In the South, all through the war thousands of slaves freed themselves by running to the Union lines. As one military chaplain described it, "Blacks illustrated what the history of the world has rarely seen—a slave population . . . leaving its bondage of centuries . . . individually or in families. . . . Their comings were like the arrivals of cities." Leaving one's family to seek freedom behind the Yankee lines was difficult, both emotionally and physically. When his father escaped, Levi McLaurin's son recalled, "I was present when he left and I told him goodbye. He said he would be back after us all." The son "saw men put dogs on his tracks and heard dogs running after my father." Another male slave joined McLaurin but turned back after three miles "because I could not leave my family."

If freed people running toward the Union lines were caught by their masters, they were whipped or even killed. One newly freed man, John Boston, escaped to a regiment from Brooklyn that was stationed in Virginia. Missing his still-enslaved wife, he wrote her: "My Dear wife It is with grate joy I take this time to let you know Where I am[.] i am now in Safety in the 14th Regiment of Brooklyn[.] this Day i can Adress you thank god as a free man[.] I had a little trouble in giting away." He added, "I trust the time Will Come When We Shal meet again[.] And if We dont met on earth We will Meet in heaven."

As the war progressed, more women, particularly if they did not have small children, accompanied the men. Former slave woman Maggie Dixon recalled that when "the Union cavalry came past our plantation, told us to quit work, and follow them, we were all too glad to do so." Slaves were especially eager to leave the plantations after soldiers destroyed the food supplies there.

At the beginning of the war, the federal government had no policy regarding the

In this cartoon, slaves abandon their master and run to Fort Monroe. General Benjamin Butler, who was in command of that Virginia fort, had declared such runaways "contraband" and had allowed them to stay with the Union forces.

treatment of escaping slaves. However, the sheer number of fleeing slaves soon pushed Congress and the Union army into forming a plan to deal with the slaves' aspirations for freedom. As soon as the Union army approached, slaves from neighboring plantations ran to its lines, hoping for their freedom. But to the slaves' disappointment, Northern soldiers in the early part of the war returned runaway slaves to their masters. Not all the Yankee generals agreed with this policy. In May 1861, General Benjamin Butler, stationed in Virginia, declared the runaway slaves "contraband," or property taken during war, and allowed them to stay with the army. Butler later explained, "I was always a friend of southern rights, but an enemy of southern wrongs." Butler's policy of freeing individual slaves who escaped to the Union army was tolerated by the federal government. Nevertheless, when other Union generals issued more sweeping orders freeing all the slaves in territories under their command, President Lincoln overrode them.

To help clarify the status of the slaves, in August 1861 Congress passed the first Confiscation Act, which kept slave owners from reenslaving runaways. Union soldiers occasionally continued to act as slave catchers and forced escaped slaves to go back to their masters. Finally, in March 1862, Congress passed a law forbidding Union soldiers from returning escaped slaves. Then in July 1862, Congress passed the second Confiscation Act, which more broadly freed the slaves of any master helping the Confederacy. Together, these measures began slowly to change the focus of the war toward a struggle for liberation by the slaves.

Throughout the war, the Union army had the practical problem of what to do with all the people fleeing to it. The army quickly put the men to work as drivers, cooks, blacksmiths, and construction workers, but the women, children, and elderly were more difficult to employ. For the fleeing slaves, the military established areas called contraband camps, usually near Union encampments. These contraband camps were often overcrowded and unsanitary. Moreover, when the soldiers moved on to fight another battle, their departure jeopardized the safety of the freed people living in the camps. White Southerners sometimes raided the camps, killing or recapturing their former slaves. Still, African Americans often established lasting friendships while living in the camps.

The composition of the contraband camps changed after July 1862 when the federal government began to allow African-American men to serve in the Union army. Once the men left, the women, children, and men unable to serve remained. Afraid that civilian freed people were becoming too dependent on government aid in the camps, U.S. officials decided to put them to work. The military therefore removed slave women, children, and men unfit for military duty from the contraband camps and placed them on abandoned plantations. There they became part of the first major experiment with non-slave labor in the South. These plantations were run either by Northern white men or by Southern planters who had taken a loyalty oath. In many areas, the employers had to promise not to whip the freed workers or use physical punishments against them.

These free laborers were supposed to be paid, but often they received very low wages or no compensation at all. Their labor contracts also contained many restrictions. Some required, for instance, that the workers carry passes when they left the plantations, in a system reminiscent of slavery. Also, food and clothing were usually in short supply. Adult workers were charged for their food and that of their children. Compounding these problems, Confederates sometimes raided these plantations and reenslaved the workers.

By the end of 1862, the women typically stayed in contraband camps or on plantations as wage laborers on Union-controlled plantations, while African-American men served in the army. The North was slow to see the value of enlisting African Americans, whether slave or free. As soon as the war started in 1861, many white abolitionists and blacks lobbied for enlisting African-American men into the army. When African-American men in the North tried to enlist, army recruiters turned them away. As one man from Ohio wrote to the secretary of war, "We beg that you will receive one or more regiments (or companies) of the colored of the free States. . . . We are partly drilled and would wish to enter active service immediately. . . . To prove our attachment and our will to defend the government we only ask a trial." The federal government refused, however, because officials were afraid that white soldiers would not want to fight alongside blacks. As the war dragged on, however, fewer white men wanted to serve in a war with such high casualties. As voluntary enlistments dropped off, the federal government instituted a draft that proved highly unpopular with many Northern whites. In July 1863 whites rioted against the draft in New York City, blaming African Americans for the war, and rampaged against them. Rioters murdered blacks and burned down an African-American orphanage and a church. The administrator of the orphanage managed to remove all the children to safety before the building was torched, however.

In July 1862, the government decided to allow African Americans to join the Union army. Although some of those who served in all-black regiments were free Northern blacks, such as Frederick Douglass's sons, most African-American

The U.S. Colored Artillery practices gun drills. Forced to serve in segregated regiments, black men faced unfair treatment by the federal government. They were paid less than white soldiers, often used inferior weapons, and received inferior medical treatment.

soldiers were former Southern slaves. Many runaways chose to enlist, although some were given little choice by Union officers needing to make their quotas of recruits.

African-American soldiers faced many more obstacles than white men in trying to join the army. According to one report, when a group of African-American men in Kentucky enlisted in the Union army, "a mob of young men . . . followed these black men from town, seized them and whipped them most unmercifully with cow hides." Afterward "they declared that 'negro enlistments should not take place.'" On occasion white men beat, whipped, and even killed African Americans who tried to join the Union army.

Although the army paid white soldiers thirteen dollars a month, African-American soldiers received only ten dollars, with three dollars deducted for their clothing allowance. In protest, African-American soldiers in the 54th Massachusetts Infantry refused to accept any money until Congress guaranteed them equal pay, which it did in 1864. As one corporal in the 54th pointed out to President Lincoln: "We have done a Soldiers Duty. Why cant we have a Soldiers pay? . . . We feel as though, our Country spurned us, now we are sworn to serve her." Soldiers were also concerned about what receiving less money meant for their families.

African Americans served in segregated regiments, and the government refused to allow them to become officers. Blacks resisted these unfair policies. As one African-American sergeant wrote, "All we ask is to give us a chance, and a position higher than an orderly sergeant, the same as white soldiers, and then you will see that we lack for nothing." The government finally reversed itself and allowed African Americans to become officers.

African-American soldiers often worked not as fighters but as laborers, digging trenches, building forts, setting up camps, burying dead soldiers, cleaning, picking up garbage in camp, and other noncombat labor. In addition, African Americans used poorer quality weapons than whites while in the service. They also often received poorer medical attention. As one white doctor confessed, "Very few surgeons will do precisely the same for blacks as they would for whites."

Occasionally, women were able to accompany their men into the army, if they became army washerwomen and cooks. As army widow Elizabeth Kane explained, "I was with him [her husband] in the army. I washed for him during his entire service in the army. . . . The officers let me live in a tent with my husband." And when he was ten years old, Robert Paul, whose father served in the infantry and whose mother worked as a laundrywoman for the army, explained that he "stayed with my father at the barracks a good deal" and "was well known by all the Company men." Black women following the army tried to stay close to their male family members, but the army felt that the presence of families undermined army discipline, so women and children were occasionally forced out of the barracks. African-American soldiers resented that white officers kept their wives in their own barracks but often forbid African-American women from living with their men.

When they remained on their old plantations, wives of the African-American soldiers faced retaliation from their slave owners. As one wife expressed to her husband in a letter: "You do not know how bad I am treated. They are treating me worse and worse every day. Our child cries for you." The letter ended hopefully, though, with "do the best you can and do not fret too much for me for it wont be long before I will be free and then all we make will be ours." Receiving such letters caused mixed reactions. Some soldiers wanted to leave the army and rescue their families; others became more motivated to stay and fight for freedom.

Many Northern whites believed that slavery produced men too docile and cowardly to fight. Because of such prejudices some whites doubted that blacks had the competence to fight in an orderly military fashion. Once former slaves had fought as Union soldiers, however, the doubters quickly changed their minds. As one white newspaper reporter raved, "It is useless to talk any more about negro courage. The men fought like tigers, each and every one of them." Whites were surprised when African-American regiments fought bravely at Port Hudson and Milliken's Bend, Louisiana; Fort Wagner, South Carolina; and the Battle of the

Crater, near Petersburg, Virginia. At Port Hudson in May and at Fort Wagner in September 1863, African-American troops battled fiercely against tremendous Confederate advantages. Union deaths from the battles ran as high as forty percent. The battle at Milliken's Bend took place just ten days after the one at Port Hudson. At first the Confederates seemed certain of victory. Outnumbered, the African Americans fought with bayonets in hand-to-hand combat against the Confederate charge. The Confederates could not defeat them. After initially falling back, the black troops held their line and the Confederates finally retreated.

At Big Black River in Mississippi (May 1863), under fire from Confederate soldiers, the African-American soldiers burned a railroad bridge the Confederates needed to bring in supplies. The soldiers also destroyed a section of railroad track. One general described the African-American soldiers: "Of this fight I can only say that men could not have behaved more bravely. I have seen white troops fight in twenty-seven battles and I never saw any fight better." Military strategists utilized African-American soldiers as an element of surprise in the opening charge against Confederate soldiers. Such maneuvers proved effective.

The Confederate government tried to counteract this development by threatening to refuse to grant black troops the status of prisoners of war if captured. It announced that captured African-American soldiers would be resold into slavery or perhaps even killed. This policy was calculated to increase the risk to African-American soldiers if they enlisted in the Union army. One general recalled that in one fight "such of the Colored Soldiers as fell into the hands of the Enemy during the battle were brutally murdered." Nevertheless, the Confederate government's refusal to recognize the rights of African-American prisoners did not deter the soldiers. One answered his commander's warning that "it may be slavery or Death to some of you today" by saying, "Lieutenant, I am ready to die for Liberty." In July 1863, President Lincoln announced that he would not exchange Confederate soldiers for Union prisoners if African-American men were not treated the same as white prisoners of war.

Although some Confederate soldiers treated African Americans as legitimate prisoners of war, others were far more brutal. In April 1864, for instance, Confederate soldiers killed unarmed African Americans trying to surrender at Fort Pillow, Tennessee. This massacre became a symbol of Confederate brutality against African-American troops. One black New Yorker wrote to President Lincoln: "If the murder of the colored troops at Fort Pillow is not followed by prompt action on the part of our government, it may as well disband all its colored troops for no soldiers whom the government will not protect can be depended upon."

In spite of their own and their families' hardships, African Americans were proud of their wartime contributions. As one African-American soldier explained, "This was the biggest thing that ever happened in my life. I felt like a man with a uniform on and a gun in my hand." These soldiers fought for freedom for themselves and their families. "If roasting on a bed of coals of fire would do away with the curse of slavery, I would be wiling to be the sacrifice."

African-American men made up almost a quarter of the navy during the Civil War. One reason is that sailors did not have to contend with as much discrimination as soldiers. For example, the Confederate policy of not exchanging African-American soldiers for whites did not apply to sailors. And because the ships of the time were too small to set up racially segregated facilities, blacks and whites worked, ate, and bunked in the same quarters. Particularly toward the end of the war, few ships sailed without African-American crew members. They even made up the majority of the crew on a few ships.

Besides serving as soldiers, former slaves also acted as spies for the Union army. They were able to maneuver in and out of Confederate lines with more ease than Northern white men could. Southerners rarely suspected African Americans of carrying out covert activities. For instance, Harriet Tubman spied during the war for the Union. She went to South Carolina, where for three years she gathered information for the military by talking to slaves living in Confederate-held areas.

Slaves contributed, often unwillingly, to the Confederate war effort. They frequently accompanied their masters into Confederate army camps to serve as personal servants. The Confederate government used slave labor to build fortifications: They cut wood, dug foundations, and did carpentry work. Slave men also moved supplies. The army paid the masters for their slaves' services. A few African-American soldiers did serve in the Confederate army. In New Orleans, free African Americans formed two regiments, not in defense of slavery but to defend their homes against Yankee attack. Once the North took control of New Orleans, however, many of these African-American Confederate soldiers went over to the Union army, revealing the tenuousness of their commitment to the Confederacy. In March 1865, a month before the Civil War ended, the Confederacy, in desperation, finally allowed African-American soldiers to fight in return for their freedom.

When the North's African-American soldiers marched into Richmond, Virginia, as the capital of the Confederacy surrendered, white Southerners must have recognized that the war had destroyed slavery forever. Thousands of slaves had freed themselves by crossing over the Union lines. African-American soldiers served their country proudly in the Civil War, and many died for the honor. For their part, African-American women and children, crowded into contraband camps, endured the war as best they could. Many also worked on plantations and became part of the Northern plan of freed labor that started during the war. The military policies regarding such labor influenced the working relationships between the freed people and their former owners during the period of Reconstruction that followed the war. The Civil War brought freedom to the nation's slaves, but just what this freedom would mean for the formerly enslaved people was unclear.

Freedom: "Take Your Freedom, My Brothes and Sisters"

After President Lincoln issued the Emancipation Proclamation in September 1862, Union soldiers went to the plantations and announced the slaves' freedom. The newly freed people, who had long yearned for freedom, greeted the news with great excitement and much celebration. Interviewed during the 1930s, Harry Bridges vividly recalled the day when three federal cavalrymen rode onto Major Sartin's plantation in Mississippi, where as a boy, Bridges had been enslaved. While looking for Sartin, they chanced upon a group of slave women hoeing cotton. Going before the women, a slave man was helping loosen the soil by plowing. As Bridges described it, "The Yankees stopped their horses and the leader called to the old negro at the plow and asked for the owner of the place.... The soldiers then inquired of him who the negroes were working for and if they had been told that they were free." When the women overheard the soldiers, "knowing a change had taken place" they "rushed to the quarters telling the news to the other women and children." Sartin had refused to tell his slaves that they were free, but the Union soldiers "told them of their freedom. One negro woman who was unable to believe the news asked if they might leave the plantation at the moment to go where they wished and of course she was answered in the affirmative much to her surprise."

The freeing of Major Sartin's slaves illustrates two important themes of the Reconstruction period. The first is that former slave owners and Southern whites generally resisted treating African Americans as free and no longer slaves. When they finally did reconcile themselves to the end of slavery, former owners never believed that African Americans were equal to and should be granted the same rights as whites. The second is that freed people had to define freedom for themselves, like the woman described above. Typical definitions of freedom often included living where one wanted and receiving payment for one's labor. One woman recalled in the 1930s that the freed people had expressed the desire to "do like dey please wid no boss over dem, an' den dey wanted to go places an' have no patroller ketch dem."

Gradually, the federal government began to plan for the former slaves becoming free. In September 1862, after the Union forces won at Antietam, Maryland, President Lincoln issued his Emancipation Proclamation, declaring freedom for the enslaved people in the Confederacy effective January 1, 1863. Lincoln deliberated for quite a while before changing the focus of the Civil War from a war to save the Union to one to end slavery. Although he personally opposed slavery, he had acted cautiously because of political considerations, fearing opposition from such loyal slave states as Maryland and Missouri. He favored gradual, compensated emancipation, with slave masters receiving payment if they voluntarily freed their slaves. Lincoln slowly began to agree with those who thought that the fastest way to break the South's resistance and end the war would be to free the slaves. He also wanted to preempt the possibility of Great Britain's entering the war on the side of the South, because England depended on the South's cotton. He believed that the anti-slavery sentiment in Great Britain would keep that country out of the Civil War if a Northern victory were to free the slaves.

Of course, thousands of former slaves had already freed themselves by taking refuge among the Union soldiers, and thousands more would follow them. Where African Americans were already free, they celebrated January 1, 1863, as Emancipation Day. In Washington, D.C., for instance, one freedwoman changed the lyrics of the song "Go Down, Moses" to "Go down, Abraham, away down in Dixie's land, Tell Jeff Davis to let my people go." Although the Emancipation Proclamation did not free slaves throughout the nation (specifically in the border states), it did declare freedom for those slaves in Confederate-held territory and it did allow Union soldiers in the future to liberate slaves, like Major Sartin's, wherever they found them.

As soon as the Civil War began, slaves—believing that the war would free them—traded information about the progress of the war and Union troop movements. As the noted African-American educator Booker T. Washington recalled, "Though I was a mere child during the preparations for the Civil War and during the war itself, I now recall the many late-at-night whispered discussions that I heard my mother and other slaves on the plantation indulge in." Washington added, "These discussions showed that they understood the situation, and that they kept themselves informed of events by what was termed the 'grapevine telegraph.'"

With emancipation, discussion among African Americans intensified as to their vision of life as freed men and women. In 1865, just before the Civil War ended, twenty African-American ministers met in Savannah, Georgia, with Secretary of War Edwin Stanton and Union General William Tecumseh Sherman to consider the future of the newly freed people. When the ministers were asked about the meaning of freedom, one responded that "freedom, as I understand it, . . . is taking us from under the yoke of bondage, and placing us where we could reap the fruit of our labor, take care of ourselves and assist the Government in maintaining our freedom." When asked how the government could best assist freed people, one minister answered, "The way we can best take care of ourselves is to have land, and turn it and till it by our own labor."

The primary desire for independence expressed by the ministers was echoed by many freed people. "I had a kind master," one former slave explained, "but I didn't know but any time I might be sold away off, and when I found I could get my freedom, I was very glad; and I wouldn't go again, because now I am for myself." Freed people held definite opinions about what freedom meant. For all, from the youngest to the oldest, it meant being allowed to live with their families without the threat of any of them being sold.

Former slaves, like the ministers who met with Secretary Stanton, also interpreted freedom as being able to live where they chose, to own land, and to be paid for their labor. Freedom also meant being able to travel freely.

Jourdon Anderson, a runaway slave during the Civil War, understood that freedom involved mobility and separating oneself from one's master. After Anderson escaped to Ohio in 1865, his former master requested his return to Tennessee, promising Anderson and his wife, Mandy, their freedom and compensation for their labor. Anderson's remarkable letter to his former owner explained his concept of emancipation, which included decent wages, proper respect, education for his children, and a place of worship of his choosing. Addressing his former master as an equal, Anderson described his new life in Ohio: "I get twenty-five dollars a month, with victuals and clothing; have a comfortable home for Mandy (the folks here call her Mrs. Anderson) and the children, Milly, Jane and Grundy, go to school and are learning well."

Freed people characteristically defined freedom as the ability to make choices about how they would look and act. As one said, former slaves "wanted to make money like de white folks an' do deir own buyin'." They did not want to dress as they had during slavery, particularly on special occasions. Freed women typically bought new cloth for dresses to wear to church or on holidays because new clothes symbolized their new status. No longer slaves, they could choose their own apparel.

Freed people regarded the use of surnames as a sign of respect, as had Jourdon Anderson in Ohio. Whites had never called slaves by their surnames but demanded this courtesy from blacks. After the war, freed people began to choose their own last names. Even though some enslaved people had used last names, many had not. Sometimes freed people adopted the last name of their master at the time of the war or chose one of an earlier master. As one man explained, taking a master's surname "was done more because it was the logical thing to do and the easiest way to be identified than it was through affection for the master." This man chose, however, not to use his master's name. "I made up my mind I'd find me a different one. One of my grandfathers in Africa was called Jeaceo, and so I decided to be Jackson." When an army officer asked one soldier, "Do you want to be called by your old master's name?" he responded tersely, "No, sur, I don't. I'se had nuff o' ole massa."

Above all, freedom equaled autonomy, the ability to make decisions for oneself and in the best interests of one's family and community. Ultimately, it involved not having to take orders from a white master. As one former domestic slave, whose owner used to ring a bell when she wanted her, insisted, "answering bells is played out." African Americans also wanted to drop slavish mannerisms toward whites. They wanted the right to refuse to yield the right-of-way to whites when they met on the street or paths, to refuse to remove or tip their hats to white men who never reciprocated, and to be called by their surnames like an adult, not by their first names without a title, like a child. Grown African-American men resented being referred to as "boy" by whites. And freed people's expectations of freedom were interrelated: The ability to travel allowed both for slave families who had been separated to reunite and for those needing employment to move to new jobs.

Part of the quest for autonomy involved the desire of the freed people to own land and become economically independent rather than continue to work for whites. Francis L. Cardozo, an African-American minister, educator, and politician, spoke in favor of land redistribution at the South Carolina constitutional convention after the Civil War. He argued that "in the North . . . every man has his own farm and is free and independent" and demanded, "Let the lands of the South be similarly divided. . . . We will never have true freedom until we abolish the system of agriculture which existed in the Southern States." Freed people argued that they deserved land because during slavery they had worked without compensation to make their owners wealthy. When asked by his former master to come work for him, Jourdon Anderson astutely suggested that his former master show good faith by giving Anderson and his wife "back pay" as slaves. "This will make us forget and forgive old scores, and rely on your justice and friendship in the future. I served you faithfully for thirty-two years and Mandy twenty years. At twenty-five dollars a month for me, and two dollars a week for Mandy, our earnings would amount to $11,680." Anderson even suggested that his former owner keep the interest on the unpaid money to pay for the clothing and medical care that Anderson and his family had received as slaves. Of course, Anderson did not really expect his former master to pay him back wages. Rather, he was pointing out the inequality of slavery as opposed to being a free person.

Freed people initially had reason to believe they would receive land from the federal government. In a few areas, the government divided up plantations deserted by slave owners who had escaped the Union soldiers. The government experimented with dividing land off the coast of South Carolina and at Davis Bend, Mississippi. Davis Bend was part of the plantations of Confederate President Jefferson Davis and his brother Joseph. Some freed people did receive small plots, although the government sold or rented the vast majority of the land to white Northerners or Southerners loyal to the Union.

Concerned about the number of escaping slaves during the war, General William Tecumseh Sherman, on January 16, 1865, ordered parts of South Carolina near the coast and on the Sea Islands to be cultivated by freed slaves. According to Sherman's Special Order No. 15, the military would give each family forty acres. Sherman also encouraged the army to lend the families army mules for plowing. He wanted freed families to become self-sufficient so that they would not depend on army supplies. In Georgia, freed people also established their own farms on land seized by the military. They worked hard to raise crops on these plots of land, did quite well, and also set up a limited local government in some areas. At the time, some military officers were so pleased by the results that they promised the land to the freed people, although such commitments were not honored after the war.

In March 1865, to encourage land ownership, Congress passed legislation stating that to "every male citizen, whether refugee or freedman, there shall be assigned not more than forty acres of land." However, this legislation was never put into effect because President Andrew Johnson vetoed the bill. In 1865, Johnson returned the plantations to the former owners once they promised loyalty to the U.S. government. Many years later, former slaves continued to express a sense of betrayal. More than sixty years after the war ended, Sally Dixon recalled, "We was told when we got freed we was going to get forty acres of land and a mule. 'Stead of that, we didn't get nothing."

Although the federal government did not give land to freed people, Congress did pass other laws to aid the former slaves. In the Senate, Charles Sumner of Massachusetts sponsored civil rights legislation and laws to aid the newly freed slaves, including provisions for having the federal government help establish schools. Before the Civil War, Sumner had been such a vocal critic of slavery and pro-slavery senators that he infuriated Representative Preston Brooks of South Carolina, who severely beat Sumner with a cane while he sat at his Senate desk. Sumner never fully recovered from the beating.

While Senator Sumner led the fight for freedmen's equity in the Senate, Thaddeus Stevens championed the cause of civil rights for African Americans in the House of Representatives. As a lawyer in Pennsylvania, Stevens had defended runaway slaves, arguing against their return. As a congressman, he bitterly opposed the Fugitive Slave Act that was passed as part of the Compromise of 1850. This act gave Southern whites the right to reenslave escaped slaves who had run away to the free states in the North. In spite of severe heart trouble, until his death in 1868 Stevens chaired the important Ways and Means Committee, which controls budgetary issues. With Sumner, Stevens was a member of the Joint Committee on Reconstruction that shaped Congressional Reconstruction policy regarding the South.

Under the leadership of men like Sumner and Stevens, the Republican-controlled Congress passed three amendments to the Constitution concerning the newly freed people. These changes were accepted with the necessary two-thirds congressional majorities, after which three-fourths of the state legislatures voted for the amendments. They then became part of the Constitution. The 13th Amendment, abolishing slavery in the United States, was adopted by the states in 1865. The 14th Amendment, granting citizenship to freed people, was added to the Constitution in 1868. This right had been denied to slaves in an 1857 Supreme Court decision. The 15th Amendment guaranteed the right of African-American men—but not women—to vote. It was adopted in 1870. The 14th and 15th Amendments also allowed African-American men to vote for new state constitutions and state legislatures during the period known as Congressional Reconstruction, from roughly 1867 to 1869, when Congress implemented its plan for rebuilding the South. Congressional Reconstruction differed from Presidential Reconstruction, which had occurred from 1865 to 1867, by supporting the political rights of freedmen. During this era, African-American men ran for office, and won, while white Southern men who had supported the Confederacy were either temporarily disenfranchised or refused to vote, to protest the suffrage granted to African-American men.

TO THE

Freedmen.

WENDELL PHILLIPS

ON LEARNING TO READ AND WRITE.

BOSTON, July 16, 1865.

My Dear Friend:

You ask me what the North thinks about letting the Negro vote. My answer is, *two-thirds* of the North are willing he should vote, and *one* of these *thirds* is determined he *shall* vote, and will not rest till he does. But the opposition is very strong, and I fear we may see it put off for many a year.

Possibly there may be an agreement made, that those who can read and write shall vote, and no others.

Urge, therefore, every colored man *at once* to learn to read and write. His right to vote may very likely depend on that. Let him lose no time, but learn to read and write *at once.*

Yours truly,

Mr. JAMES REDPATH. WENDELL PHILLIPS.

This public letter from reformer Wendell Phillips urges blacks to educate themselves so they can assume the duties of citizenship.

Besides passing these three amendments, Congress overrode President Johnson's veto to establish the Bureau of Refugees, Freedmen, and Abandoned Lands, known as the Freedmen's Bureau. Its mission was to help freed people make the transition from slavery to freedom. The bureau gave out food to both Southern whites and African Americans if they needed it. It also provided an opportunity for former slaves to legalize their marriages, by issuing marriage licenses. Once the freed people realized they would not obtain land, bureau agents helped negotiate labor contracts between the freed people and their new employers and settle labor disputes. Establishing schools and hospitals was another part of the Freedmen's Bureau's work, particularly as it became clear that white Southerners wanted facilities that excluded African Americans.

Understaffed and underfunded, the Freedmen's Bureau did not always work the way Congress intended. Sometimes its employees living in the South were overly sympathetic to white employers and prejudiced against African Americans. Also, freed people found it hard to take time off from work to walk to the bureau in the closest town and make a claim against an employer.

Besides passing legislation to set up the Freedmen's Bureau, Congress tried to protect freed people's rights through other laws. Congress passed the Civil Rights Act of 1866 to overturn the discriminatory Black Codes that Southern states had passed after 1865 to limit the rights of African Americans. Although President Johnson demanded that the Southern states abolish slavery by ratifying the 13th Amendment, he encouraged Southern state legislatures to reject the concepts of African-American suffrage and equality.

Immediately after the Civil War, during what is referred to as Presidential Reconstruction, Southern state legislatures under the control of whites sympathetic to the Confederacy passed laws that applied only to African Americans. These laws, passed from 1865 to 1866, attempted to thwart African Americans' visions of freedom and their quest for individual and community independence. These Black Codes bestowed certain legal rights on former slaves, such as the right to enter into contracts legally. As a result, freed people gained the right to marry and acquire personal property.

More significantly, however, the Black Codes limited various aspects of African Americans' lives. Most states passed vagrancy laws, which meant that African Americans had to prove they were employed by whites or risk arrest. To further ensure that African Americans were available for employment by whites, the states passed strict rules enforcing yearlong labor contracts so that workers could not change employers for at least a full year, even for higher wages. In Florida, employees who broke their contracts could suffer physical punishment or be required to provide a full year's labor without pay. Mississippi passed some of the most repressive laws, such as legislation prohibiting African Americans from possessing guns and leasing or renting land in rural areas. Some Black Codes also allowed former masters or other whites to apprentice or have the children of former slaves work for them if the courts ruled that the children's parents were destitute. Thus, former slave owners could keep African-American boys until they reached twenty-one and girls until they turned eighteen without paying them or their parents anything for their labor. The Black Codes also forbade interracial marriage and prohibited African Americans from serving on juries. Although the Black Codes allowed African Americans to be witnesses in court, they could not testify against a white person.

Along with the passage of the Black Codes, white vigilante groups sprang up throughout the South to terrorize African Americans and keep them from exercising their vision as free people. The best-known such organization was the Ku Klux Klan, which was formed in Tennessee in 1866. An early leader of the Klan was Nathan Bedford Forrest, a Confederate soldier and former slave owner whose men were responsible for butchering African-American men at Fort Pillow, Tennessee, during the Civil War. The Klan and other groups targeted whites and African-American men and their families who were active in the Republican party as well as white and African-American schoolteachers. They also attacked black landowners and African Americans refusing to behave in a manner subservient to whites.

Through their dealings with Southern whites, African Americans learned that freedom could not be easily attained but would involve struggle. Freed people adopted a variety of methods to try to ensure what they considered freedom. When possible, they made complaints to the Freedmen's Bureau regarding white injustices. On plantations they joined together to demand better wages and working conditions. Within their communities they established their own churches and schools. With the passage of the 14th Amendment to the Constitution, African-American men, along with women and children, marched to polling places. There, the men cast their votes for Republican candidates to help ensure civil rights for themselves and their communities.

Politics: "Slavery Is Not Abolished Until the Black Man Has the Ballot"

As a young child, Robert Smalls was a well-treated house servant. When he was twelve, his master hired him out as an urban slave. He worked on the docks at Charleston, South Carolina, and learned sailmaking. Then in May, 1862, in his twenties, Smalls and his wife, Hannah, decided to escape slavery by stealing a Confederate boat and sailing it to freedom. The one they took was a boat Smalls worked on, which had a slave crew and three white officers. There were sixteen people, including Smalls's family, on the ship early one morning while the white crew members were still sleeping onshore. With a straw hat hiding his face, Smalls guided the boat past the Confederate posts, correctly signaling the Confederate codes. Some Confederates thought the boat was out patroling very early, but they allowed it through the checkpoints. After passing the last point, Smalls dropped the Confederate flag and raised a white bed sheet as a sign of surrender. Then he sailed to Charleston, which the Union forces controlled, and turned over the boat to the

Union soldiers. Smalls not only won his freedom but the U.S. Congress paid him a reward for providing the Union army with a working Confederate war vessel.

Robert Smalls went on to serve as a second lieutenant in the Union navy. In 1864, while in Philadelphia, he was thrown off a streetcar. The protests that resulted from this incident led the streetcar companies to integrate their cars. After the war, Smalls continued his political activism. As he grew more successful, Smalls compensated as a free adult for his lack of formal education during slavery. From five to seven o'clock each morning, he studied on his own and, for the next two hours, had private lessons. To improve his reading ability, he subscribed to a newspaper. He became a delegate to the South Carolina constitutional convention. In 1870, he won a seat in the South Carolina Senate and served as a U.S. congressman. Smalls became one of the most influential politicians in South Carolina during Reconstruction, supporting public education and voting rights for African-American men.

During Reconstruction, for the first time, African Americans in the South held office in local and state governments and even became lawmakers in the U.S. Congress. Some of these lawmakers had been free before the war, but others, like Smalls, were formerly enslaved. Guaranteeing and protecting the right of African-American male suffrage was important to these leaders, as it was to Smalls. In the face of intense—even violent—opposition, they served in public office.

Before the end of the Civil War, African Americans participated in meetings, organizations, and conventions to voice their political concerns and aspirations. In 1864, African Americans met in Syracuse, New York, to form the National Equal Rights League. The League encouraged the formation of state branches. African Americans in New Orleans formed their own chapter. Calling for African-American male suffrage, the League championed other civil rights issues and demanded, for example, that African Americans be permitted to sit wherever they wanted on streetcars rather than being relegated to the dirtiest, most crowded cars or having to stay on the platform outside.

During Reconstruction, African Americans throughout the country participated in civil rights groups called Union Leagues. Many of the leagues were racially segregated, but some included both African-American and white Republicans, working together to oppose the former Confederates, who were Democrats. Union Leagues often supported reforms on the local level such as protesting all-white juries and raising money to build schools and churches. Committed to the issue of workers' rights, the leagues provided advice on negotiating for better wages and even organized strikes in Alabama and South Carolina. To keep mobs of whites from interrupting their meetings, the league often encouraged African-American men to arm themselves when attending. On some of these occasions, black women kept guard over stacks of weapons.

During and after the war, African Americans organized state conventions to advance the political and economic issues of significance to them. These conventions demanded such rights as being allowed to serve on a jury, gain an education, and carry guns. "We claim exactly the same rights, privileges and immunities as are enjoyed by white men—we ask nothing more and will be content with nothing less," declared a statement from the 1865 Alabama convention. It continued: "The law no longer knows white nor black, but simply men, and consequently we are entitled to ride in public conveyances, hold office, sit on juries and do everything else which we have in the past been prevented from doing solely on the ground of color." At the South Carolina convention, William B. Nash, who later became a state senator, summed up several of these demands: "We ask that the three great agents of civilized society—the school, the pulpit, the press—be as secure in South Carolina as in Massachusetts, or in Vermont. We ask that equal suffrage be conferred upon us, in common with the white men of this state." At first it was the African Americans who had been free before the war who controlled the convention agendas, but increasingly freedmen became active.

Immediately after the war, Southern and Northern blacks began to agitate for voting privileges for African-American men. Frederick Douglass argued that "slavery is not abolished until the black man has the ballot." African-American men petitioned the government to grant them the right to vote, arguing that "if we are called on to do military duty against the rebel armies in the field, why should we be denied the privilege of voting against rebel citizens at the ballot box?"

Tying the vote to military service automatically excluded African-American women from being considered for suffrage. Neither political party endorsed woman suffrage, and the issue lost in several state referenda across the country. Failure to receive the vote did not keep African-American women from other kinds of political activity, however, such as declaring their loyalty to the Republican party through wearing campaign buttons, attending meetings, and marching with their men to the voting places.

President Lincoln favored limited African-American male suffrage, for "the very intelligent, and [for] those who serve our cause as soldiers," but he did not make the advocacy of black male suffrage part of his plan for the South. When he became confident that the North would win the Civil War, he began to work out measures to deal with the Southern states involved in the rebellion. Under Lincoln's policy, men highly placed in the Confederate army or government would not immediately regain their right to vote, but most Southern men would not be punished if they promised to support the U.S. government and accept the end of slavery. Lincoln's plan allowed that after ten percent of a state's 1860 voting population declared its loyalty to the Union, the state could establish a new government. Only three Confederate states agreed to Lincoln's policy: Louisiana, Arkansas, and Tennessee. Because Lincoln developed this plan during the war, it remains unclear how he would have dealt with the South once the war ended.

Members of Congress reviewing Lincoln's plan felt it was too conciliatory to Confederates and did not go far enough in protecting the newly freed slaves.

Congress exercised its prerogative not to allow representatives from Louisiana, Arkansas, or Tennessee to join the U.S. Congress. Additionally, Congress countered Lincoln's policies with the Wade-Davis Bill, which temporarily placed the former Confederate states under military control. Rather than automatically having these states represented in Congress, as in Lincoln's plan, this bill had the president appoint governors to oversee the transition within the former Confederate states. Under these governors, a majority of the voting population (as opposed to Lincoln's ten percent) had to swear loyalty, after which each state was required to pass a new state constitution outlawing slavery. Like Lincoln's plan, in this one high-ranking Confederate government and military men could not vote. In addition, only men who swore that they had not supported the Confederacy or fought against the Union could vote for delegates to write the new state constitutions. This test of loyalty was referred to as the "ironclad oath." The Wade-Davis Bill also provided freed people with limited civil rights. Because Lincoln refused to sign the Wade-Davis bill, it never became law.

Lincoln and Congress were never able to work out a compromise for reconstructing the South. On April 14, 1865, while enjoying a play with his wife at Ford's Theatre, in Washington, a pro-slavery actor named John Wilkes Booth shot the president in the head with a pistol. Booth himself fell onstage, breaking his left leg. Some members of the audience thought he yelled in Latin, "Thus be it ever to tyrants." Booth limped outside and rode away. Early the next day, President Lincoln died. On April 26 a soldier who was trying to capture Booth shot and killed him.

Upon Lincoln's death, Vice President Andrew Johnson assumed the presidency. Johnson, a former slave owner, had remained loyal to the Union. He was a compromise candidate for vice president, chosen to appease the border states and slave owners not in rebellion. Johnson's plan for Reconstruction, referred to as Presidential Reconstruction, was in effect from 1865 until 1867. It differed from Congress's later plan, referred to as Congressional Reconstruction. Johnson's proposals included making white Southerners from Confederate states take loyalty oaths to the Union and called for the writing of new Southern state constitutions. They specified the election of new state governments before a state's representatives to the U.S. Congress would be accepted. Johnson demanded that Southern whites owning more than twenty thousand dollars worth of property request a special presidential pardon as a way of further humiliating them.

Unlike many members of Congress, Johnson showed little concern over the status of freed people, believing that they needed to be controlled by Southern whites. After presenting his plan for Reconstruction, Johnson vetoed a bill funding the Freedmen's Bureau and the Civil Rights Act of 1866. However, Congress obtained the two-thirds majority required to override a veto, and both bills became law. Johnson tried to undercut Congress's position by attempting to sabotage its efforts at Reconstruction of the South. The ongoing disagreements between Johnson and Congress over governmental policies regarding Reconstruction caused a widening rift between the executive and legislative branches of government. Congress passed a law that the president could not remove presidential appointments approved by the Senate, but Johnson ignored it. Hostilities grew to the point where the Congress actually impeached the president, although in 1868 it voted not to remove him from office.

The Southern states were quick to accept many facets of Johnson's plan for Reconstruction because much of it was more agreeable to them than Congress's. In 1865-66, white men—many of whom were former Confederates and slave owners—were elected as delegates to rewrite the state constitutions and soon after became state legislators. Although the states' revised constitutions recognized the end of slavery, the state legislatures in most Southern states also passed the Black Codes, which restricted African Americans' civil rights.

Angered in part by the Black Codes, by white attacks against African Americans in race riots in Memphis and New Orleans in May and July 1866, and by the Southern states' unwillingness to accept civil rights for newly freed slaves, the U.S. Congress decided that a plan tougher than Johnson's was needed. For one thing, Congress refused to accept senators and representatives elected from the states that had adopted Johnson's Reconstruction plan. Then, in 1866, Congress passed the 14th Amendment to the U.S. Constitution, which granted citizenship to African Americans and ensured that they were counted in the population for representation purposes in the House of Representatives. Congress further declared that any man who had supported the Confederacy could not be elected to any state or federal office unless Congress approved. This provision incidentally helped promote the Republican party in the South because most of the men disenfranchised were Democrats. Although accepting the 14th Amendment was a prerequisite for congressional recognition of a state's representatives and senators, all the Southern state legislatures except Tennessee initially voted against the 14th Amendment. It ultimately passed in 1868.

In 1867, Congress acted on its own Reconstruction plan. Congress placed military commanders with federal troops in charge of the former Confederate states. Although the Southern states complained about having Union troops stationed in the South, by the end of 1866 only thirty-eight thousand remained, mostly in frontier areas.

Another part of Congressional Reconstruction was its requirement that the former Confederate states rewrite their constitutions to supersede those passed during Presidential Reconstruction. A state could then set up a state legislature and, if it ratified the 14th Amendment, be readmitted into the Union and have its representatives accepted in the U.S. Congress. To guarantee African-American men the right to vote, Congress also passed the 15th Amendment to the United States Constitution. It was ratified by the states in 1870.

The new state constitutions written during Congressional Reconstruction were often the most democratic ones passed in the South. They provided funds for public schools, railroad construction, and other improvements needed in part because of war damage. They supported services for the poor and physically disabled as well as the establishment of orphan asylums. The state constitutions also included such progressive measures as abolishing imprisonment for owing money and public whippings as punishment for crimes. Through the revised constitutions and new state laws, much of the racially discriminatory legislation passed under the Black Codes was eliminated.

The Republican-dominated Congress supported African-American male suffrage, in part because some members believed that blacks would achieve equity and justice only if they received suffrage. Congress also knew that freed people would be more likely to vote for the Republican rather than the Democratic party. African Americans supported the Republican party because Republicans endorsed equal rights and the end of slavery, whereas the Democrats had opposed the federal government's ending of slavery.

Congressional Reconstruction made available unprecedented political opportunities for African-American men in the South. Even Northern African Americans headed South to become community leaders and officeholders. On the local level, African Americans became increasingly active, electing men to positions as mayors, police chiefs, school commissioners, and state militia officers. They sat on juries and became policemen and tax collectors. Nineteen African Americans in Louisiana and fifteen in Mississippi became sheriffs. African-American coroners as well as racially integrated juries and sheriffs helped African Americans receive the justice denied to them as slaves. Local black leaders built coalitions with other African Americans to help influence state policies and aid in electing African Americans to offices at the state level.

African Americans voted in large numbers for state delegates to the new state constitutional conventions at a time when many white Democrats who had supported the Confederacy were refusing to vote. With these elections, African Americans became part of the constitutional delegations in the South. Whites, including both Northern Republicans who had moved to the South as well as Southern whites who had stayed loyal to the Union during the war, made up the majority of the delegates. Only in Louisiana and South Carolina were African Americans the majority in the delegations.

When state elections were held after the ratification of the new state constitutions, male voters of both races overwhelmingly elected Republicans, both white and African American. Many black delegates to the state constitutional conventions later became state legislators. African Americans representatives advocated land redistribution, equal access to public schools, women's rights, a ten-hour workday rather than having laborers work from sunup to sundown, and prohibitions against family violence. They also argued for racially integrated restaurants, hotels, theaters, and transportation systems. Although African-American legislators disagreed among themselves on many of these issues, almost all wanted full political rights for African Americans.

The Mississippi legislature of 1874–75 includes several black representatives. At the time, Mississippi had more African-American officeholders than most other states.

Besides serving at the state and local levels, African Americans were also elected to national office. Sixteen African-American men served in the U.S. Congress during Reconstruction. In 1870, Hiram Revels from Mississippi became the first African-American U.S. senator. He took the Senate seat once held by Jefferson Davis, who had resigned to become president of the Confederacy. Before the war, Revels's parents, as free blacks, had lived in North Carolina. Revels attended college, became a minister at the African Methodist Episcopal Church in Baltimore, and was a chaplain for an African-American regiment stationed in Vicksburg, Mississippi. Revels also recruited black soldiers for the Union army.

Blanche Kelso Bruce also served as a U.S. senator. As a slave in Missouri, Bruce had become a printer. During the war, he ran a school for African-American children. Then he went to Mississippi, where he became a sheriff and a tax collector. After election to the Senate, he worked on such issues as Indian policy, improvements to the Mississippi River, and racial equity.

Joseph H. Rainey of South Carolina was the first African American to serve in the U.S. House of Representatives. Rainey had been a free African American before the Civil War and had worked in Charleston, South Carolina. Robert P. Elliot was a delegate to the South Carolina constitutional convention and served in the South Carolina House of Representatives, becoming speaker in 1874-76. He was also a U.S. congressman. In Alabama, three African Americans served as congressmen including James T. Rapier. Rapier supported expanding public funds for education rather than relying solely on private schools, and he helped freed people obtain land in the West.

Alonzo J. Ransier, born in England, was another South Carolina congressman. Free before the war, he worked as a clerk for a shipping office. John R. Lynch, the son of a slave woman and a white man, became free during the Civil War. After serving as justice of the peace, he was elected as a representative to the Mississippi legislature and served two terms in the U.S. House of Representatives. He advocated voting rights for African-American men.

In the South during Reconstruction, most of the highest state offices were held by whites. Only Louisiana had an African-American governor, Pinckney B. S. Pinchback. He supported African-American male suffrage, education for freed people, and integrated accommodations on trains and boats. Mississippi and South Carolina both had African-American lieutenant governors. In Louisiana and South Carolina, African Americans served as state treasurers. African Americans became secretary of state in Florida, Mississippi, and South Carolina. Arkansas, Florida, Louisiana, and Mississippi had African-American superintendents of education during Reconstruction. In some states, these officials oversaw the development of the first state public school systems for whites as well as blacks.

The African-American lawmakers serving at the state level came from a variety of backgrounds. Some, like James Lynch of Mississippi, were free Northern African Americans before Reconstruction. Educated in Pennsylvania, he went to

Mississippi after the war to work for the Methodist Episcopal Church. During the war, Lynch served as a cook in the army. As he wrote in his diary, "I have convictions of duty to my race as deep as my own soul. . . . They impel me to go [to] a Southern state, and unite my destiny with that of my people." Lynch campaigned for the Republican party, organized a Loyal League to support it, and became secretary of state in Mississippi. On July 4, 1865, speaking to freed people in Augusta, Georgia, Lynch argued that "all that my race asks of the white man is justice." Francis L. Cardozo worked as a carpenter, saved his earnings, and went to Europe for an education. A minister, he traveled in the South to train African-American teachers. Cardozo, a delegate to the South Carolina state constitutional convention, later became the first African-American secretary of state.

More than six hundred African-American men were elected to state legislatures in the South, although whites continued to chair most of the important committees. Except in Louisiana and South Carolina, most of the black legislators were former slaves.

During Reconstruction, resistance was fierce to African-American lawmakers and Northern-born as well as Southern white Republicans who dominated Southern legislatures. Whites formed secret organizations such as the Ku Klux Klan and White Camelia. Well-armed groups like the Red Shirts, rifle clubs, and white leagues like the Klan tried to keep African-American men from voting and killed or drove out African-American politicians from their homes, even sometimes out of the South. As historian Eric Foner has explained, "In effect, the Klan was a military force serving the interest of the Democratic party, the planter class, and all those who desired the restoration of white supremacy." One freedman recalled that Klansmen assaulted African Americans and once "ravished a young girl who was visiting my wife." He explained, "The cause of this treatment, they said, was that we voted the radical [Republican] ticket."

Ku Klux Klan violence devastated the Loyal League and made holding mass political meetings increasingly difficult for African Americans. One African-American minister recalled being terrorized by the Klan: "The republican paper was then coming to me from Charleston. It came to my name. They said I must stop it, quit preaching, and put a card in the newspaper renouncing republicanism, and they would not kill me; but if I did not they would come back the next week and kill me." In his testimony to Congress, one African-American justice of the peace in Tennessee stated that Klansmen assaulted him "because I had the impudence to run against a white man for office, and beat him." An attempted murder of an African-American politician in Alabama was justified by whites, according to testimony about Klan activities, on the grounds that he "was going around instructing and enlightening negroes how to act and how to work for their rights, and to make contracts to get their rights." The Klan sent a message to a black Georgia congressman expressing its contempt: "For we swear by the powers of both *Light and Darkness* that no Negro shall enter the Legislative Halls of the

South." Even faced with such opposition, African Americans continued to serve at the national, state, and local levels. Georgia state senator Aaron Bradley, along with other African Americans, fought against the Klan. He wrote a public notice to the "KKK and all Bad Men" that stated, "If you strike a blow the man or men will be followed, and house in which he or they shall take shelter, will be burned to the ground."

African Americans resisted white vigilantism, but they could not fight the combined legal and illegal methods whites used to disenfranchise black voters. In Alabama, African Americans told Klansmen that "they were willing to go out into an open field and 'fight it out.'" But such courageous stands could not effectively protect white and African-American Republicans. Resistance to the Klan and other white violence was dangerous because local whites often did not support African Americans' attempts to retaliate against the Klan. Also, the Klan often possessed superior weapons. African Americans correctly feared that armed confrontation with Klan members and other white vigilantes would increase the likelihood that whites would retaliate and spread the violence against African Americans. During 1870 and 1871, the United States passed Enforcement Acts, which expanded the use of federal courts against election fraud, and in 1871, the Ku Klux Klan Act gave the federal government the right to use federal courts as well as troops against groups conspiring to keep people from voting, sitting on juries, or holding public office. When troops were used in South Carolina, violence declined for a short time in the South.

Nonviolent means were also used to keep African Americans from participating in government. In Georgia in 1868, the state legislature refused to allow duly elected African-American members to attend state congressional sessions, on the grounds that because of their race, the African Americans did not possess the right to serve as lawmakers. The black legislators were finally seated by order of the U.S. Congress. Many white Republicans involved in political coalitions with African Americans preferred that the blacks not hold office but simply elect white Republicans to represent them. The majority of Southern whites never fully accepted the idea of African-American male suffrage, and many secretly hoped to subvert it once the federal government removed its troops from the region.

After a lull during the election of 1872 because of federal intervention, violence flared again. In Mississippi, an African-American sheriff pleaded in a letter to the governor for federal troops to protect African-American officeholders and voters. He observed, "A perfect state of terror reigns supreme throughout the county." During the election of 1875, when violent white mobs tried to keep African-American men from voting, one black policeman told his former master, "We are gwine to have this election; we mean to get it by fair means if we can, but we are bound to have it anyhow." Besides violence aimed at keeping African-American men from voting, Southern whites also refused to rent them land or give them credit or jobs if they supported the Republican party. As one African-American lawmaker recalled, "I always had plenty of work before I went into politics, but I never got a job since." He conjectured that whites refused to hire him "because they think they will break me down and keep [me] from interfering with politics."

During the 1870s, Northern commitment to Reconstruction began to wane. Republicans split over issues such as corruption, tariffs, and free trade. Corruption in government, including bribery of officials, was a problem nationwide after the war. Economic growth and particularly the expansion of the railroads were accompanied by attempts to sway politicians, whether by lawful or unlawful methods. While corruption and graft were much greater in the North than the South, Reconstruction was often blamed for the dishonesty in government. White Southern politicians received much more in illegal payments and railroad stocks than the African-American lawmakers, but some black lawmakers were also found to have accepted bribes. Railroad companies handed out money or stock to gain state legislators' support for their projects, inducing politicians to vote for projects in which they had an economic interest. U.S. Congressman Robert Smalls of South Carolina, along with others, was convicted of taking a bribe, although he was later pardoned.

In the North, whites wearied of the turmoil of Reconstruction. Many began to believe that peace would occur only if the Southern whites, particularly the planters, controlled Southern state governments and African Americans, even though this meant that white domination would subvert the ideal of equal rights. After 1872, the federal government became increasingly unwilling to use federal troops to stop violence against African-American voters and lawmakers. In that same year, Congress gave back the right to vote to most Confederate supporters. As a result of whites voting once more, the desertion of some Southern whites from the Republican party, and the disenfranchisement of some African-American male voters through violence and other means, more Democrats were elected and took control of state governments in the South. As one African-American politician noted, "The whole South—every state in the South—had got into the hands of the very men that held us as slaves." These men favored a white supremacist government and society, with African Americans subservient to whites in their political, economic, and social relationships. These white legislators enacted various methods of keeping blacks from voting. Along with moving polling places into white areas and providing fewer ones where African Americans lived, they also passed poll taxes and established property qualifications for voting. Poor African Americans who could not afford to pay the poll tax could not vote. As a result, fewer African American lawmakers were elected. White officials also increasingly barred blacks from serving on juries.

In 1876, the federal government withdrew even its marginal support for Reconstruction. In the presidential election of that year, the Democratic candidate,

Samuel J. Tilden, won the popular vote over the Republican nominee, Rutherford B. Hayes. Because in some states, particularly in the South, the votes were contested with both parties declaring victory, Tilden did not gain the needed electoral college votes. In 1877 Congress worked out a compromise through a special election commission that decided in favor of Hayes by one vote. Meanwhile, Republican and Democratic leaders informally decided that if Southern congressmen would accept Hayes, he would withdraw federal troops from the South. Such a policy, which Hayes had favored even before the election, would allow white Southerners to disenfranchise Southern black men without federal interference. Southern Democrats also wanted more control over federal jobs in the South and federal help in financing road construction, bridge repair, and other such improvements.

The African-American men who held office during Reconstruction provided Southern blacks with more legal equity than they had previously received as slaves or would gain under legislatures controlled by the Democrats after Reconstruction. The new constitutions passed during Reconstruction instituted many reforms within the South. The political failure of Reconstruction, during and after the Reconstruction era, was that these achievements were often undermined.

Labor: "I Mean to Own My Own Manhood"

Major Martin Delaney, one of the few African Americans to become an officer in the U.S. Army during the Civil War, went to South Carolina as a Freedmen's Bureau agent in 1865. He delivered a speech encouraging freed people to refuse to accept poor working conditions. First he reminded them of the wealth produced by slaves: "People say that you are too lazy to work, that you have not the intelligence to get on yourselves.... You men and women, every one of you around me, made thousands and thousands of dollars. Only you were the means for your master to lead the idle and inglorious life, and to give his children the education which he denied to you for fear you may awake to conscience." Then Delaney denounced the inequity of free (non-slave) labor: "Now I look around me and I notice a man, bare footed covered with rags and dirt. Now I ask, what is that man doing, for whom is he working. I hear that he worked for thirty cents a day. I tell you that must not be. That would be cursed slavery over again." Delaney's speech raised significant issues for freed people such as low wages and the failure of African Americans to receive just compensation for their servitude. He also stressed that even with freedom, few blacks were reaching the degree of economic independence from whites that they desired.

Most blacks failed to achieve the level of economic well-being that Major Delaney and the freed people hoped for immediately after the war. During Reconstruction, a small minority of African Americans became landowners with small family farms. In South Carolina, for instance, the state government helped some gain small homesteads. But those who became landowners were the exception. By the end of Reconstruction, most African Americans in the South still worked at agricultural labor for white employers, doing the same kind of work they had done as slaves—but now they expected to be paid for it.

Freed people expected free labor, in contrast to slavery, to mean fewer work hours and more control over their work. Freedom meant no more overseers, no more beatings. Workers now expected to be able to leave their employers at will, for better wages or improved working conditions. The former slave masters, however, often disagreed with this definition of free labor. They expected their laborers to go on working from sunup to sundown as before, with one payment at the end of the year, and under many of the same restrictions as under slavery. The agricultural and domestic work environment thus set the scene for struggles between freed people and their employers over their conflicting definitions of free labor.

As 1865 ended, freed people were becoming reluctant to work for white employers because at that time they expected to receive their own land from the federal government. As one man argued, "Gib us our own land and we take care of ourselves; but widout land, de ole massas can hire us or starve us as dey please." And after refusing to work for twenty-five cents a day for his former owner, another worker declared, "I mean to own my own manhood, and I'm goin' on to my own land, just as soon as when I git dis crop in, an' I don't desire for to many change until den. . . . I'm not goin' to work for any man for any such price." Freed people argued that they deserved the land because they had never been paid for their labor as slaves.

Regardless, President Johnson returned to the former slave owners the land the freed people had gained during the war. Most white Northerners agreed with Johnson's decision to advocate wage labor rather than land ownership for former slaves. They believed that land confiscation was too radical a practice for the federal government to promote. Agents from the Freedmen's Bureau therefore traveled throughout the South explaining that the government was not, in fact, going to distribute land. These agents also insisted on having labor contracts between employers and freed people in order to provide fair wages and working conditions for employees and give planters a reliable labor force. Such contracts were agreements between workers and employers indicating wages to be paid and the kind of work to be performed. Other clauses were often included as well, such as statements on deportment. In one case, workers were "required to be orderly industrious people and observe the rules of the place." Contracts also restricted when workers could have guests, as in stipulations such as "no neighboring negroes will be allowed to remain in the quarters [housing for former slaves] longer than twelve hours, without reporting to [the employer]."

At first, African Americans resisted signing labor contracts because they wanted to hold out for owning their own land. They were afraid of "signing them-[selves] back to their masters" as one Freedmen's Bureau agent said. A freedman declared, "If I can't own de land, I'll hire or lease land, but I won't contract." Hoping for more economic independence from whites, some African Americans organized to protest these yearlong labor contracts. Other freed people tried to exist on abandoned lands, as self-employed families, by planting crops, hunting, and fishing.

With or without labor contracts, freed people eventually began to work for white employers simply because they were poor and needed the work. And as part of the Black Codes, state governments passed vagrancy laws that punished African Americans by jailing them if they were not employed by a white person. Even when pressured into working for wages, freed people resisted as much as they could. Workers turned the yearly signing of labor contracts into negotiating sessions in which they discussed working arrangements. They held out as long as possible to work out the best deals. Immediately after the war, labor shortages developed in the South that not only kept wages competitive but also allowed laborers to gain extra concessions, such as the right to keep their own garden patch and to have more say in managing the plantation.

The majority of the freed men and women worked in the fields growing cotton, rice, and other crops. Planters continued to need agricultural workers, but few postwar Southern households employed as many house servants as they had previously. Former slave owners hired some freedwomen as maids and cooks, but the contracts show that they also performed other work related to food production.

Wages for agricultural workers varied. Monthly wages ranged from ten dollars to twenty dollars for men and eight dollars to ten dollars for women and children older than twelve. These wages did not buy very much. For example, one freedwoman bought a bar of soap for fifty cents from a store located on the plantation where she was working. This purchase alone probably represented five percent of her monthly income. Often the sugar plantations paid the highest wages because the owners were paid better prices for this crop than others. Some planters calculated a monthly wage and would agree to pay with cash only when they sold the crops. Other farmers paid by giving workers a share of the crop, which the employer usually sold after harvesting. He would then divide the money between himself and the workers. Shares for the work force ranged from one-half to one-quarter of the crop. Occasionally, planters would give the workers' share of the crop directly to them and let them divide it among themselves. At first, planters used the same labor contract for many workers, whether they were related or not. Over time, however, contracts became narrower, with only one family per contract.

Initially, the former slave owners anticipated ruling their employees with the same authority masters had exercised over slaves. Despite their acceptance of the demise of slavery, they could not accept a free labor system in which African Americans would be able to exercise the same rights as whites, such as changing employment or working without physical coercion. As a result, employers sometimes reacted violently to any challenge to their dominance. As one Mississippi newspaper summarized the attitude of most former slave owners, "The true station of the negro is that of a servant. The wants and state of our country demand that he should remain a servant."

The freed people believed, however, that they were entitled to protest labor conditions they considered unfair. Workers and employers argued not only over wages but also about nonpayment of wages. The latter represented the largest number of complaints brought to the Freedmen's Bureau by freed people. As one argued, "I craves work, ma'am, if I gets a little pay, but if we don't gets pay, we don't care—don't care to work." To justify not paying workers their wages, planters typically used the defense that the laborers had bought items in the employer-owned stores on the plantations and had in this way already spent their wages. Employers also deducted stiff fines for missed work, as much as fifty cents or a dollar a day. This rate was often much higher than what employees were paid per day. Freed men and women complained that their employers routinely found trivial excuses to dismiss them after the harvest, to avoid paying them. Since they lived where they worked, when planters ordered laborers off the plantations, the workers lost their homes as well as their jobs.

The former slave owners' reluctance to accept the loss of restrictions on workers such as had existed under slavery was compounded by their own economic difficulties. They had, in fact, very little money to pay their workers with, in part because after the war the federal government declared the Confederate dollar worthless. Even before the war, much of the planters' wealth had depended on their slaves and land. The planters lost their slaves without compensation, and in parts of the South some of the land and property was ruined by the war. In general, land values declined after the war. On top of this, the years 1866 and 1867 witnessed agricultural disaster throughout many areas of the South. Bad weather and an invasion of army worms, which are particularly voracious caterpillars, contributed to crop failures. In 1867 and 1868 when cotton prices decreased from wartime highs (although not to the levels of prewar prices), interest rates rose as planters' ability to borrow tightened. Planters were often in debt to merchants for their supplies.

Planters often proved unable to pay their workers or were unwilling to share the very small profits they had achieved at the end of the year. Given these financial woes, planters wanted a docile labor force willing to work for low wages. Employers were convinced that African Americans would not work without being compelled to through stringent vagrancy laws, restrictive labor contracts, and the threatened use of the whip. Whites saw work as labor for white employers, not African-American self-employment. They feared economically independent African Americans because they believed they would be harder to control.

As Democrats regained majorities in Southern state legislatures, they passed laws that helped planters assert authority over African-American workers. They enacted legislation that made it more difficult for workers to get paid by allowing planters to pay merchants and other creditors before paying their laborers. Furthermore, to keep African Americans more financially dependent on planters and merchants, laws were passed that limited their rights to hunt and fish. During Reconstruction, the Ku Klux Klan perpetrated violence against workers if it thought that they were not sufficiently subservient to whites. The Klan especially targeted African Americans who were self-employed and therefore not dependent on whites. As one freedman explained, the Klan "do not like to see the negro go ahead."

Besides difficulties over the payment of wages, conflicts erupted between freed people and planters over how work should be done and when. The former slave owners wanted their workers to labor in groups referred to as "gangs." After the war, planters hired men they referred to as agents or foremen to do the work of overseers. Workers resented these agents (even in the rare cases where they were African American) and refused to work in the field with them. One planter reported that his workers told him, "We won't be driven by nobody." Freed people insisted on working in smaller groups, often with family members, without continual white oversight.

In addition to resisting working in gangs under close supervision from whites, blacks also protested the use of violence, such as whipping, to discipline workers. Although labor contracts often forbade whippings, many white employers were convinced that blacks needed the threat of violence to make them work.

Workers protested their conditions in various tangible ways. Some joined together to resist violent behavior. In Mississippi, when one overseer tried to harm a field worker, the others turned on him so that he "had to run for [his] life," according to his testimony to the congressional Joint Committee on Reconstruction. One planter's wife wrote about a group of workers who reacted to abuse perpetrated by an employer's son by becoming "a howling, cursing mob with the women shrieking, 'Kill him!' and all brandishing pistols and guns." The son was quickly sent to a private school away from the plantation.

In July 1876, workers in the rice fields of South Carolina went out on strike because the planters had paid them with scrip that could be redeemed only in plantation stores. These stores often had higher prices than outside places. Feeling cheated, the workers wanted the freedom to make their own decisions about how and where to spend their wages. This strike ended in partial victory for the laborers. Although the strike organizers were jailed, the planters agreed to stop paying their workers only in scrip.

Freed African Americans now refused to perform labor not expressly negotiated in their contracts or not associated with the actual raising of the crops. For instance, some freed people resisted repairing fencing or feeding livestock. They demanded opportunities to make more decisions about the crop they were raising, particularly when they were working for a share of it. They wanted to decide early on with the planter how much of each crop to plant and when and where to sell it. Planters preferred waiting until the end of the year to pay them, however, to help ensure that the workers performed noncrop-related labor during the rest of the year.

Planters continued to believe, as Major Martin Delaney pointed out, that freed people did not work as hard as they might. But increasingly, they came to realize that giving laborers a share of the crop was a better incentive than contracting with them for cash. When signing labor contracts, freed people tried to negotiate for the form of payment they preferred. For example, freed people who never received the cash wages they were promised wanted a share of the crop, feeling more assured of such payment.

Disputes also developed over freed people's intention to work fewer hours than they had as slaves. They resisted working from sunup to sundown. They now began to demand Saturday as well as Sunday as days off. Besides working for their regular earnings, freed people cultivated gardens or sometimes rented a small plot of land to raise vegetables and other crops to sell on their own. Having fewer hours of field work provided new spare time for such activities. Freed people also came to expect to spend more time with their families, friends, and neighbors. Although planters opposed any changes from slave conditions, freed people expected the needs of their families to be considered in decisions on how much time freedwomen and children should devote to outside employment. African Americans now wanted their children to go to school, not work in the fields.

Freedwomen's tasks for their families increased after the war. Under slavery, breakfast and dinner were often eaten in the fields. The master would typically designate an elderly black woman to look after all the children while their parents worked. With freedom, cooking and making clothes now often ceased to be communal activities. Besides doing the cooking, washing, sewing, and gardening, freedwomen took charge of caring for their own children. Pregnant and nursing mothers wanted to give up outside work. Mothers sometimes argued with their employers about giving their babies more attention instead of working in the fields. One planter complained in his journal, "Harriet and Amelia nursing over twelve months, disobeyed order to quit suckling [nursing]." A few planters even reacted violently against mothers who spent more time with their families than employers allowed. William Jenkins, the employer and former master of a freedwoman named Annette, once whipped her because she arrived late to work. When Jenkins ordered her to strip off her clothes for the beating, she pleaded, "Master William I had my children to tend to made me so late." Jenkins then gave her two hundred lashes with his rawhide whip. Clearly he had not yet made the transition from a slavery mentality to one of freedom.

Freedwomen's need to spend more time with their children without constant interference from white employers was only one of the factors that encouraged the growth of postwar sharecropping. Sharecropping spread at different rates in

Women wash clothes outdoors, under South Carolina pines, around 1880. Although they engaged in such communal activities, freedwomen tried to spend as much time as possible with their own families, caring for children and husbands.

different parts of the South. It was often preceded by other labor experiments, including monetary wage contracts and the practice of working in small groups referred to as squads. Sharecropping usually involved a planter's paying his workers a part of the crop, up to as much as half, for their labor. The planter generally provided the tools and seed.

Sharecropping developed because freed people did not receive land and because employers often failed to pay promised wages on a regular basis. For freed people, sharecropping also meant less direct supervision by white overseers and the ability to work in groups smaller than gangs. It allowed women to balance their time between field work and doing their own families' domestic tasks. Under sharecropping, freedmen could make more choices about how to use their family resources and labor. Freed people also tried to arrange their field work so that their children were able to attend school. The planters ultimately came to accept sharecropping, although they preferred the gang system of labor under the supervision of a white overseer.

Although sharecropping allowed freed people more independence than they had under slavery, it had severe drawbacks. Since sharecroppers bought their food, clothing, and other items from the plantation store, they often finished the year in debt or with very little profit. And as cotton prices fell, sharecropping increasingly became economically devastating for African Americans, poor whites, and the South as a whole. As one freedman summed it up, his people had received "freedom without giving us any chance to live to ourselves and we still had to depend on the southern white man for work, food, and clothing, and he held us through our necessity and want in a state of servitude but little better than slavery." As another wrote, "No man can work another man's land . . . even for half and board and clothe himself and family and make any money. The consequence will be the freedmen will become poorer and poorer every year."

Many of the newly freed wanted to leave their plantations to seek out better economic opportunities and education for their children. However, when they migrated into either Southern or Northern cities following the war, they found the employment opportunities very limited. Often, the men found jobs as blacksmiths, bricklayers, or carpenters if they had done these jobs as slaves. They also found work as barbers and as waiters in restaurants and hotels. The Republican party helped some African Americans gain politically appointed jobs as postal clerks, mail carriers, deputy sheriffs, county clerks, and customs workers. A few blacks attempted to start their own businesses, but many of these failed in the wake of the depression of 1873. Freedwomen typically became domestics and washerwomen.

African-American men, like other Americans, looked to the West for better employment opportunities. Although they found more diverse types of employment in the West than in the North or South, they also faced discrimination. As African-American men moved West during Reconstruction, they joined cattle drives as cooks and cowboys and drove cattle in Kansas and Texas. According to his book, Nat Love, who drove cattle, earned the nickname Deadwood Dick by winning a roping contest in Deadwood, Arizona. Some African Americans became farmers in the West by taking advantage of the Homestead Act, which offered free land to those who agreed to cultivate it. Others went west as soldiers. In 1866 the U.S. Army formed African-American regiments of the 9th and 10th Cavalry and organized the 24th and 25th Infantry in 1869. The troops went west and southwest to protect the settlers moving out there. They also built roads, constructed telegraph lines, captured cattle rustlers, protected workers constructing the railroads, and guarded the mail. African-American men tried other kinds of employment in the West and Southwest, such as becoming railroad workers and miners, because these jobs paid more than field work. In San Francisco, where most African Americans were single males, men worked as sailors and railroad personnel. Black women in western cities were still primarily limited to domestic work; some found employment as laundresses.

In Charleston, workers shovel coal. Such unskilled labor was often the only choice for black men, who faced discrimination by white employers.

Some African-American men in the West became very successful. In 1865, blacks in San Francisco owned tobacco and soap factories as well as laundries and real estate offices. A few men formed mining companies, such as the Colored Citizens of California. African Americans also owned silver mines in Nevada, Montana, Colorado, and Utah. In 1870, Clara Brown, who cooked and washed for miners, became the first African-American member of the Colorado Pioneer Association. A few African-American entrepreneurs were quite successful, including the founders of the Cosmopolitan Coal & Wood Company.

Increasingly, after the war—in both the North and the West—black skilled workers like carpenters, blacksmiths, and barbers, who often had received their training during slavery, found that gaining employment was difficult. White employers did not want to hire them, partly because white workers, fearing the competition of blacks, often refused to work with them. On occasion, whites hired African Americans to replace better-paid whites or used African Americans as strikebreakers, which promoted racial hostility. In 1865, white workers in Baltimore drove off African-American carpenters and caulkers from their jobs. Another reason white employers did not hire blacks was that they preferred to rely on the labor of immigrants, who were considered easier to control. Skilled African-American workers were often therefore forced into unskilled labor, doing the lowest-paying, dirtiest, least skilled jobs. By 1870, most African Americans were unskilled laborers or service workers.

Lack of union support also increased the labor difficulties of skilled African Americans. Unions often refused to allow blacks to join, although a few did organize segregated locals, which separated white and African-American workers. Typical was the experience of Lewis Douglass, the son of Frederick Douglass. Lewis Douglass was prohibited from joining the Typographical Union in Washington, D.C., even though he had worked in his father's print shop and had excellent experience. The inability to join a union kept African-American youth from apprenticing themselves to skilled workers and learning a trade. In December 1869, the National Negro Labor Union was established to enable African Americans to join a union and fight for better wages and working conditions. The great majority of African-American workers, however, even those living in the cities, remained outside unions.

In cities as well as the countryside, white employers paid African-American workers less than whites. Tobacco factory workers in Richmond, Virginia, complained that "we the Tobacco mechanicks of this city and Manchester is worked to great disadvantage.... They say we will starve through laziness that is not so. But it is true we will starve at our present wages." Collective action by African-American workers such as washerwomen and day laborers to protest their low wages and poor working conditions was not uncommon. African-American urban workers organized strikes, but they often failed to achieve either higher wages or better working conditions.

During Reconstruction, African Americans were ultimately unable to fulfill their dreams of economic independence. Poor agricultural conditions, labor restrictions, legal and illegal discrimination, failure to obtain land, and the worsening economic times during the depression of 1873 guaranteed poverty for the majority of Southern African Americans. The economic plight of the nation's freed people represented one of Reconstruction's biggest failures.

Family: "My Name Was Peggie, One of the Children of Prince and Rose"

Freedwoman Maria Clark recalled in some detail her relationship with her husband, specifically how it began during slavery and survived the war: "I had been with my young mistress about three years when I married Henry Clark in 1859, I fix the date by knowing it was about two years before the late war broke out. My Master performed the marriage ceremony, he did not give me or my huband papers to show for our marriage, but gave us a great treat for all the slaves on the plantation." The couple "remained on the Clark Plantation in Hinds County [Mississippi] thru [the] battle of Vicksburg end[ing] in 1863, which was the first time we knew we were free, all the slaves in the surrounding county was gathered into a camp on a plantation about five miles from Vicksburg."

Henry and Maria Clark stayed in the contraband camp until Henry and many of the other men were enlisted in the Union army. Maria then followed her husband into the army to cook for the soldiers. "When the troops moved off many of us were sent upon the Paw Paw Island where I rented ground to make my living in his absence. I received news that he was very sick in [a] Hospital at Memphis, Tenn. As soon as I could raise money I went there with the determination to take care of him, when I arrived there I found him some better." Clark was discharged soon after his wife arrived and she took him home, although he was "very weak and complained of great suffering. While on the journey, when the boat struck the landing at Paw Paw Island we met several of our friends, who were acquainted with him before he entered the service they assisted me in getting him from the boat." Clark died six months later.

As Maria Clark's narrative shows, slavery did not destroy all African-American families. Some slave couples remained devoted to each other in spite of hardship, even though slave marriages were not legal. Such marriages provided the foundation for many African-American families after the war.

Even though couples could not legally marry during slavery, slave families sustained each other through its day-to-day rigors. Slave couples participated in marriage ceremonies, often with permission of the masters, who sometimes allowed slave weddings to be held on holidays such as the Fourth of July. But the three-day Christmas holiday, which most masters gave as time off from work, was the favorite time to get married. The weddings of house slaves were often quite elaborate, with food and dancing. When a slave named Susan Drane married fellow slave Charles Hooven, a white preacher conducted the ceremony in the owner's parlor. The event was attended by the master's family "and a number of invited guests. They had a grand supper upon the occasion." At some ceremonies the master read from the Bible.

Some slaves did not have a wedding ceremony. One formerly enslaved father remembered that when his daughter married a man from another plantation, "I gave my consent and both the owners agreeing, he came on a certain night and they went to bed together and after that time he visited and cohabitated with her as his wife." He added that "there was no formal ceremony, but they considered themselves husband and wife and were so regarded by others." The father recalled that he had been married the same way as his daughter.

Slavery constantly threatened such marriages. The marriage registers of freed people kept by the Freedmen's Bureau have provided an indication of how long slave marriages generally lasted. One historian has determined that approximately eighteen percent of slave marriages ended involuntarily. Others have calculated that almost thirty-nine percent of slave marriages were "broken by the master."

Emancipation brought legalized marriage to the formerly enslaved couples. During the Civil War, African-American couples kept Union army chaplains busy performing marriage ceremonies. Lucinda Westbrooks recalled being "married by a white man preacher Miller—who came there with the first Yankees and went around marrying the soldiers. He married lots of other soldiers the same day." Chaplains often held soldiers' weddings for several couples at once. Freed people referred to legal marriages as marriages "under the flag." Army regulations promoted such marriages because the military allowed only legally married spouses to visit soldiers.

After the war, couples delighted in the festivities accompanying weddings, either for new couples or as second weddings for those who had been married during slavery. Freed people viewed their slave marriages as binding even after emancipation. However, the Freedmen's Bureau discounted slave marriages because they had not been legal and regarded these new weddings as celebrating first marriages.

African Americans' reasons for wanting to marry after the war varied. For many, marriages symbolized freedom because a master's permission was no longer required. Legalized marriage also meant that children now belonged to their mother and father and could not be sold. Furthermore, church membership often required legalized marriage. The First African Baptist Church of New Orleans, for one, passed such a policy after the abolition of slavery, declaring, "Any person wishing to become members of this church who may be living in a state of illegitimate marriage shall first procure a license and marry." As one woman recalled, "We got married by license, because the church we joined required every one to be married by license." Many freed people marrying after the Civil War sought out a church with an African-American congregation and preacher. As one Freedmen's Bureau official wrote in 1865, freed people "all manifest a disposition to marry in the church, and prefer a minister of the Gospel to unite them."

Former slaves acquired a second family during slavery if they were sold and then remarried. These circumstances, as well as other marital problems often made worse by poverty, caused abandonment by spouses. Desertion brought about particularly serious consequences for African-American women with children. In one case, Nathan Williams, after nine years of marriage to his wife, Louisa, left her and "married again leaving her with one child without means of support," according to a Freedmen's Bureau agent. Such abandonments could be emotionally painful for the spouse left behind. Once a Northerner inquired of a freedwoman, "You have no husband?" The woman responded, "I had one . . . but he ran away one day with another woman. . . . Feel like it most killed me at first. I get over it now."

Marital disagreements occasionally led to domestic violence. When this happened, African-American women felt justified in leaving abusive husbands. One black woman named Amanda Fay had a slave husband who, according to her pension examiner, used to "whip her and treat her roughly," so "she quit him because he treated her badly, and; because she thought she had a perfect right to [do] so." Often, members of the extended family would intervene in marriages when violence became a pronounced problem.

While thousands of men and women married as slaves later remarried, some African Americans chose not to go through a formal marriage ceremony. Some refused to marry because a new marriage would jeopardize the woman's pension from the U.S. government. When Union soldiers died, whether during or after their service, their widows were entitled to a pension, or payment, from the government. These widows' pension (eight dollars a month for a private's wife) sometimes made women reluctant to remarry after a husband's death. The federal laws relating to the dispensation of pensions forbade women who remarried or lived with a man from claiming a military pension. Some widows believed they could hide the reality of their living with a man more easily than they could disguise remarriage because cohabitation did not create records such as a marriage certificate.

Such relationships after the war were just like marriages, except that they were not legalized. Couples lived together, with the woman adopting her man's surname. They cared about each other's well-being, and they were sexually intimate. After explaining that she and Thomas Toller had never married but had "lived together until he died," from 1866 to 1904, freedwoman Isabella Toller elaborated, "I had the name Carter and was called Isabella Toller and have not been called or known by any other name since." She noted that when their first child was born, "It was his child and he said it was and we agreed, he and I and my mother, that we would go together for all time." As soon as the pension office discovered these relationships, through intensive questioning of whites or African Americans who knew the women, they ceased paying pensions to them.

When a freedman did marry, he became the legal head of the family. During slavery, the slave masters had held all legal rights to slave families, including the power to sell family members. Even so, a slave father played a part in his family's life. When the master distributed blankets or clothing, for example, to the head of each slave family, the slave father rather than mother usually received them if the couple lived together on the same plantation. Slave men also held leadership positions on plantations as drivers, artisans, and preachers.

After slavery, the freedman, as husband and father, rather than the master assumed legal responsibility for his family, including guardianship of his children. When employers refused to pay their wives or drove their families off of plantations, husbands represented their family members before the Freedmen's Bureau agent or in court. Men tried to protect their spouses and children, particularly from beatings by employers. One freedman defended his shooting of a white man by arguing that the man had "abused [his] wife." Sometimes men signed labor contracts for the entire family and received the whole family's wages.

Increasingly, after the war, employers put labor contracts and accounts at the plantation store in the husband's name, even when other members of the family also worked there.

After the war, freedmen greatly expanded the economic responsibilities they assumed for their families. According to testimony from a pension examiner, one freedman began thinking about his new role while serving in the army: "He had a chance to marry in the service, but could not take care of a wife like he ought to in the army, and did not marry." Four years after the end of the war, once he found work, he did marry. One will left by a freedman showed the extent to which men thought of their wives' economic well-being. Although few freed people left such documents because they often lacked property and were illiterate, freedman Daniel Sanders dictated a will to his employer. He directed that "after my burial expenses are satisfied and all of my just debts are paid which is few I will all I have to go to my wife Leather as long as she lives, And then to be disposed of as she may see fit." Sanders also made provision for his wife's grandson. The Sanders estate "consist[ed] of one mule, one cow, and some debts due me."

Men and women performed different tasks for their families. Freedwomen took on more child care than they had during slavery. They also did such household work as cooking, washing clothes, and cleaning the houses or cabins. Although freed men and women considered the husband the main provider in the family, freedwomen also worked, either as field laborers or as domestic servants for white families. A freedwoman's contributions were important to the welfare of her family. Women sometimes raised vegetables or other crops for the family outside of any wage labor or a sharecropping arrangement. For example, in 1868, when Robert Shackleford signed a contract concerning yearly wages for himself and his sons, the employer also agreed "to let the wife of said Robert Shackleford have for cultivation a certain piece of land . . . for her sole care and benefit" as well as land for a garden.

Purchase records from plantation stores reflect the differences in men's and women's family activities as well as distinctions in their dress. In January 1868, on the Oakwood plantation in Mississippi, men bought pants, caps, shirts, boots, and hunting and fishing gear like shot, fishing line, powder, hooks, and buckets. Women purchased material for clothes making like cotton plaid, but no pants or shirts. Men and women both bought whiskey, tobacco, lamp oil, and thread. Freedwomen wore dresses, or skirts and blouses for field labor, while African-American men wore pants and shirts. Women decorated their outfits by adding ribbons and, when they could afford it, enjoyed wearing jewelry, often buying earrings. They willingly spent part of their pay on their attire. Freedwoman Hattie Jefferson purchased a dress upon receiving her first wages for picking cotton. Women elaborately styled their hair by wrapping it with strips of cloth, particularly on special occasions. Wrapping hair and wearing decorative handkerchiefs were both African traditions.

Whites often ignored a freedman's place as head of a family. When husbands who had been separated from their families either by slavery or war returned, whites often resisted their efforts to reclaim their families. Employers did not want men reuniting with their families if it meant losing workers before harvest time.

Whites, particularly employers, refused to recognize either the right of freed people to form independent families or African-American women's right to choose their own sexual partners. Along with attempts to keep family members separated, white men sometimes sexually abused black women. On occasion, although less often than during slavery, whites sexually harassed and even raped African-American women. Particularly during the period of Presidential Reconstruction, local courts often refused to take African-American women's complaints against white men seriously because they believed these women to be less moral than white women. Whites argued that black women's innate seductive behavior provoked the attacks, a charge the freed men and women denied.

During the days of slavery, rapes of slave women by whites generally went unpunished, but state legislatures in the South in the antebellum period passed laws prohibiting interracial marriage. This was to further ensure the inferior status of African Americans and to keep the races legally separated. In the South, interracial relationships had been without legal standing before the war, and immediately after it, the state legislatures passed new laws as part of the Black Codes to reestablish these restrictions. White Southerners especially feared having African-American men marry white women because such unions destroyed any claims whites might make to racial superiority. Later, during Congressional Reconstruction, state legislatures made up of whites and blacks repealed such laws. After Reconstruction, as segregation grew, the Southern states reinstated them.

One significant threat to the African-American family during Presidential Reconstruction was the apprenticing by whites of African-American children. In this era, state legislatures controlled by white former Confederates passed laws allowing whites to keep African-American girls until age eighteen and boys until twenty-one without paying them or their parents for their labor. In order to remove African-American children from their parents' custody, whites were supposed to prove to the courts that the children's parents were incapable of caring for them.

In Mississippi, as in other states, the law gave former slave owners preference in taking the children. Given that the courts were sympathetic to former slave owners immediately after the war and given the freed people's prevailing poverty, whites could easily convince judges of the parents' inability to provide for their children even when it was not true. The parents of apprenticed children often went to the Freedmen's Bureau for help in getting their children back. African Americans resented the apprenticing of their children and the ongoing attempts by whites to break up their families. "I think very hard of the former owners," said one freed person, "for Trying to keep My blood when I kno that Slavery is

WHAT MISCEGENATION IS!

—AND—

WHAT WE ARE TO EXPECT

Now that Mr. Lincoln is Re-elected.

By L. SEAMAN, LL. D.

The title page of this racist pamphlet, published around 1865, graphically illustrates white fears of miscegenation, or interracial marriage. After the war, state legislatures in the South passed laws to prohibit marriages between blacks and whites.

dead." If a child's parents died, other relatives such as grandparents, aunts, uncles, brothers, and sisters would petition the Bureau to gain the release of the child from apprenticeship.

Such concern for family members, whether immediate or extended family, began when children were small. After the war, freedwomen came to depend on their older children to assist in providing care for younger siblings. This was often necessary because women had to work in the fields for wages or a share of the crop even when they preferred to be with their children. Children only a couple of years older helped watch over sisters and brothers. Freedwoman Sarah Robinson recalled, "When I got big enough I 'toted' my brother about." At twelve, Rose Dowan cared for children from the time "they [were] borned and nursed them from that time up until they was large enough to care for themselves."

Knowledge of their lineage was important to African Americans so that their children would know their people. Children learned about their fathers even if they had died or were separated from their mothers when the children were young. Before and after the war, on many of the larger plantations, extended kin lived with their families. In addition, stepfamilies, like extended families, were often relied on as part of the family network.

After the war, women relied on relatives when they did not have a husband. Widows received help from their parents or brothers and sisters when they asked. After the death of her husband, a soldier during the war, freedwoman Helen Thomas Shaw lived with her mother and father. She recalled that "her father helped support me till he died."

Being part of an extended family meant that people cared for their elderly relatives when they were able to. Aged former slaves discovered that finding jobs after the war was difficult. Employers hired only the most physically fit men and women to do agricultural labor. Worn out from slavery, the elderly were forced to depend on their children and other family members to provide for them. Freed people tried to support their parents, but given their own poverty, found it difficult. Immediately after the war, when freed people needed help, they turned to the Freedmen's Bureau. The Bureau was reluctant to incur the cost of providing for aging former slaves, but it did build hospitals for the freed people. When necessary, it transported the destitute or sick to medical facilities.

Local governments, particularly those under Democratic control, resisted taking responsibility for older former slaves unable to work. Even though African Americans paid taxes, local municipalities refused to provide services for blacks in need. During Presidential Reconstruction, local governments passed specific "pauper" taxes, which only African Americans had to pay, but whites still continued to claim that they could not provide assistance to African Americans. However, during Congressional Reconstruction, more hospitals and orphanages were built, due in part to the lobbying by African-American lawmakers.

Families of freed people in the South showed both continuity and change from the days of slavery. As with slave families, the extended family continued to play an important part in people's lives. Unfortunately, white denigration of the male role in the black family and whites' sexual abuse of African-American women carried over from slavery. The practice of whites' apprenticing freed people's children also affected family unity. These issues all stemmed from attempts by white Southerners to establish their racial domination after the war. Even though whites did not fully recognize freed people's right to make decisions for their own families, African Americans were able to exercise much more control over their family life than they had been able to as slaves. Men became the legal heads of their households, and men and women alike were able to raise their children without constant white intervention. Racial oppression failed to extinguish the strength of African-American families during Reconstruction.

Community: "It Was a Whole Race Trying to Go to School"

During the Civil War, the Reverend William H. Hunter, a chaplain in the U.S. Army, returned to North Carolina, where he had been a slave, and preached the following sermon.

> A few short years ago I left North Carolina a slave. I now return a man. I have the honor to be a regular minister of the Gospel in the Methodist Episcopal Church of the United States and also a regularly commissioned chaplain in the American Army. . . . I am proud to inform you that just three weeks ago today, as black a man as you ever saw, preached in the city of Washington to the Congress of the United States; and that a short time ago another colored man was admitted to the bar of the Supreme Court of the United States as a lawyer. One week ago you were all slaves; now you are all free.

Hunter, like many freed people, saw the Civil War in religious terms: "Thank God the armies of the Lord and of Gideon has triumphed and the Rebels have been driven back in confusion and scattered like chaff before the wind."

The political nature of Hunter's sermon is representative of others during Reconstruction, for community activities within the church served as a power base for African-American leadership. Throughout the country, barriers against African Americans' full participation in U.S. society began to fall during Reconstruction, as blacks struggled during and after the war to achieve equal rights in both the South and the North. They also formed their own organizations such as churches, schools, and social clubs.

These new institutions took the place of the slave communities that were then breaking up on the plantations. As sharecropping developed, freed people gradually moved out of their old slave quarters—rows of cabins, often attached to each other—and into individual cabins built on the land on which they worked.

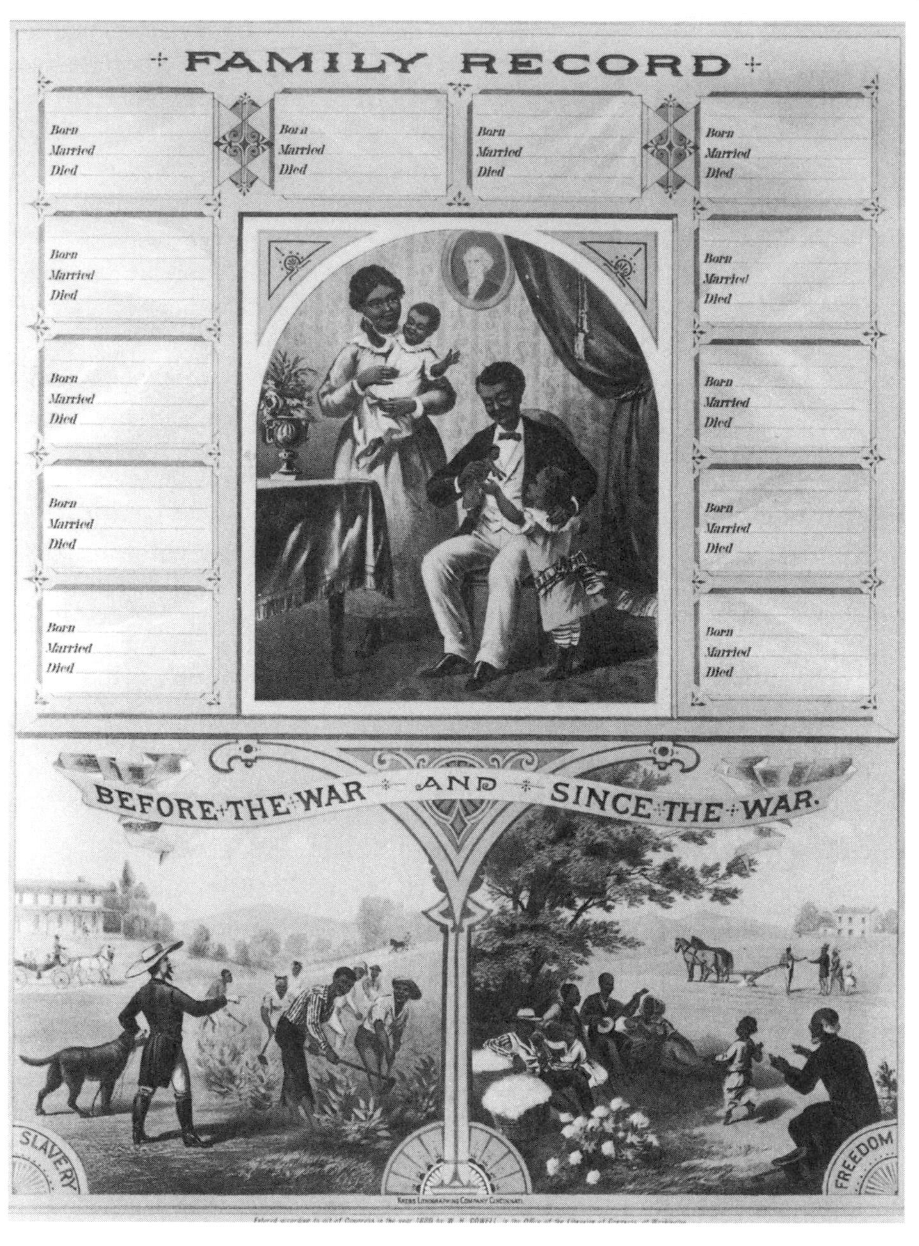

African Americans could use forms like this one to record their family history and list the networks of relatives on which many families depended. It includes, at bottom, a sentimental depiction of what life was like for blacks during slavery and after the war.

Workers usually rented these places. While no longer in the close living quarters of slavery, freed people continued to socialize. Weekends, particularly Saturday night and Sunday, and holidays were a perfect time to get together. Friends and neighbors gathered at church services, weddings, and funerals.

Such closeness did not mean the absence of tension among African Americans, however. Most complaints brought to the Freedmen's Bureau were about white employers not paying their workers, but occasionally freed people brought grievances against one another. Occasionally, an African-American employer did not pay his employees, or lack of fencing sometimes caused friction when a mule or cow invaded a neighbor's garden.

Conflict between individuals did not keep freed people from working toward common goals, such as education for themselves and their children. Education fulfilled practical needs, such as being able to read labor contracts, and it increased the possibility of the next generation's upward mobility. As one freedman said, "I wishes the Children all in School. it is better for them then to be their Serveing a mistes." Being educated was also a way to counter the racist myth that African Americans were innately intellectually inferior to whites.

During the war, many freed people received their first formal lessons from Northern teachers who visited army and contraband camps. One teacher commented on soldiers stationed in Vicksburg: "I have taught in the North . . . and have never seen such zeal on the part of pupils, nor such advancement as I see here." Education was as important to black soldiers as their freedom. One soldier proudly declared, "A large portion of the regiment have been going to school during the winter months. Surely this is a mighty and progressive age in which we live."

Groups such as the American Missionary Association arranged for teachers to travel south to instruct both soldiers and civilians. Charlotte Forten, an African American from Philadelphia whose relatives were prominent abolitionists, taught former slave children during the war on the Sea Islands off the coast of South Carolina. She wrote in her journal: "I enjoyed it much. The children are well-behaved and eager to learn. It will be a happiness to teach them." Besides instructing her students in the fundamentals of reading and writing, she taught history, such as the overthrow of French rule in Haiti led by Toussaint L'Ouverture. Forten "talked to the children a little while to-day about the noble Toussaint. They listened very attentively. It is well that they sh'ld know what one of their own color c'ld do for his race. I long to inspire them with courage and ambition (of a noble sort) and high purpose."

Northern teachers set up makeshift schools on plantations that were under Union control. Southern planters and the Northerners leasing plantations were unenthusiastic about any educational efforts, fearing they would interfere with their disciplining of the labor force. During and after the war, freed people established their own schools. Sometimes they received help from the Freedmen's

The main building of Howard University in Washington, D.C., in 1870. Founded only three years earlier, Howard was one of several black colleges established after the war that provided professional training in medicine and other fields.

Bureau or Northern societies set up to aid the newly freed slaves, but they also opened schools without outside assistance.

Along with primary schools, during Reconstruction institutions of higher education for African Americans were also founded. Among these were Howard University, Fisk University, Atlanta University, Clark University, Alcorn State University, Bethune-Cookman College, Hampton Institute, and Richmond Theological Seminary. Many of these institutions were founded as teachers' colleges to train African Americans as educators, although they also taught other job skills.

After the war, the Freedmen's Bureau established 740 schools with more than one thousand white and African-American teachers. More significantly, during Congressional Reconstruction, under pressure from blacks, Southern states developed school systems financed by public rather than private funds. Throughout the South, schools of whatever sort were segregated, although African Americans made attempts to integrate them.

While children attended schools during the day, adults went to night school after a full day of work. As the African American educator Booker T. Washington explained, "Few people who were not right in the midst of the scenes can form any exact idea of the intense desire which the people of my race showed for education. It was a whole race trying to go to school. Few were too young, and none too old, to make the attempt to learn." At one school in Atlanta, for example, children attended school until two o'clock in the afternoon, followed by adults; evening classes were held until ten o'clock at night. "The parents are delighted with the idea of their children learning to read, and many take great pleasure in visiting the schools," one educator reported, "and asking the teacher to pay 'ticular pains to our children, as we wish them to get all the learning they can, 'caus you know Miss, I's got no learning myself consequently I know how much I loses without it."

Many Southern whites remained distinctly hostile to formal education for African Americans. Resentful about being taxed to pay for their education, whites were afraid that once blacks gained an education, they would fight white supremacy with even greater determination. Planters typically preferred African-American children to work in the fields rather than attend school. They feared that once their laborers gained an education, they would refuse field work and domestic service in favor of higher-paying jobs with better working conditions.

Because white Southerners refused to rent rooms to Northern teachers of African-American students, the teachers often had trouble finding places to live. Local whites, including the members of the Ku Klux Klan, sometimes threatened teachers, forcing them to leave. Also, whites often resisted former slaves' attempts to buy land to build schools. Occasionally, they took the extreme measure of burning down African-American schools, or they destroyed books. Other, more moderate whites encouraged the establishment of segregated schools to avoid the possibility of integration.

The desire for education for their children and more autonomy in the workplace caused thousands of rural African Americans to leave their plantations and go north and west or into Southern cities. Oppressive economic, social, and political conditions in the South caused thousands of African Americans to go west, particularly in the late Reconstruction period. The West seemed to promise fewer racial restrictions and more opportunities, although before the war, many Western territories had restricted the settlement of free African Americans. In the Wyoming territories, however, African-American men were allowed to vote.

During Reconstruction, African Americans achieved some measure of equality, aided by a coalition of white Republicans. In the North and West, blacks utilized the civil rights acts passed by Congress to end discrimination and gain access to public facilities. In the West, even though their numbers were small, African Americans agitated for equality during Reconstruction. Under the influence of the dominant Republican party, legalized discrimination diminished in the West. Minnesota and Iowa granted suffrage to African-American men even before the ratification of the 15th Amendment. In 1865, Illinois and Ohio repealed many of their discriminatory laws, including those prohibiting blacks from serving on juries. In California, African Americans began a petition drive to support the right of black men to testify in court, which was granted in 1863. Several Western states started to desegregate their streetcars. In San Francisco, as elsewhere, transportation was desegregated, but some public facilities were segregated and restricted seating to separate areas.

African-American political involvement grew noticeably after the 15th Amendment was ratified. In the West, as in the South, blacks were overwhelmingly Republican. In Detroit, men formed the Lincoln Sixth Ward Republican Club, and blacks later ran for public office there with only limited success. In Colorado, African-American men served as delegates to Republican conventions.

African-American communities grew in the West, despite their small populations. California contained the largest number of African Americans in the Far West—more than four thousand. In the Midwest, more than seventeen thousand blacks lived in Kansas, far more than in any other Western state. There were some six hundred African-American ministers in the West, about two hundred in Kansas alone. In 1864 an African Methodist church was formed in Carson City, Nevada, even though the entire population of blacks in the whole state was only 367. Fraternal and social clubs and newspapers were all started, and San Francisco had two African-American newspaper editors.

Reconstruction also had an impact on the Northern African-American population as well as on blacks in the South and West. African Americans made up less than two percent of the population in the North, but they had long agitated there for equal rights. In Massachusetts, African Americans integrated various public places for the first time. In 1867, Philadelphia allowed African Americans to sit with whites on streetcars. However, only with the passage of the 15th Amendment could African-American men vote throughout the North. And once they were able to vote, their small proportion in the overall population made it difficult for them to achieve significant political power. As a result, very few Northern African-American men were elected to office.

As opposed to the South, where only New Orleans allowed white and African-American children to attend school together, several states in the West and North desegregated their public school systems. Rhode Island in 1866 and Connecticut in 1868 allowed white and African-American children to go to school together. In many large cities, such as Chicago, black children were educated alongside whites. Michigan desegregated its schools in 1867, although the Detroit school board did not comply until 1871. African-American parents protested that the board had earlier ignored the desegregation ruling, and their activism helped persuade it to end the practice of having separate schools. In the 1870s, Nevada and Oregon allowed integrated schools, and in San Francisco, blacks met and passed resolutions opposing separate schools. The state courts there ruled that schools could be separate but

Students from an integrated school in New Orleans. Although some Western and Northern cities allowed integrated schools after the war, in the South only New Orleans approved such an arrangement.

they must have equal facilities. In 1875, the segregated schools were abolished in San Francisco. The measure passed in part as a response to the declining economy of the 1870s, which made maintaining separate school systems more difficult.

In the North, African Americans gained access to state funded colleges that had previously denied them admission. Discrimination continued to be a problem there, however. In Cincinnati, one African American pointed out that racism "hampers me in every relation of life, in business, in politics, in religion, as a father or as a husband."

Along with moving to the North and West, African Americans also settled in Southern cities in an attempt to find freedom. In the five-year period after the war, the African-American population doubled in several Southern cities. Violence on the plantations was part of what motivated blacks to move to the cities. As one African-American state representative pointed out, "People who get scared at others being beaten go to the cities." In the cities, African Americans joined newly established churches, voluntary associations such as burial societies (which insured funds for funerals), savings and loan associations, and clubs—both social and political—established by and for African Americans. Lodges such as the Colored Masons and Colored Odd Fellows were founded. Blacks also formed their own volunteer fire companies such as the Victor Engine Company and the Bucket and Ladder Company in Raleigh, North Carolina, in part because Southern whites refused to integrate those already in existence. The state militia also developed all-black units. In Southern cities, African Americans lived in areas that became increasingly segregated from whites, in substandard housing, often at the edge of town.

Southern cities did not offer an escape from unequal treatment. Occasional outbreaks of violence, including rioting against African Americans in Memphis and New Orleans in 1866, made blacks wary. Public facilities were usually segregated, with African Americans rarely receiving the same level of service or accommodations as whites. Theaters allowed African Americans to attend, but let them sit only in certain sections, often those with the least desirable seats. Some places, such as the New Orleans Opera House, that did not racially segregate people often openly refused admittance to African Americans. In many cities—including Charleston, New Orleans, Richmond, Mobile, Nashville, Louisville, and Savannah—African Americans organized campaigns to integrate streetcars but had limited success. Often, they had to settle for segregated cars.

Both in the cities and in rural areas after the war, freed people established their own places to worship. Those who as slaves had gone with their masters to church services and listened to white preachers exhort them to be obedient to their masters now organized churches independent and separate from those of whites. To this effort, blacks throughout the South gave their money. For example, in Charleston, South Carolina, by 1866 African Americans had established eleven churches. White churches became increasingly segregated as whites refused to integrate their facilities or allow blacks to hold leadership roles. In rural areas, freed people attended church services in cabins or held outside prayer meetings away from their former masters and other whites. Most blacks gravitated to African-American-controlled Baptist churches, but others joined the African Methodist Episcopal Church. In certain parts of the South, particularly in New Orleans, African Americans practiced Catholicism.

Churches forged vital links within the freed African-American community. Particularly in the cities, attendance was so great that churches often offered three, rather than the normal two, services on Sunday. Services sometimes lasted two hours, during which ministers read letters from former slaves wanting to know about family members separated during slavery. Church buildings also provided school classrooms and places for meetings and lectures. And social life often centered around the church.

Entire religious communities encouraged and celebrated the individual's salvation, which brought a person into the religious congregation. "Saw a wonderful sight to-day, 150 people were baptized in the creek near the church," remarked Charlotte Forten. "They looked very picturesque—many of them in white aprons, and bright dresses and handkerchiefs. And as they, in procession, marched down to the water, they sang beautifully. The most perfect order and quiet prevailed throughout."

Religion also played a role in encouraging education. Because many freed people held deeply felt religious convictions, wanting to read the Bible provided them with another strong incentive to learn to read.

During Reconstruction, freed people used the church—the African-American institution least controlled by whites—to promote political participation. Ministers freely mixed religion with political activism. As one religious leader in Florida explained, "A man in this State cannot do his whole duty as a minister except he looks out for political interests of his people." During Reconstruction, more than one hundred ministers served in Southern state legislatures. Involvement with the church for both the clergy and lay officials as with organizing schools and burial and fraternal societies gave African-American men experience as leaders within their own institutions and helped train them to become effective politicians.

As with religion, whole communities of African Americans participated in political events. Loyal Leagues, formed to support the Republican party, held social gatherings including dances. In at least one Mississippi community, freed people gathered at the church and walked together to local polling places. Women and children marched with the men voters in these parades.

Politics was important to the entire community of African Americans. Freed people often thought of the vote as belonging to the community of freed people rather than to just one person. African-American women, like the men, hoped that having black men vote would ensure a redistribution of land, better schools, equal opportunity for jobs, and equal access to public facilities. African-American men voted overwhelmingly for the Republican party, sometimes with a turnout as high as ninety percent, and African-American women supported their men's decisions. As one Northern teacher described the scene at a polling place, "The colored women formed a line of one hundred or more, and ran up and down near the line of voters, saying . . . 'Now Jack, ef you don' vote for Lincum's men I'll leave ye.'" Planters complained that their field laborers left work to attend political rallies. In Richmond, Virginia, during the Republican state convention, the owners of tobacco factories had to shut down because so many of their African-American workers had gone to the convention.

During Reconstruction, the old, tightly knit slave communities on the larger plantations began to disperse, especially with the spread of family sharecropping and the building of separate cabins. After the war, a sense of having shared interests and goals strengthened collective efforts in education, religion, and politics, widening freed people's vision of the meaning of community. Despite fierce white opposition that included violence, African Americans persevered to establish their own churches and schools.

Resisting intense hostility, African Americans participated in America's political life through meetings, conventions, protests for the integration of public facilities, and voting. Even with the ultimate failure of Reconstruction and the return of Democratic party rule, the new autonomy compared favorably to slavery, and African-American families, churches, and schools endured to provide a lasting legacy.

Chronology

1441

Portuguese explorers capture Africans off the coast of Mauritania, signaling the start of a European trade in African slaves.

1479

Spain and Portugal sign the Treaty of Aláçovas, granting Portugal the right to supply the Spaniards with all the African slaves they needed.

1494

The first Africans arrive in Hispaniola with Christopher Columbus. They were free persons.

1502

African slavery introduced in Hispaniola, thereby inaugurating the institution in the Americas.

1522

First rebellion by African slaves in the Americas occurs in Hispaniola.

1539

The black explorer Esteban encounters the Zuni Indians in New Mexico and is killed.

1542

The Spanish Crown abolishes Indian slavery and the *encomienda* system.

1550

First slaves to arrive in Brazil directly from Africa disembark at the city of Salvador.

1565

Africans help construct St. Augustine in Spanish Florida, the oldest non-Indian town in North America.

1586

Francis Drake frees Africans in the Spanish Caribbean but fails to make them part of England's colony at Roanoke.

1595

Spanish Crown awards the first *Asiento,* or monopoly contract, to supply the colonists with slaves.

1609

Runaway slaves in Mexico, led by Yanga, sign a truce with the Spaniards and obtain their freedom and a town of their own.

1617

The town of San Lorenzo de los Negros receives its charter in Mexico, becoming the first officially recognized free settlement for blacks in the Americas.

1619

About twenty Africans disembark from a Dutch ship at Jamestown, Virginia.

1644

For the first time, New England merchants send three ships to Africa to trade for gold dust and Negroes.

1662

Virginia statute declares that all children born in the colony are to inherit the status of the mother.

1663

England creates the Company of Royal Adventurers into Africa, replaced in 1672 by the Royal Africa Company.

1700

Slavery becomes legally sanctioned in the colonies of Pennsylvania and Rhode Island.

1708

Africans in South Carolina are more numerous than Europeans, making it the only English mainland colony with a black majority.

1731

African-born Samba Bambara plans slave revolt in French Louisiana and is executed with his co-conspirators.

1733

The Spanish king issues an edict granting freedom to any English slaves escaping to St. Augustine, Florida.

1739

Slaves kill their masters in Stono Rebellion in South Carolina, but their efforts to reach Florida fail.

1765

Anti–Stamp Act demonstrations in Charleston, South Carolina, lead to rumors of a slave plot and black calls for liberty.

1770

Black sailor Crispus Attucks leads an attack on British soldiers and is killed in the Boston Massacre.

1772

The decision of Lord Mansfield in the Somerset Case puts slavery on the road to extinction in England.

1773

African-born Phillis Wheatley, age nineteen, publishes her book, *Poems on Various Subjects, Religious and Moral.*

1775

Virginia governor, Lord Dunmore, issues a proclamation offering freedom to slaves joining the British cause against the colonists.

One of the first independent black Baptist congregations develops in Silver Bluff, South Carolina.

1776

American Declaration of Independence proclaims that all men are created equal.

1777

Blacks in Massachusetts and New Hampshire petition for freedom based upon principles of the Declaration of Independence.

1778

Black businessman Paul Cuffe and his brother John refuse to pay taxes, claiming taxation without representation.

1780

Pennsylvania enacts first gradual emancipation law.

Blacks in Newport, Rhode Island, form the first Free African Union Society.

1783

Massachusetts outlaws slavery by court decision in the Quok Walker case.

1786

Black Poor Committee formed in London to aid needy African-American immigrants.

1787

British abolitionists found the Society for the Abolition of the Slave Trade, and British reformers establish the colony of Sierra Leone to receive black American immigrants in London and other freed slaves.

American Constitutional Convention develops a new government protecting slavery.

Northwest Ordinance forbids slavery in American territory north of the Ohio River and east of the Mississippi.

Richard Allen and Absalom Jones form the Free African Society in Philadelphia.

1788

Massachusetts prohibits all foreign blacks, except those from Morocco, from living in the state for more than two months.

1790

Charleston's free black people organize the Brown Fellowship Society.

1791

Haitian revolution begins.

1793

Eli Whitney's cotton gin spurs economic expansion and tightens the bonds of slavery.

1794

Slavery is abolished in the French Empire.

In Philadelphia, the St. Thomas African Episcopal Church opens its doors, and Richard Allen establishes Bethel African Methodist church.

1798

Toussaint L'Ouverture expels the British and becomes the most powerful leader in French colony of Saint Domingue (Haiti).

1799

New York's manumission law frees the children of slaves born after July 4.

1800

Gabriel Prosser's planned revolt against slavery in Virginia fails; Prosser and his followers are hanged.

1802

Napoleon reinstitutes slavery in the French Empire.

1804

New Jersey becomes the last Northern state to pass a manumission act.

Haiti becomes an independent nation.

1808

The foreign slave trade is closed; Africans are no longer legally imported into the United States.

1811

Led by enslaved leader Charles Deslondes, about four hundred slaves revolt and flee plantations in St. Charles and St. John the Baptist parishes in Louisiana.

1816

The American Colonization Society is formed by white Americans. Their aim is to send African Americans back to Africa.

1817–18

African Americans join the Seminole Indians in their fight to keep their Florida homelands.

1820

The Missouri Compromise allows Missouri to enter the United States as a slave state but outlaws slavery north of the 36th parallel.

1822

Denmark Vesey, a free African American, plans a revolt against the arsenal at Charleston and surrounding plantations. He is betrayed before the revolt begins, and Vesey and his followers are hanged.

The American Colonization Society buys land in Western Africa for the few blacks who want to return; the nation is called Liberia.

1827

Freedom's Journal, the first African-American newspaper, is published by Samuel Cornish and John Russworm.

1829

David Walker issues his *Appeal,* in which he denounces slavery and calls on African Americans to rise up and throw off the yoke of slavery.

More than half of the black people of Cincinnati flee the city in response to white mob violence. Riots in other Northern and Western cities force blacks to migrate to Canada and elsewhere.

1830

African-American delegates from New York, Pennsylvania, Maryland, Delaware, and Virginia meet in Philadelphia in what was the first of many conventions to devise ways of bettering the condition of free and enslaved blacks.

1831

Nat Turner leads about seventy fellow slaves in uprising against the slaveholders of Southampton, Virginia. He and his followers are captured and hanged after they kill about sixty whites.

1833

The predominantly white American Anti-Slavery Society is formed, signaling the beginning of organized white protest against slavery.

1835

Fugitive slaves join the Seminoles against the militias of Florida, Georgia, and Tennessee to keep their homelands.

1847

Frederick Douglass publishes abolitionist newspaper the *North Star.*

1850

The Compromise of 1850 is passed with the most repressive fugitive slave law ever put into effect in the United States.

1852

Black activist and abolitionist Martin Delany publishes *The Condition, Elevation, Emigration, and Destiny of the Colored People of the United States,* in which he argues that emigration to Central or South America or some area in the American West offers the best prospects for black freedom.

1854

The Republican Party is formed on the premise that slavery must be kept out of the Western territories.

1857

In *Scott* v. *Sandford*, the Supreme Court rules that blacks are not citizens and therefore have no legal rights, that blacks are property, and that whites who possess such property can treat them however they please and can take them wherever they want.

1859

White abolitionist John Brown leads a slave revolt against the federal arsenal at Harpers Ferry, Virginia. Brown is captured and hanged. Revolt spreads fear among slaveholders across the nation.

1860

Arkansas expels all free blacks from the state. Other Southern states had debated expulsion of free blacks but only Arkansas passes an expulsion law.

Abraham Lincoln is elected president on the Republican platform of non-extension of slavery. Seven Southern states secede in reaction to his election.

April 12, 1861

Civil war begins when Confederates fire on a U.S. ship sent to resupply Fort Sumter, in South Carolina. Four more Southern states secede and join the Confederacy.

August 6, 1861

First Confiscation Act prevents slave owners from reenslaving runaways.

April 16, 1862

Slavery is abolished in Washington, D.C.

July 17, 1862

Congress permits the enlistment of black soldiers.

January 1, 1863

Lincoln's Emancipation Proclamation goes into effect.

July 13, 1863

Draft riots begin in New York.

April 12, 1864

Fort Pillow, Tennessee, massacre of Union soldiers, including blacks.

June 15, 1864

Congress approves equal pay to African-American soldiers.

March 3, 1865

Congress establishes Bureau of Refugees, Freedmen, and Abandoned Lands.

April 9, 1865

General Robert E. Lee surrenders to General Ulysses S. Grant at the town of Appomattox Court House, Virginia.

April 14, 1865

Lincoln is assassinated; Vice President Andrew Johnson becomes president.

April 1, 1866

First national Ku Klux Klan convention.

April 9, 1866

Congress passes Civil Rights Bill.

1868

President Andrew Johnson is impeached by the House of Representatives, but the Senate votes not to remove him from office.

July 28, 1868

14th Amendment, granting citizenship to freed people, is adopted.

February 25, 1870

Hiram Revels of Mississippi is elected to the U.S. Senate and takes the seat once held by Jefferson Davis.

May 30, 1870

15th Amendment, granting freedmen but not women the right to vote, is ratified.

December 11, 1872

Pinckney B. S. Pinchback becomes governor of Louisiana.

March 1, 1875

Congress passes Civil Rights Act.

1877

Rutherford B. Hayes becomes president with agreement to remove federal troops from the South.

1879–1881

First major migration of African Americans from the South to Kansas and Western territories occurs.

Further Reading

General African-American History

Anderson, James D. *The Education of Blacks in the South, 1860–1935.* Chapel Hill: University of North Carolina Press, 1988.

Aptheker, Herbert, ed. *A Documentary History of the Negro People in the United States.* Vols. 1–2. New York: Citadel Press, 1951.

Aptheker, Herbert, ed. *A Documentary History of the Negro People in the United States.* Vols. 5–7. Secaucus, N.J.: Carol Publishing, 1994.

Bennett, Lerone, Jr. *Before the Mayflower: A History of Black America.* 6th rev. ed. New York: Viking Penguin, 1988.

———. *The Shaping of Black America.* New York: Viking Penguin, 1993.

Berry, Mary Frances, and John W. Blassingame. *Long Memory: The Black Experience in America.* New York: Oxford University Press, 1982.

Blackburn, Robin. *The Overthrow of Colonial Slavery, 1776–1848.* New York: Verso, 1988.

Boles, John B. *Black Southerners, 1619–1869.* Lexington: University Press of Kentucky, 1983.

Conniff, Michael, and Thomas J. Davis. *Africans in the Americas: A History of the Black Diaspora.* New York: St. Martin's, 1993.

Cooper, Anna Julia. *A Voice from the South.* 1892. Reprint, New York: Oxford University Press, 1988.

Foner, Philip S. *History of Black Americans: From Africa to the Emergence of the Cotton Kingdom.* Westport, Conn.: Greenwood, 1975.

Franklin, John Hope, and August Meier, eds. *Black Leaders of the Twentieth Century.* Urbana: University of Illinois Press, 1982.

Franklin, John H., and Alfred A. Moss, Jr. *From Slavery to Freedom: A History of African Americans.* 8th ed. Boston: McGraw-Hill, 1999.

Garwood, Alfred N., comp. *Black Americans: A Statistical Sourcebook 1992.* Boulder, Colo.: Numbers and Concepts, 1993.

Gates, Henry L., Jr. *A Chronology of African-American History from 1445–1980.* New York: Amistad, 1980.

Genovese, Eugene. *From Rebellion to Revolution: Afro-American Slave Revolts in the Making of the Atlantic World.* Baton Rouge: Louisiana State University Press, 1979.

Giddings, Paula. *When and Where I Enter: The Impact of Black Women on Race and Sex in America.* New York: Bantam, 1984.

Gutman, Herbert G. *The Black Family in Slavery and Freedom, 1750–1925.* New York: Vintage, 1977.

Harding, Vincent. *There Is a River: The Black Struggle for Freedom in America.* San Diego: Harcourt Brace, 1981.

Harris, William H. *The Harder We Run: Black Workers Since the Civil War.* New York: Oxford University Press, 1982.

Hine, Darlene C., et al., eds. *Black Women in America.* New York: Carlson, 1993.

Hornsby, Alton, Jr. *Chronology of African-American History: Significant Events and People from 1619 to the Present.* Detroit: Gale Research, 1991.

Jaynes, Gerald David, and Robin M. Williams, Jr. *A Common Destiny: Blacks and American Society.* Washington, D.C.: National Academy Press, 1989.

Jones, Jacqueline. *Labor of Love, Labor of Sorrow: Black Women, Work, and the Family from Slavery to the Present.* New York: Basic Books, 1985.

Levine, Lawrence. *Black Culture and Black Consciousness: Afro-American Folk Thought from Slavery to Freedom.* New York: Oxford University Press, 1977.

Litwack, Leon, and August Meier. *Black Leaders of the 19th Century.* Urbana: University of Illinois Press, 1988.

Mintz, Sidney W., and Richard Price. *The Birth of African-American Culture: An Anthropological Perspective.* Boston: Beacon, 1992.

Nash, Gary B. *Red, White, and Black: The Peoples of Early America.* Englewood Cliffs, N.J.: Prentice-Hall, 1992.

Quarles, Benjamin. *The Negro in the Making of America.* 3rd ed. New York: Macmillan, 1987.

Rice, C. Duncan. *The Rise and Fall of Black Slavery.* Baton Rouge: Louisiana State University Press, 1975.

Salzman, Jack, David Lionel Smith, and Cornel West, eds. *Encyclopedia of African-American Culture and History.* 5 vols. New York: Simon & Schuster Macmillan, 1996.

Savage, William Sherman. *Blacks in the West.* Westport, Conn.: Greenwood Press, 1976.

Chapter 1

Histories and Accounts of Africa and the Americas

Curtin, Philip D., ed. *Africa Remembered: Narratives by West Africans from the Era of the Slave Trade.* Madison: University of Wisconsin Press, 1968.

Curtin, Philip D., Steven Feierman, Leonard Thompson, and Jan Vansina. *African History.* New York: Longman, 1978.

Knight, Franklin. *The Caribbean: The Genesis of a Fragmented Nationalism.* 2nd ed. New York: Oxford University Press, 1990.

Lockhart, James. *Spanish Peru, 1532–1560: A Colonial Society.* Madison: University of Wisconsin Press, 1967.

Lockhart, James, and Stuart Schwartz. *Early Latin America: A History of Colonial Spanish America and Brazil.* New York: Cambridge University Press, 1983.

Palmer, Colin A. *Slaves of the White God: Blacks in Mexico, 1570–1650.* Cambridge: Harvard University Press, 1976.

Rodney, Walter. *How Europe Underdeveloped Africa.* Rev. ed. Washington, D.C.: Howard University Press, 1982.

Rout, Leslie B. *The African Experience in Spanish America, 1502 to the Present Day.* New York: Cambridge University Press, 1976.

Schwartz, Stuart B. *Sugar Plantations in the Formation of Brazilian Society: Bahia 1550–1835.* New York: Cambridge University Press, 1986.

Thornton, John. *Africa and Africans in the Formation of the Atlantic World, 1400–1680.* New York: Cambridge University Press, 1992.

Van Sertima, Ivan. *They Came Before Columbus.* New York: Random House, 1976.

Slavery and the Slave Trade

Bowser, Frederick P. *The African Slave in Colonial Peru, 1524–1650.* Stanford, Calif.: Stanford University Press, 1974.

Curtin, Philip D. *The Atlantic Slave Trade: A Census.* Madison: University of Wisconsin Press, 1972.

Davidson, Basil. *The African Slave Trade.* New York: Little, Brown, 1988.

Donnan, Elizabeth, ed. *Documents Illustrative of the Slave Trade to America.* 4 vols. Washington, D.C.: Carnegie Institution, 1930–35.

Equiano, Olaudah. *The Interesting Narrative of the Life of Olaudah Equiano, or Gustavus Vasa the African.* Edited by Paul Edwards. 2 vols. London: Heinemann, 1967.

Genovese, Eugene. *From Rebellion to Revolution: Afro American Slave Revolts in the Making of the Modern World.* Baton Rouge: Louisiana State University Press, 1979.

Klein, Herbert. *African Slavery in Latin America and the Caribbean.* New York: Oxford University Press, 1986.

Lovejoy, Paul E. *Transformations in Slavery: A History of Slavery in Africa.* New York: Cambridge University Press, 1983.

Phillips, William D., Jr. *Slavery from Roman Times to the Early Atlantic Slave Trade.* Minneapolis: University of Minnesota Press, 1985.

Rawley, James A. *The Transatlantic Slave Trade.* New York: Norton, 1981.

Reynolds, Edward. *Stand the Storm: A History of the Atlantic Slave Trade.* Chicago: Ivan R. Dee, 1993.

Schwartz, Stuart B. *Slaves, Peasants, and Rebels: Reconsidering Brazilian Slavery.* Urbana: University of Illinois Press, 1992.

Thomas, Hugh. *The Slave Trade.* New York: Simon & Schuster, 1997.

Watson, Alan. *Slave Law in the Americas.* Athens: University of Georgia Press, 1989.

Chapter 2

Slavery and Slave Culture

Aptheker, Herbert. *American Negro Slave Revolts.* New York: Columbia University Press, 1943.

Berlin, Ira. *Many Thousands Gone: The First Two Centuries of Slavery in North America.* Cambridge: Harvard University Press, 1998.

Burnside, Madeleine, and Rosemarie Robotham. *Spirits of the Passage: the Transatlantic Slave Trade in the Seventeenth Century.* New York: Simon & Schuster, 1997.

Ferguson, Leland. *Uncommon Ground: Archaeology and Early African America, 1650–1800.* Washington, D.C.: Smithsonian Institution Press, 1992.

Franklin, John Hope, and Loren Schweninger. *Runaway Slaves: Rebels on the Plantation.* New York: Oxford University Press, 1999.

Frey, Sylvia. *Water from the Rock: Black Resistance in a Revolutionary Age.* Princeton, N.J.: Princeton University Press, 1991.

Frey, Sylvia, and Betty Wood. *Come Shouting to Zion: African American Protestantism in the American South and British Caribbean to 1830.* Chapel Hill: University of North Carolina Press, 1998.

Gomez, Michael A. *Exchanging Our Country Marks: The Transformation of African Identities in the Colonial and Antebellum South.* Chapel Hill: University of North Carolina Press, 1998.

Higginbotham, A. Leon, Jr. *In the Matter of Color: Race and the American Legal Process: The Colonial Period.* New York: Oxford University Press, 1978.

Holloway, Joseph E., ed. *Africanisms in American Culture.* Bloomington: Indiana University Press, 1990.

Johnson, Charles, Patricia Smith, and the WGBH Research Team. *Africans in America: America's Journey Through Slavery.* New York: Harcourt Brace, 1998.

Jordan, Winthrop D. *White Over Black: American Attitudes toward the Negro, 1550–1812.* Chapel Hill: University of North Carolina Press, 1968.

Kaplan, Sidney, and Emma Nogrady Kaplan. *The Black Presence in the Era of the American Revolution.* Rev. ed. Amherst: University of Massachusetts Press, 1989.

Kolchin, Peter. *American Slavery, 1619–1877.* New York: Hill & Wang, 1993.

Mullin, Michael. *Africa in America: Slave Acculturation and Resistance in the American South and the British Caribbean, 1736–1831.* Urbana: University of Illinois Press, 1992.

Piersen, William D. *From Africa to America: African American History from the Colonial Era to the Early Republic, 1526–1790.* New York: Twayne, 1996.

Raboteau, Albert J. *Slave Religion: The "Invisible Institution" in the Antebellum South.* New York: Oxford University Press, 1978.

Scherer, Lester B. *Slavery and the Churches in Early America, 1619–1819.* Grand Rapids, Mich.: William B. Eerdmans, 1975.

Smith, Billy G., and Richard Wojtowicz. *Blacks Who Stole Themselves: Advertisements for Runaways in the Pennsylvania Gazette, 1728–1790.* Philadelphia: University of Pennsylvania Press, 1989.

Stuckey, Sterling. *Slave Culture: Nationalist Theory and the Foundations of Black America.* New York: Oxford University Press, 1987.

Thomas, Hugh. *The Slave Trade.* New York: Simon & Schuster, 1997.

Regional Studies

Breen, T. H., and Stephen Innes. *"Myne Owne Ground": Race and Freedom on Virginia's Eastern Shore, 1640–1676.* New York: Oxford University Press, 1980.

Greene, Lorenzo Johnston. *The Negro in Colonial New England.* New York: Columbia University Press, 1942.

Hall, Gwendolyn Midlo. *Africans in Colonial Louisiana: The Development of Afro-Creole Culture in the Eighteenth Century.* Baton Rouge: Louisiana State University Press, 1992.

Hanger, Kimberly S. *Bounded Lives, Bounded Places: Free Black Society in Colonial New Orleans, 1769–1803.* Durham, N.C.: Duke University Press, 1997.

Hodges, Graham Russell. *Slavery and Freedom in the Rural North: African Americans in Monmouth County, New Jersey, 1665–1865.* Madison, Wis.: Madison House, 1997.
Holton, Woody. *Forced Founders: Indians, Debtors, Slaves, and the Making of the American Revolution in Virginia.* Chapel Hill: University of North Carolina Press, 1999.
Ingersall, Thomas N. *Mammon and Manon in Early New Orleans: The First Slave Society in the Deep South, 1718–1819.* Knoxville: University of Tennessee Press, 1999.
Landers, Jane. *Black Society in Spanish Florida.* Urbana: University of Illinois Press, 1999.
Littlefield, Daniel. *Rice and Slaves: Ethnicity and the Slave Trade in Colonial South Carolina.* Baton Rouge: Louisiana State University Press, 1981.
Morgan, Edmund S. *American Slavery, American Freedom: The Ordeal of Colonial Virginia.* New York: Norton, 1975.
Morgan, Philip D. *Slave Counterpoint: Black Culture in the Eighteenth-Century Chesapeake and Lowcountry.* Chapel Hill: University of North Carolina Press, 1998.
Olwell, Robert. *Masters, Slaves, and Subjects: The Culture of Power in the South Carolina Low Country, 1740–1790.* Ithaca, N.Y.: Cornell University Press, 1998.
Piersen, William D. *Black Yankees: The Development of an Afro-American Subculture in Eighteenth-Century New England.* Amherst: University of Massachusetts Press, 1988.
Sensbach, Jon F. *A Separate Canaan: The Making of an Afro-Moravian World in North Carolina, 1763–1840.* Chapel Hill: University of North Carolina Press, 1998.
Sobel, Mechal. *The World They Made Together: Black and White Values in Eighteenth-Century Virginia.* Princeton, N.J.: Princeton University Press, 1987.
Tate, Thad W., Jr. *The Negro in Eighteenth-Century Williamsburg.* Charlottesville: University Press of Virginia, 1966.
Usner, Daniel H., Jr. *Indians, Settlers, and Slaves in a Frontier Exchange Economy: The Lower Mississippi Valley Before 1783.* Chapel Hill: University of North Carolina Press, 1992.
Williams, William H. *Slavery and Freedom in Delaware, 1639–1865.* Wilmington, Del.: Scholarly Resources, 1996.
Wood, Betty. *Slavery in Colonial Georgia, 1730–1775.* Athens: University of Georgia Press, 1984.
Wood, Peter H. *Black Majority: Negroes in Colonial South Carolina from 1670 through the Stono Rebellion.* New York: Knopf, 1974.

Biographies and Literature

Edwards, Paul, ed. *Equiano's Travels.* London: Heinemann, 1967.
Gordon-Reed, Annette. *Thomas Jefferson and Sally Hemings: An American Controversy.* Charlottesville: University Press of Virginia, 1997.
Grant, Douglas. *The Fortunate Slave: An Illustration of African Slavery in the Early Eighteenth Century.* New York: Oxford University Press, 1968.
Shields, John C., ed. *The Collected Works of Phillis Wheatley.* New York: Oxford University Press, 1988.
Yates, Elizabeth. *Amos Fortune, Free Man.* New York: Dutton, 1950.

Chapter 3

The American Revolution

Berlin, Ira. *Many Thousands Gone: The First Two Centuries of Slavery in North America.* Cambridge: Harvard University Press, 1998.

Berlin, Ira, and Ronald Hoffman, eds. *Slavery and Freedom in the Age of the American Revolution.* Charlottesville: University Press of Virginia, 1983.

Davis, David Brion. *The Problem of Slavery in the Age of Revolution, 1770–1823.* Ithaca, N.Y.: Cornell University Press, 1975.

Flexner, James T. *George Washington: Anguish and Farewell (1793–1799).* Boston: Little, Brown, 1972.

———. *George Washington in the American Revolution (1775–1783).* Boston: Little, Brown, 1968.

Frey, Sylvia R. *Water from the Rock: Black Resistance in a Revolutionary Age.* Princeton, N.J.: Princeton University Press, 1991.

Greene, Jack P. *All Men Are Created Equal: Some Reflections on the Character of the American Revolution.* Oxford: Clarendon Press, 1976.

Hirschfeld, Fritz. *George Washington and Slavery: A Documentary Portrayal.* Columbia: University of Missouri Press, 1997.

Horton, James Oliver, and Lois E. Horton. *In Hope of Liberty: Culture, Community, and Protest Among Northern Free Blacks, 1700–1860.* New York: Oxford University Press, 1997.

Kaplan, Sidney, and Emma Nogrady Kaplan. *The Black Presence in the Era of the American Revolution.* Amherst: University of Massachusetts Press, 1989.

Morgan, Edmund S. *The Birth of the Republic, 1763–89.* Chicago: University of Chicago Press, 1992.

Nash, Gary. *Race and Revolution.* Madison, Wis.: Madison House, 1990.

Quarles, Benjamin. *The Negro in the American Revolution.* Chapel Hill: University of North Carolina Press, 1961.

Wood, Gordon. *The Creation of the American Republic, 1776–1787.* Chapel Hill: University of North Carolina Press, 1969.

Revolution in France and Haiti

Cole, Hubert. *Christophe: King of Haiti.* London: Eyre & Spottiswoode, 1967.

Fick, Carolyn E. *The Making of Haiti: The Saint Domingue Revolution from Below.* Knoxville: University of Tennessee Press, 1990.

Geggus, David P. *Slavery, War, and Revolution: The British Occupation of Saint Domingue, 1793–1798.* Oxford: Clarendon Press, 1982.

Hunt, Alfred N. *Haiti's Influence on Antebellum America: Slumbering Volcano in the Caribbean.* Baton Rouge: Louisiana State University Press, 1988.

James, C. L. R. *The Black Jacobins: Toussaint L'Ouverture and the San Domingo Revolution.* Rev. ed. London: Allison & Busby, 1980.

Korngold, Ralph. *Citizen Toussaint: A Biography.* New York: Hill & Wang, 1965.

Logan, Rayford W. *The Diplomatic Relations of the United States with Haiti, 1776–1891.* Chapel Hill: University of North Carolina Press, 1941.

McCloy, Shelby T. *The Negro in the French West Indies.* Lexington: University of Kentucky Press, 1966.

Ott, Thomas O. *The Haitian Revolution, 1789–1804.* Knoxville: University of Tennessee Press, 1973.

Rude, George. *Revolutionary Europe, 1783–1815.* New York: Harper, 1964.

African-American Culture and Society

Andrews, William L. *To Tell a Free Story: The First Century of Afro-American Autobiography, 1760–1865.* Urbana: University of Illinois Press, 1986.

Berlin, Ira. *Slaves Without Masters: The Free Negro in the Antebellum South.* New York: Oxford University Press, 1974.

Bolster, W. Jeffrey. *Black Jacks: African American Seamen in the Age of Sail.* Cambridge: Harvard University Press, 1997.

Chaplin, Joyce E. *An Anxious Pursuit: Agricultural Innovation and Modernity in the Lower South, 1730–1815.* Chapel Hill: University of North Carolina Press, 1993.

Egerton, Douglas R. *Gabriel's Rebellion: The Virginia Slave Conspiracies of 1800 and 1802.* Chapel Hill: University of North Carolina Press, 1993.

Fitts, Leroy. *A History of Black Baptists.* Nashville, Tenn.: Broadman Press, 1984.

Fitts, Leroy, and Charles T. Davis. *The Slave's Narrative.* New York: Oxford University Press, 1985.

Gewehr, Wesley M. *The Great Awakening in Virginia, 1740–1790.* Gloucester, Mass.: Peter Smith, 1965.

Hall, Gwendolyn Midlo. *Africans in Colonial Louisiana: The Development of Afro-Creole Culture in the Eighteenth Century.* Baton Rouge: Louisiana State University Press, 1992.

Hatch, Nathan O. *The Democratization of American Christianity.* New Haven: Yale University Press, 1989.

Hodges, Graham Russell. *Root and Branch: African Americans in New York and East Jersey, 1613–1863.* Chapel Hill: University of North Carolina Press, 1999.

———. *Slavery and Freedom in the Rural North: African Americans in Monmouth County, New Jersey, 1665–1865.* Madison, Wis.: Madison House, 1997.

Isaac, Rhys. *The Transformation of Virginia: Community, Religion, and Authority, 1740–1790.* Chapel Hill: University of North Carolina Press, 1982.

Jordan, Winthrop D. *White Over Black: American Attitudes Toward the Negro, 1550–1812.* Chapel Hill: University of North Carolina Press, 1968.

Kulikoff, Allan. *Tobacco and Slaves: The Development of Southern Cultures in the Chesapeake, 1680–1800.* Chapel Hill: University of North Carolina Press, 1986.

Littlefield, Daniel C. *Rice and Slaves: Ethnicity and the Slave Trade in Colonial South Carolina.* Baton Rouge: Louisiana State University Press, 1981.

Miller, Floyd J. *The Search for a Black Nationality: Black Colonization and Emigration, 1787–1863.* Urbana: University of Illinois Press, 1975.

Morton, Louis. *Robert Carter of Nomini Hall: A Virginia Tobacco Planter of the Eighteenth Century.* Charlottesville: University Press of Virginia, 1941.

Mullin, Gerald W. *Flight and Rebellion: Slave Resistance in Eighteenth-Century Virginia.* New York: Oxford University Press, 1972.

Mullin, Michael. *Africa in America: Slave Acculturation and Resistance in the American South and the British Caribbean, 1736–1831.* Urbana: University of Illinois Press, 1992.

Nash, Gary B. *Forging Freedom: The Formation of Philadelphia's Black Community, 1720–1840.* Cambridge: Harvard University Press, 1988.

Nell, William C. *The Colored Patriots of the American Revolution.* 1855. Reprint, Salem, N.H.: Ayer, 1986.

Payne, Daniel A. *History of the African Methodist Episcopal Church.* 1891. Reprint, New York: Arno, 1969.

Porter, Dorothy, ed. *Early Negro Writing, 1760–1837.* Boston: Beacon Press, 1971.

———. *Negro Protest Pamphlets: A Compendium.* New York: Arno, 1969.

Raboteau, Albert J. *Slave Religion: The "Invisible Institution" in the Antebellum South.* New York: Oxford University Press, 1978.

Robinson, William H. *Black New England Letters: The Uses of Writings in Black New England.* Boston: Trustees of the Public Library, 1977.

———. *Early Black American Prose: Selections with Biographical Introductions.* Dubuque, Iowa: William C. Brown, 1971.

Ruchames, Louis. *Racial Thought in America: A Documentary History. Volume I: From the Puritans to Abraham Lincoln.* Amherst: University of Massachusetts Press, 1969.

Sernett, Milton C. *Black Religion and American Evangelicalism: White Protestants, Plantation Missions, and the Flowering of Negro Christianity, 1787–1865.* Metuchen, N.J.: Scarecrow Press, 1975.

Sidbury, James. *Ploughshares into Swords: Race, Rebellion, and Identity in Gabriel's Virginia, 1730–1810.* New York: Cambridge University Press, 1997.

Simms, James M. *The First Colored Baptist Church in North America. Constituted at Savannah, Georgia, January 20, A.D. 1788.* 1888. Reprint, New York: Negro Universities Press, 1969.

Smith, Charles S. *A History of the African Methodist Episcopal Church.* Reprint New York: Johnson, 1968.

Sobel, Mechal. *Trabelin' on: The Slave Journey to an Afro-Baptist Faith.* Westport, Conn.: Greenwood Press, 1979.

Stuckey, Sterling. *Slave Culture: Nationalist Theory and the Foundations of Black America.* New York: Oxford University Press, 1987.

Walls, William J. *The African Methodist Episcopal Zion Church: Reality of the Black Church.* Charlotte, N.C.: A.M.E. Zion Publishing House, 1974.

Wilmore, Gayraud S. *Black Religion and Black Radicalism: An Interpretation of the Religious History of Afro-American People.* 2nd ed. Revised and enlarged. Maryknoll, N.Y.: Orbis, 1983.

Wood, Gordon S. *The Radicalism of the American Revolution.* New York: Knopf, 1992.

Yentsch, Anne Elizabeth. *A Chesapeake Family and their Slaves: A Study in Historical Archaeology.* New York: Cambridge University Press, 1994.

Slavery and the British Empire

Drescher, Seymour. *Capitalism and Antislavery: British Mobilization in Comparative Perspective.* New York: Oxford University Press, 1987.

Fyfe, Christopher. *A History of Sierra Leone.* London: Oxford University Press, 1962.

Porter, Dale H. *The Abolition of the Slave Trade in England, 1784–1807.* New York: Archon Books, 1970.

Wilson, Ellen Gibson. *The Loyal Blacks.* New York: G. P. Putnam, 1976.

Winks, Robin W. *The Blacks in Canada: A History.* New Haven: Yale University Press, 1971.

Biographies

Bedini, Silvio A. *The Life of Benjamin Banneker.* New York: Scribner, 1972.
Crawford, George W. *Prince Hall and His Followers. Being a Monograph on the Legitimacy of Negro Masonry.* 1914. Reprint, New York: AMS Press, 1971.
George, Carol V. R. *Segregated Sabbaths: Richard Allen and the Rise of Independent Black Churches, 1760–1840.* New York: Oxford University Press, 1973.
Hodges, Graham. *Black Itinerants of the Gospel: The Narratives of John Jea and George White.* Madison, Wis.: Madison House, 1993.
Robinson, William H. *Phillis Wheatley and Her Writings.* New York: Garland, 1984.
Thomas, Lamont D. *Rise to Be a People: A Biography of Paul Cuffe.* Urbana: University of Illinois Press, 1986.

Chapter 4

Slavery and Free Blacks

Berlin, Ira. *Slaves Without Masters: The Free Negro in the Antebellum South.* New York: Random House, 1974.
Blassingame, John W. *The Slave Community: Plantation Life in the Antebellum South.* Revised. New York: Oxford University Press, 1979.
Botkin, B. A., ed. *Lay My Burden Down: A Folk History of Slavery.* Chicago: University of Chicago Press, 1945.
Genovese, Eugene. *Roll, Jordan, Roll: The World the Slaves Made.* New York: Random House, 1974.
Gutman, Herbert. *The Black Family in Slavery and Freedom, 1750–1925.* New York: Pantheon, 1976.
Johnson, Michael, and James L. Roark. *Black Masters: A Free Family of Color in the Old South.* New York: Norton, 1984.
Kolchin, Peter. *American Slavery 1619–1877.* New York: Hill & Wang, 1993.
Lebsock, Suzanne. *The Free Women of Petersburg: Status and Culture in a Southern Town, 1784–1860.* New York: Norton, 1984.
Litwack, Leon F. *North of Slavery: The Negro in the Free States, 1790–1860.* Chicago: University of Chicago Press, 1961.
Meier, August, and Elliot M. Rudwick. *From Plantation to Ghetto: An Interpretive History of American Negroes.* 3rd ed. New York: Hill & Wang, 1976.
Nash, Gary B. *Forging Freedom: The Formation of Philadelphia's Black Community, 1720–1840.* Cambridge: Harvard University Press, 1988.
Osofsky, Gilbert, ed. *Puttin' On Ole Massa. The Slave Narratives of Henry Bibb, William Wells Brown and Solomon Northup.* New York: Harper & Row, 1969.
Richardson, Marilyn, ed. *Maria W. Stewart, America's First Black Woman Political Writer: Essays and Speeches.* Bloomington: Indiana University Press, 1987.
Sweet, Leonard L. *Black Images of America, 1784–1870.* New York: Norton, 1976.
White, Deborah Gray. *Ar'n't I a Woman? Female Slaves in the Plantation South.* New York: Norton, 1985.

Williamson, Joel. *New People: Miscegenation and Mulattoes in the United States.* New York: Free Press, 1980.

Biographies and Autobiographies

Andrews, William L., ed. *The Oxford Frederick Douglass Reader.* New York: Oxford University Press, 1996.

Douglass, Frederick. *Narrative of the Life of Frederick Douglass, an American Slave.* New York: St. Martin's, 1993.

Gilbert, Olive. *Narrative of Sojourner Truth.* New York: Oxford University Press, 1991.

McFeely, William S. *Frederick Douglass.* New York: Norton, 1991.

Chapter 5

General Histories of the Civil War and Reconstruction

Bercaw, Nancy D. *Gendered Freedoms: Race, Rights, and the Politics of Household in the Delta, 1861–1875.* Gainesville: University Press of Florida, 2003.

Edwards, Laura F. *Gendered Strife and Confusion: The Political Culture of Reconstruction.* Urbana: University of Illinois Press, 1997.

Foner, Eric. *Reconstruction: America's Unfinished Revolution, 1863–1877.* New York: Harper & Row, 1988.

McPherson, James M. *Battle Cry of Freedom: The Civil War Era.* New York: Oxford University Press, 1988.

African Americans During the Civil War Era

Bardaglio, Peter. "The Children of Jubilee: African American Childhood in Wartime." In *Divided Houses: Gender and the Civil War.* Edited by Catherine Clinton and Nina Silber. New York: Oxford University Press, 1992.

Berlin, Ira, et. al. *Free At Last: A Documentary History of Slavery, Freedom, and the Civil War.* New York: New Press, 1992.

Billington, Ray Allen, ed. *The Journal of Charlotte L. Forten: A Free Negro in the Slave Era.* New York: Dryden Press, 1953.

Daniels, Douglas Henry. *Pioneer Urbanites: A Social and Cultural History of Black San Francisco.* Philadelphia: Temple University Press, 1980.

Davis, Ronald L. F. *Good and Faithful Labor: From Slavery to Sharecropping in the Natchez District, 1860–1890.* Westport, Conn.: Greenwood, 1982.

Du Bois, William E. B. *Black Reconstruction in America, 1860–1880.* New York: Atheneum, 1962.

Foner, Eric. *Freedom's Lawmakers: A Directory of Black Officeholders During Reconstruction.* New York: Oxford University Press, 1993.

Frankel, Noralee. *Freedom's Women: Black Women and Families in Civil War Era Mississippi.* Bloomington: Indiana University Press, 1999.

Franklin, John Hope. *Reconstruction After the Civil War.* Chicago: University of Chicago Press, 1961.

Gerteis, Louis S. *From Contraband to Freedman: Federal Policy toward Southern Blacks, 1861–1865.* Westport, Conn.: Greenwood, 1973.

Glatthaar, Joseph I. *Forged in Battle: The Civil Alliance of Black Soldiers and White Officers.* New York: Free Press, 1990.

Holt, Thomas. *Black over White: Negro Political Leadership in South Carolina during Reconstruction.* Urbana: University of Illinois Press, 1977.

Horton, James Oliver, and Louis E. Horton. *Black Bostonians: Family Life and Community Struggle in the Antebellum North.* New York: Holmes & Meier, 1979.

Jaynes, Gerald David. *Branches Without Roots: Genesis of the Black Working Class in the American South, 1862–1882.* New York: Oxford University Press, 1986.

Katzman, David M. *Before the Ghetto: Black Detroit in the Nineteenth Century.* Urbana: University of Illinois Press, 1973.

Kolchin, Peter. *First Freedom: The Responses of Alabama's Blacks to Emancipation and Reconstruction.* Westport, Conn.: Greenwood, 1972.

Leckie, William H. *The Buffalo Soldiers: A Narrative of the Negro Cavalry in the West.* Norman: University of Oklahoma Press, 1967.

Litwack, Leon E. *Been in the Storm So Long: The Aftermath of Slavery.* New York: Knopf, 1979.

McPherson, James M. *Marching toward Freedom: Blacks in the Civil War, 1861–1865.* New York: Facts on File, 1991.

———. *The Negro's Civil War: How American Negroes Felt and Acted during the War for the Union.* New York: Vintage, 1965.

Miller, Edward A. *Gullah Statesman: Robert Smalls from Slavery to Congress, 1839–1915.* Columbia: University of South Carolina Press, 1995.

Mohr, Clarence L. *On the Threshold of Freedom: Masters and Slaves in Civil War Georgia.* Athens: University of Georgia Press, 1886.

Pearson, Elizabeth Ware, ed. *Letters from Port Royal, 1862–1868.* New York: Arno, 1969.

Quarles, Benjamin. *The Negro in the Civil War.* Boston: Little, Brown, 1969.

Rabinowitz, Howard N. *Race Relations in the Urban South, 1865–1890.* New York: Oxford University Press, 1978.

Ransom, Robert L., and Richard Sutch. *One Kind of Freedom: The Economic Consequences of Emancipation.* New York: Cambridge University Press, 1977.

Rawick, George P. *The American Slave: A Composite Autobiography.* Westport, Conn.: Greenwood, 1972.

Schwalm, Leslie. *A Hard Fight For We, Women's Transition from Slavery to Freedom in South Carolina.* Urbana: University of Illinois Press, 1997.

Shaffer, Donald R. *After the Glory: The Struggle of Black Civil War Veterans.* Lawrence: University Press of Kansas, 2004.

Picture Credits

Courtesy American Antiquarian Society: 96; Archivo General de la Nación de México: 32; Courtesy of the Billy Graham Center: 188; Boston Athenaeum: 211; By Permission of the British Library: 167; Chicago Historical Society: 64, 83, 174, 200, 222, 232; Courtesy of the Charleston Museum, Charleston, S.C.: 202; Giraudon/Art Resource, NY: 43; Courtesy of the John Carter Brown Library at Brown University: 115; Library Company of Philadelphia: 21, 126, 191; Library of Congress: 28, 70, 87, 91, 110, 111, 130, 152, 177, 241, 249, 269, 272; Maryland Historical Society, Baltimore, Md.: 157; Metropolitan Museum of Art, Rogers Fund, 1942 (42.95.19): 147; Moorland-Spingarn Research Center, Howard University Archives: 274; Museo de América, Madrid: 46; Collection of the New York Historical Society: 100, 184, 186; New York Public Library, I. N. Phelps Stokes Collection, Miriam and Ira D. Wallach Division of Art, Prints and Photographs: 35, 61; Schomburg Center for Research in Black Culture, New York Public Library, Astor, Lenox, and Tilden Foundations: ii, 73 (Slavery-Documents Collection), 164, 170 (Slavery-Labor Collection), 230 (Organizations-U.N.I.A.); Courtesy Gary Tong: 6, 12; Walter P. Reuther Library, Wayne State University: 262.

Contributors

The Editors

Robin D. G. Kelley is Professor of Anthropology and African-American Studies at Columbia University. Author of several prize-winning books, including *Race Rebels: Culture, Politics and the Black Working Class* and *Yo' Mama's DisFunktional!: Fighting the Culture Wars in Urban America*. His most recent publication is *Freedom Dreams: The Black Radical Imagination*. He lives in New York City.

Earl Lewis is Provost and Asa Griggs Candler Professor of History and African-American Studies at Emory University. He is the author or editor of seven books, among them *In Their Own Interests: Race, Class and Power in Twentieth-Century Norfolk, Virginia*; *Love on Trial: An American Scandal in Black and White* (with Heidi Ardizzone); and *Defending Diversity* (with Patricia Gurin and Jeffrey Lehman).

The Authors

Noralee Frankel is assistant director on women, minorities, and teaching at the American Historical Association. She is co-editor of *Gender, Class, Race, and Reform in the Progressive Era* and author of *Freedom's Women: Black Women and Families in Civil War Era Mississippi*. In addition, she has published several articles dealing with the issues of race and gender.

Daniel C. Littlefield is Carolina Professor of History at the University of South Carolina. He is the author of *Rice and Slaves: Ethnicity and the Slave Trade in Colonial South Carolina*.

Colin A. Palmer is Distinguished Professor of History at the Graduate School and University Center of the City University of New York. He was previously the William Rand Kenan, Jr., Professor of History at the University of North Carolina at Chapel Hill, where he chaired the history department, and African and Afro-American. He is the author of *Passageways: A History of Black America to 1865; Slaves of the White God: Blacks in Mexico, 1570–1650;* and the forthcoming *Africa's Children: The Pre-emancipation Experiences of Blacks in the Americas*, among other publications.

Deborah Gray White is professor of history at Rutgers University. She holds a Ph.D. from the University of Illinois at Chicago. Dr. White is the author of *"Ar'n't I A Woman?" Female Slaves in the Plantation South,* for which she won the Letitia Brown Memorial Book Prize, and *Too Heavy a Load: Black Women in Defense of Themselves, 1894–1994.* She has also contributed articles to *Before Freedom Came: African-American Life in the Antebellum South,* and *Visible Women: New Essays on American Activism.*

Peter H. Wood is a Rhodes Scholar and Harvard Ph.D. who teaches early American history at Duke University. His first book, *Black Majority,* examined slavery in colonial South Carolina and received a National Book Award nomination. Wood is the co-author of *Powhatan's Mantle: Indians in the Colonial Southeast* and *Created Equal: A Social and Political History of the United States.* In 2004 he published *Weathering the Storm: Inside Winslow Homer's 'Gulf Stream,'* a book exploring one of the great black images in American art.

Index